NIGHT PHOTOGRAPHY AND LIGHT PAINTING

NIGHT PHOTOGRAPHY AND LIGHT PAINTING

Finding Your Way in the Dark

LANCE KEIMIG

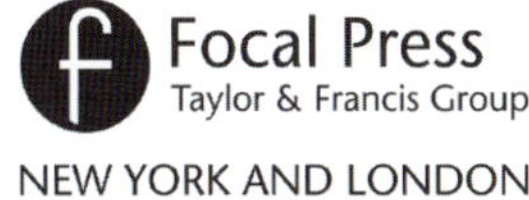

Focal Press
Taylor & Francis Group

NEW YORK AND LONDON

Second edition published 2016
by Focal Press
70 Blanchard Road, Suite 402, Burlington, MA 01803

and by Focal Press
2 Park Square, Milton Park, Abingdon, Oxon OX14 4RN

Focal Press is an imprint of the Taylor & Francis Group, an informa business

First edition published by Focal Press 2010

Library of Congress Cataloging in Publication Data
Keimig, Lance.
   Night photography and light painting : finding your way in the dark /
   by Lance Keimig. — [2nd edition].
      pages cm
   ISBN 978-0-415-71898-1 (pbk.) — ISBN 978-1-315-86774-8 (ebook)
   1. Night photography. I. Title.
   TR610.K387 2015
   778.7'19—dc23   2014041223

ISBN: 978-0-415-71898-1 (pbk)
ISBN: 978-1-315-86774-8 (ebk)

Typeset in Univers
By Keystroke, Station Road, Codsall, Wolverhampton

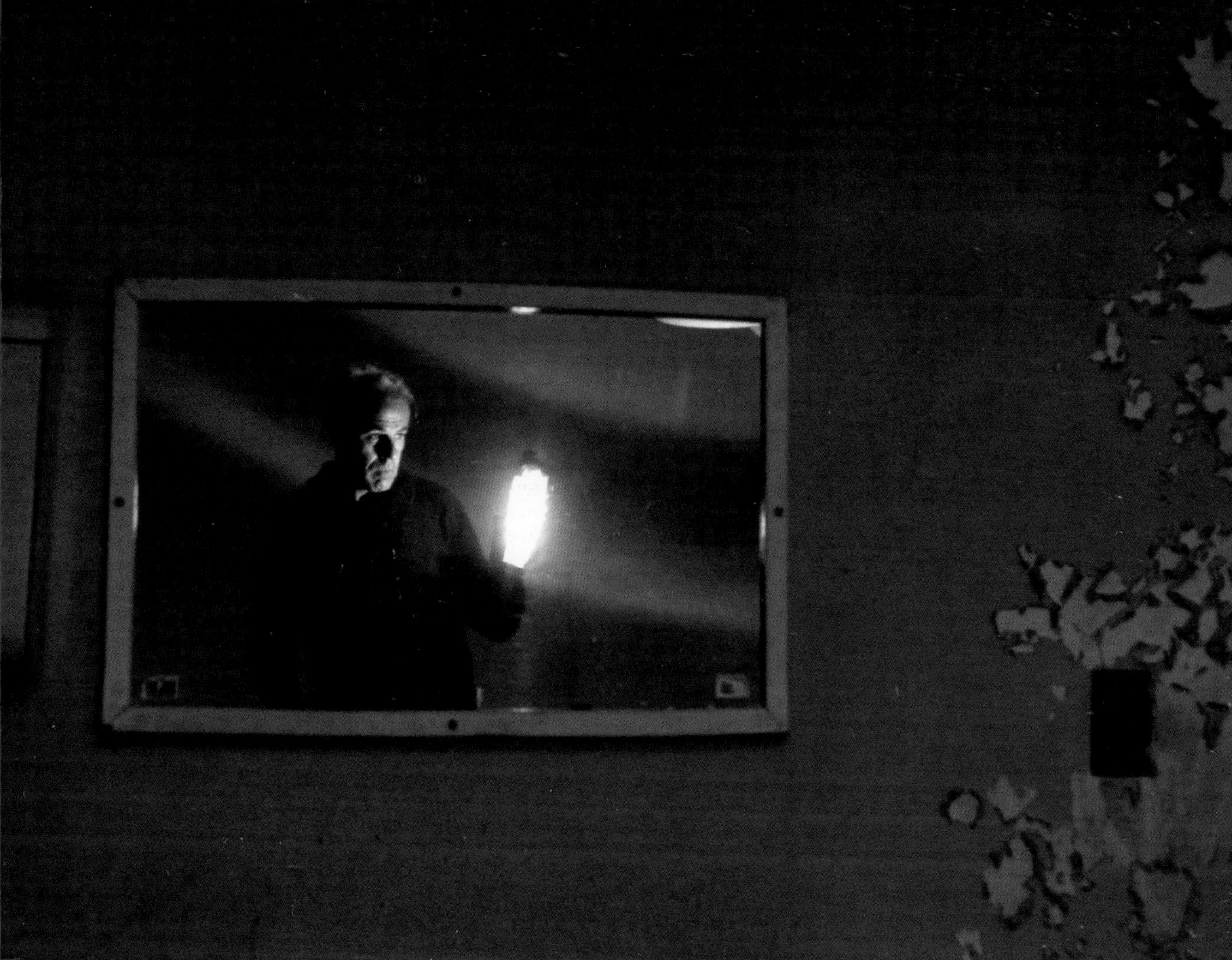

Self-portrait, Steve Harper, 1980

This book is dedicated to my friend and mentor, Steve Harper. Your teaching, encouragement, and friendship over the past 25 years have shaped my career. I'm quite sure that this book, or the first edition, would never have been written if I'd not discovered your classes so long ago. You inspired a generation of night photographers, and I am proud to be one of them. Thank you Steve.

Contents

Foreword

TIM BASKERVILLE

"On any given night . . . "

I first met the author in 1991 through an introduction by fellow night photographer Steve Harper. Lance Keimig had recently moved from the East Coast to San Francisco, essentially to study night photography with Harper; I was a former student of Steve's, busy working on an exhibit of night photography—*The Nocturnes*—featuring the work of Bay Area photographers who were exploring the expanding genre. It was clear from this auspicious meeting that Lance had more than a passing interest in the transformative nature of night photography; thus began a working relationship that has now surpassed 20 years—and many cold nights spent photographing the abandoned, the forgotten, and the unobserved. In 1996 both our work was showcased on the newly developed Nocturnes website, and in 1997 we began planning The Nocturnes Workshop Series, which launched with three workshops the following year. Shortly afterward, Lance relocated back to the East Coast and continued to exhibit and teach there, as well as "commuting" to California for workshops where we taught together. In hindsight, I think this expanding reach of our workshops, exhibits, and other efforts set the stage to accommodate the explosive growth of interest in night photography, mirroring the accelerated evolution of digital photography. At this point we were true evangelists of night photography, owing a huge debt to Steve Harper's tutelage and mentorship.

For the past 20 years, Lance has shown an inspiring commitment to the art and craft of night photography, to fostering night photography education, and to a philosophy of it. Lance and I (like Steve Harper before us) are of the same mind: that there is something special, something unique about night photography—an intrinsically transformative quality in its nature that you don't find in other kinds of photography.

This "philosophy of night photography "—what is it, what does it involve? Well, it is a bit like the Slow Food movement (or the other "Slow" initiatives: Slow Art, Slow Technology, etc.), encouraging a contemplative approach to the making (as opposed to the *taking*) of an image. It involves an emphasis, less on gear and gadgets (things), and more on the creative process, experimentation, and the experiential nature of the act of photographing at night.

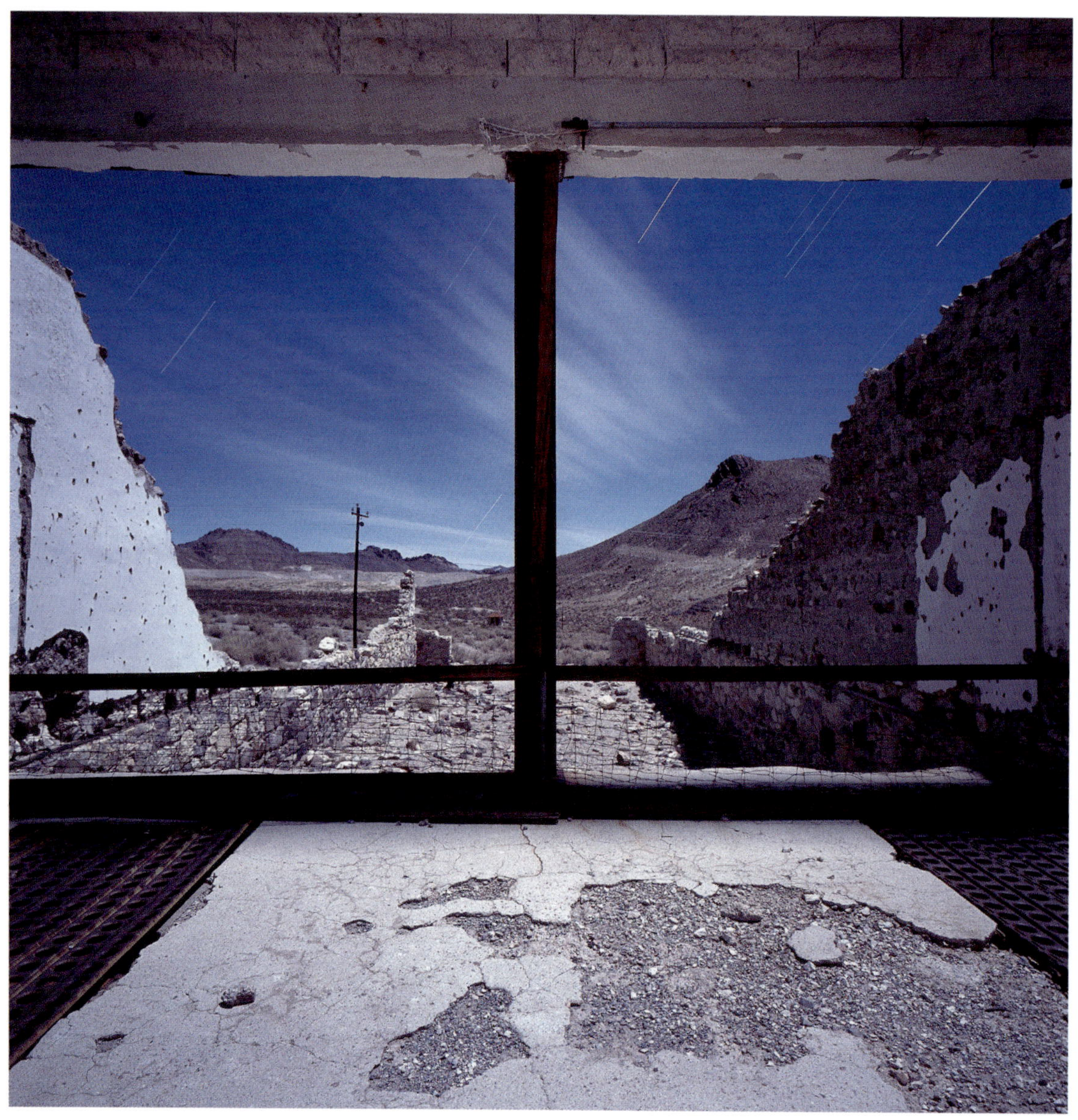

Rhyolite, Tim Baskerville. Porter Brothers Store, rhyolite, NV Hasselblad 500/CM, 80 mm planar, 22 minutes, f8, at ISO 64, tungsten balanced film.

Nowhere is this more evident than in photographing the landscape and the night sky. Long exposures (again, "slow") reveal the inherent transformative potential of night photography. In minutes (or hours) long exposures of straight lines (actually, long arcs) etched onto film or a camera sensor do not trace, as it would seem, the stars' movement across space, but instead, our movement, this planet's rotation, relative to those stars' positions. We don't ordinarily see the quantitative element of "distance over time" rendered in such an aesthetic manner. As Lance points out: "In Night Photography, time is compressed—it's almost like shooting a movie and the camera jams, so the entire film is recorded onto a single frame—and that one photograph may represent 10 minutes, or 20 minutes . . . or six hours!"

Transformative experiences rely on rituals to organize and codify those encounters, and night photographers, from the earliest days of the genre, have their own set of self-organizing rituals. One such ritual would find "full moon" photo enthusiasts from Edward Steichen to Troy Paiva out in the cold night air, every full moon cycle (approximately 29.5 nights—photographing two nights *before* the full moon rises—in addition to the actual night of the full moon, and maybe (depending on the season and early sunsets) one night *after* the full moon.

The cornerstone of this "slow" philosophy of night photography is in distinct counterpoint to the ever-escalating pace of technology and of life in the 21st century. Even the photographic tools we use—while we love them for what they enable us to do—are a result of this ongoing parade of technological "wonders." We long for some solace, a retreat into the calm of night.

How then does this timeless ethos of night photography square with the breathtaking pace of technological innovation in digital photography? It is as if the very thing that has helped advance night photography in recent years is the thing that many seek escape or refuge from. Can the author help us "re-find" our way in the dark? When I was first asked by Focal Press to review the proposal for a new edition of *Finding Your Way in the Dark*, I wondered how such an already highly regarded and successful text could be improved. But, I think that Lance has done it, making the hard choices (e.g., dropping the film section) while surveying the current state of the art today.

In this new edition, the author addresses recent developments in high-ISO photography (both for low-light testing and for astrophotography), as well as the increasing interest in light painting and *light drawing* (finally, a distinction has been made!). For this new edition, Lance has again invited several photographers from the night photography community to contribute—a fitting measure, indicative of the cooperation and openness that characterizes the night photography community. As I've often said: "Some of the nicest people I have ever met are night photographers!"

Acknowledgments

When the first edition was published in August 2010, I never imagined that a book on night photography would go on to be reprinted several times, and translated into six different languages. It is a testament to the ever-increasing popularity of the subject, one that has been deeply personal to me for nearly 30 years. Night photography has been the cornerstone of my life's creative efforts and I feel truly fortunate to have been able to make it the foundation of my photographic career. I owe a real debt of gratitude to the many hundreds of students and workshop participants who have studied with me over the years. It has been one of the greatest pleasures I've known to see the spark of night photography catch fire in so many of the wonderful photographers I have had the privilege of working with over the last 16 years of teaching.

This revised and expanded edition of *Night Photography and Light Painting: Finding Your Way in the Dark* has been a long time coming. First and foremost, I want to thank Kimberly Duncan-Mooney at Focal Press, who first contacted me in January of 2013 about a second edition. Thank you also to my editors at Focal, Alison Duncan, Anna Valutkevich, and Nicola Platt and Emma Elder at Taylor & Francis for your persistence, patience, and encouragement along the road to producing this new version of the book. Thanks also to Matthew Scotti at Focal for your help with researching images and copyright holders for the history of light painting. Thank you also to Jason Page for your help with the history chapter. Your research into the history of light painting has become the foundation of all knowledge on the subject.

Many thanks to Tim Baskerville of The Nocturnes for his excellent Foreword and editing suggestions. To the many photographers and light painters whose words and images grace the pages of this book, thank you. Your images and willingness to share your knowledge are a big part of the success of this book. I want to thank Alister Benn, J. Michael Sullivan, and especially Keith Kiska, who all wrote guest sections that were ultimately cut due to space limitations. Your excellent work is appreciated and I'm sorry that it didn't make it to print. Thank you also to Rick Whitacre, Troy Paiva, and Michael Frye for your informative articles.

Peggy Hansen quickly figured out just the right balance between encouragement and space for me to work. I have so much to thank you for. You helped make this project possible in a very real way. Scott Martin has been my friend, mentor, and workshop partner since 2007, and my advancement into the digital age has been skillfully guided by his great knowledge, and kindness. Thanks also to my friend Tom Paiva; knowing you and seeing your fine work over these many years has been, and continues to be, an inspiration. A huge thank you to Susanne Hupfer, my 2 am editing specialist. Christian Waeber and Katherine Moxhet were present during the creation of many of the images in both versions of this book, and their nocturnal camaraderie over these many years has been a welcome constant on many a dark and stormy night. Katherine, thank you also for your gentle nudges that helped to keep me on track, for your heroic last-minute work reviewing the proofs, and for continuing to carry the torch for film-based night photography. I hope you never let it die out, and I look forward to many more *Acros Adventures* with you.

My son Skye helped with editing, and your music kept me going through many a long night while writing this book. You are my biggest inspiration. My mother has loved me as only a mother could, through thick and thin, and the longest, darkest nights. Your belief in me has kept me going at times when little else could.

Introduction

In August 2008 I was invited to write a book on night photography by Focal Press, something I had thought about doing for many years. I was at Mono Lake in California's Eastern Sierra teaching a workshop on the subject when I received the call; ironically, my friend Jill Waterman, whose own night photography book had just been published, was a guest at the workshop with me. Jill had freshly printed copies of her book with her, and I was eager to recommend it to my students. Along with Andrew Sanderson's earlier film-based night photography book,

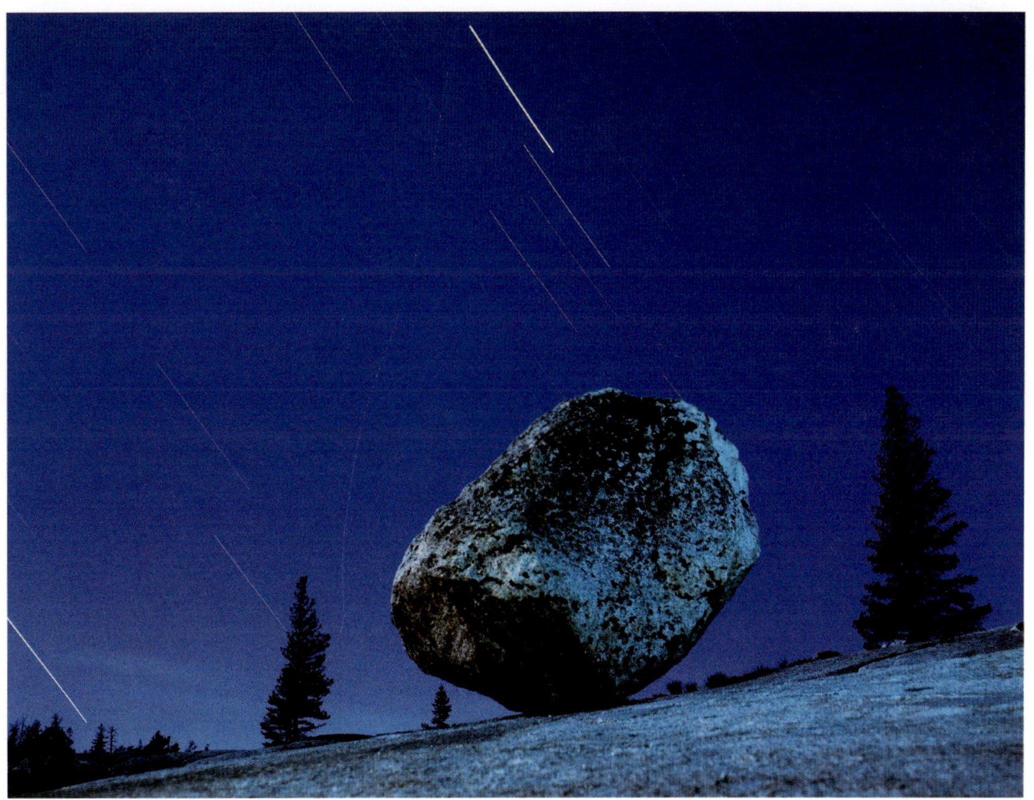

Steve's Rock, Olmsted Point, Yosemite National Park, CA, 1991

This is the original image of the boulder in Yosemite that is known to a generation of night photographers as Steve's Rock. Steve Harper shared his passion for night photography with hundreds of students during his many years teaching in San Francisco from the late 1970s to the early 1990s. Had I not made the fateful decision to move across country to study with him shortly before he retired, this book may never have been written. Thank you Steve.

Jill's was one of the few books on the subject to embrace night photography for its own unique characteristics and not simply to teach people how to shoot fireworks and ferris wheels at the county fair. Jill had the misfortune of publishing just at the time when digital technology had advanced to the point where night images taken with digital cameras were as good or better than those shot on film. Because of the long production time required to write, edit, design, and print a book of this nature, she had been working on the book while digital cameras were still struggling to cope with the extreme demands of night photography, and film shooters still made up a large percentage of night photographers. This, combined with the fact that Jill was (and still is) primarily a film photographer, made for a book that lacked much of the technical information on digital night photography that people were craving.

Still, *Night and Low-Light Photography: Techniques for Commercial and Artistic Success* is an inspiring book. My favorite thing about it is that Jill took a collaborative, community-based approach to writing it. Night photographers have always banded together to share images and experiences. Perhaps in part because no one else understood our passions and obsessions—especially security and law enforcement personnel—and also because of the many common experiences shared by night photographers everywhere, a collaborative project made perfect sense. Jill included the writing and images of many different photographers, all with different interests and points of view. Rather than producing a book with a single perspective, Jill presented the collective experience of some of the best night photographers of the time in one publication.

On the other hand, I was fortunate that my first book was published at just the right moment: digital technology had finally caught up with film, and interest in the subject was growing exponentially. Still, I never imagined that the book would be as successful as it has been. The first edition of this book is now outdated, having been written in 2009. Technology has continued to advance at a staggering pace; cameras, lenses, postprocessing software, and even flashlights and batteries have evolved dramatically.

Probably the biggest technological change is the ever-increasing quality of images shot at high ISO. When the first edition was written, I advised that photographers should stick to their camera's native ISO whenever possible for optimal image quality. Many current DSLRs are capable of producing high-quality images at 3200, 6400, and even 12,800 ISO, and the possibilities offered by this new technology are practically limitless. We can now photograph a moonless landscape and night sky with exposures as short as 10 seconds, rendering the stars as points of light rather than the star trails that come with long exposures shot at 100 or 200 ISO.

One other recent advance worth mentioning is the introduction of smaller mirrorless and other compact digital cameras that are capable of excellent image quality even under the demanding conditions of night photography. None of these cameras can rival the image quality of a full frame DSLR, but not everyone needs to have that level of quality, and these smaller, more affordable cameras help to make the exciting world of night photography and light painting accessible to an ever-widening audience. An overview of these new cameras, their advantages, and their limitations is included in the equipment chapter.

I chose the same approach as Jill when writing the first edition of this book, and invited several colleagues with specific knowledge and insights to contribute to the project, and I believe that *Night Photography: Finding Your Way In The Dark* was a better book for it. This new edition also contains contributions from several guest photographers and writers who each specialize in a specific aspect of night photography.

It is with some regret that I omit the chapter on film-based night photography from the first edition, but as there are fewer and fewer films, papers, and photo labs to work with each year, as well as fewer photographers using them, it only makes sense to remove it from this revised edition of *Finding Your Way in the Dark*. I photographed at night with black and white film for over 25 years, and although I rarely venture out with my view camera anymore, at times I do miss the darkroom and the craft of working with film. If you are interested in shooting film at night, I recommend Jill Waterman's and Andrew Sanderson's books, or the first edition of this book, all of which cover the subject in depth.

The first edition of *Finding Your Way in the Dark* opened with a chapter on the history of night photography, which was, if truth be told, my favorite part of the book. Steve Harper always began his classes with a historical overview, giving his students a glimpse into the challenges that earlier generations of night photographers had overcome. I've always remembered those lessons, and usually start my own workshops and classes the same way. This edition begins with a history of light painting, starting with some of the earliest uses of added light in photography.

When Tim Baskerville and I began teaching night photography workshops together at Rayko Photo Center in San Francisco during the late 1990s, we were practically the only ones in the US routinely teaching the subject. We are both alumni of Steve Harper, who developed and taught the first college-level class on night photography at the Academy of Art in San Francisco in the 1980s, and have been proud to take the torch and carry it for him ever since. These days (perhaps I should say these nights), there are workshops with very specific themes, such as light painting in automotive junkyards, cemeteries, or ghost towns, and night photography in urban environments with artificial light, or in national parks using long exposures and star trails or short exposures using high ISOs to capture images of the Milky Way. With these increases in accessibility and popularity of night photography, there is an ever-expanding range of available resources, and I am happy to include a listing of classes, workshops, books, eBooks, and online resources for those interested in additional information or inspiration.

Night Photography and Light Painting: Finding Your Way In The Dark was written for aspiring amateur photographers and artists interested in exploring the creative possibilities of night photography and light painting. It is assumed that the reader will have at least a basic understanding of photographic principles such as manual exposure mode and depth of field. At least rudimentary familiarity with RAW file image development will be invaluable in understanding the contents of the text. My own postprocessing workflow is straightforward and Lightroom-centric, and I avoid using Photoshop except in cases where Lightroom can't do the job, such as image stacking for long star trails or expanded depth of field, or for exposure blending using layers. I never presume that my way is the only way or the best way; I just do and teach what works for me. I encourage you to explore any and all the techniques you can, both in the field and behind the computer.

This book is suited for advanced beginners through professional photographers, but those with very limited photographic experience may be better served by my friend and fellow night photographer Gabriel Biderman's *Night Photography: From Snapshots to Great Shots*. If you have an eagerness to explore the night and the many artistic possibilities it offers, and have a good understanding of basic photography principles, then *Digital Night Photography and Light Painting* is for you. As Gabe likes to say, *carpe noctem*—seize the night!

PART I
GETTING STARTED

THE HISTORY OF LIGHT PAINTING

FROM FLASH POWDER TO FLASHLIGHTS

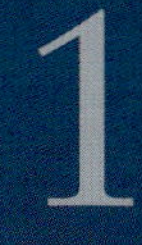

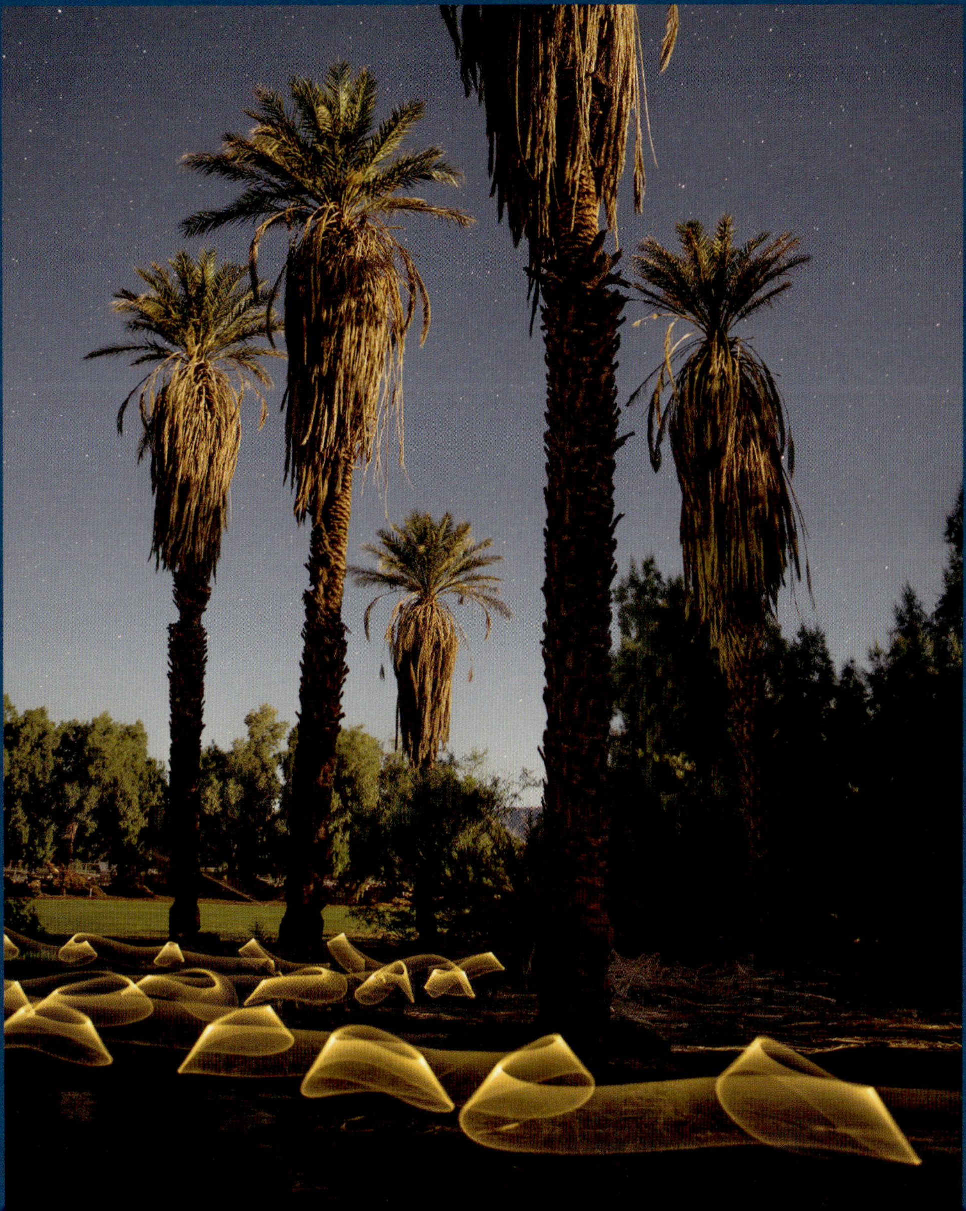

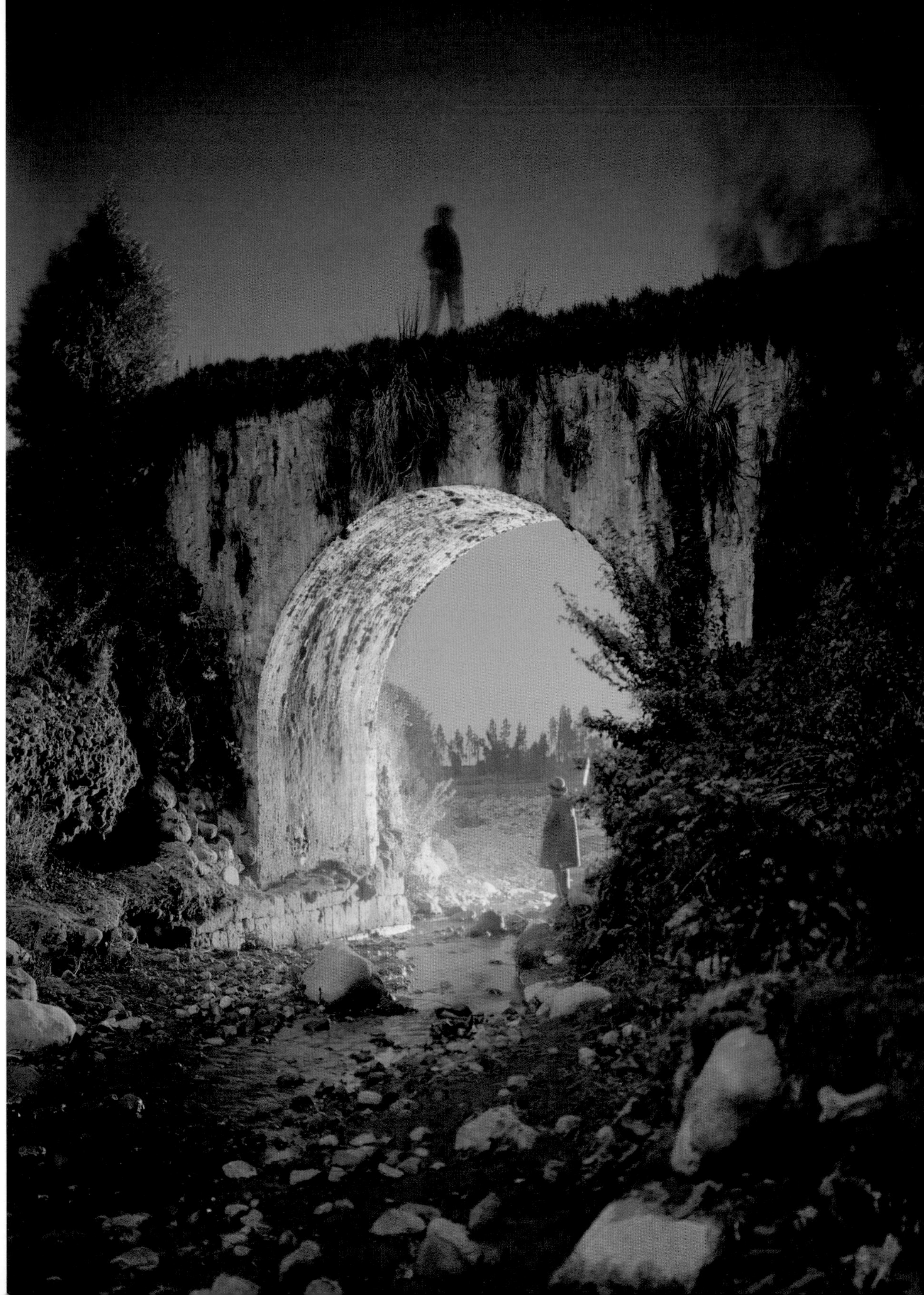

In the first edition of this book, I wrote about the history of night photography, a subject that has fascinated me for a quarter of a century. Rather than simply reprint that chapter here (available for free as a PDF on my website: thenightskye.com/FYWITD_ch1.pdf), the following pages introduce the history of light painting. Like night photography, light painting and drawing have become increasingly popular in recent years. It has been used frequently in advertising in print and on television, and there are a variety of highly specialized light painting tools that have been developed by light painters, and even a few that are sold commercially.

This book conforms to the common usage of the general term "light painting," which refers to lighting added by a photographer and combined with a long exposure to make an image, either at night or in a darkened interior. Light painting includes both using added light to illuminate a scene, and any lights pointed back toward the camera to create patterns of light. The term "painting with light" is defined as the use of a handheld light source that is usually moved during the exposure to light part or all of the scene in a photograph, and the term "drawing with light" is used when a handheld light is pointed back toward the camera to create shapes, text, or abstract designs. In painting with light, the added light *illuminates* the subject. In drawing with light, the light added by the photographer actually *is* the subject. Light painting includes both painting with light and drawing with light. The more traditional placement of stationary lights that are used to light all or part of the scene is referred to simply as location lighting. It is somewhat awkward and unfortunate wordage, but we need to distinguish between the different types of lighting, and this is the common terminology. Hopefully, it will all make sense once you start reading through the chapters.

This chapter might be more accurately called *A History of Photography with Added Light*, as it follows the development of location lighting, and eventually drawing with light and painting with light, concurrently with the development of night photography from the early years of the medium up until about 1990. Tracing the origins of light painting as an art form is fraught with dead ends and pitfalls because there is scant photographic or written documentation of early experiments. The genre had never been clearly defined or even established as a medium until very recently. The coalescence of a light painting "community" brought together by the internet and photo sharing sites like Flickr and 500px is a welcome and very recent development. It is impossible to say who was the first, or who first intended, to illuminate a photograph by painting or drawing with light. Most 19th-century photographers who used artificial light in their images did so out of necessity, rather than for artistic purposes. The early photographic materials were not very light

---

"Nocturne: Aqueduct of Izcuchaca," Arequipa, Peru, Carlos and Miguel Vargas, ca. 1920

Underappreciated pioneers of night photography and light painting, the Vargas brothers were probably the first to apply light painting techniques for artistic purposes. It is just possible to make out a faint image of one of their assistants holding a bottle filled with flash powder. Their Nocturnes were clever, beautiful, and technical masterpieces of the time.

"View in the Catacombs," Paris, Nadar
[Gaspard Félix Tournachon], 1861

Nadar is credited with a number of firsts,
including the first aerial photographs, which he
took from a hot air balloon. In the early 1860s,
he photographed the sewer tunnels, and the
catacombs that were discovered underneath
Paris during the construction of the Metro.
In the lower right-hand corner of this image,
a crude magnesium lamp is visible. He used
these lamps to light the passageways of the
catacombs.

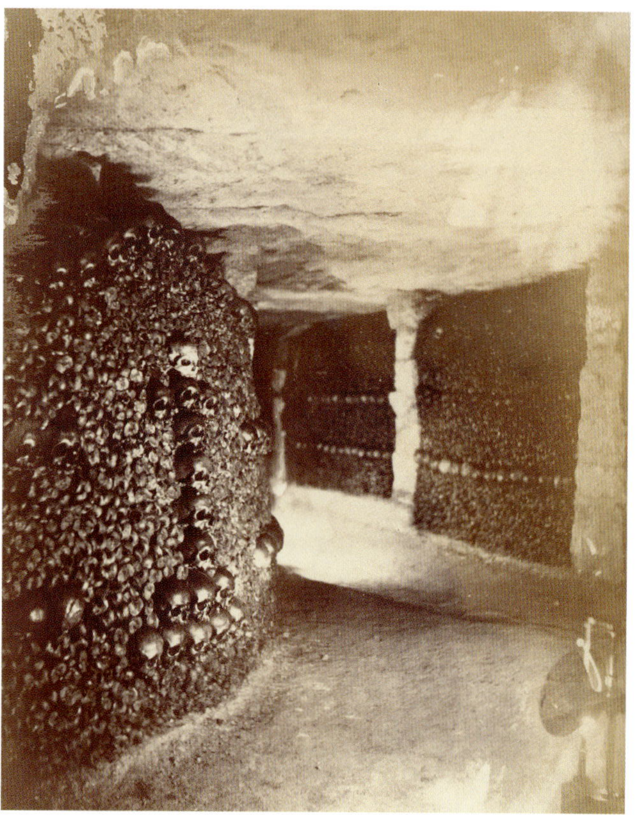

sensitive, and were difficult to use. Before the introduction of the dry plate negative in the 1870s, simply managing to make images in the dark was a major accomplishment.

The French photographer Nadar was one of the first to add artificial light to a scene in order to photograph it. Nadar photographed the catacombs and sewers below Paris, making about one hundred wet-plate glass negatives between 1861 and 1862. He used both lamps that burned strips of magnesium wire and electric lights powered by primitive batteries for these photographs, and employed mannequins to represent workers, because of the lengthy exposures.[1] The wet-plate collodion process that Nadar used was a significant technical advance over the earlier Daguerreotype, but these plates had to be exposed and developed before the emulsion dried. The lengthy exposures required underground made wet-plate photography impossible without added artificial light.

Étienne-Jules Marey and Georges Demeny were French physiologists working together in the 1880s to study and understand movement and locomotion. They were contemporaries of Edward Muybridge, and concurrently developed an alternative method of recording movement that recorded multiple images on a single film as opposed to Muybridge's method, where each image was recorded on a separate frame. Marey and Demeny's invention was a precursor to the motion picture camera, and Marey would later work with the Lumière brothers during the development of their camera.[2] This work was not directly related to light painting per se, and they were using photography for scientific rather than artistic purposes. However, in 1888–1889, Demeny used a technique known as the Quénu method to record patterns of both involuntary movements such as tremors, and also to understand the physiology of locomotion. The Quénu technique involved attaching incandescent light bulbs to the joints of a subject in order to more easily observe movements.[3] Demeny advanced the technique by making long exposure photographs, resulting in what are now presumed to be the first light drawing photographs.[4]

Edward Steichen made a significant contribution to the genre of night photography and light painting with his series of 1908 photographs of the French sculptor Rodin's sculpture of Balzac. These images were made primarily by the light of the Moon at Rodin's suggestion.[5] Although there had been various other efforts to photograph by moonlight before Steichen, most notably by John Frith of Bermuda, who made moonlit exposures of up to six hours in 1887,[6] it is the

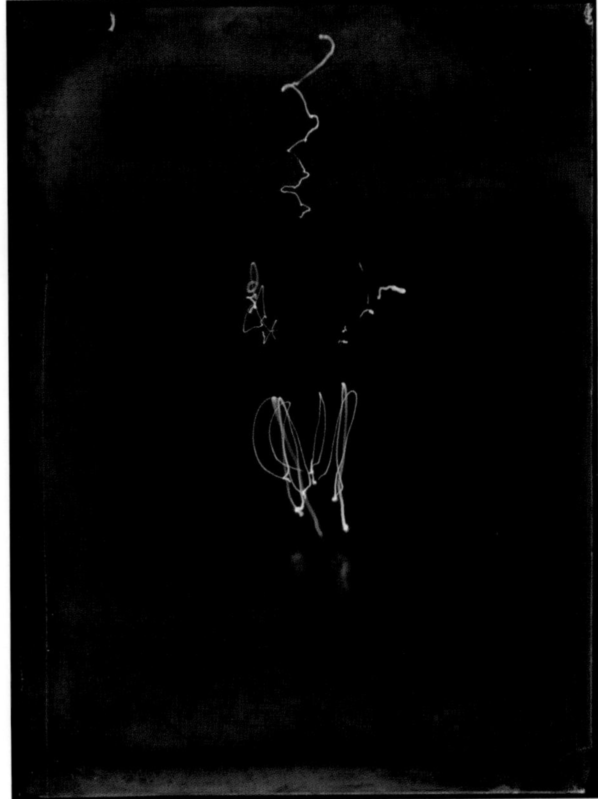

"Pathological Walk in Front," Georges Demeny and Étienne Jules Marey, 1889

This image is considered the first light painting photograph. Demeny and Marey were physiologists studying human locomotion, and they created this image by attaching small lights to the joints of a figure who walked toward the camera during a long exposure in a darkened room. Many early light painting photographs were made for scientific rather than artistic purposes.

Balzac photographs that are the best extant examples of early moonlight photographs. Because there was no precedent for determining exposures, Steichen made a series of exposures ranging between 15 minutes and an hour over two nights by moonlight, dusk, dawn, and even one by flash.[7] This may be the first incidence of long exposure combined with added light, which would become the basis for all light painting in the future.

Frank Gilbreth began his career as a bricklayer, but was frustrated by the inefficiencies in the way that masons performed their work. He believed that there was "one best way"[8] to do every task, and devised a system of motion study using photography that he called stereo chronocyclegraph (time-motion-writing). He and his wife further developed the techniques of Marey and Demeny, attaching blinking lights to workers' arms and legs to record and study their movements in photographs. Like the French physiologists, the Gilbreths had no artistic ambitions; photography for them was a tool to aid them with their work. Where Marey and Demeny's objective was to study and understand movement, the Gilbreths' objective was to find the most comfortable and efficient way to perform a worker's task, increasing productivity for the company and comfort for the worker.

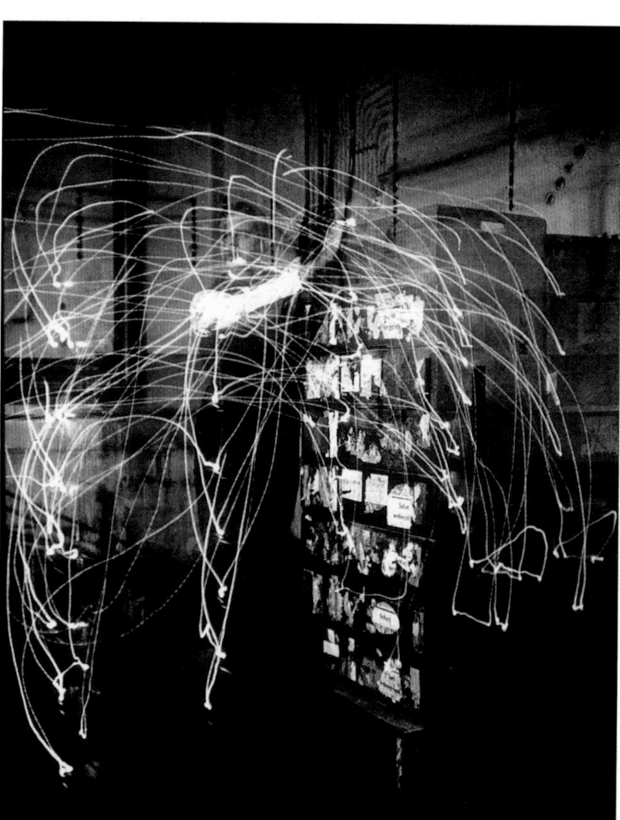

"Efficiency Study," Frank and Lillian Gilbreth, 1918

Like Demeny and Marey, Gilbreth made light painting exposures for scientific research rather than for art. The Gilbreths worked to improve working conditions by improving efficiency in the workplace.

Carlos and Miguel Vargas Zaconet were two brothers who operated a commercial photography studio in Arequipa, Peru from 1912 to 1927. They were among the first to combine long moonlight exposures. What distinguishes the Vargas brother's work from Steichen's Balzac images is that the brothers carefully staged a series of nighttime images with multiple light sources, refining their techniques over a period of years. They placed lights in various locations, both within the scene they were photographing, and outside the frame. They thoughtfully illuminated key elements of the scene, and used moonlight to expose the background over the course of long exposures. They balanced their own added light with the existing light, be it moonlight or streetlights. Photographers before this time had used added light without much regard for aesthetics, but the Nocturnes of the Vargas brothers were carefully designed for maximum visual impact. Indeed, they orchestrated complex scenes with numerous posed figures who often had to hold a pose for extended periods of time. Their creation of their imagery was intentionally choreographed in collaboration with each other and their subjects. The photo historian Peter Yenne surmises that it was advances in photographic technology and the advent of electric light that initially led to this body of work. In an article accompanying an exhibit of the brothers' work entitled *The Vargas Brothers, Pictorialism, and the Nocturnes*, Yenne writes that, "Taking a cue from the silent screen, they concocted a series of elaborate tableaux using moonlight, lanterns, bonfires, flash powder and street lamps. These theatrical scenes required exposures of up to an hour, and meticulous attention to detail."[9]

Although the Vargas brothers' photographs are not widely known outside of Peru, their night photographs were more sophisticated than anything that anyone else would do for decades to come. It is unlikely that their photographs were seen by their contemporaries in the US or Europe, lest others would no doubt have copied their efforts. As it was, there doesn't seem to be a comparable body of work until the late 1950s in the iconic railroad imagery of O. Winston Link and his colleagues. In between the Vargas brothers' Peruvian Nocturnes, and Link's railroad images, there were plenty of other photographers photographing at night and experimenting with using light in new ways.

The Hungarian photographer Brassaï produced some of the best-known night photographs of Paris in the 1930s,[10] but in terms of lighting, he mainly used the contemporary equivalent of an on-camera flash—a narrow tray of magnesium flash powder held overhead alongside the camera. It was Brassaï's use of explosive flash powder that led Picasso to give him the nickname of "The Terrorist."[11] The great surrealist photographer Man Ray, who was also living in Paris in the 1930s, made what may have been the first photographs using the technique of drawing with light for artistic expression. Ray's 1935 series of images entitled *Space Writing* were thought to be scribbles of light until photographer Ellen Carey discovered Ray's signature written with light camouflaged in one of the images after a conversation with a curator from the Smithsonian about Carey's own drawing with light work.[12]

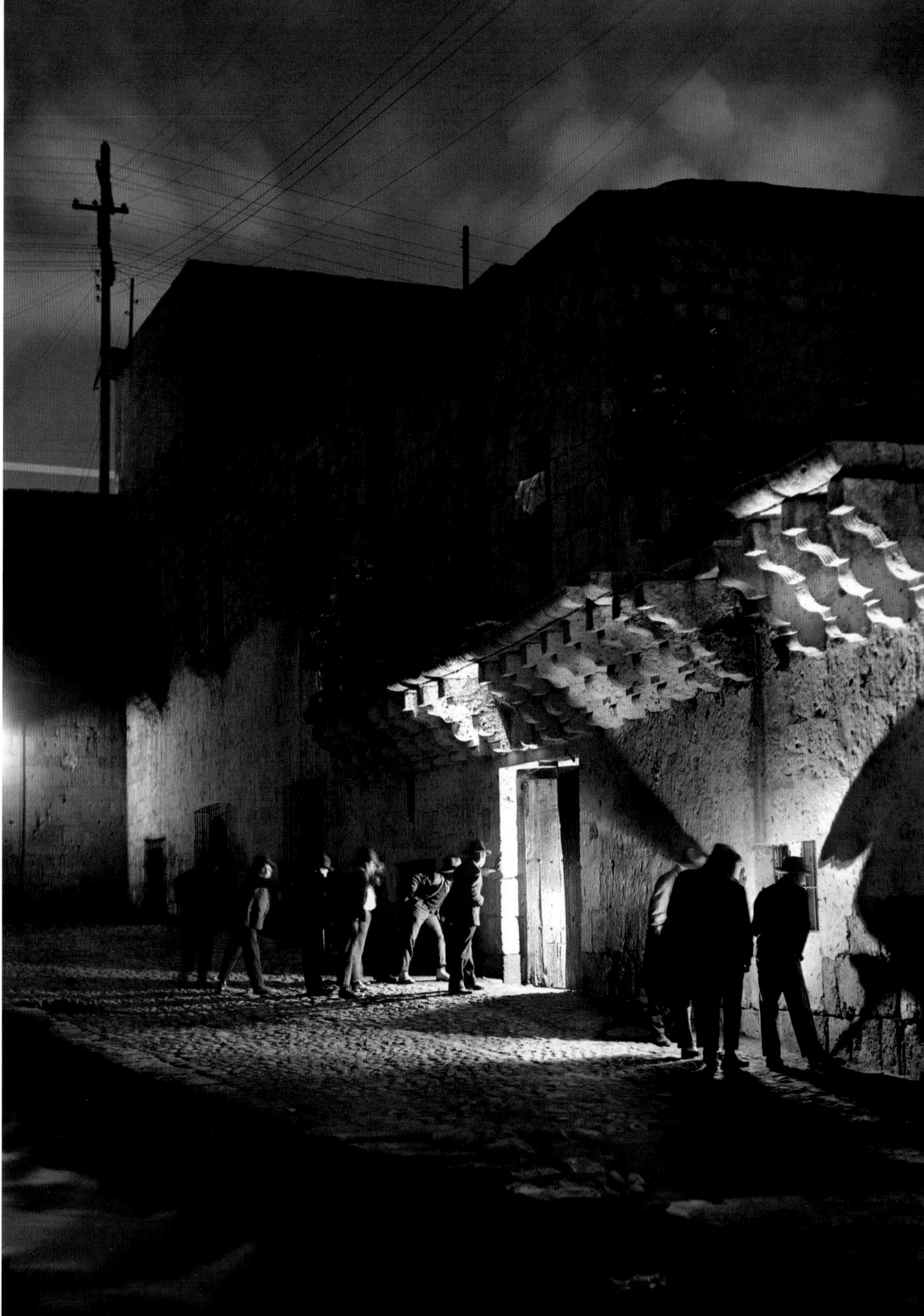

"Nocturne: Entrance to the Cabezona," Carlos and Miguel Vargas, 1920

According to historian Petter Yenne, there's reason to think that the picture of the men outside a tavern entrance is part of a series commemorating a political uprising protesting the dominance of the central government over the southern provinces. The Cabezona still stands—it was a rambling apartment complex owned by a woman with a big head (hence the name), which also housed a tavern/whorehouse that was in all likelihood patronized by local artists and bohemians, including the Vargas brothers.

Bill Brandt, an English photographer who apprenticed with Man Ray in Paris in 1930, was one of many photographers influenced and inspired by Brassaï's seminal book, *Paris de Nuit*. He also created several bodies of nighttime images during the 1930s and 1940s, including those published in his book entitled *A Night in London*,[13] and photographs of a darkened London taken by moonlight during the German Blitz in 1939 and 1940.[14]

Brandt was less concerned with recording reality the way that Brassai did with his documentary images than he was with creating something dark and mysterious and transforming a scene through the use of staging and darkroom manipulation. Brandt's use of lighting was rudimentary, but he often staged his night photographs using friends and family as models. It is Brandt's use of pre-visualization to create a photograph that he saw in his mind rather than what he saw in the viewfinder that distinguished him from his peers. Brandt used whatever techniques were available to him to shape an image the way he saw it in his mind, regardless of whether the result was fact or fiction. He said, "Photography is still a very new medium and everything must be tried and dared . . . photography has no rules. It is not a sport. It is the result which counts, no matter how it is achieved.[15]

Life magazine photographer Gjon Mili began working with Harold "Doc" Edgerton, who was a pioneer in short duration flash photography at the Massachusetts Institute of Technology (MIT), at the beginning of 1937. There, they experimented with flash to create stop action images of fast-moving objects. Edgerton's famous pictures of an apple exploding as a bullet passes through it, and a playing card being split by a bullet, are prime examples. This work indirectly led to the images that Mili would be best known for, as he experimented with lighting techniques throughout his career. These images have come to be called *Picasso's Light Drawings*.

Mili had photographed figure skaters with small lights attached to their ice skates and made long exposures while they glided across the ice in a darkened rink. The lights traced the path of the skaters' routines, creating a permanent record of their movements on film. When *Life* sent Mili to France to photograph Picasso, Mili showed these images to Picasso in order to convince him to collaborate on a portrait of the artist drawing with light. He agreed, and Picasso was so impressed with the result that the two did four more sessions together. In total Mili recorded a total of 30 Picasso light drawings, many of which were published in *Life* magazine in 1949.[16] The technique involved Picasso using a small electric light in a darkened room to make the

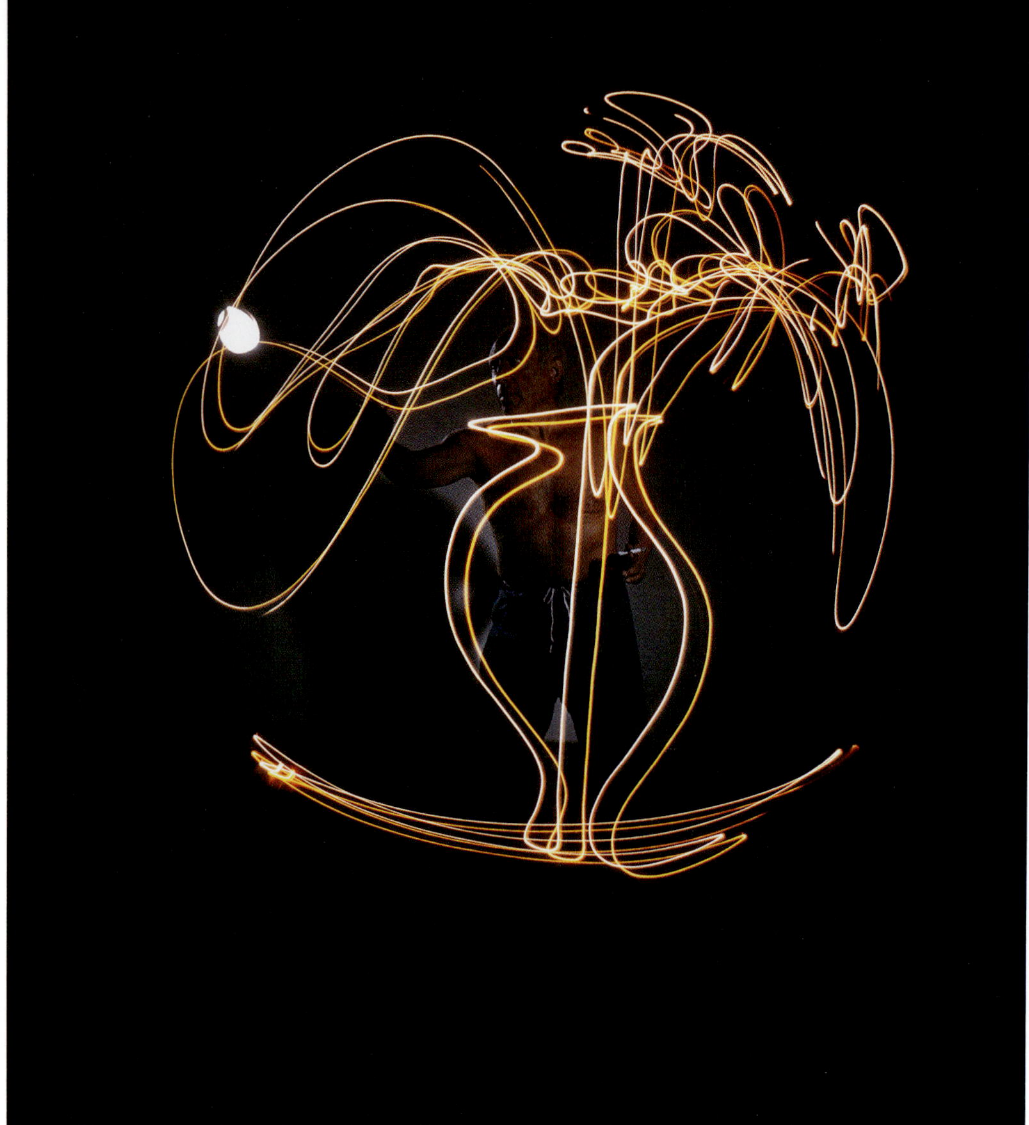

Picasso drawing with light in his studio, Gjon Mili, 1949

Mili was assigned to photograph Picasso for *Life* magazine, and after showing the Spanish painter some of his images of figure skaters with lights on their skates, Picasso decided to try drawing with light for himself.

drawing, and Mili firing a flash one or more times to record the artist's portrait along with the light drawing.

During the 1970s, more and more photographers and artists began to use light in novel ways in their photographs. The drawing with light techniques that Man Ray and Picasso had used in the 1930s and 1940s evolved and grew in new directions. In the decades between when Ray and Picasso made their light drawings and the 1970s, conceptions about photography were changing, as was the technology that made drawing and painting with light a more practical endeavor. Photographers increasingly thought of themselves as artists rather than technicians or documentarians. Flashlights and other lighting tools became brighter, lighter, and more portable, a phenomenon that would repeat itself again at the dawn of the 21st century when flashlights became exponentially brighter, and batteries longer lasting and more powerful.

Photographers also began to work outdoors at night, which provided considerably more freedom than the confines of a small interior space. Two New York photographers in particular took the light drawing technique to new levels. Both David Lebe and Eric Staller created their pioneering images from the 1970s without any awareness of light painting as a genre or art form, but their work evolved naturally out of curiosity and experimentation as part of their creative process.

David Lebe came to light drawing while looking for a way to make expansive, uncluttered images in a cramped apartment one night in 1976. Stoned, and working in the dark, he opened

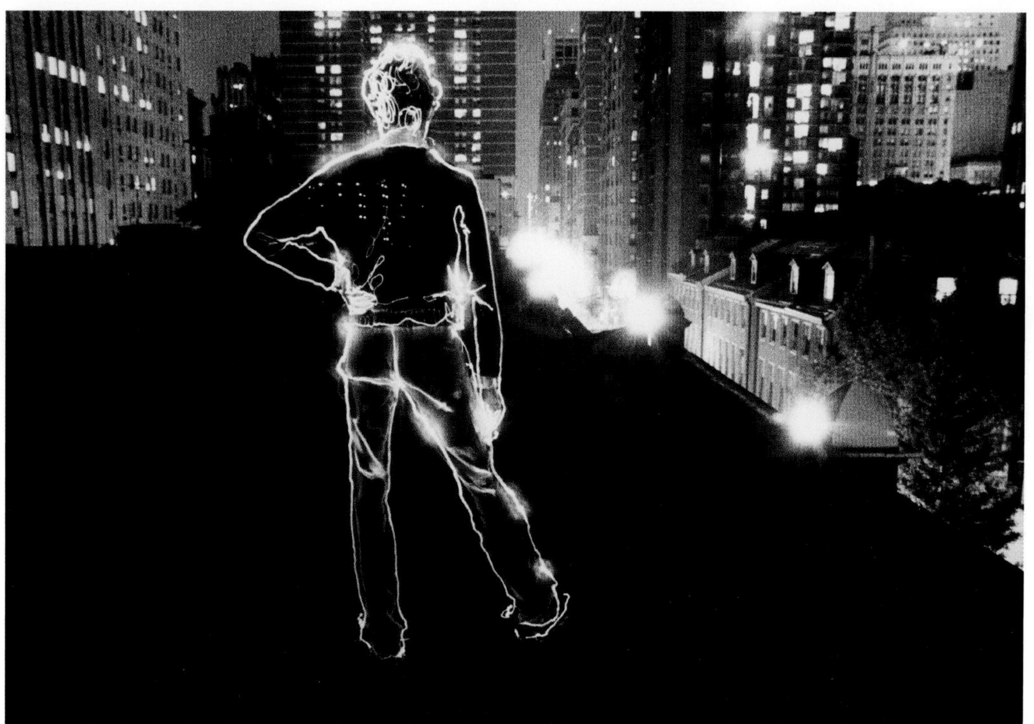

"Angelo on the Roof," 15th and Pine Streets, Philadelphia, David Lebe, 1979

Lebe developed his light drawing technique over a period of several years after having the idea to trace a figure with a penlight during a long exposure. This is his best-known image, and was featured recently on the cover of *Transformational Imagemaking: Handmade Photography Since 1960* by Robert Hirsch.

the shutter for a long exposure and traced an outline of himself while pointing a flashlight back at the camera, resulting in a minimalist image of a glowing figure on black and white film. Lebe had seen images of car headlights and taillights tracing lines of light in photographs, and therefore didn't feel like he had invented anything new, but that he was "expanding a phenomenon native to the medium."[17] He realized that there was great creative potential in this technique, and he continued experimenting with what he called "light drawings," making images both indoors and out over a period of almost twenty years. Later in the mid-1980s, Lebe created still life images by tracing flowers and other objects with a penlight as a means to escape temporarily from the turmoil in his life. One night, after realizing that he had forgotten to bring home flowers to use in these light drawings, he decided to simply create the flowers with light, and the "Scribbles" series was born. He showed his light drawings in galleries in New York and Philadelphia in the early 1980s, when he also used the term "painted photograms," which was designed to blur the lines between painting and photography.[18]

Eric Staller saw the quiet nighttime streets of his neighborhood as stages waiting to be transformed by his magic wand—the Fourth of July sparkler. In the mid- to late 1970s, Staller drove around New York scouting locations for what he called his, "choreographies of light."[19] Initially, he used a single handheld sparkler that burned for about a minute to trace objects in front of his camera. He would plan the shot, light the sparkler, and run through the scene outlining objects, or simply drawing lines, hoping to finish before the sparkler burned out. Impressed by the architectural uses of the human figure in Fritz Lang's film *Metropolis* and old *Busby Berkeley* films, Staller began to think of the geometry of his body. By attaching a newly discovered sparkler that lasted for ten minutes to a broomstick, he was able to fill large volumes of space with his light drawings, moving in front of the camera while the shutter was open. He was not recorded in the image because he moved constantly, never remaining in any one place long enough to register on the film. In time his work became more complex, and Staller built lighting tools including a hoop with Christmas lights, and an illuminated cube on wheels that he used to create geometric shapes in space. Staller came to think of the making of his images as "light performances," as "Crowds of curious garbage men, night watchmen, workaholic Wall Streeters and the homeless gathered to watch the lunatic with the blazing broomstick!"[20] Eric Staller's brother Jan is also a well-known night photographer who published the influential books of color night photography *Frontier New York* in 1979, and *On Planet Earth* in 1997.

Steve Harper is better known for his role as a pioneering educator in the field of night photography than for his images, and he influenced a generation of photography students in the San Francisco Bay Area. Many of those former students including the author are still involved in night photography and light painting a quarter of a century later. He developed and taught the first college-level class in night photography at the Academy of Art College in San Francisco beginning in the late 1970s. Harper was one of a group of photographers experimenting with

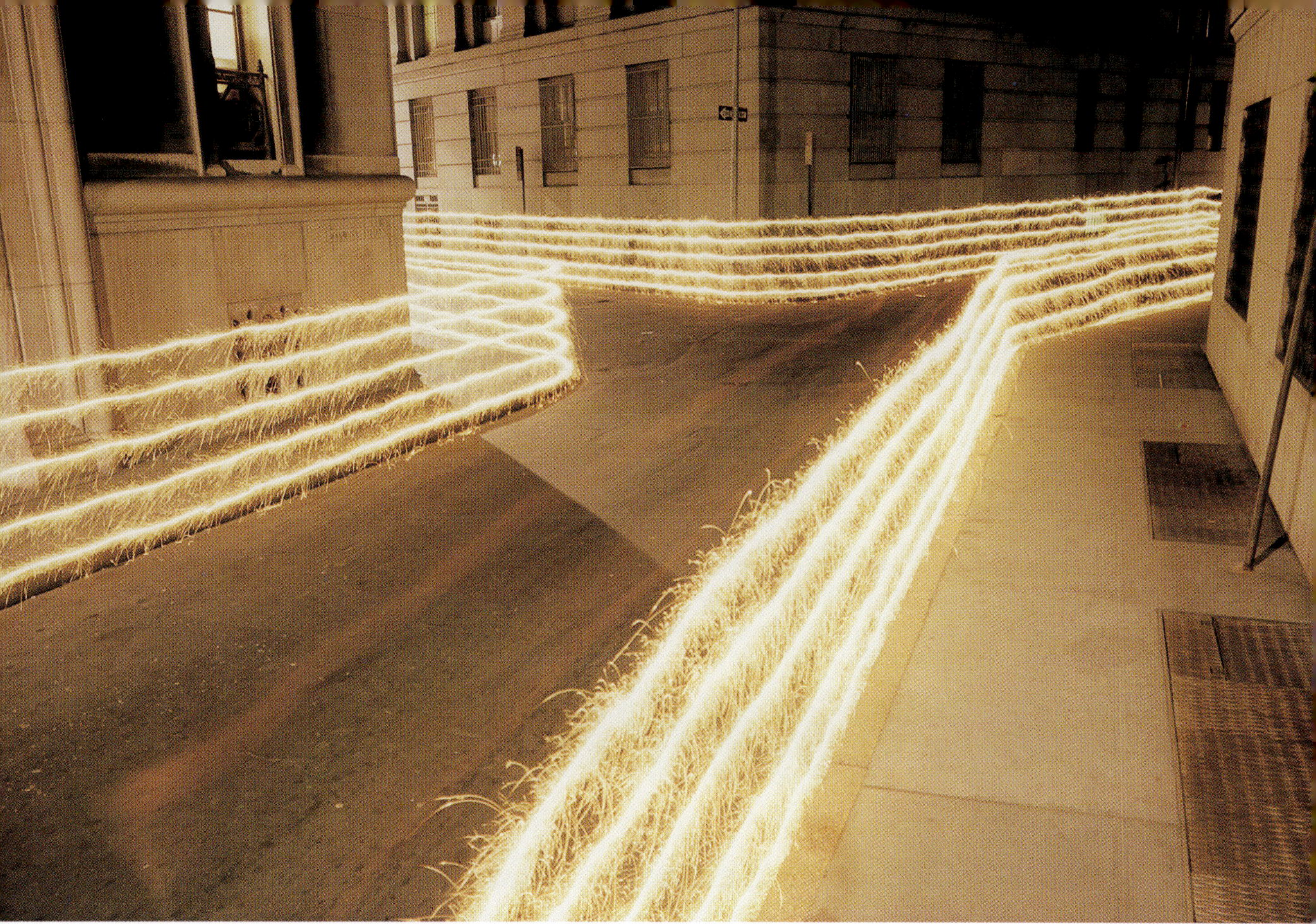

"Ribbon on Hanover Street," Eric Staller, 1978

Staller attached five sparklers to a broomstick, which he held at arm's length as he walked down Hanover Street in lower Manhattan, much to the amusement of curious garbage men, night watchmen, and homeless people who he says gathered to watch the lunatic with the blazing broomstick.

night photography in the Bay Area in the 1970s, which included Richard Misrach, Arthur Ollman, Steve Fitch, and Jerry Burchard. Before he retired from teaching, sharing the results of his experiments with his students was perhaps as important as the resulting images for Harper. He often collaborated with students during field sessions, experimenting with different films, development and lighting techniques, and encouraging students to push themselves to do something new, and also to work with each other as part of the creative process.

Steve Harper has always been acutely aware of color, and before digital cameras he preferred to work with tungsten balanced slide film. He used both flashlights and strobe for light painting—whichever was more appropriate to the shot. He frequently used colored filters on his light sources, and encouraged his students to do the same to control mood of the image, and to achieve a pleasing color balance at a time when most other light painters and night photographers were more concerned simply with getting a good exposure.

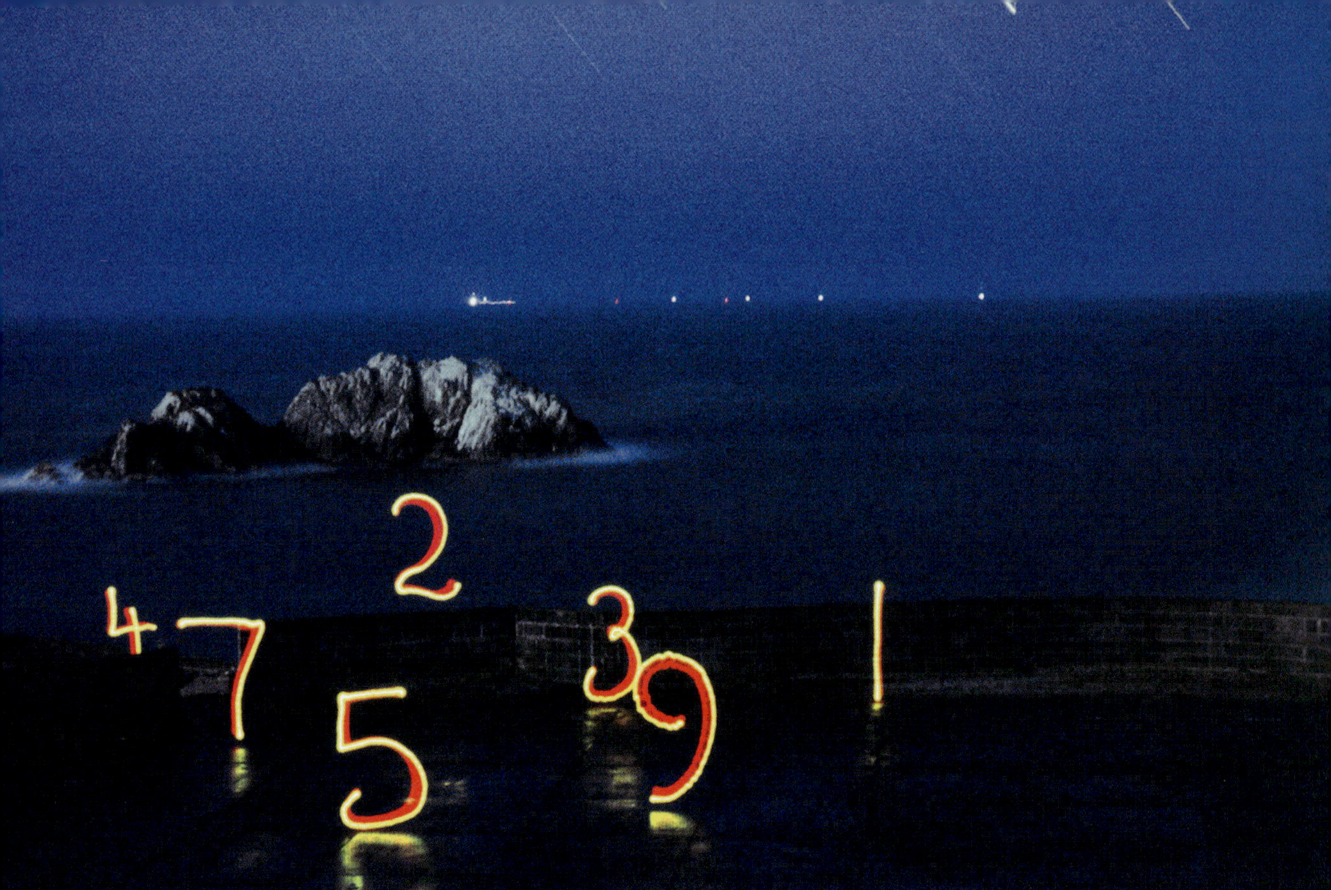

"1, 2, 3, 4, 5, 9, 7," Steve Harper and Kiyoshi Sekizuka, 1981

Harper often photographed with his students, which may be partly why he was so influential on so many photographers in the Bay Area in the 1970s and 1980s. In this photograph, 6 and 8 were on break during this exposure made in San Francisco.

Vicki DaSilva was exposed to the images of Marey and Demeny, as well as Mili's Picasso images while studying the history of photography in art school in the early 1980s. These images, along with her interests in performance art, text-based art, minimalism, and graffiti were the impetus for her to explore the mediums of painting and drawing with light. She experimented and tried many different techniques over a period of years, slowly developing her style and finding meaning in her work. She eventually came to think of her work as a means of socio-political expression as text became an increasingly important part of her work. In 1986, she met her husband Antonio, an electrician, and together they devised a complex system involving moving long fluorescent tubes on a track system to create huge fields of colored light for what may be her best-known work. Da Silva's current projects address current events and political causes, and she often collaborates with non-profit organizations who use her images as fund-raising tools for causes that she supports. DaSilva was one of the first people to use light painting photography as a tool to achieve other goals, rather than simply as a form of expression. This phenomenon has become increasingly popular in recent years as light painting is used both commercially and politically to express ideas in the media.

William Lesch began his photographic career as a large format black and white photographer in the tradition of Ansel Adams in the 1970s. He became interested in the appearance of objects that moved during long exposures, first in the work of early photographers who had no choice but to use long exposures, and then later in his own work. He experimented with neutral density filters to extend his exposure times, and began working with color film about 1980. He moved from the midwest where he had grown up to the Sonoran desert in Tucson, AZ. He struggled to make photographs, trying to capture the intensity of the desert, and frustrated by the apparent stillness and lack of activity. The techniques he employed in his earlier work no longer served him. Eventually, he realized that in the desert, it was the light that changed more than anything else, as shadows moved across the landscape and colors intensified at the beginning and end of each day. In the early 1980s, Lesch began working with multiple exposures on the same sheet of color film using red, blue, and green color separation filters. The results were interesting, but impossible to control. A major breakthrough occurred with his work when he started making just two exposures, one during the day and one at night, without moving the camera, on one sheet of film. These images usually included a foreground that was in shadow during the daytime shot, which he would paint with light during the night exposure, using a car headlight covered with colored gels and connected to a motorcycle battery.[21] Lesch had great success with this technique, creating wildly colorful images that were different from any other light painting photography that had come before. He published a book of these images entitled *Expansions* in 1992.

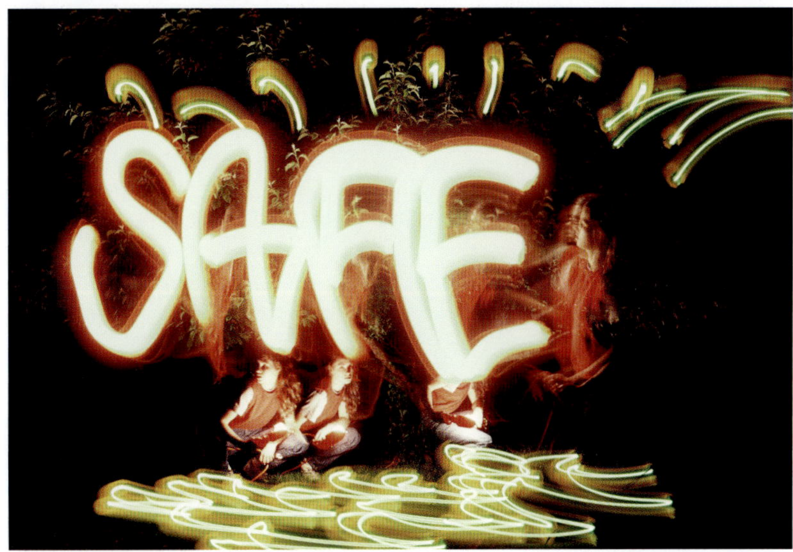

"Safe," Vicki DaSilva, 1984

Much of DaSilva's art has been influenced by her activism working for social justice, and she considers this image a defining moment in the direction of her work.

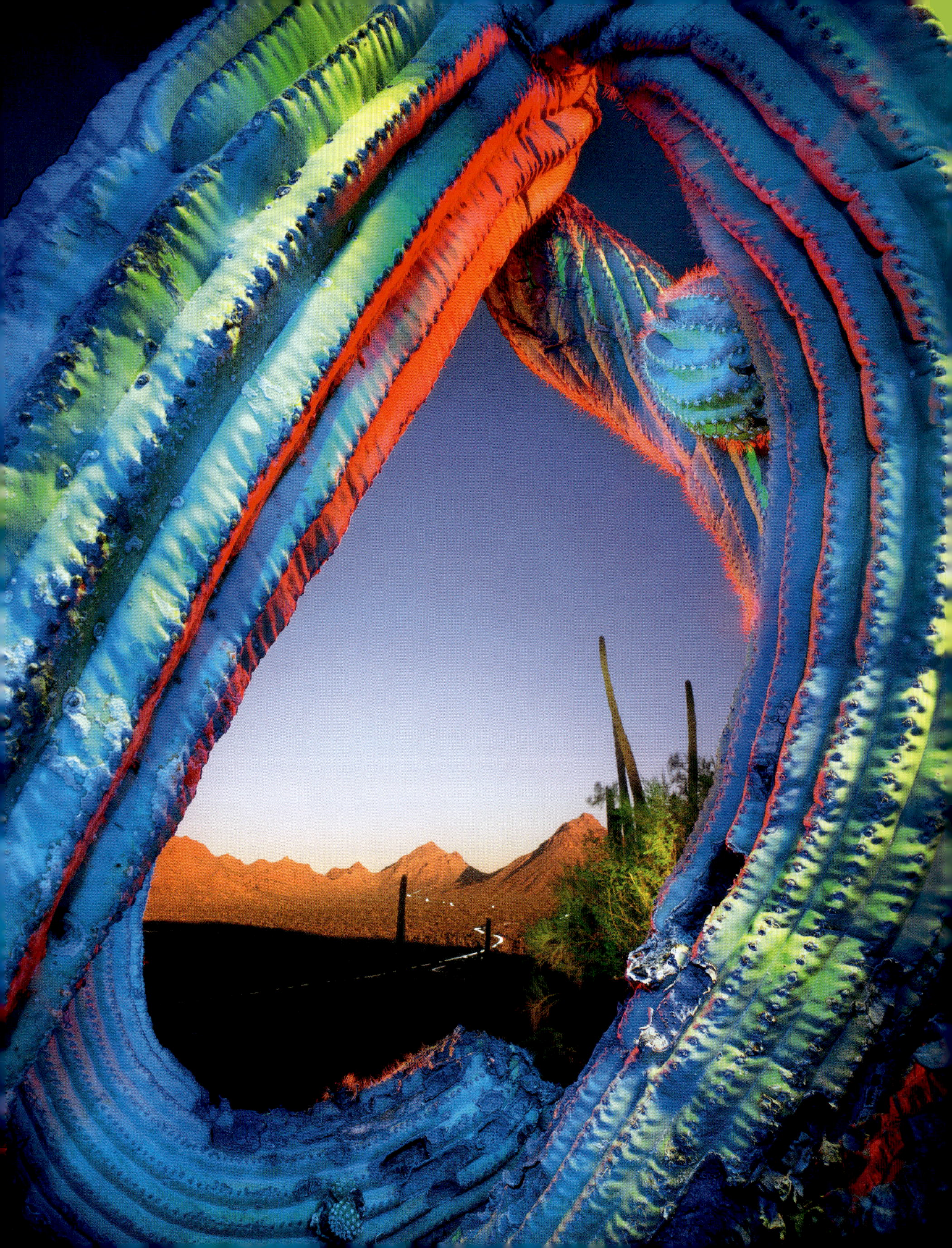

"Heart of Saguaro," William Lesch, 1984

This image was the culmination of a process of photographically exploring the Sonoran desert over many years. The image was used by Kodak in the early 1990s to promote their Ektachrome EPY film.

Troy Paiva is a self-taught photographer and light painter who has photographed abandoned and ruined towns and structures in the California and Nevada deserts since 1989 when he saw his brother Tom's work from a class with Steve Harper. He sat in on a few of Harper's classes, and was instantly hooked on night photography and fairy quickly started to use intensely colored lights to illuminate the shadows of his photographs. After being exposed to the bold use of color in both Chip Simons' and William Lesch's work, Paiva developed his own style, initially using handheld flashes with colored gels for his primary light source. By the mid-1990s, Paiva was also using maglite flashlights when the situation called for a continuous light source, and then with the advent of LED flashlights and more powerful batteries at the turn of the century, he switched to flashlights almost exclusively.

Paiva's lighting style has been emulated by many photographers over the years, because he has posted hundreds of images on his own website, and thousands on Flickr, many times filling in the back story on his locations with text about the colorful places he photographs. He says, "I've been able to see places and things that virtually no one else has, day or night, and I get to night-shoot 'em. I like the adventure, the challenge and difficulty."[22] Paiva is driven to explore and photograph, and being copied has forced him to push himself to evolve and break new ground with both locations and techniques. He is one of the most passionate and prolific night photographers and light painters working today.

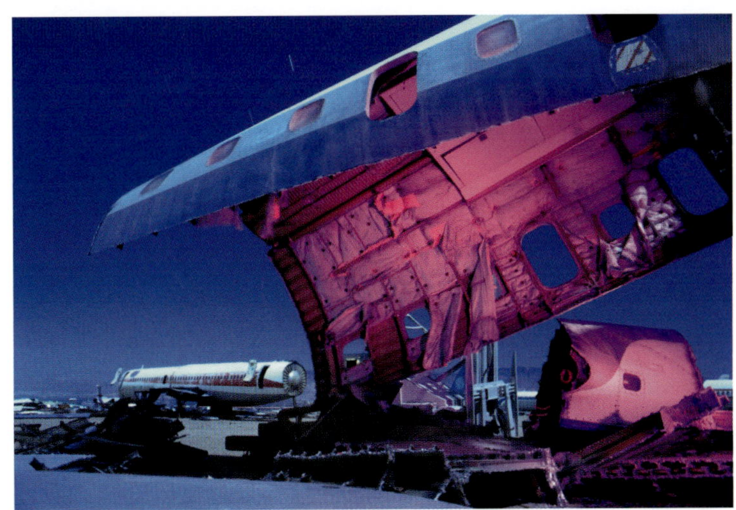

"DC-8 and 880," Troy Paiva, 1989

Paiva says, "I had only been night shooting a few months when I made this image." In those pre-9/11 days access to this amazing junkyard only took a couple of phone calls. Today Mojave Airport has a strict "No photography beyond the flight line" policy, and access is all but impossible. Both of these aircraft disappeared into the smelter shortly after I took this.

This brief chapter barely scratches the surface of the difficult-to-define genre of light painting photography. There are no doubt dozens of other artists and photographers whose work could be included here. Much of it rests in obscurity in forgotten files, unseen for decades. Because light painting as a motif is a relatively recent phenomenon, there are few references in books, journals, and museum collections. Still the photographers and images presented here help to trace the evolution of added light photography, light painting photography, and light drawing as art forms. There has been an explosion of interest in light painting since the beginning of the 21st century, largely brought about by advances in technology—digital cameras, flashlights, and batteries, as well as social media and the internet. As night photography and light painting become increasingly common, it is the truly creative and dedicated artists whose work will catch our attention and hold our imagination in the future, and no doubt there will be a better historical record of light painting photography going forward thanks to websites like www. LightPaintingPhotography.com and www.lpwalliance.com. We explore the images of some of those photographers in the chapters on light painting and light drawing later in the book.

NOTES

1 Naomi Rosenblum, *A World History of Photography*, Abbeville Press, Fourth Edition (January 29, 2008), p. 248.

2 Michel Frizot (editor), *A New History of Photography*, Konemann, 1998 English Translation Edition, p. 256.

3 Ibid., p. 274.

4 Jason Page, LightPaintingPhotography.com, Page in California, and Sergey Churkin in Russia have done extensive research on light painting history, and to date have not been able to find any earlier examples of light painting or drawing.

5 http://www.musee-rodin.fr/en/rodin/educational-files/rodin-and-steichen#references

6 *Anthony's Photographic Bulletin*, April, 1871, pp. 589–590.

7 Ibid., pp. 34–36

8 Frank Bunker Gilbreth, *Motion Model and the Age of Measurement*, Dodge Idea, no. 32 (1916), p. 662.

9 From email correspondence with Peter Yenne, July, 2009.

10 Brassaï's book, *Paris de Nuit*, published by Arts et Metiers Graphiques in 1933 was the first book of night photographs ever published. It has been reprinted twice, and the 1987 Parthenon edition is a faithful reproduction of the original, which was printed in rich photo gravure. It is an essential volume for any night photography library.

11 Paul Delany, *Bill Brandt, A Life* (Jonathan Cape, 2004), p. 77.

12 Krystian Von Speidel, Man in the Mirror, *Venü* magazine (March/April 2011), pp. 54–55.

13 Unfortunately, *A Night On London* has never been reprinted, and original copies are extremely rare and expensive.

14 Bill Brandt, *Blackout in London* (Lilliput, December, 1939) and Bill Brandt, *London Under Blackout* (*Life* magazine, January 1, 1940).

15 A Photographer's London, Introduction to Bill Brandt, *Camera in London*, Focal Press, 1948.

16 *Life* magazine, December 12, 1949.

17 From email correspondence with David Lebe, January, 2014.

18 Ibid., Lebe.

19 Eric Staller, *Out of My Mind*, Staller Studio Nederland, 2006, Introduction.

20 Ibid., Staller.

21 From email correspondence with William Lesch, January, 2014.

22 From email correspondence with Troy Paiva, February, 2014.

NIGHT PHOTOGRAPHY EQUIPMENT

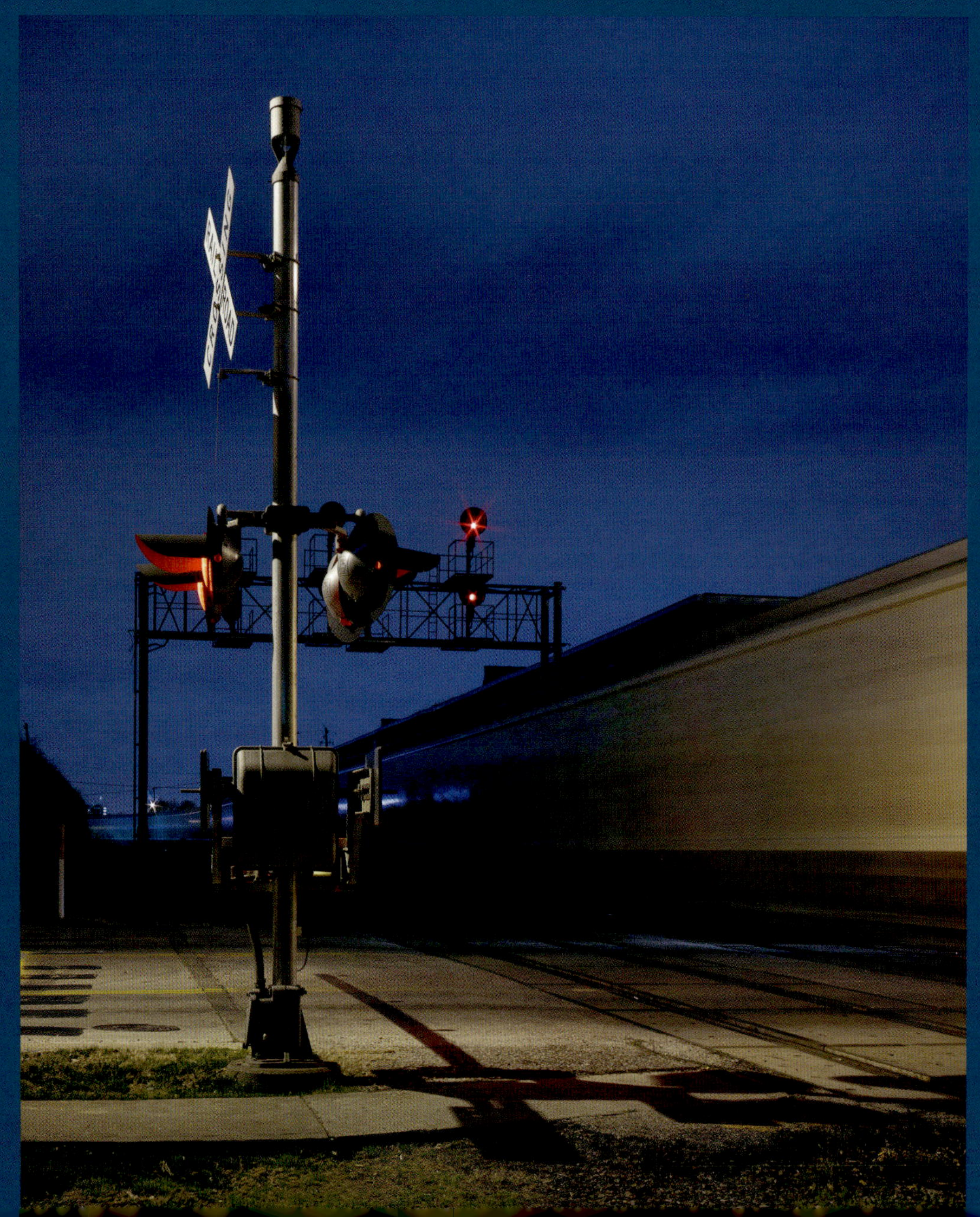

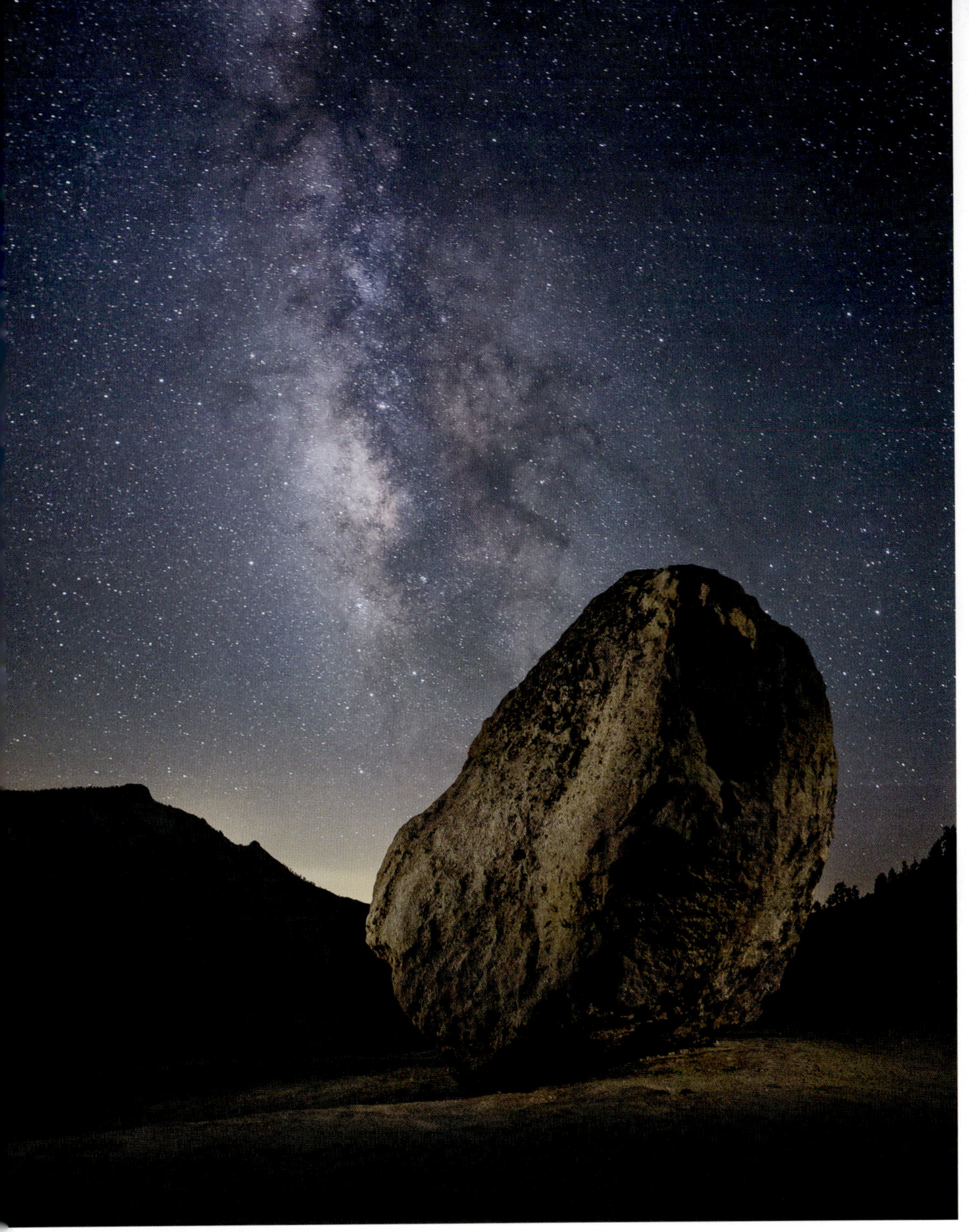

2

"Steve's Rock and Milky Way," Olmsted Point, Yosemite National Park, CA. 25 seconds, f4 at ISO 12,800. Canon 6D, Rokinon 24 mm f1.4. Low-power LED flashlight from camera left and right. Recent Model cameras and new, less expensive optics make this kind of image much easier to create than in past years.

In this chapter, we explore equipment options and talk about how they relate to the processes and challenges of night photography and light painting. The selection of cameras, lenses, tripods, and other gear is mostly a matter of personal choice, but a brief discussion of the essential night photographer's tool kit is presented to help the reader make informed decisions about equipment choices. I reluctantly mention a few specific camera models as examples of certain features, knowing that new models with new features and capabilities are released all the time. Even so, the cameras mentioned in this chapter will still make excellent choices, even after they have been replaced, especially for those shopping for good value in a used camera.

As night photography becomes increasingly popular, many people are "sub-specializing" in specific forms of night photography once they have experienced some of the many possibilities afforded by advances in digital camera technology. A current generation full-frame DSLR (Digital Single Lens Reflex) or mirrorless camera is the best choice for "astro-landscape," or star point and Milky Way photography, but is probably overkill for someone primarily interested in urban night photography. Just a few years ago DSLRs were the only viable camera choice for night photography, and those with full-frame sensors were the default choice for anyone serious about shooting at night. Current APSC (Advanced Photo System type-C) sensor DSLRs are quite capable in almost every situation, and many of the new mirrorless, micro four-thirds, and advanced compact cameras provide increasingly viable options for those looking for a lighter, or less potentially less expensive option.

CAMERA CHOICE

Almost any camera that can be mounted on a tripod has a manual exposure control and the ability to do extended exposures can be used for night photography. All DSLR cameras can be used at night, but in most cases the newer the model, the better the results are likely to be. The biggest advantage to the most recent DSLR cameras is that they produce less long exposure and high-ISO noise than older cameras, and this is especially true of the more expensive full-frame sensor cameras. Full-frame sensor cameras will almost always produce lower noise levels than smaller sensor cameras, but noise is becoming less of an issue as each successive generation of cameras and RAW processing software continues to improve. If image quality is your primary concern and you plan to make prints 20 × 30 inches or larger, consider a camera with a full-frame sensor. If you are primarily interested in photographing the landscape on moonless nights to capture star points and the Milky Way, a full-frame sensor camera will be a worthwhile investment, as these are the cameras that perform best at the extreme ISOs required for this type of work. Another consideration in favor of full-frame sensor cameras is the availability of wide-angle prime and manual focus lenses. To get the extreme wide-angle views favored by many night photographers, those with APSC sensor cameras are generally limited to zoom lenses, which have some limitations for night photography. Those limitations are explained in the next section.

The Canon 6D and Nikon D610 are both really excellent choices, and are the first full-frame sensor cameras available for less than $2000. Nikon's mid-level full-frame D750 offers a few extra features like a built-in intervalometer, and an articulated screen that makes photographing at low camera angles easier. Full-frame DSLRs like the D810 and 5D MK III offer modest advantages over the entry-level full-frame cameras mentioned above, and are certainly worth considering if you have a substantial budget. However, your money might be better spent on quality lenses unless you have a specific need for more advanced features or higher megapixel counts. In general, the top-of-the-line cameras primarily designed for photo journalists like the Nikon D3x, D4s or Canon 1Dx are not worth the cost for night photography alone because the high-end features that make these cameras so expensive, like high frame rate and superfast autofocus, are irrelevant at night.

More megapixels does not necessarily mean better image quality, and megapixel count shouldn't be a top priority when choosing a camera. Megapixels correlate more closely with maximum possible print size than with image quality, which is more a factor of the size of individual photo sites on the sensor. Bear in mind that the huge files generated by cameras with high megapixel counts require a lot of processing power, and you may need to upgrade your computer, and image storage capacity. A camera with 12–18 megapixels has more than enough resolution for most people. Nikon and Canon have the lion's share of the market, and they each have their advantages. In general, the Nikons have a wider dynamic range (which is especially relevant for urban night photography), and slightly better image quality, while Canon cameras have better live view, which enables easier focusing in low light, and automatic long-exposure noise reduction (LENR), which is more efficient and useful than simply on or off modes.

There are other options. Pentax has developed a unique solution to the problem of stars rendering as lines during long exposures due to the Earth's movement, called Astrotracer. It combines the use of Pentax's in-camera image stabilization with a hotshot-mounted GPS unit. Rather than build image stabilization into their lenses as Canon and Nikon have done, the sensors in Pentax camera bodies move to compensate for vibration during exposure. The Astrotracer function takes advantage of this feature by slowly shifting the sensor to account for the Earth's rotation during an exposure. It allows for exposures of up to 5 minutes in length, compared to the 10–30-second exposure limitation with fixed sensor cameras. Astrotracer takes some effort, but it is a great option for astro-landscape photography. It is relatively inexpensive when compared with full-frame sensor cameras.

In late 2013, Sony released the first full-frame mirrorless cameras: the A7 and A7r. The A7r is reported to have the same sensor as the Nikon D800, automatically moving it to the head of the pack in image quality while maintaining a fairly compact size. In mid-2014, Sony released the full-frame A7s that has remarkable image quality at very high ISOs. As sales of low to midrange mirrorless cameras have been hindered by the ever-increasing quality and ubiquity of cell phone cameras, expect to see camera manufacturers introducing more high-end mirrorless cameras like the Sony. They could be the next evolutionary step in digital cameras. There have been major advances in compact DSLR, mirrorless, interchangeable lens cameras in recent years, and one of these cameras would be good for travel photography at night, or anyone else who is concerned with carrying a lot of weight. Fuji's X series, the Olympus OMD cameras, and the Sony NEX7 are good examples of this type of camera that can be used successfully at night. Olympus offers a unique feature called Live Bulb, which allows the user to view an image, and its histogram as it builds during the exposure, so that the exposure can be stopped at just the right moment. The image quality of most of these cameras is not as good as APSC or full-frame sensors, but the cameras are considerably smaller and lighter. One exception is the fantastic Fujifilm X-T1, which sports a 16 MP APSC sensor, and is the top performer in its class for high-ISO shooting. In general, compact fixed lens or high-end point and shoot cameras still have too many limitations to be truly useful for night photographers. Few if any have a bulb or time setting for unlimited exposures. Features to watch out for with point and shoots are the ability to save RAW files, a bulb, or long exposure mode, manual exposure mode, and access to all ISOs and shutter speeds at all times. For example, the Canon G16 (which is otherwise a fine camera) yields decent quality images at ISOs up to 1600, but as soon as the shutter speed reaches 30 seconds or longer, the camera is locked in at ISO 80! With a 250-second maximum exposure length, this is extremely limiting for anyone wanting to photograph by moonlight, or in other very dark environments. Still, the G16 (or G1X with its larger sensor) would be good backup or travel cameras for those who need to travel lightly. Medium format digital cameras and backs are generally not well suited to night photography due to limitations of shutter speed and ISO, not to mention the risk of theft or damage to such an expensive piece of equipment in the field.

Choosing a camera is a very personal decision, as well as a substantial investment that you are likely to live with for a long time. You should choose one after careful consideration of your specific needs and budget, not simply on someone else's recommendation. Just as the camera needs of a wildlife photographer and a wedding photographer are quite different, the same is true of night photographers. Our needs are closest to those of landscape photographers, which makes sense since night photographers often photograph the landscape—at night! Going to a professional camera store with a knowledgeable sales staff and spending time handling each of the cameras under consideration is a great way to decide if a camera is right for you or not. Ergonomics and menu navigation vary tremendously from one camera to the next, and the only way to evaluate these things is by actually using the camera. The very best way to get a good feel for a camera would be to rent the various cameras that you are thinking about purchasing from a service like BorrowLenses.com or LensRentals.com.

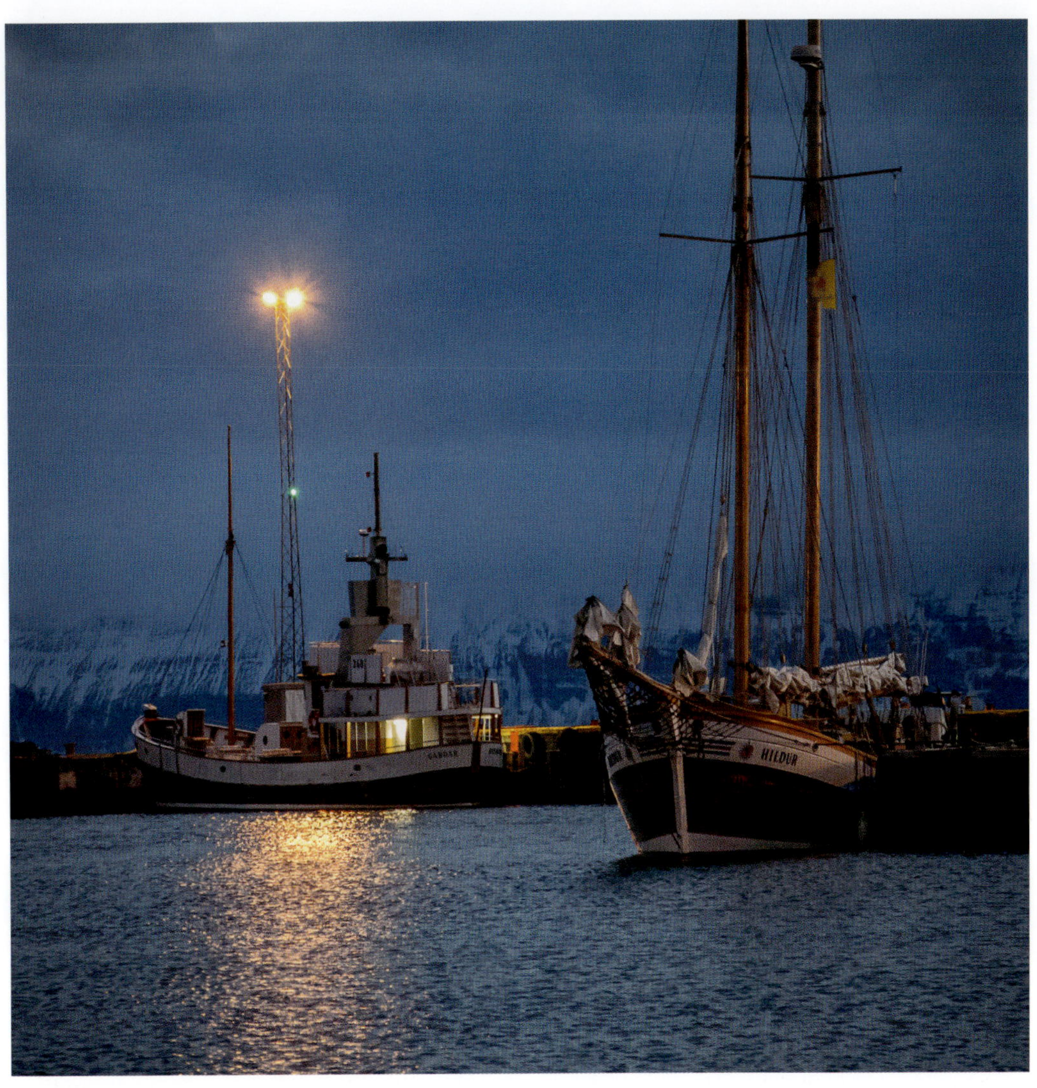

Husavik, Iceland in twilight. 1/20 second, f3.2 at ISO 1250. Canon G15 camera. Images shot at such high ISOs were rarely of print quality until very recent compact cameras. Most can't compare in image quality to a DSLR, but the convenience of such a small camera for travel is often worth the sacrifice.

Digital cameras are one commodity where you truly get what you pay for, and it generally is a good strategy to buy the newest and most expensive model you can afford—assuming that you plan to print your images. If you don't expect to print your photographs and will only display them online or on your own computer, a lesser or older camera will more than suffice.

Main features to look for in digital cameras for night photography:

1. First and foremost is the ability to shoot RAW files, and full manual exposure controls with a bulb shutter speed setting. These are a given with all DSLRs.
2. Effective Live View is extremely helpful for focusing and determining composition.
3. High-ISO capability (at least 6400 for native 100 ISO cameras, and 12,800 for native 200 ISO) is important for performing test exposures in moonlight. Even if the image quality is mediocre at these ISOs, you'll still be able to use them for exposure, composition, and focus checks. 6400 is the standard ISO for astro-landscape photography.
4. Availability of a shutter release with built-in timer or intervalometer. Aftermarket timers are about one-third of the price of name brand timers. Again, this is a given with DSLRs, but not so with compact or point and shoot cameras.
5. In-camera LENR buffering that allows you to keep shooting without waiting for the LENR to finish processing the previous image. Currently, this is limited to the Canon 5D series, 6D series, and 7D series.
6. Auto LENR, or at least the ability to turn LENR on and off. A few cameras have it permanently switched on, which renders the camera useless for stacking and time lapse photography.
7. A full-frame sensor. They generate cleaner files with less noise, and there is a wider selection of available lenses. Full-frame sensor cameras can almost always be used at higher ISOs than smaller sensor cameras. Cameras with good image quality at ISO 6400 or higher will allow you to photograph the landscape with short exposures, preserving the stars as points of light rather than creating star trails. Sony's A7, A7s, Nikon's D610, D750, and D810, and Canon's 6D and 5D MK III are good examples. Future generations of DSLRs will no doubt continue to have improved image quality at high ISOs.
8. Weatherized and durable construction.
9. Easily accessible ISO controls for switching between high and low ISOs for test shots.
10. Easy access to camera settings and functions on the rear LCD with adjustable brightness. Auto brightness is even better.
11. Customizable exposure modes—cameras that have custom exposure modes allow for easy switching between night and daytime, or high-ISO test, and native ISO camera settings.
12. Logical, intuitive, and easy-to-navigate menus. You shouldn't have to pat your head and rub your belly while standing on one foot in the dark to change the ISO, aperture, or shutter speed.

LENSES

After the camera, lens selection is the next important equipment consideration. Any lens can be used for night photography, but most photographers tend to favor wide-angle lenses, which capture more of the atmosphere that makes for successful night photography. There is no reason why longer focal length lenses cannot be used effectively at night, but they generally have smaller maximum apertures, which makes them harder to compose and focus in the dark. Telephoto lenses may require stopping down considerably to get a reasonable depth of field, necessitating longer exposures or higher ISOs, and in turn risking noisier images. Telephoto lenses are most successfully used at night for photographing the rising moon against a silhouetted horizon, or other distant vistas.

As a general rule, fixed focal length or prime manual focus lenses yield the best results, and are the easiest to work with in low-light situations. Autofocus does not work very well in low-light conditions. Even though autofocus lenses generally can be switched to manual focus mode, they are optimized and engineered for autofocusing. Focusing speed is of primary concern for lenses to be able to focus on moving subjects. As a result, the "throw," or amount the lens must rotate to focus from near focus point to infinity, is greatly reduced on autofocus lenses. The short throw in combination with low tension on many lenses makes them difficult to focus manually with any precision. Another engineering concession that was made to preserve the autofocus motor on modern lenses is that they will focus beyond infinity. By extending the throw beyond infinity, it puts less stress on the motor when the lens comes into focus at the infinity setting. What this means for those who are focusing manually is that you cannot simply turn the lens until it stops to set focus to infinity. If a lens is accidentally focused beyond infinity, nothing will be sharp in the resulting images.

Prime lenses also usually have larger maximum apertures than zoom lenses, which makes it easier to focus and compose with them in the dark. Additionally, astro-landscape photography requires pushing the limits of ISO, shortest shutter speed possible, and widest possible aperture. Prime lenses with a maximum aperture of between f1.4 and f2.8 are highly desirable for this type of work. Many primes also yield better image quality and performance than even the best zoom lenses. Primes are designed for a single purpose, while zooms are required to do the job of several lenses, often at a lower price point. Primarily because they are convenient, zoom lenses are much more prevalent than prime lenses today. Zoom lenses can certainly be used with a little extra care, but fixed focal length, manual focus primes still have several advantages for night photography. The image quality of zoom lenses has dramatically improved in recent years, and the problem of reduced sharpness, resolution, and flare from stray light is less of an issue than it was even ten years ago, especially with professional-level lenses. Zooms also tend to be considerably larger and heavier than primes, particularly the most useful ones with wide maximum apertures. Moreover, the complex optical design of zoom lenses means that there are more glass surfaces to reflect light and cause flare. If zoom lenses are to be used, it is best to avoid the inexpensive kit lenses that come with many cameras, as well as lenses that cover a very wide range of focal lengths. While undeniably convenient, a lens that ranges from 18 mm (wide angle) to 200 or even 350 mm (telephoto) and costs only a few hundred dollars cannot be expected to perform as well as a prime lens, especially under the challenging conditions of night photography. For the most part, money spent on top quality prime lenses is well spent. Zeiss makes superb quality (and very expensive) fast, manual focus prime lenses in Nikon and Canon mounts. These lenses are designed to stand up to the demands of high megapixel full-frame DSLRs.

Another increasingly popular option are the ultrafast manual focus prime lenses manufactured in Korea by Samyang, and marketed under the names of Samyang, Bower, and Rokinon. The three brands are simply marketing names, and the lenses are identical except for the branding, so choose whichever one has the best price. There is a 14 mm f2.8, a 24 mm f1.4, a 24 mm f3.5 tilt/shift lens for architectural work, a 35 mm f1.4, and an 85 mm f1.4. These lenses all offer exceptional value, costing between one-fifth and one-third of the cost of the Canon or Nikon lenses. The superfast maximum apertures are useful for astro-landscape and street photography at night. The 14 mm and 24 mm lenses are not quite as sharp as the name brand lenses, but they offer a huge advantage for night photographers in that they do not suffer from the often severe comatic aberration seen in the much more expensive Canon and Nikon lenses. Comatic aberration, or coma, is generally only a problem for photographs that contain point light sources near the edge of the frame—starry skies for example. Coma causes stars or other light sources near the edges of the frame to look like a comet with a tail or birds in flight, which is why coma is sometimes referred to as the "seagull effect." It is generally agreed in the night photography community that the minimal tradeoff in sharpness with the Samyang produced lenses is made up for with coma-free images.

These Korean lenses offer great value with excellent image quality, but there is a catch. The manufacturer continues to have quality control issues, and the production and assembly is inconsistent. If you choose to purchase one of these lenses, it is essential to test them for sharpness upon receipt of the lens. By photographing a grid on a copy stand, or simply a brick

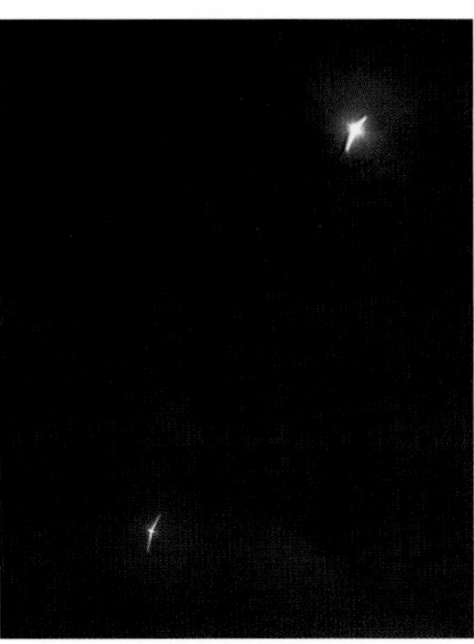
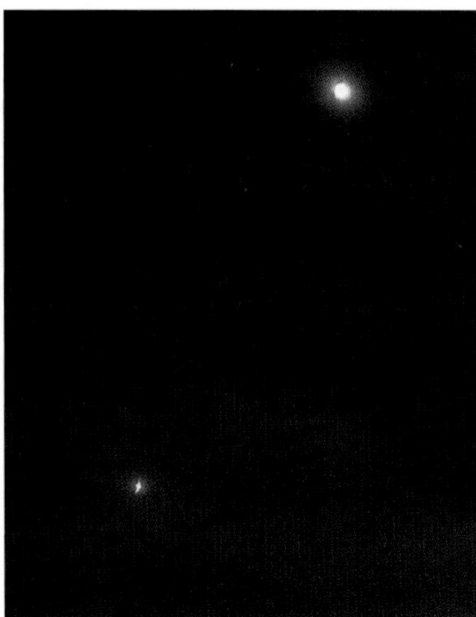

Comparison of comatic aberration in Canon and Rokinon 24 mm f1.4 lenses. These two 100 percent magnification details of images were shot with Canon's 24 mm f1.4 on the left, and Rokinon's 24 mm f1.4 on the right. Overall, the Canon lens is slightly sharper, but suffers from severe coma, but the Rokinon has almost no coma at all. The Canon lens costs more than three times as much as the Rokinon, but the Rokinon lenses have a reputation for inconsistency. (Images courtesy of Rick Whitacre.)

wall from about 6–8 feet away with a level, tripod-mounted camera, you can check for uneven sharpness from edge to edge. The test should be performed with the lens wide open, and while some falloff in sharpness at the edges of the frame is to be expected, it should be even in all four corners. If one side or one corner is noticeably less sharp than the others, return your lens for another, and be sure to test the second one as well. Some people will no doubt be put off by this inconsistency in build quality, but if you are willing to do the testing to make sure you have a sharp lens, it is worth the effort, and you'll save over $1000. Sigma's "Art Lens" line also has some great options for primes, such as their 35 mm f1.4 and 50 mm f1.4.

Under $1500	Under $2500	Under $4000
Current entry-level Canon or Nikon DSLR	Nikon D7100 or Canon70D/7D	Canon 6D or Nikon D610
Tokina 11–16 mm f2.8	Tokina 11–16 mm f2.8 Lens	Rokinon 24 mm 1.4
	Rokinon 24 mm 1.4	Rokinon 14 mm 2.8
		Rokinon 35 mm 1.4

Manual focus primes from the 1970s and 1980s are another option, offer great value for money, and there is a good supply of them on the used market. However, these lenses have been recently rediscovered by night photographers, and the widest lenses are becoming harder to find. They are usually not as good as modern primes, but offer a great return for minimal investment, and have the added advantage of being small, lightweight, and designed for manual focus.

When Canon and Nikon (who have long dominated the SLR market) first released autofocus cameras in the mid-1980s, the two companies took different approaches to engineering the new cameras and lenses. Canon chose to start from scratch, and designed a completely new lens mount, while Nikon chose to keep their existing lens mount to enable photographers to continue to use their old lenses. This resulted in Canon's early autofocus lenses performing faster and more smoothly than the Nikons. This disparity has now been eliminated, and some feel that Nikon even has a slight advantage in autofocus performance. The advances in autofocus technology have been primarily in focusing speed, rather than in low-light performance.

Unless you are using a Nikon DSLR with Nikon lenses, you'll need an adapter to mount the lens to the camera. Fortunately, these adapters are inexpensive and easy to find. Most manual focus Nikon lenses can be adapted to a variety of contemporary DSLRs. Canon manual focus (FD) lenses cannot be used on Canon DSLRs without an adapter that includes an additional glass element in the adapter, which usually reduces image quality. These extra elements act as teleconverters, increasing the focal length and severely limiting wide-angle photography. Ironically, and fortunately for Canon shooters, Nikon, Olympus, Leica, M42 screw mount, and

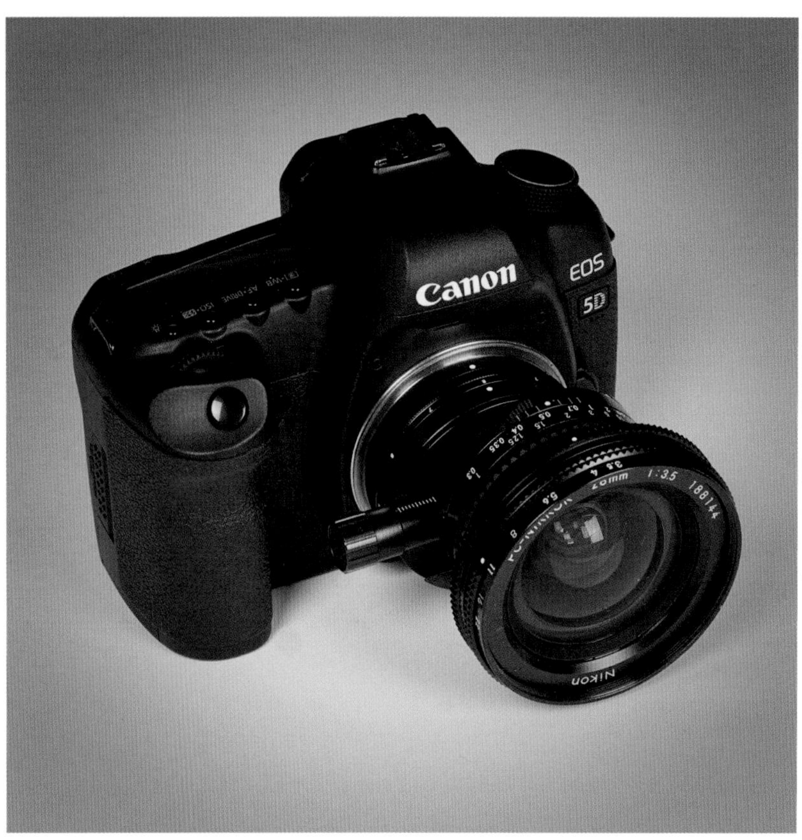

PC Nikkor 28 mm f3.5 lens mounted on a Canon 5D MK II camera. Many of the images in this book were made with this late 1980s' vintage Nikkor manual focus lens. The ability to have in-camera perspective control makes for better image quality and no loss of image area due to postprocessing perspective control. There are many inexpensive adapters to enable mounting of lenses with different mounts. Film camera lenses were made for 35 mm film, and as such have large image circles and generally excellent image quality. Look for multi-coated lenses that do reduce reflection, increase transmittance, and generally do a better job preventing lens flare.

Contax manual focus lenses can all be easily adapted to fit on Canon cameras without an additional lens element.

There are two major drawbacks to adapting other manufacturers' lenses to your DSLR. Due to the thickness of the adapter that goes in between the camera body and lens, the distance scale on the lens may not be accurate. If a lens adapter is used, focusing must be done visually rather than with the distance scale on the lens barrel. No adapter is required to use manual focus Nikon lenses on Nikon DSLRs, and the distance scale can be used for hyperfocal focusing, a technique discussed in Chapter 3. Additionally, these lenses will need to be stopped down to the working aperture manually. This is simple enough to do, but it is a common and annoying mistake to forget to stop down the lens before starting an exposure. Because these lenses must be stopped down and focused manually, they are not suited for other types of photography that require spontaneity and a quick response time.

Perspective control (PC) lenses are especially useful for photographers who shoot primarily architectural subjects and want to avoid converging vertical lines from tilting the camera upwards to capture the tops of buildings. PC lenses are also great for creating panoramas from two images taken with the lens shifted to the extreme left and extreme right. The perspective doesn't change when PC lenses are shifted, and this enables images to be seamlessly blended using Photomerge, a feature in Photoshop that automatically combines multiple images into a single panoramic image. Older PC lenses can be easily adapted to fit DSLRs and are substantially less expensive than their contemporary counterparts. The recently released Rokinon/Bower/Samyang Tilt-Shift 24 mm f3.5 ED AS UMC lens costs about half as much as the equivalent Canon or Nikon lenses, but is not quite as sharp as the other lenses by this manufacturer. Modern PC lenses have considerably better optics and coatings than PC lenses from the 1970s and 1980s; they are therefore sharper and suffer less from chromatic aberration and flare. I have found the Olympus OM series of shift lenses to be of exceptional quality. The most useful focal lengths of PC lenses range from 17 to 45 mm.

A basic selection of prime lenses for night photography would include an extreme wide-angle lens such as a 14–18 mm focal length, a moderate wide lens such as a 24–28 mm focal length, and a normal perspective lens in the 35–50 mm range. Of course, if you tend to favor one particular lens or focal length in the daytime, there's no reason not to use it at night. If you have already invested in high-quality autofocus zoom lenses, by all means use them; just be aware that they will be harder to focus at night.

Extreme wide-angle primes for APS sensors are very limited, and frequently expensive. For this reason, a high-quality wide-angle zoom might be the best option. Currently, the best choice is probably the Tokina AT-X 116 PRO DX-II 11–16 mm f2.8, which offers excellent performance and great value. For slightly more money, the Sigma 18–35 mm f1.8 DC HSM lens is the first zoom lens to offer a consistent f1.8 maximum aperture across all focal lengths, but it lacks the super wide angle of the Tokina lens. If you have the resources and are willing to spend $2000 on a lens, the venerable Nikon AF-S Zoom Nikkor 14–24 mm f2.8G ED AF lens is probably the finest wide-angle zoom lens ever made. It is so good that many Canon shooters use this lens with an adapter on their Canon bodies, sacrificing the autofocus. For a night photographer planning to stick with the APSC format, the Tokina 11–16 mm f2.8 combined with a Samyang/ Rokinon 24 mm f1.4 would make an excellent and compact lens complement. Alternatively, the Sigma 18–35 mm f1.8 DC HSM lens combined with a Rokinon 14 mm f2.8 is another good combination. You'll gain a stop on the aperture of your primary lens, but sacrifice the super wide-angle field of view. If you prefer extreme wide angles, go with the Tokina. If you'd rather have a faster lens, choose the Sigma.

TRIPODS

The next important equipment selection is a tripod. It is well worth the money to purchase a professional-quality tripod because inexpensive consumer models do not provide adequate stability and support for long exposures in even the gentlest breeze. It is also very common for inexpensive tripods to have a very weak connection between the camera and tripod, often with a plastic plate instead of a metal one to attach the camera to the tripod. These should be avoided at all costs. It is important to consider stability against size and weight, as even expensive carbon fiber tripods may vibrate or blow over in windy conditions if they are extremely light. Although these tripods may be adequate for exposures of a few seconds, the long exposures required to photograph by moonlight dictate that a sturdier tripod should be used. Some tripods have a hook at the bottom of the center column on which you can hang a stabilizing weight on windy nights. Quality tripods are sold as separate components—the head and the legs. You should choose tripod legs that extend high enough that you rarely have to raise the center column because doing so effectively makes your tripod considerably less stable. Tripods that have only three leg sections are also more stable than travel tripods that have four or five leg sections for compactness. Most tripod legs are made from either aluminum or carbon fiber. Aluminum tripods are less expensive, and carbon fiber tripods are lighter, and don't feel as cold against bare skin. Carbon fiber is not inherently more stable. The reduction in weight with a carbon fiber tripod is really the only reason to spend the extra money. There are two main types of tripod heads: the pan-tilt head, and the ball head. Pan–tilt tripod heads have three knobs for adjusting the camera angle separately in each direction, while ball heads move freely in all directions when the adjustment knob is loosened. Pan–tilt heads are often preferred by photographers who shoot architectural subject matter because the camera can be positioned and aligned to the subject with more precision. They tend to be larger and more cumbersome, but are usually less expensive than ball heads of comparable quality. Ball heads use a ball and socket mechanism to adjust the camera position, and the camera can be adjusted in all directions with the release of a single control. Better ball heads also have a tension adjustment that makes them easier to control, but this feature often adds considerably to the price. Ball heads are preferred by photographers who work with the landscape and with moving subjects like people, and need to respond and adjust the camera position quickly and frequently. The distinction between these types of heads isn't significant for most night photography, as long as you choose one that is stable, and easily adjustable. In my own experience, I have found that Induro and Manfrotto tripods and heads offer the best value and great quality, but there are many excellent options to choose from. If possible, as with cameras, it is a good idea to actually handle a tripod before you buy it rather than simply buying one online.

CABLE OR REMOTE RELEASES

The shutter speed range on most cameras does not extend past 30 seconds in manual mode, and although this is sufficient for brightly lit night scenes, most night scenes require much longer exposures. To take very long exposures, you'll need to set the shutter speed or mode to bulb, and use either a cable release or wireless remote release. These are available for almost all cameras from the manufacturer and also as less expensive after-market products. A manual shutter release is basically a locking switch that holds the shutter open as long as the switch is engaged, or until the camera's battery runs out. Although newer cameras have camera or brand-specific releases, older film cameras, as well as most medium and large format cameras, use a universal mechanical cable release. For anyone who will be doing long exposures on a regular basis, or anyone interested in star trails, an intervalometer, or shutter release with a built-in time, is highly recommended. The price difference between brand-name and aftermarket releases can be substantial. It appears as though the Canon and Nikon timed releases are manufactured by another company and then rebranded, and the aftermarket timers sell for about one-third of the cost. The great advantage to these timed releases is that they can be programmed to take single or multiple exposures of almost any length sequentially or at programmable intervals. With a manual shutter release, you must time the exposure with a watch or phone, and manually close the shutter at the correct time.

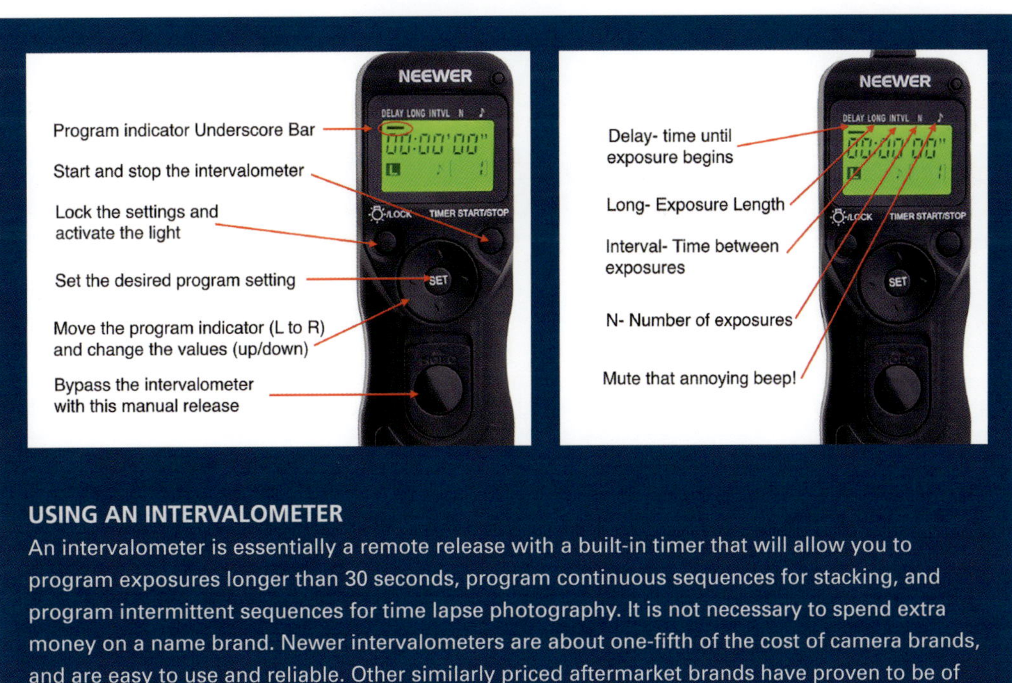

USING AN INTERVALOMETER

An intervalometer is essentially a remote release with a built-in timer that will allow you to program exposures longer than 30 seconds, program continuous sequences for stacking, and program intermittent sequences for time lapse photography. It is not necessary to spend extra money on a name brand. Newer intervalometers are about one-fifth of the cost of camera brands, and are easy to use and reliable. Other similarly priced aftermarket brands have proven to be of inconsistent quality.

LENS SHADES AND FLARE BLOCKING DEVICES

Flare from light sources just outside of the frame can be a major problem at night. For this reason, it is essential to always use a lens shade, hood, or other flare-preventing device. It is important to choose a shade or hood that is made specifically for the lens you are using. A shade for a longer lens will result in vignetting on a wide-angle lens, and a wide-angle shade will not provide adequate protection on a longer lens. The butterfly-style lens shades that are designed for zoom lenses are compromised to accommodate for the variable focal length of the lens, and do not block the light from many potential sources of lens flare. A handy alternative or complement to a lens shade is a hot shoe- or tripod-mounted arm with a clip that holds a dark card. With these devices, the card can be placed in almost any position, and is more effective than a shade alone. There are numerous such devices, some of which include Dinkum Systems Lens Shades, the Flex Lens Shade, FM Photography McClamps, and the Flare Buster. Attaching

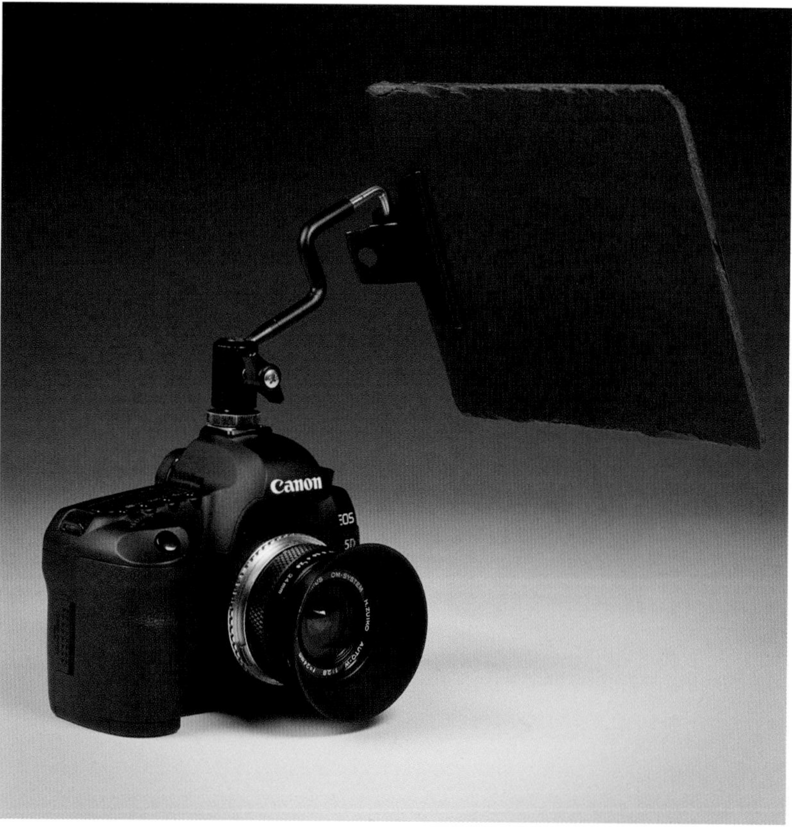

An articulated hot shoe-mounted clamp for holding a gobo—essentially a piece of black cardboard for preventing lens flare. This one is made by Ebony, a Japanese view camera manufacturer. Other options have clamps on both ends; one for a tripod leg and the other for a gobo.

one of these devices to the camera hot shoe on a windy night risks camera movement during long exposures because the card will catch the wind like a sail. If you have a very stable tripod, the tools that attach to the tripod are less likely to cause motion blur, but even these are bad news on a windswept night. On windy nights, simply holding a black card to shade the lens or clamping the shade to a separate light stand or tripod would be better options.

OTHER EQUIPMENT BASICS

These are the basic necessities for night photography, but there are just a few other things that will make your work easier and more comfortable in the field. Although battery technology has improved along with cameras, a second or even third camera battery assures that your camera will have enough power to last the night. A small penlight or flashlight that can be attached to a lanyard and worn around your neck is an invaluable aid for finding things in your camera bag or controls on your camera. This should be a relatively weak light, preferably a red one, to preserve your night vision in dark environments. Using a bright light to adjust your camera when your eyes have been dark-adapted is most unpleasant, and can also draw unwanted attention to yourself. However, if you will be photographing primarily in nature, inside of abandoned buildings, or other very dark environments, a powerful flashlight to use as a focusing aid will be extremely helpful, if not essential. If you plan to photograph mostly in urban areas with street lighting, this is much less of an issue. Flashlights are discussed in depth in the light painting chapter (Chapter 8).

Lens filters are mostly of little use at night, with the exception of a UV or simple protective filter in wet conditions, especially near the ocean where salt spray can ruin a good lens in a short time. UV filters do add a layer of protection to the front element of your lens, but they also add two more reflective surfaces that are likely to increase lens flare, especially if they are not the very best quality optical glass and are exceptionally clean. If you invest in top-quality lenses, it makes no sense to put an inexpensive, poor-quality filter in front of it. Fingerprints, dust, and condensation either on the front or rear of your filter may not affect image quality much in the daytime, but they are more problematic at night when multiple light sources often cause severe lens flare. Unless you tend to be clumsy, or are especially hard on your gear, I suggest avoiding lens filters except in the rain or near the ocean.

A raincoat for your camera can make the difference between calling it a night and sticking it out to get a great shot if it starts to rain. There are several options for high-tech (and expensive) camera protection, but a disposable hotel shower cap weighs next to nothing, doesn't take up much space, and does the job nicely in light rain and drizzle. A plastic bag and rubber band will also work in a pinch, and keeping a plastic trash bag handy is a great way to keep your camera bag dry or clean if you need to put it down in the muck. Lens tissue or a small chamois or microfiber cloth is also helpful to keep your lens clean and dry. Digital camera EXIF data records exposure, camera, and lens data, but many photographers carry a digital voice recorder to make notes about location, exposures, or detailed descriptions of light painting. Of course, an old-fashioned note pad and pencil will work too. Taking exposure notes is essential for film photographers because the best way to learn to gauge exposures is by comparing negatives or transparencies to carefully recorded notes. There's not much else you'll need in terms of equipment, except for more powerful flashlights, a battery-powered strobe, or other portable light sources if you plan to do light painting; these are discussed in Chapter 8.

DRESSING FOR NIGHT PHOTOGRAPHY

Now that your camera bag is fully loaded, you'll want to make sure that you are dressed appropriately for night photography, and have whatever creature comforts you may want in the field. It may seem obvious to wear warm clothes on a cold night, but many people are surprised with how cold they get standing around waiting for long exposures. Dress in layers, and bring a hat and gloves if the temperature is expected to fall below about 50°F (15°C). Mittens with flip tops that open to expose your fingers are a good way to avoid the need to take your gloves off to adjust your camera. If you prefer gloves, spending the extra money on a close-fitting pair that doesn't impede your dexterity too much is a worthwhile investment. After having tried many different gloves and mittens, and not being happy with any of them, I finally discovered Aquatech Sensory Gloves, which are designed especially for photographers. They have a tiny, stretchable hole for your thumb and fingertip to adjust your camera, but do a great job at keeping out the cold. They work well in conjunction with chemical hand warmers. These disposable, activated charcoal packs that are worn inside of your gloves can make a huge difference in your comfort level on cold nights so keeping a few in your bag assures they'll be there when you need them. The kind made for shoes actually work better with flip-top mittens because they come with an adhesive strip that will keep them in place when you open your mittens. These chemical hand and foot warmers are available from camping or outdoor outfitter stores, as well as in the sporting goods department of big-box stores.

Wearing dark-colored clothing serves a dual purpose. If you inadvertently walk in front of the camera, or intentionally walk into the shot to add light, wearing black will minimize the chances of showing up in the image as long as you don't remain in the same place for too long. You'll also be less likely to attract attention to yourself if you happen to be trespassing or just want to work unnoticed. Sensible shoes that offer a reasonable amount of protection when you'll be putting your feet down in unfamiliar territory are also a good idea. Wearing flip-flops for night photography is not a good idea. A thermos of coffee, bottle of water, and a snack (brownies are the traditional choice) will also serve you well on a cold night. Being well fed and dressed appropriately can make all the difference on long, productive nights. Finally, keeping a few samples of your work with you may go a long way in explaining your motives should you be accosted by police or security guards—an occasion that is bound to happen at some point in

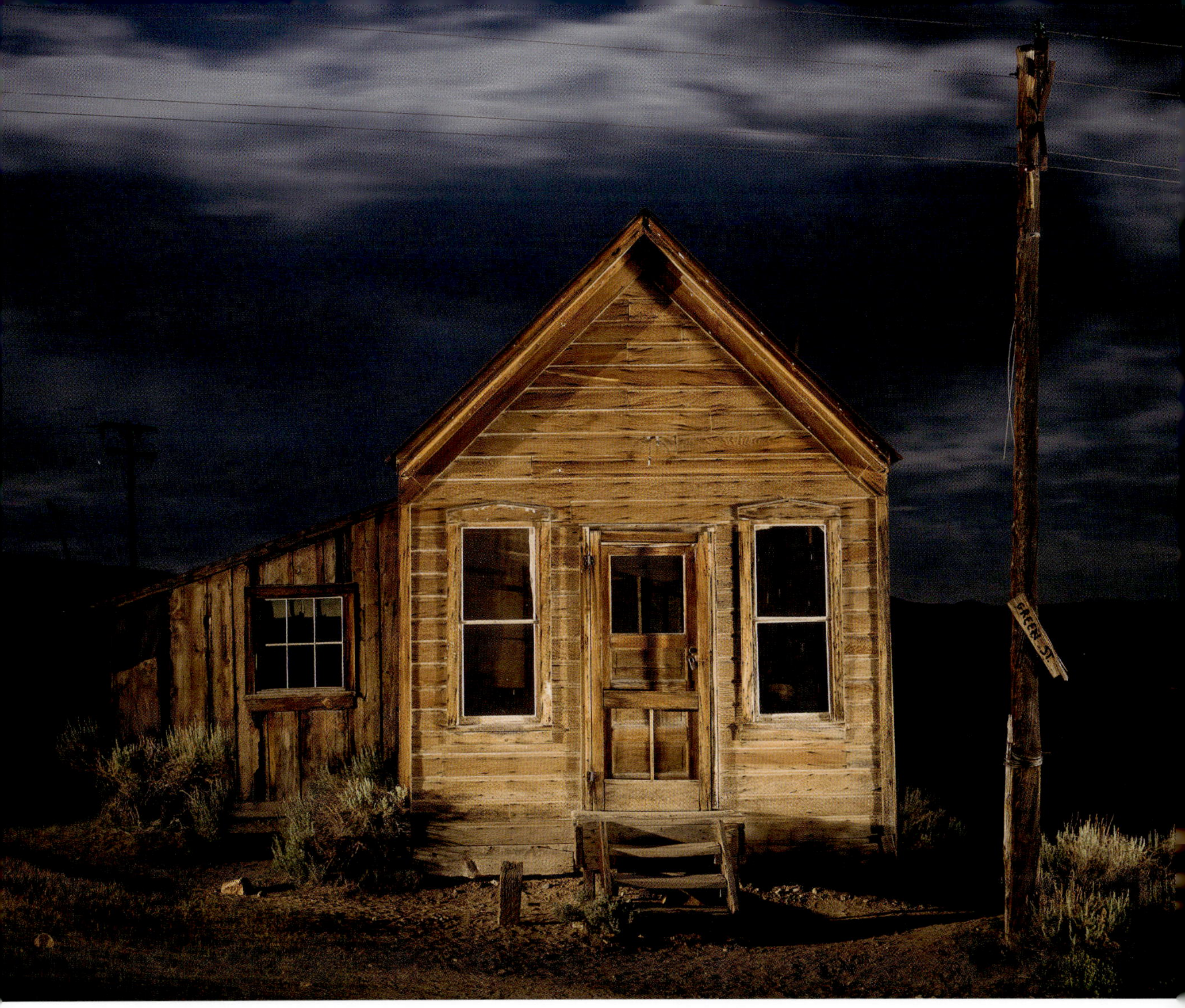

Green Street, Bodie Ghost Town, CA. 30 seconds, f4.5 at ISO 800. Canon 6D, 35 mm f2.8 Zuiko Shift lens. Feeling like I needed exercise, I decided to do a series of 30-second light-painted house portraits at Bodie last summer. This required starting the exposure with a 2-second delay, and then running (at 8,400 feet of elevation) to first one side and then the other to rake light across the house, hitting the ground with the light in front as I passed. In this case, I also had to light the electric pole and sign. Working at 800 ISO meant that I didn't need much light to get the job done, and usually finished before the shutter clicked. The Moon behind the clouds made for a great sky—at least for the houses on this side of the street.

urban areas. Being prepared with the right equipment, clothing, and comfort items will make your experience much more enjoyable, and help you to stay focused on the task at hand.

When buying photo gear—be it for day or night—the most important thing is to really understand your needs, and then buy the best equipment you can afford. Too many people get hung up on having the latest and best of everything without giving much thought to what they will do with it once they buy it. Consider your intentions: will you make large prints or simply show images online? Will you do primarily long exposures with star trails or short exposures at high ISO to capture star points and the Milky Way? Do you favor extreme wide angles or a normal or telephoto perspective? Does your computer have the processing power to handle 36 megapixel RAW files? Can you really afford that $2000 lens? Renting equipment, either from a professional camera dealer if you live in a large metro area, or from one of the excellent online rental companies like BorrowLenses.com or LensRentals.com, is a great way to try out a camera or lens before committing to an expensive purchase that may not be what you really want or need.

THE BASICS OF NIGHT PHOTOGRAPHY

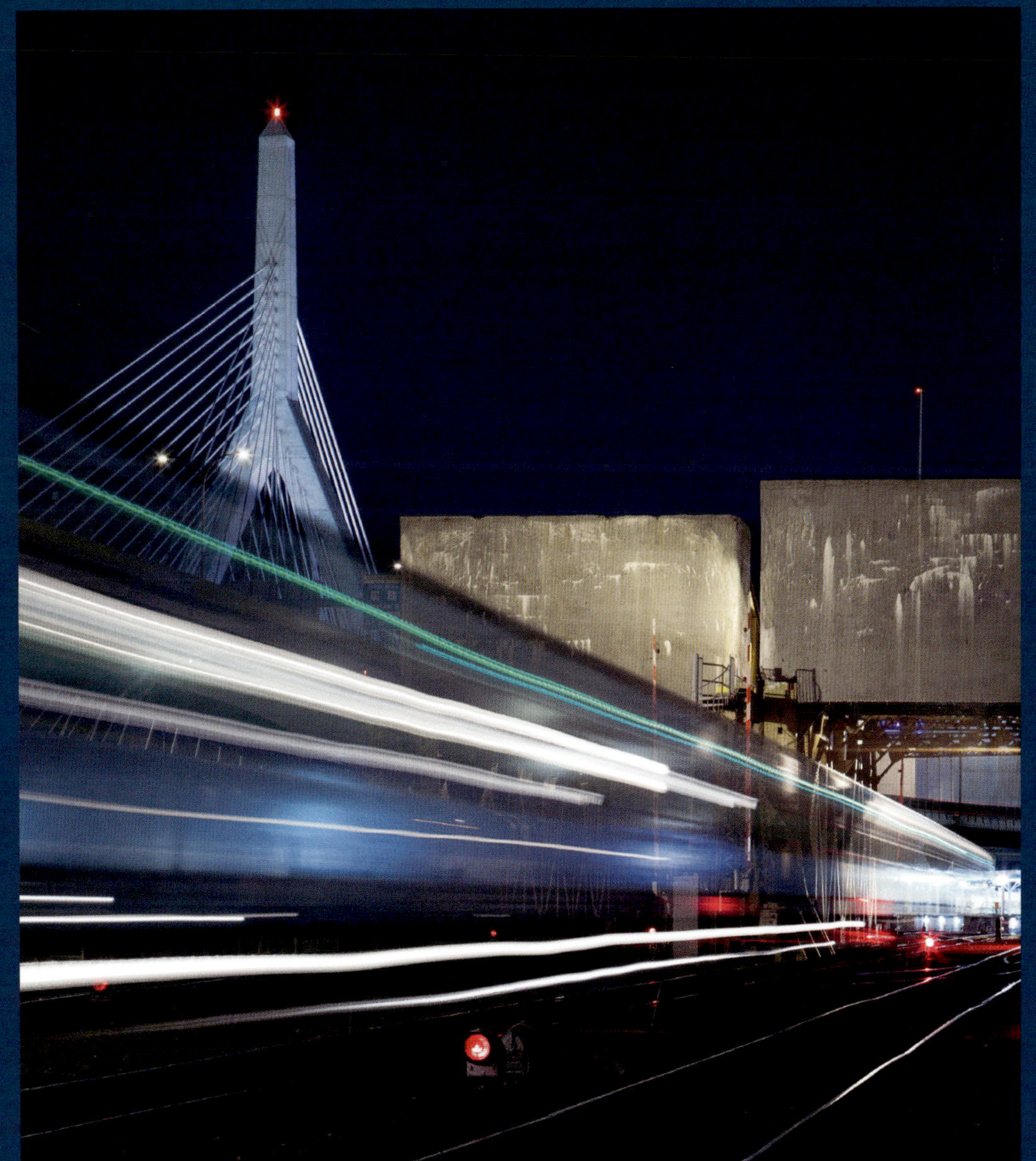

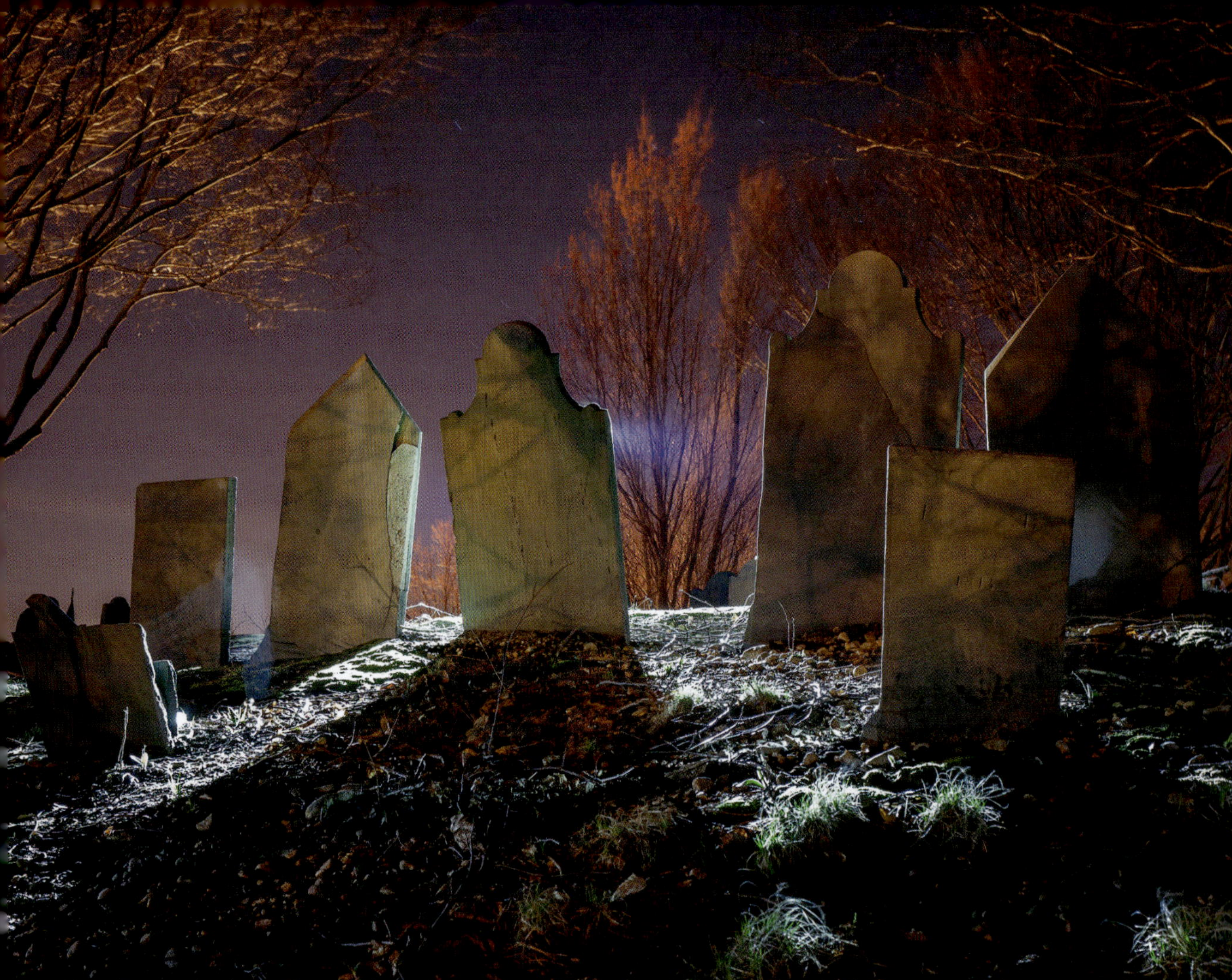

3

"Old Gravestones," Plymouth, Massachusetts. 4 minutes, f5.6, ISO 400 Canon 5D MK II, Rokinon 24 mm f1.4 lens. Nearby sodium vapor streetlights turn the treetops orange and the sky purple, as backlighting from a bluish LED flashlight highlights the gravestones.

THE NIGHT PHOTOGRAPHY MIND-SHIFT

Night photography presents numerous technical challenges, but also countless opportunities. Photographing at night requires one to look at the world from a different perspective. Night photography should not be considered merely an extension of daytime photography because night light transforms the known world into something unfamiliar and strange. In much the same way that moving into the studio after photographing outdoors with natural light demands a different approach, photographing at night requires many different considerations. Of course your photographic skills and knowledge will serve you well, but there are surprises ahead, many new things to learn, and exciting discoveries to be made. As the light at night is such a huge part of what makes nocturnal photography special, scouting locations during the daytime is often ineffective. Returning to a location at night to photograph a scene observed during the day can lead to disappointment, as the circumstances at night may make the photograph you envisioned impossible to take. This is especially true in urban situations with artificial light. Conversely, scenes that simply must be photographed jump out at you at night, but go unnoticed, or simply don't exist, in the daylight due to the different lighting conditions.

Natural landscapes are less likely to offer up as many surprises at night, and planning these kinds of images in advance can be a big factor in capturing a successful image. There are a number of photo planning apps for smartphones that can help you to be in the right place at the right time. The best is Photography to Pills, which even has a feature that lets you visualize where and when the Milky Way will appear in the sky. Currently, it is only available for iPhone. If you have an android phone, your best bet is The Photographer's Ephemeris.

BEING PREPARED
Dressing appropriately for the weather and your intended location, packing your camera bag in a logical and orderly way, and being confident using your camera's frequently accessed controls are all steps you can take to increase your comfort and productivity in the field. Unless you are accustomed to working on a tripod, chances are that slowing down to the night photographer's pace will require an adjustment in attitude and approach. Night photography is not a spontaneous act, and working in a methodical and deliberate fashion minimizes user error. Simple things like always keeping each item in your bag in the same place means that you won't have to fish around for it with a flashlight—you can just reach in and grab what you need. Although some people prefer to use a headlight, they tend to be brighter than you really need, draw unwanted attention to yourself, and most importantly it can ruin your shot when you forget to turn it off and walk around inadvertently shining it all over the place. After 15 or 20 minutes, your eyes will have adapted to the lower light levels to the point where you may not need a light at all, and not using a flashlight will preserve your night vision. Another simple thing you can do to facilitate your fieldwork is to place a small piece of adhesive Velcro on the back of your cable release or timer and attach it to your tripod leg. Most releases have unnecessarily long cords, and Velcro will keep the device within easy reach rather than dangling from the camera. Simple things like this can have a surprising impact on your overall experience. Every step that you take to standardize your workflow in the field helps to minimize technical errors that can ruin a shot.

In many years of teaching classes and workshops on night photography, the one thing I've seen most often that frustrates people new to it is the lack of basic familiarity with their cameras. Being able to navigate the menu system, finding and enabling or disabling features, and knowing which buttons serve which functions may seem fairly basic until you find yourself in the middle of nowhere in total darkness on a moonless night without your camera manual.

Everything is harder in the dark—especially if you are in unfamiliar territory, on uneven ground, in a place where your safety may be in question, or if it is freezing cold and you are wearing gloves.

Sit down with your camera and manual for an hour, and learn the menu features and button locations by memory. It is a lot easier to learn in the comfort of your own home rather than out in the cold, dark night. At the very least, you should be able to adjust aperture, shutter, ISO in the dark, and be able to find the image review button and histogram functions easily, as well as be able to activate and use magnified live view for focusing without the aid of a flashlight.

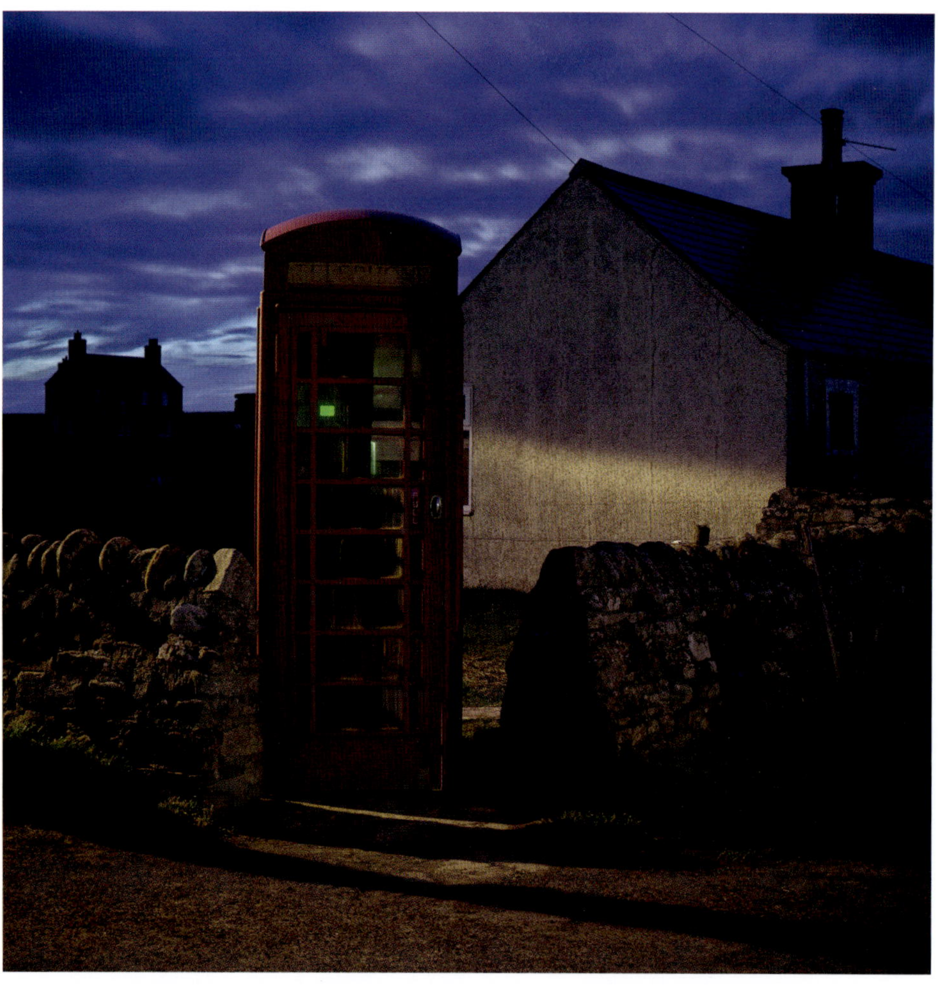

"Phone Home," Birsay, Orkney, Scotland. 30 seconds, f8, ISO 320. Canon 5D MK II, 28 mm f3.5 Nikkor PC lens. The "Simmer Dim" as the endless twilight of midsummer is known in Scotland. This image was taken at 2:30 am, but it never really gets dark in summer at such high latitudes. The mix of sodium vapor and twilight makes for dramatic lighting.

Learning how to program your intervalometer is key too. Ideally, you should only need to use a flashlight to illuminate your focus point or for light painting.

A basic understanding and awareness of the lunar cycle, the path of the Moon through the sky—where it rises and sets, where and when the Milky Way will appear in the sky, celestial events like eclipses, meteor showers, and comets, and a heightened awareness of weather will serve you well as you decide when, where, and what to photograph. Adding a lunar calendar to your desktop or phone keeps this useful information at your fingertips, and you'll probably find yourself reserving a couple of nights a month around the new moon and full moon for photography. Planning ahead is always beneficial, but being prepared to venture out and photograph should a dense fog or some other favorable condition arise without warning will lead to unique opportunities. Allow yourself the spontaneity to make the most of special circumstances. Hopefully, your significant other will do the same. If your mate is suspicious of your nocturnal activities, invite him or her to join you. If he or she accepts, you'll either have a new partner in crime, or never be questioned again when you declare that you are going out to photograph on a dark and stormy night.

MANY VARIABLES

There are more variables than constants with night photography, and many of them are beyond the control of the photographer. Some find this frustrating, others find it exciting. Whichever the case, learning how your camera will respond under different conditions is a big part of understanding what works and what doesn't when shooting at night. Extreme contrast and a wide dynamic range are the most challenging obstacles to urban night photography. Varying amounts of moonlight over the course of the lunar cycle, or even a single night as the Moon rises or sets, can make deciding on exposures a challenge in a natural environment. We often have to contend with noise created by high temperatures, long exposures or high-ISO settings. Figuring out the right combination of ISO, aperture, and shutter speed for different situations can be daunting. Composing and focusing in low-light levels can also be cumbersome and difficult. Lens flare from the multitude of light sources in the nighttime environment is often problematic and can be difficult to predict. In this chapter, we explore solutions to these technical challenges as well as other uncontrollable variables like working with existing light sources. Simply getting acclimated to working in the dark takes some getting used to, but it makes a big difference in your night photography comfort level.

COMPOSITION AND SUBJECT MATTER

Night photographers photograph a wide range of subject matter in a variety of conditions and locations. Landscapes, cityscapes, grand vistas, and intimate tableaux are all part of the oeuvre. Many night photographers specialize in a particular type of photography. Some photograph mainly the natural landscape—either using short exposures to record star points, or long exposures to record star trails—others photograph mainly in industrial areas. Many people involved in the urban exploration movement also photograph during their adventures. Urban explorers venture into abandoned buildings—factories, schools, and psychiatric hospitals are particular favorites. Climbing bridges, antenna towers, and the exteriors of skyscrapers—always illegally, so it must be done at night—has attracted a growing following of professional thrill seekers recently, and these young daredevils always document their adventures. Light painting, or the use of portable handheld lights to illuminate or create subject matter, has also become increasingly popular in recent years, largely proliferated through photo-sharing websites like Flickr, 500px, and even Google+ and FaceBook. Anything that can be photographed in the daytime can be shot at night although it will probably look completely different. Even in the absence of all light, it is possible to photograph with the addition of light from flash, flashlights, glow sticks, or even fire.

A mid-fifties Ford outside a bodega on the streets of Havana. 6 seconds at f8, ISO 100, Canon G1X at 27 mm. The subject is placed at the intersection of two-thirds, anchoring the image, and the strong diagonal lines of the street create a sense of depth, and take the viewer visually into the photograph. The mixed lighting and anonymous figures talking in the background add interest too.

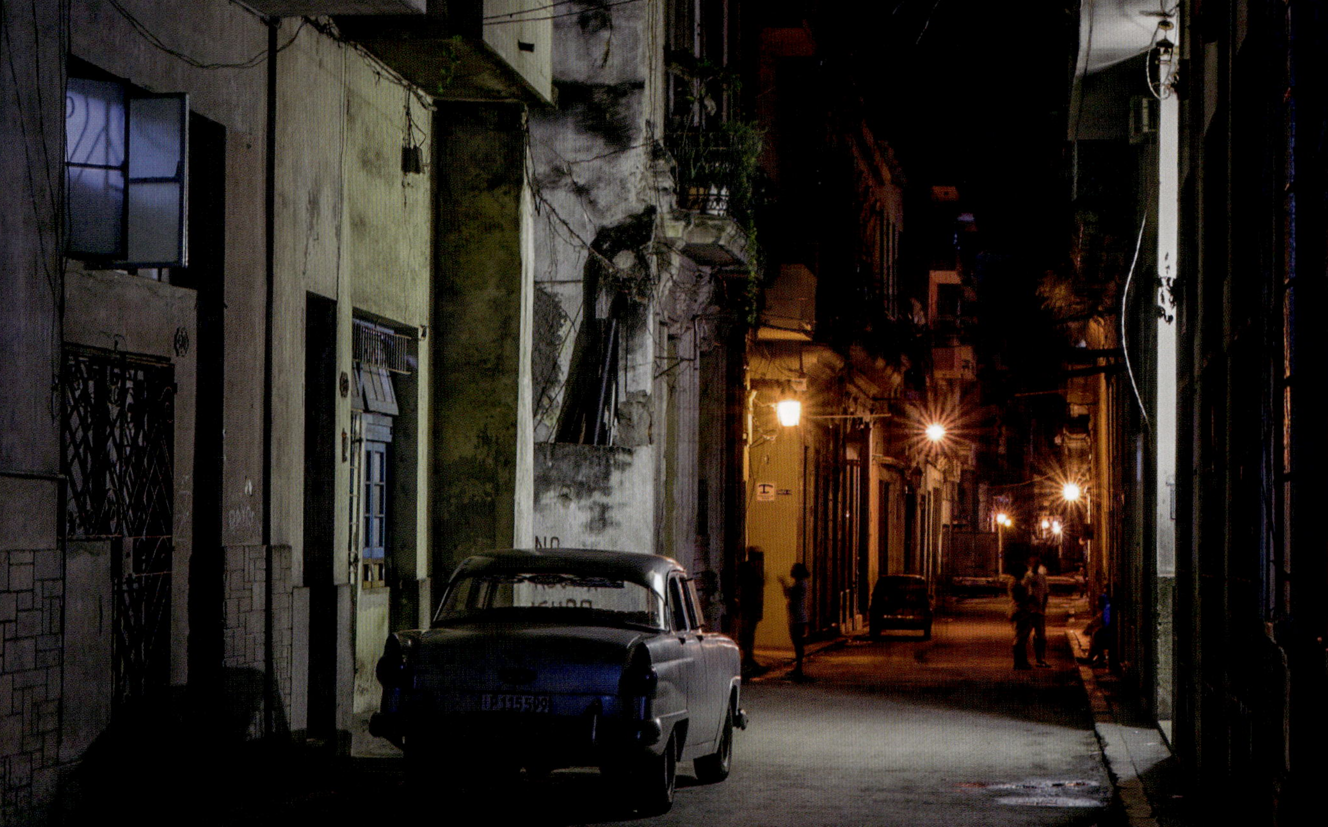

In many ways, composing a night photograph is not that different from composing a daytime image. The rules of design apply equally in the dark as in the light, and they are still made to be broken. Compositional devices like the rule of thirds, diagonal lines, exaggerated perspective, and repetition make for dynamic compositions any time of day or night. The most interesting images are ones where the viewer's gaze is kept in motion, moving from one spot to another within the frame. Consider the direction of lighting, be it streetlights, moonlight, or your own added light, the relationship of foreground to background elements, and don't be afraid to break the rules. For example, by adding some light to the foreground, using the Moon as a backlight has the potential to create real drama. Sometimes, it may be necessary to modify a composition to exclude bright light sources from the image. Such a modification may be a compromise of the ideal composition, but if it restricts the dynamic range of the scene to that of the camera's capability, it may be justified. Bright areas at the edge of an image always draw the viewer's attention, and this is particularly true at night. A light or brightly exposed area near the edge of the frame can lead the eye away from the subject, and away from the image entirely.

COMPOSING AND FOCUSING

Composing both your shot and focusing can be difficult in low-light conditions, simply because it is hard to see the image in the viewfinder. Fortunately, there are simple solutions to deal with these problems. Digital cameras afford us the luxury of being able to view the image immediately after capture, and it is easy enough to adjust the camera position and recompose as needed. Setting your camera to the highest ISO setting and doing a series of handheld test exposures is a good way to refine a shot. Even if the light level requires exposure times of a few seconds, most people can hold the camera steady enough to get a reasonable idea of what the final image will look like. This technique is a great way to predict and correct for potential problems like flare, and also to spot stray objects at the edges of the frame that might have otherwise gone unnoticed. When you first arrive at a location, spend some time getting to know the area. Even if it is a familiar place, chances are that it looks and feels different at night. As your eyes adjust to the darkness, walk around and see what catches your eye. Once you have some ideas, make some handheld exposures at your cameras highest ISO and lens' widest aperture to find the best vantage point, the best perspective, and to look for potential issues or problems. As you gain more experience, this will come naturally, and you'll soon be ready to get to work.

Live view is an extremely useful feature that can be used in combination with a flashlight to make focusing in darkness more manageable. A bright flashlight can aid both composing and focusing your night shots. By shining the light around in the image while looking through the viewfinder, it may be easier to find the corners of the frame. It is a common mistake for both day and night photographers to concentrate their attention strictly on the subject, and to ignore the edges of the composition. Night photographers should pay extra attention to the entire image, both because it can be difficult to see, and because night photographs generally require a greater commitment of your time and energy. It is always disappointing to invest 15 or 20 minutes in a single exposure only to later find an unnoticed object in the shot that could have been easily avoided with a little more care. A great trick for determining the edges of your image in a very dark and confined environment, for example inside a building, is to shine your flashlight through the camera viewfinder, and observe where the light falls. This can be a very useful technique, but it will only work with DSLRs, a very bright flashlight, and in a confined space that is almost completely dark. Flashlights are also very useful as focusing aids.

Although your camera's autofocus system will probably work in a bright urban environment, autofocus does not usually work well in very low light. Infrared (IR) assist beams on some cameras will be helpful for autofocus in certain situations, but these are more commonly found built into flash units than cameras. Focusing manually is the best option at night, and there are several ways to achieve accurate focus. As discussed in Chapter 2, manual focus (MF) lenses are better suited for night photography. Autofocus lenses (AF) are engineered to focus as quickly and accurately as possible—in autofocus mode. Unfortunately, what works best for autofocus is not what works best for humans. The short "throw" between closest focusing point and infinity, as well as the low tension of most AF lenses, makes them super sensitive and very difficult to focus precisely by hand. Additionally, to protect the AF motor during rapid focusing, the throw actually extends beyond infinity. Unlike most MF lenses, which can be racked to the end of the throw and will reliably stop at infinity, almost all AF lenses rotate just past infinity, and no part of the image will be sharp if the lens is accidentally set this way.

Focusing techniques	Useful for/with	Reliability
Manual focus, shining flashlight on subject	Very accurate focusing with bright flashlight and live view	Best
Manual focus, placing flashlight in scene at the point of focus	Works well with or without live view	Best
Unassisted manual focus	Manual focus lenses, brightly lit scenes with or without live view	Good
Hyperfocal focusing	Convenient and maximizes depth of field	Good
Autofocus	Brightly lit scenes, lots of ambient light	Limited
IR-assisted autofocus	Use your flash's IR assist beam for focusing with relatively short focus distances	Limited
Zone focusing	Similar to hyperfocal, but does not include infinity focus	Limited
Auto or manual infinity focusing using moon- or streetlight	Wastes much of your depth of field	Last resort

Just as your flashlight can be helpful when composing a shot, it is also a useful tool for focusing. The most obvious technique is to stand behind the camera, and shine the light on the area to be focused. Then, while still holding the light in position, focus manually while looking through the viewfinder. Focusing utilizing this technique in conjunction with live view is even better. The live view image may not be bright enough to use for focusing without the aid of a flashlight, but combining the zoom feature on live view with a flashlight allows for extremely accurate focusing. Canon cameras have a live view mode that simulates how the exposure will look with the camera settings as they are currently set on the camera. You should disable this exposure simulation option as it may darken the image and make it harder to see in most situations. Additionally, it is not an accurate way of gauging exposure. Nikon cameras require the lens to be set at the maximum aperture to make the most out of live view for focusing. It is a good idea to experiment with your own camera to see what settings will give you the best results. Another method is to place your flashlight at the focus point in the scene, pointed back toward the camera. Return to the camera and focus on the light itself, again using live view if you have it, and then retrieve your light before taking the shot.

FOCUSING USING LIVE VIEW

The following steps will help you to use live view to effectively focus in little to no light.

1. After composing your image, either by way of the viewfinder, test shots, or both, lock down your tripod. You don't want to have to recompose once the composition is determined.
2. Activate live view. Use whichever settings give you the brightest image. Live view settings vary from one camera to the next. Exposure simulation on Canon cameras is not useful in low light.
3. Using the brightest flashlight you have (if needed), illuminate the part of the scene where you wish to focus. You may also put the light in the scene at the point where you wish to focus, and focus on the light itself.
4. Using the joystick or toggle wheel on the camera, position the small box on the LCD over the area where you wish to focus. This is much easier before magnification.
5. Now, magnify your image with the button on the back of the camera, *not* by zooming the lens.
6. Focus, and then turn off, or retrieve your light. Since live view uses a lot of battery power, turn it off after focus is achieved.
7. If you haven't already determined your exposure, do that now, and then make your image.

USING A CONSTANT APERTURE

Because there are so many variables that are beyond your control when photographing at night, it's helpful to have one fixed point to provide a frame of reference. Film shooters especially need a way to be able to compare one image to the next or images shot on different nights in different locations. Comparing results from one session to the next is a great way to learn what's working and what isn't in your photographs. It is counterproductive to always use the same white balance, as the range of color temperatures found at night varies widely. It would be inconvenient to limit yourself to a single ISO, and there's no single shutter speed that will work for every photograph. The logical fixed point is aperture. Picking one aperture that provides a reasonable depth of field and using it for the bulk of your photographs will help you to understand nighttime exposures—at least until you are comfortable photographing at night in a variety of conditions. For wide to normal lenses, f8 seems to be a good compromise between depth of field and overly long exposures from smaller apertures. If you tend to shoot with longer lenses, or a medium or large format camera, you may want to choose a smaller aperture for more DOF. If you shoot extreme wide-angle lenses, f5.6 may provide all the DOF you need. For astro-landscape photography, f2.8 is the standard aperture. The important thing is having a fairly constant aperture to be able to compare results with a fixed frame of reference. This is more important while you are first learning, and are still building confidence. If you use hyperfocal focusing, keeping a constant aperture also prevents the need to refocus for every shot. A constant aperture is also necessary if you use high dynamic range (HDR) or manual layer blending to combine several exposures as a means of contrast control. Of course, there are times when you will want to use a larger or smaller aperture for more or less DOF, and you absolutely should when it's called for. It is just good practice to vary your exposure with time or ISO rather than aperture.

HYPERFOCAL FOCUSING

Manual focus prime lenses can be prefocused using the hyperfocal distance (HFD) or zone focusing techniques. The hyperfocal distance is the nearest point for any given focal length, aperture, and camera format that will keep infinity in acceptably sharp focus. Remember, for every lens there is an exact point of focus, and an area in front of and behind the focal point that is reasonably, or acceptably, in focus. Sharpness falls off gradually as you move further away from the focal point until the image is noticeably out of focus. This zone of focus is what we call depth of field. In short, hyperfocal focusing maximizes your depth of field. When a lens is focused at the

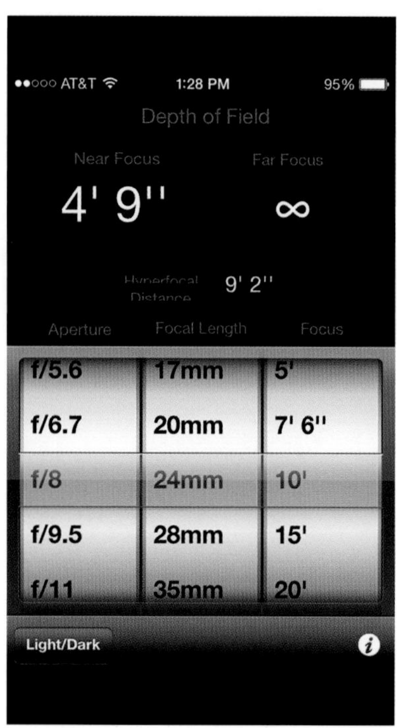

Screen shot showing the useful Tack Sharp app, which can be used to find depth of field and hyperfocal distance for any camera/lens/aperture combination. The app shows that the HFD for a 24 mm lens set at f8 on a full-frame camera is 9 feet, 2 inches, and that the depth of field extends from half of the HFD (4 feet, 9 inches) to infinity. HFD is a constant based on sensor size, focal length, and aperture. There are other similar apps that achieve the same results.

hyperfocal point, the depth of field extends from half of that distance to infinity. For example, if the hyperfocal distance for your lens/aperture/camera combination is 30 feet, then your depth of field extends from half of that distance, or 15 feet, to infinity. Technically, it is possible to use hyperfocal focusing with any lens, but with short throw zooms it is so difficult to do it with any precision that you're better off using another focusing method. Manual focus, prime lenses have a DOF scale that allows you to prefocus to the hyperfocal distance. The scale combines the use of distance markings with pairs of numbers or colored lines representing the f numbers of the lens, one on either side of the mark that represents the focal point. By lining up the infinity symbol on the distance scale with the outer number or colored line representing your working aperture, you have just focused the lens to the hyperfocal distance. The near distance in the DOF will be indicated by the inside number or colored line on the DOF scale. The scale provides only an approximation of the true DOF, and for this reason it is a good idea to use the HFD for the aperture one stop greater than your working aperture. In other words, if you are shooting at f11, focus to the HFD for f8, which ensures that infinity will be perfectly sharp, and gives you a comfortable margin of error. Zoom lenses do not have DOF scales, because the DOF changes with the focal length as the lens is zoomed in and out.

Photographers working with view cameras, or any lens that does not have a DOF or distance scale, can still use hyperfocal focusing. Carrying a hyperfocal card makes this easy, or use

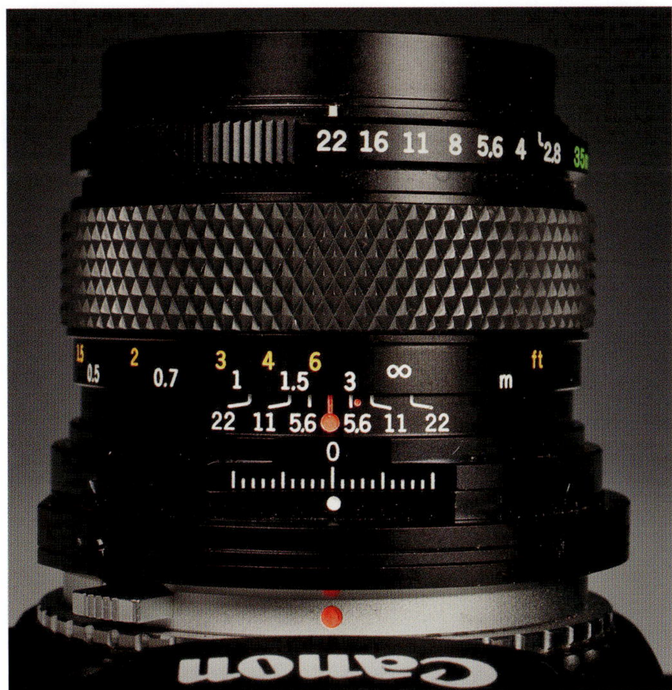

This manual focus Olympus Zuiko Shift 35 mm lens shows the depth of field scale, and is set to the hyperfocal distance for f22. By placing the infinity mark just inside the right hand 22 on the DOF scale, this sets the HFD. The actual focal point is a little more than 7 feet, and the depth of field extends from about 4 feet to infinity. The HFD increases as the aperture diameter is increased, and depth of field increases as the aperture gets smaller.

one of the many smartphone apps for this purpose. The one called Tack Sharp is easy to use, highly customizable, and accurate. When you determine the appropriate HFD from your table or calculator, walk off the distance from the camera by counting your steps and place a flashlight on the ground pointed back toward the camera. Focus on the light, and you're focused at the HFD. The average adult stride is about 3 feet, so if your HFD is 30 feet, start at the camera, and walk 10 steps into the shot, and place the light and focus at that location. Don't worry if your measurement isn't completely accurate; this is one of the reasons for calculating the hyperfocal distance conservatively by closing down the lens an extra stop.

If this all sounds confusing, rest assured that once you have your lens focused at the HFD, you can leave it there as long as you use the same aperture. Those with low vision, or who have difficulty focusing at night, should consider prefocusing their lenses before leaving home. You can measure the HFD for your working aperture with a tape measure to make sure you are focusing at the true HFD. The focus ring on the lens can then be secured with tape, ensuring the lens will remain focused all night. Of course, if you change apertures, your HFD will change, and you will need to refocus.

None of these focusing methods will work in every situation, so it's great to have several different techniques at your disposal. Now let's look at some of those uncontrollable variables and see what we can do to work around them.

CONTRAST AND DYNAMIC RANGE

The range between the darkest black and brightest white in a scene, digital file, negative, or print is called dynamic range. Daytime photographs usually involve a single light source—either the Sun or an overcast or cloudy sky. On a clear day, the Sun is a moderately high-contrast point light source that creates deep shadows, midtones, and bright highlights. Unless the scene contains specular highlights like sunlight reflected off water, glass, or metal, the dynamic range of the scene can be recorded by a DSLR sensor. An overcast sky is a diffuse light source, with much lower contrast, a smaller dynamic range, and only a couple of stops between the darkest and lightest tones in a scene. The situation in an urban area at night is completely different, because nighttime illumination involves many different localized light sources that are quite weak in comparison to the Sun or diffused skylight. A typical night scene might be described as a sea of darkness punctuated by small pools of light. Night photographs are often described as theatrical or stage-like because the light often comes from different directions and different sources. The exception to this are photographs that are taken in remote natural environments by moonlight or starlight. As you might expect, moonlit scenes have a similar dynamic range to sunlit scenes, with two important differences. The first is obvious; moonlight is much weaker because it is sunlight reflected off of the surface of the Moon. Second, because moonlight is so weak and requires long exposures, the Moon moves in the sky during the exposure. As the Moon moves, its shadow advances with it, and the edges are softened as they are washed over with light. The end result is that moon shadows are not as deep as Sun shadows. Moonlit scenes usually express a fairly narrow dynamic range, unless the camera is pointing toward the Moon.

The dynamic range between bright and dark areas in artificially lit environments can easily be 15 stops, and if light sources are included in the image that range is greater still. This exposure

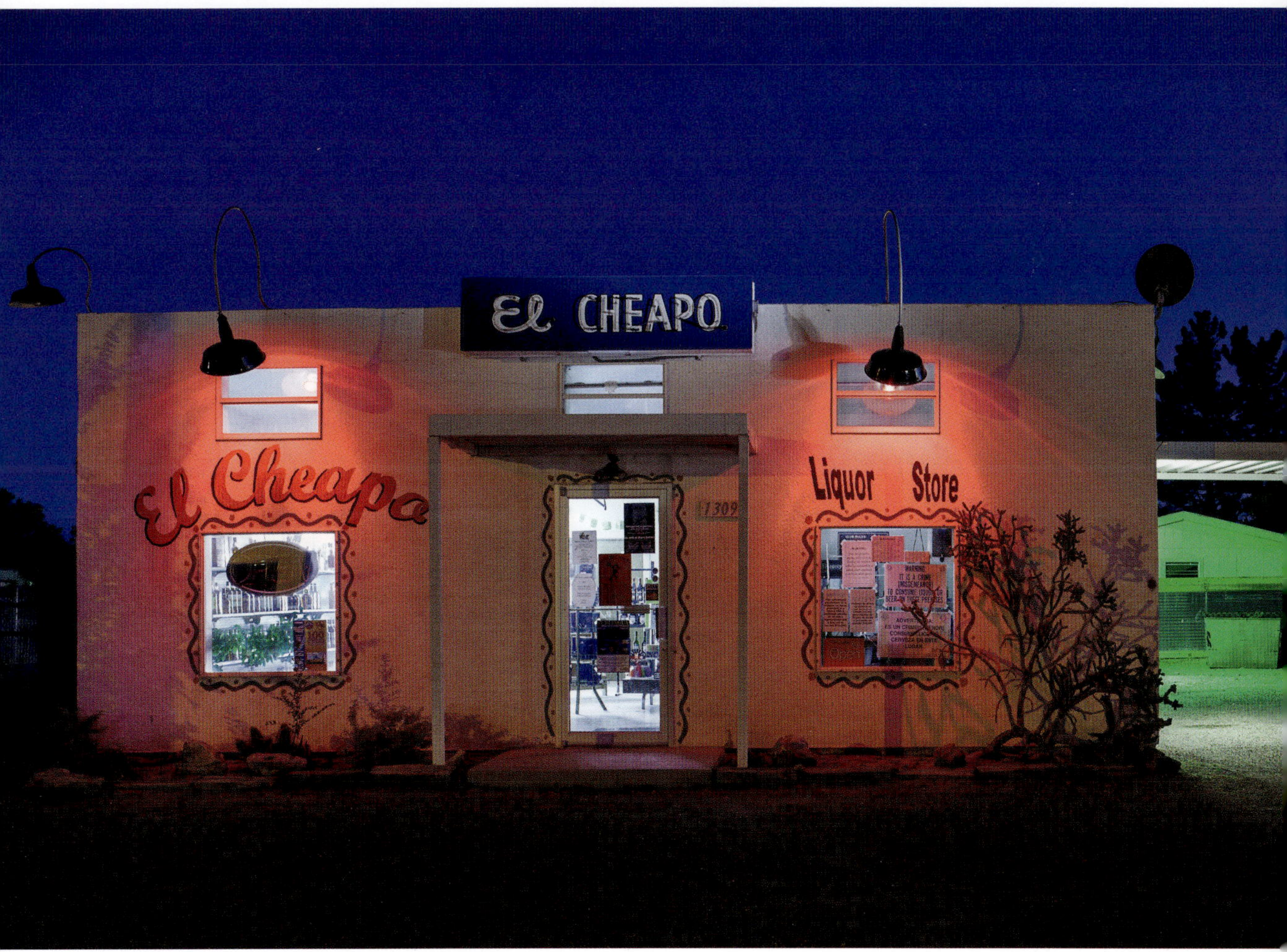

El Cheapo Liquor Store, Marfa, Texas. 30 seconds, f8 at ISO 100. Canon 5D MK II, 35 mm Zuiko Shift f2.8 lens. The El Cheapo was a landmark in the offbeat town of Marfa that sadly closed in 2013. In order to control the extreme contrast presented by the subject, my friend and I made our images as the last light was fading from the sky. As it got darker, the lights inside the store became blown out, so we asked the storekeeper if we could turn off some of the lights. Fortunately, they were amenable, and we got the shot. Red lights in the fixtures over the storefront, mercury vapor in the rear on the right, and flashlight to illuminate the burned-out neon sign. This unusual approach to scene contrast control is the kind of thinking required for successful night images.

difference between shadows and highlights is more than any camera sensor can accommodate without going to extreme measures. Sometimes an image is worth the investment in postprocessing time to try to recover an image with such high contrast, but the best way to handle such extremes is to manage them in-camera whenever possible. A slight adjustment of the composition can often reduce overall contrast. By making minor camera position adjustments, it may be possible to hide a prominent light source behind a tree, street sign, or other object in the scene. In complex situations with many light sources, finding the best camera position to hide the most problematic lights can be like solving a puzzle—move the camera to obscure one light, and another appears.

Another option might be to crop the image a little tighter to eliminate light sources near the edge of the frame that are causing lens flare and increasing the overall contrast. Sometimes a compromise of the ideal composition is the only way to photograph a particularly contrasty scene. In other instances, it simply may not be possible to capture the scene you see before you in a single image. In this situation, HDR imaging or blending multiple exposures can be considered. This can be achieved with HDR software or by manually layering images—or parts of them—in Photoshop. Taking the dynamic range of your DSLR into consideration will help guide you in determining if a scene can be effectively photographed in a single capture, or if it will require multiple exposures to record all the important detail in the scene. It is important to differentiate between important highlights where detail needs to be preserved (such as the side of a brightly lit building) and highlights that can be allowed to clip or be overexposed (like a streetlight). There is no hard rule here; it is a subjective decision made by the photographer at the time of exposure. A surprising amount of highlight detail is contained in a RAW file, and can be recovered in postprocessing. However, when there is clipping in all three channels (RGB), and the sensor sites become fully saturated, there can be no recovery of detail.

Each new generation of digital cameras expand the dynamic range that digital photographers have to work with. Early DSLR cameras had a dynamic range of about 8 stops, which had been improved to about 12 stops by 2008. The Nikon D810 has a theoretical dynamic range of 14.8 stops and[1] is the greatest of any DSLR on the market in late 2014. Currently, there is no print media that can reproduce the full dynamic range of the D810, or many night scenes, which can easily exceed 15 stops. A quality print will convey a sense of the dynamic range of the image, but it will be compressed to fit the dynamic range of the paper. Dynamic range and approaches to managing it are discussed in further detail in the next chapter.

LIGHT SOURCES AND COLOR TEMPERATURE

The color of daylight changes throughout the day depending on the amount of atmosphere that the light travels through to reach the Earth, and this depends on the elevation of the Sun above the horizon. Because there is only one primary light source during the day, most daylight

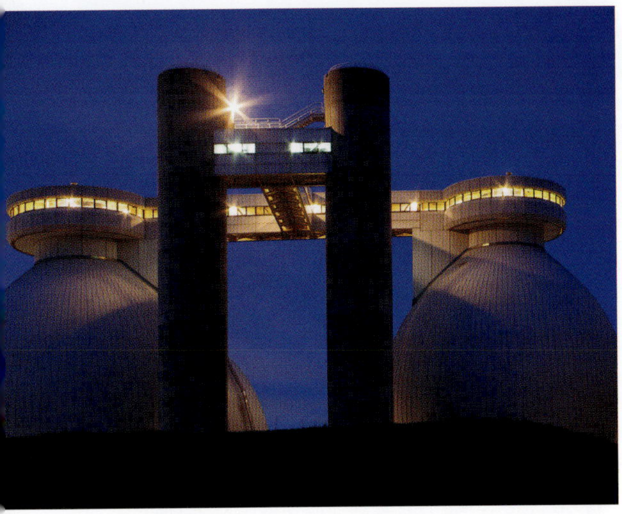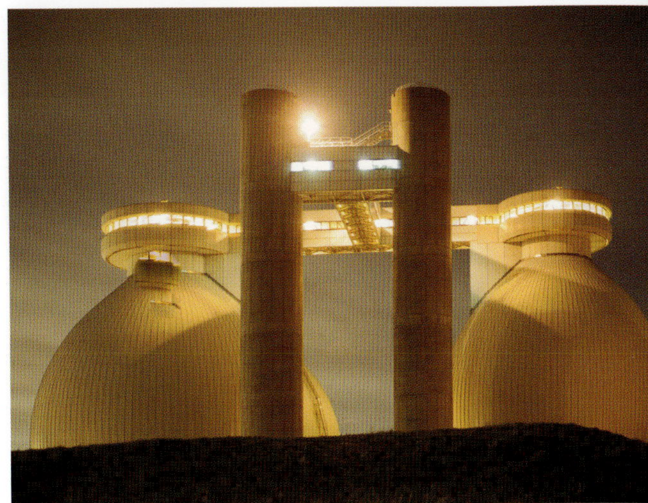

"Deer Island Sewage Treatment Plant," Boston, MA. White balance and mixed light. 30 seconds, f8 at ISO 100 for both images. These two images pictures were made 20 minutes apart with the same settings and white balance. The only thing that has changed is the ratio of daylight to artificial light, as it was twilight at the time of the image on the left and fully dark for the one on the right. Low clouds had also rolled in, which reflected the sodium vapor lights, and added a yellow cast to the sky.

pictures can be easily color balanced for that light source. However, there are many different types of light sources in our nighttime environment, and each of them has its own color balance, or temperature. Our eyes do a remarkable job of compensating for varying brightness levels, because our irises continually expand and contract the pupil based on the brightness of what we see before us. Our brains accommodate for the various color temperatures of streetlights, which we mostly think of as being neutral. When we see different types of lights adjacent to each other, the color differences are more obvious. Photography appears to exaggerate the color of light because digital sensors do not adapt to light the way our eyes do. Mixed lighting is one of the things that creates so much potential in night photography, but it can also cause some of the biggest headaches. Digital cameras have a white balance function that is generally set for the dominant light source in a scene. Cameras can be set for daylight, cloudy, tungsten, fluorescent, custom white balance, a specific color temperature, or to auto white balance (AWB). AWB generally works well, especially in recent camera models—except when there are strong multiple light sources, which is exactly the situation that is frequently found at night.

In some instances, it may be desirable to have a completely neutral and natural color balance in an image, but more often than not juxtapositions of different colored light can add to the visual impact of a photograph. Just as theatrical and Hollywood lighting designers use warm and cool colors to set the mood of a scene, night photographers can take advantage of different types of light in the same way. The first step is to learn to recognize what these light sources are, and how they are rendered in photographs.

The Kelvin temperature scale is used to quantify the color of light, which ranges from about 1500 K for candlelight, 4000 K for moonlight, 5500 K for sunlight, to as high as 12,000 K for blue sky. The lower the color temperature, the warmer (redder) the color, and the higher the color temperature, the cooler (bluer) the color. The Kelvin temperature scale is not the most accurate measurement of the color of many artificial light sources, because it actually only applies to incandescent light sources—fire, sunlight (or moonlight), gaslight, or tungsten bulbs. Gas discharge sources like fluorescent, sodium vapor, and metal halide lights, as well as light-emitting diode (LED) lights, give light that varies in hue from the red to blue in the Kelvin scale. Fluorescent, mercury vapor, and metal halide lights all contain green, which cannot be accounted for on the Kelvin scale. The fluorescent and auto white balance settings can accommodate for the green in these light sources, but the other presets use only the yellow to blue axis in determining white balance.

Most DSLRs have white balance settings that range from about 2500 K to 8000 K. White balance can also be refined with RAW processing software in postproduction, but it is best to set the white balance in-camera. The white balance setting will affect the exposure histogram, which is your primary means of determining exposure in many situations. Therefore, setting the white balance to a color temperature that renders colors close to the way that you want them will also ensure a better exposure histogram. The table below details the color temperatures on different light sources.

Light source	Color temperature	Hue	Primary use
Low-pressure sodium vapor	589.3 nm monochromatic	Deep yellow	Outdoor lighting near observatories, tunnels, more common in Europe than in the United States
Candle	1500 K	Orange	Romantic dinners
High-pressure sodium vapor	2000 K	Yellow–orange–pinkish	Most common street lights, slowly being phased out
Incandescent/tungsten	2700–3200 K	Yellow	Traditional indoor lamps
Moonlight	4100 K	Neutral to bluish	Lyncanthropes
Fluorescent	4000–6000 K + green	Neutral to greenish	Indoor lighting, illuminated signs
Metal halide	3000–20000 K (usually in the 5000 K range)	Neutral to bluish	Stadiums, parks, street lighting

Light source	Color temperature	Hue	Primary use
LED	4000–7500 K (usually in the 5000 K range)	Slightly warm to bluish	Increasingly common for street and home lighting
Mercury vapor	6500 K + green	Cyan. Similar to metal halide, with a stronger green color cast	Being phased out. Industrial areas, some street lighting

The most common artificial light sources are sodium vapor, metal halide, fluorescent, tungsten, and mercury vapor. Low-pressure sodium vapor lights are instantly recognizable for their strong monochromatic yellow–orange color. They are commonly used in Europe to alert drivers that they are about to enter a village or small town. Despite their high efficiency rating, low-pressure sodium vapor lights are rarely used for street lighting in North America because it is

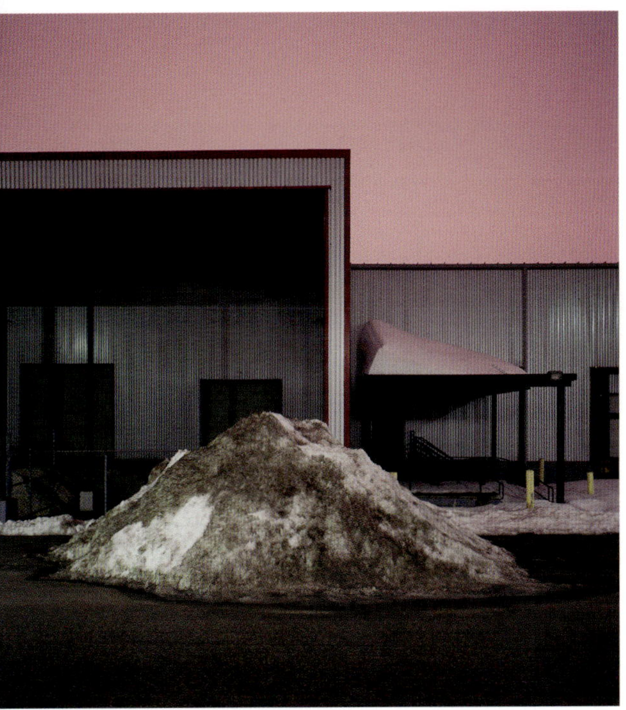
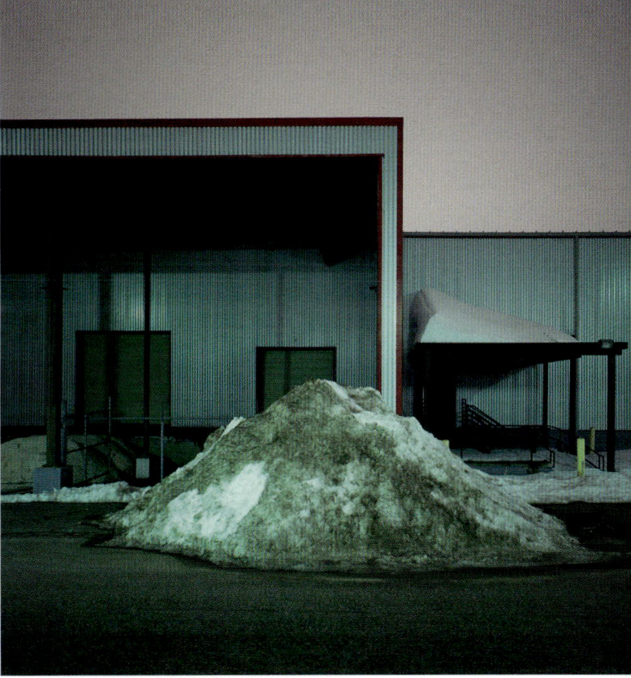

"Dirty Snow," South Boston. 30 seconds, f8 at ISO 200. The lights in this industrial area in South Boston are primarily mercury vapor, and have a cyan–green color cast. The two variations of the picture here have differing white balances. The image on the left was balanced for the mercury vapor by using the eyedropper tool in Lightroom on the corrugated metal building. The image on the right was white balanced by using the eyedropper on the sky. You may notice that the image is as bright as daytime, but it was taken late at night on a completely cloudy night.

difficult to see colors under this type of lighting. Conversely, high-pressure sodium vapor is the predominant type of streetlight found in most cities around the world. These lights have a pinkish–orange cast, and are difficult to color correct, but they appear somewhat more neutral to the eye. Mercury vapor lights emit a greenish–blue or cyan cast, as well as a fair amount of ultraviolet radiation, and remaining fixtures are mostly found in industrial settings. The sale of new mercury vapor lamps was banned in the US in 2008, and will be banned in the EU in 2015. Metal halide lights are closely related to mercury vapor, but include other elements along with mercury in the tube to produce a broader spectrum of light. Metal halide lights are increasingly common in parking lots and public parks, but the most common use is in stadiums and sports facilities because of the clean white appearance of the light. Metal halide lights can vary widely in color temperature, but most appear slightly bluish in photographs. Ceramic discharge metal (CDM) halide lamps are a new form, but it seems that LED fixtures will be the next generation of streetlights. LED or light emitting diodes are used in traffic lights, crosswalk signs, and are replacing neon tubes in sign lighting.

Los Angeles has recently completed converting its streetlights to LED, and other cities are sure to follow. They have a much more pleasing and neutral appearance to the eye, but much as

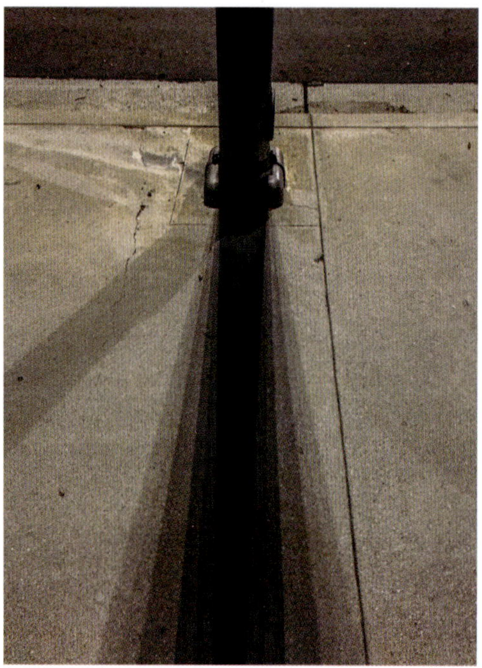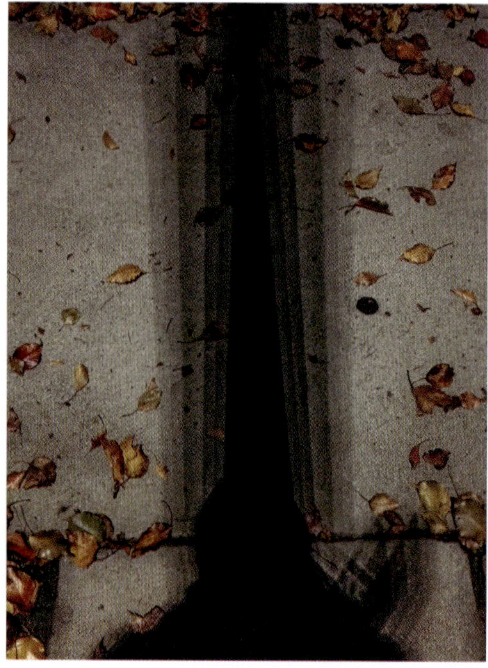

Shadows on the sidewalk in Los Angeles from a multi LED streetlight. 1/15 f2.4 ISO 800 (both exposures), Apple iPhone 5. Repeated pattern shadows caused by multiple LED lights in a single streetlight fixture.

night photographers have complained about the ugly orange light of sodium vapor, we'll miss them when the nighttime environment is illuminated entirely with even, neutral LED lighting. It is worth noting that LED streetlights often include multiple emitters, offset just enough so that each one throws its own distinct shadow. The lights in Los Angeles have a 4 × 4 emitter arrangement, so every streetlight casts 16 overlapping shadows! They are highly efficient, but expensive compared to other light fixtures. They can be manufactured in many colors, but white LEDs usually have a color balance similar to daylight, between 4000 K and 7500 K. Most modern flashlights use LEDs. Fluorescent fixtures are occasionally used outdoors, but are primarily found in office and other commercial buildings. If you photograph a city skyline at night and notice that the interiors of the buildings are glowing green, the building is illuminated with fluorescent lighting. Tungsten or incandescent lights are the familiar lights most people have in their homes, and they have a warm yellowish color balance between 2800 K and 3200 K. They too are being phased out in the US, and are being replaced with compact fluorescents (CFL) and LED bulbs. Aside from the occasional neon sign, these are the main artificial light sources that will impact your night photographs, and, as was mentioned earlier, it is worthwhile learning to distinguish among them.

WEATHER

Weather conditions can dramatically affect both the contrast and color balance of night photographs. In addition to the extremes of contrast between areas illuminated by streetlights and the surrounding darkness, there can be similar extremes between subject and sky. On clear nights, the exposure for the sky is considerably longer than the exposure for artificially illuminated scenes. The photographer must compromise the exposure by favoring either the scene at ground level or the sky. One way to compensate for this exposure disparity is to photograph on nights when there is a full, or nearly full, moon high in the sky. Moonlight will have relatively little impact on ground-level illumination, but it will add light to the sky, giving it tone and color in the photographs. On overcast nights, the clouds in the sky will reflect the light from the ground, reducing the overall image contrast and adding color to the sky. The predominant light source in the area will flavor the color of the sky, but the end result will be a combination of all of the light from the city or town mixed together and bouncing back down off of the clouds. In most locations, a cloudy sky will have a purplish hue which varies in intensity depending on the height of the cloud cover, the overall level of ground illumination, and the type of lighting in the immediate surroundings. If there is a difference in the type of subject matter illumination, and the dominant lighting of the area, there can be major differences in the color temperature between the ground and sky. These differences can make for truly interesting images, but they can also be tedious to color correct if a natural appearance is desired. Urban night photography will usually be more successful on cloudy nights or when there is a full moon on clear nights. Clear nights will generally lead to solid black skies, which don't work well for most images.

The situation is quite the opposite in natural, moonlit scenes. On clear nights, the exposure at ground level and the exposure for the sky are about the same. Of course the exposure times will be much longer if there is little or no moonlight, but even with only starlight to work with, it is possible to photograph in remote areas on clear nights. Cloudy nights in areas with little or no ground-level illumination lead to images with a bright white sky, and dark foreground with low localized contrast in the foreground, but high global contrast between the sky and ground. One solution in this situation is to add light to the foreground with light painting, but just like solid black skies, pure white skies with no detail are not very appealing. Broken, moving clouds can add visual interest to any type of night photograph, urban or rural. Positioning the camera so that the clouds are moving perpendicular to, or at least at a 45-degree angle to, the image plane makes for a more dramatic image. Clouds moving parallel to the image plane tend to blur together and wash out, creating the white sky effect.

FLARE

Night photographs can be plagued by lens flare which is caused by stray light shining directly on the lens from sources outside of the field of view. This unwanted light is scattered across the surfaces of lens elements, and can manifest in different shapes. Flare can be hexagonal or octagonal shaped, reflecting the shape of the lens aperture, or it may appear as rings or star patterns. Flare sometimes appears as a haze that washes out the image and reduces contrast, especially when there is a light source just outside the frame. Wide-angle lenses and zoom lenses are especially prone to flare problems because their complex design and numerous elements provide many surfaces that can cause light to scatter inside the lens. Filters, especially dirty ones, are also frequent contributors to lens flare. Unless you are prone to dropping your gear, or are working in windy or dusty environments, it's probably best to leave the filters at home when you go out night shooting. Lens shades or hoods are designed to prevent flare, but engineering compromises to accommodate for the variable focal length of zoom lenses reduce their effectiveness. It is often difficult to spot lens flare in the camera viewfinder because most SLR and DSLR viewfinders reveal only about 96–98 percent of the image, so flare at the edge of the frame is particularly hard to spot. The best way to check for lens flare is to walk around in front of the camera, and look at the surface of the lens, making sure not to cast your shadow on the camera or lens. If you can see any light falling directly on the lens—regardless of whether or not you are using a shade—chances are that your image will have some flare. In this case, the best solution is to shade the lens further with a black card, either held in your hand or attached to the camera or tripod with an articulating arm with a clip to hold the card. It may also be possible to shade the lens by positioning your body in between the offending light source and your camera. You'll need to be careful not to place the card in the field of view, especially with wide-angle lenses. Make sure you look closely at the image before moving the camera for the next shot, both for signs of flare and for the intrusion of your flare-blocking device. Lens hoods can also cause vignetting of the image if the hood does

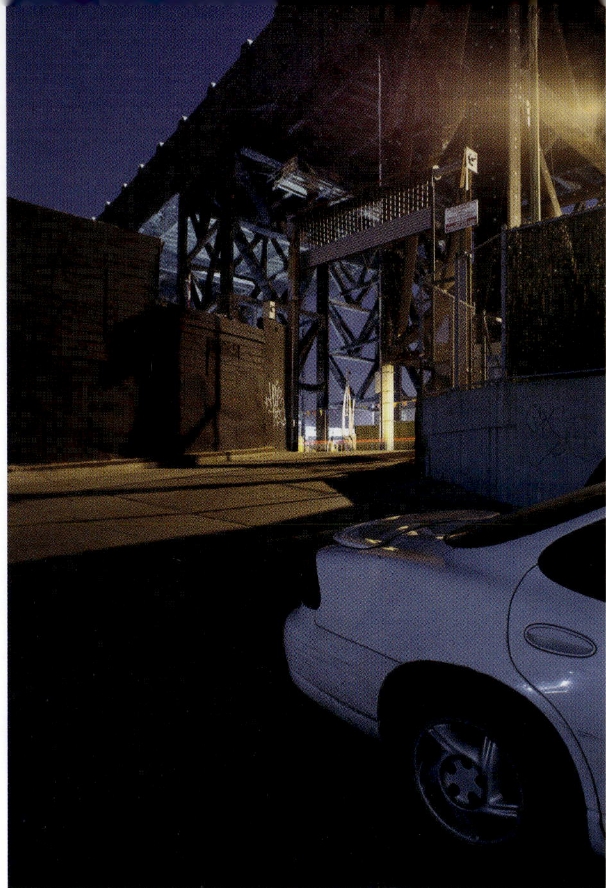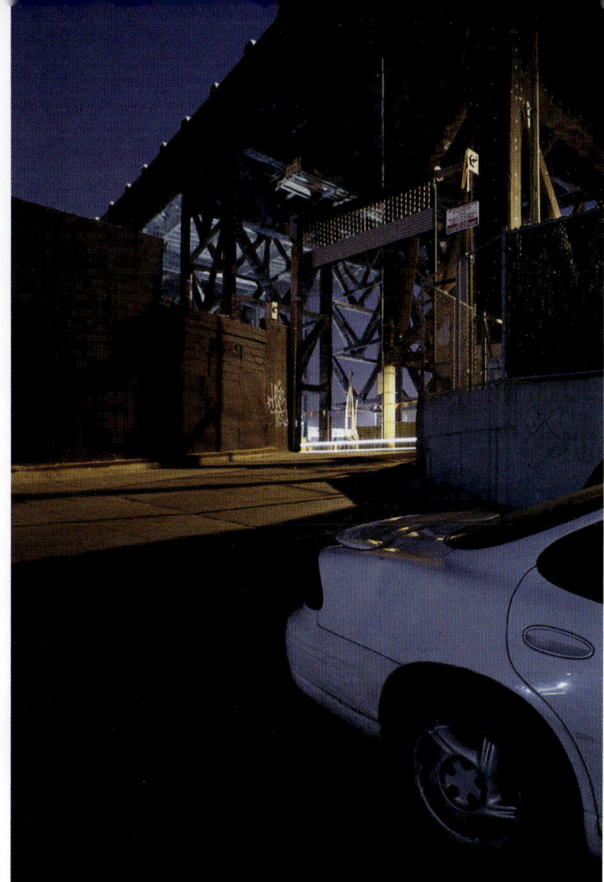

"Gowanus Canal Bridge," Brooklyn, NY. 30 seconds, f8 ISO 400, Canon 5D MK II, 24 mm f3.5 Zuiko Shift lens. The image on the left shows lens flare from a streetlight that was just out of the frame on the right. The flare was avoided in the version on the right with the use of a black card shielding the lens. This technique is more effective than a lens shade alone, although you should always use a lens shade at night regardless. It is best to move around in front of the camera, on the side opposite the offending light source, and to visually confirm that you have blocked any light that was falling on the front of the lens.

not match the lens, or if it is not properly attached to the lens. Modern twist-on shades can accidentally be misaligned or put on the lens without being fully rotated into position. Both of these common mistakes will cause vignetting. In the absence of a lens shade or black card, a hat or even your hand can be employed to do the job, but it is best to use a dark-colored object that won't reflect light back into the lens.

In Chapter 4, we look at camera settings for night photography, and develop a strategy for optimizing exposure in different nighttime situations.

NOTE

1   Dynamic range and other qualities of digital cameras are compared and analyzed on the website www.dxomark.com. This website is a very useful resource if you are considering a new digital camera but it only compares cameras on the basis of image quality. There's a lot more to a great camera than the sensor.

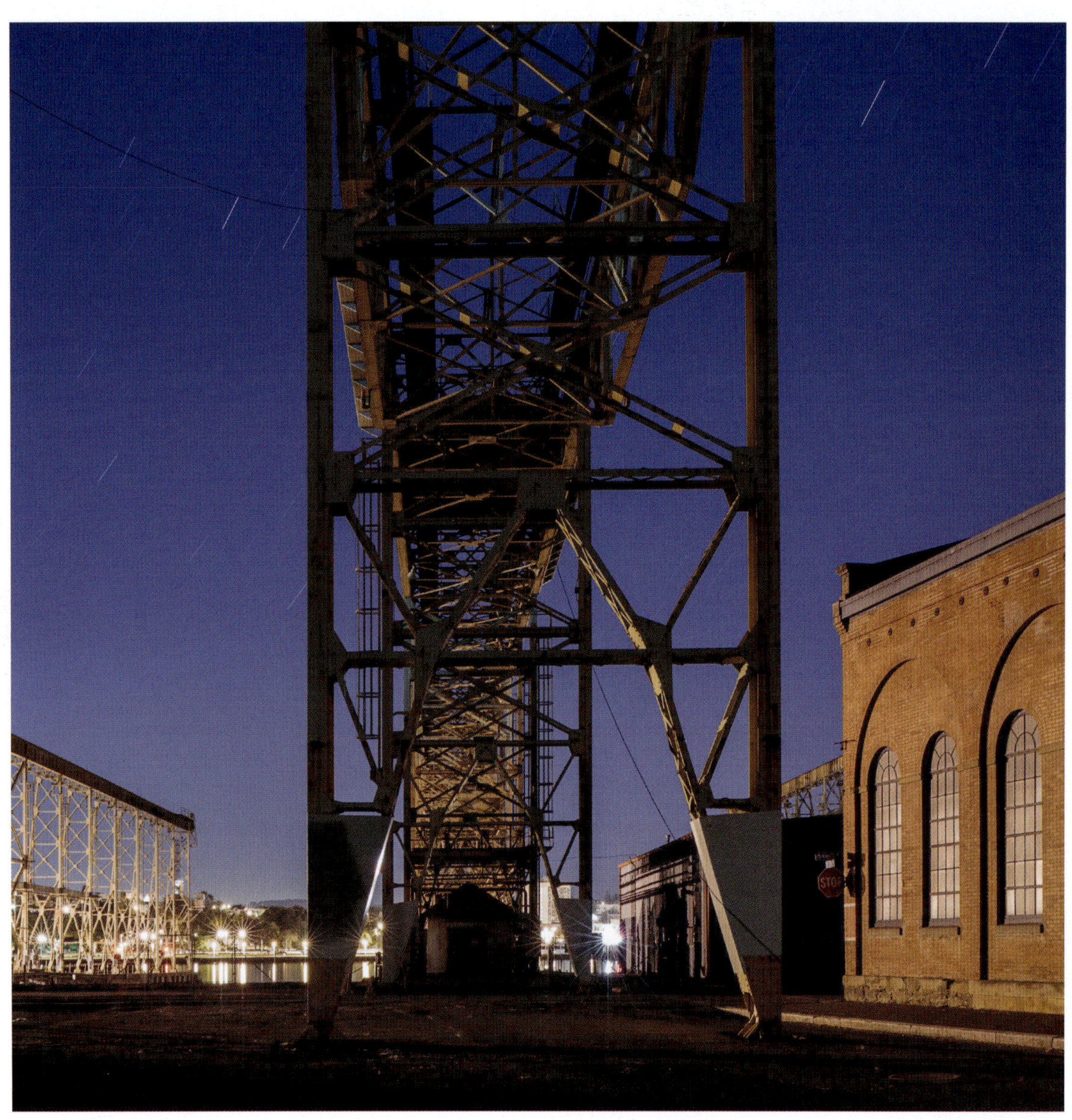

"Mare Island Naval Shipyard," Vallejo, CA. 6 minutes, f8, ISO 400. It was deceptively dark on Mare Island despite all of the lights in the distance This image still required a six minute exposure at ISO 400. Note the star trails. In a brighter area, only the very brightest stars would be recorded.

PART II
TYPES OF NIGHT PHOTOGRAPHY

KEY CAMERA SETTINGS AND EXPOSURE FOR OPTIMAL IMAGE QUALITY

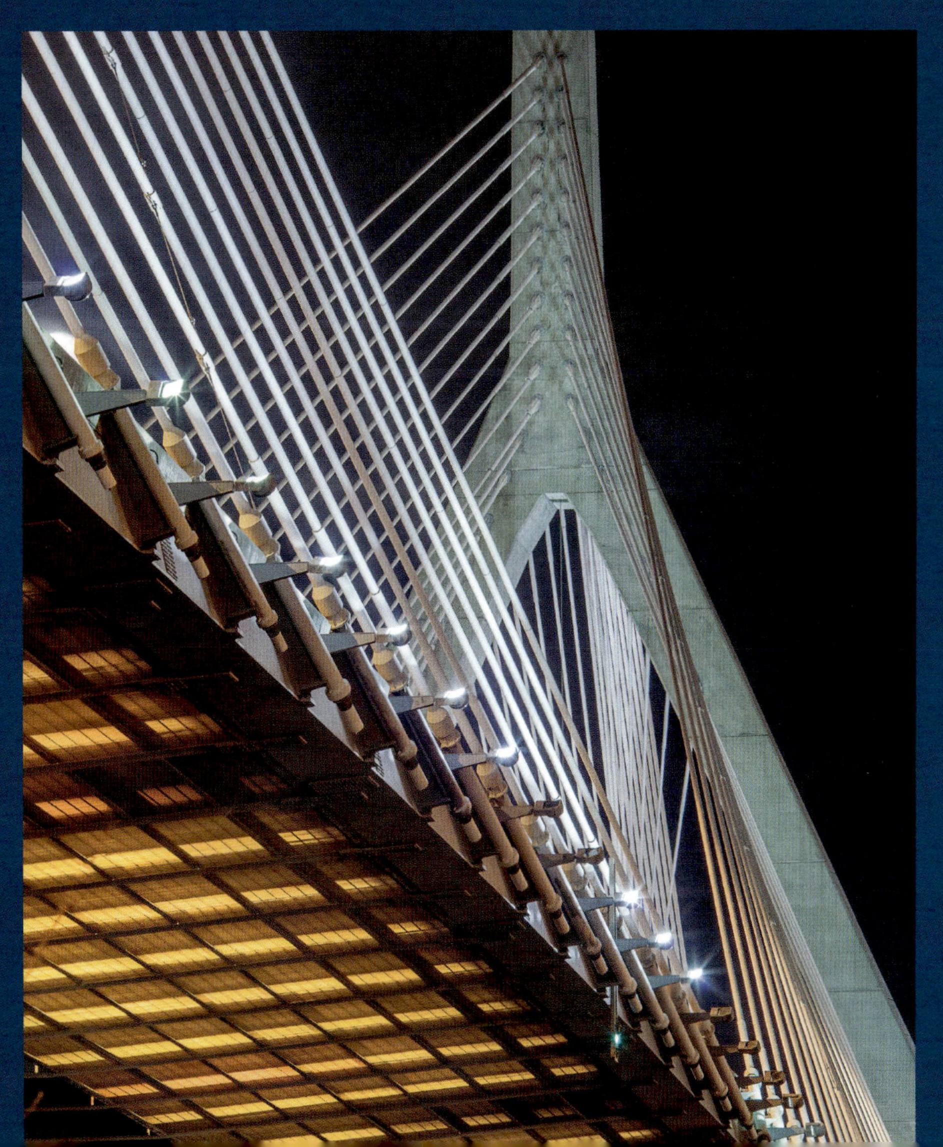

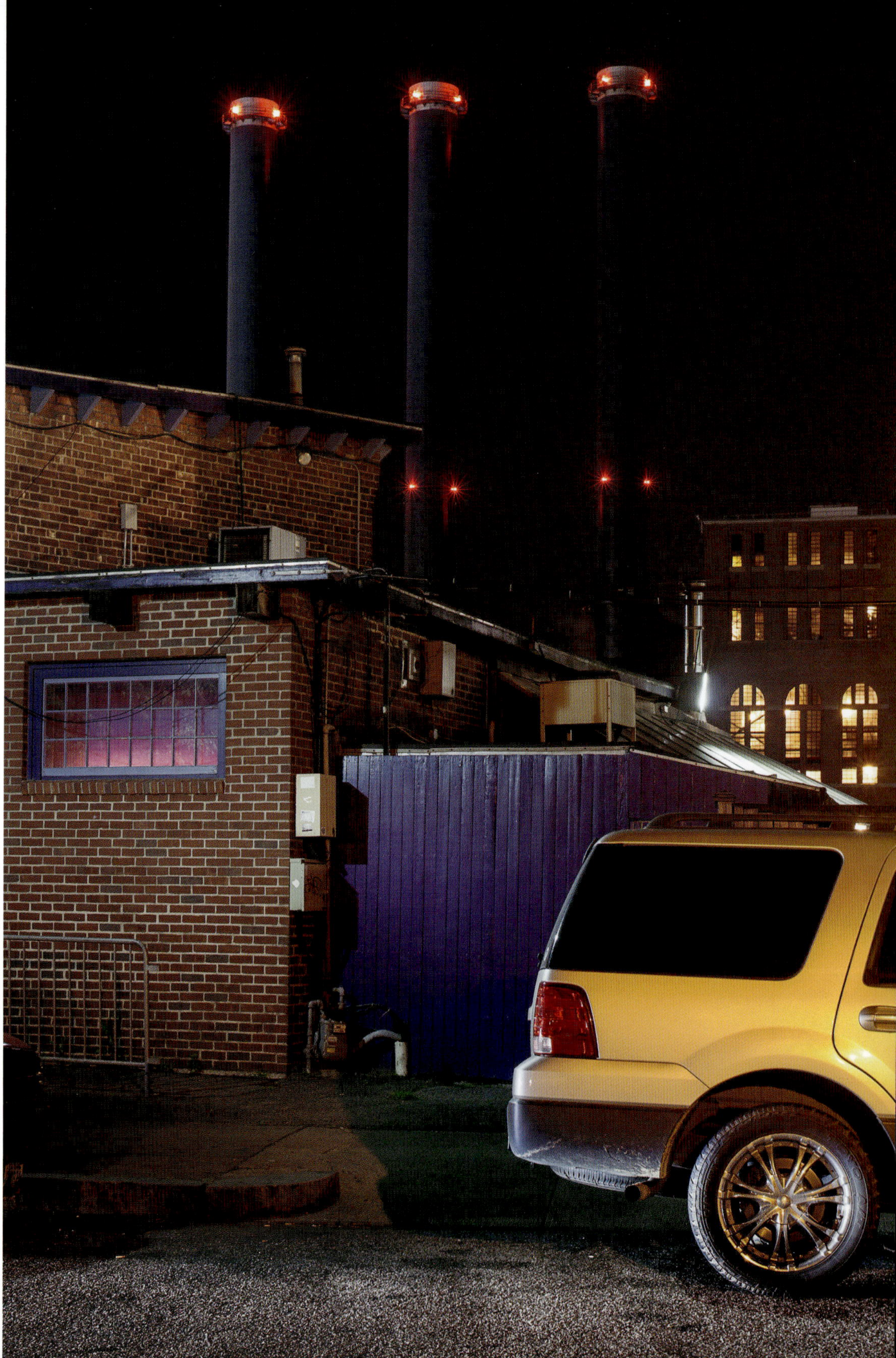

4

In this chapter, we learn how to optimize exposure and minimize noise for maximum image quality, and establish the preferred camera settings and features for night photography.

OPTIMAL EXPOSURE

There is an old adage in black and white film-based photography that says: "Expose for the shadows, and develop for the highlights." The idea is to have as much information in the shadows as you can by giving the maximum exposure that allows you to recover important highlight detail in development. In essence, optimal exposure for digital photography follows a similar principle. The ideal RAW file pushes the histogram to the right where the sensor is tonally rich. Such an exposure will probably appear overly bright straight from the camera, but will also have the information necessary to make a quality print. A RAW file is like a film negative—it contains a wealth of information that can be interpreted in many different ways. The great advantage of RAW files over JPGs is that they can be preserved in their original form indefinitely, and reinterpreted at any time. As you become more proficient working with your chosen software, or as that software improves in future versions, the original RAW file will always be available for you to work with.

The single most important technical aspect of digital night photography is optimizing exposure for RAW capture and development. There is certainly much more to successful night photography than technical perfection, but having the best possible exposure will provide you with the most artistic freedom and creative control to interpret the image according to your vision. An optimal RAW file contains the maximum possible ratio of image information (signal) to data that is an unwanted by-product of capture and processing (noise). This is known as the signal to noise ratio (SNR). Noise is inherent to all electrical processes, including digital photography, and can distort or block the signal (your image). To achieve the highest quality image, you need to achieve the highest possible SNR. Providing the sensor with the greatest possible exposure without clipping important highlights is the way to ensure the best SNR.

EXPOSE TO THE RIGHT

Understanding histograms is paramount to successful digital photography, whether it be daytime or night photography. Determining optimal exposure is based on an evaluation of luminosity and RGB histograms, the preview image, the flashing highlight indicator, and analysis of the scene based on experience. There is no such thing as an ideal or perfect histogram, as it is simply a description of tones in an image. However, a right-biased histogram—one where

"Saturday night" in Providence, RI. 10 seconds, f8, at ISO 200, Canon 5D MK II, 35 mm f2.8 Zuiko Shift lens. Distinctive smoke stacks dominate the Providence harbor, and the waterfront is always hopping on a Saturday night. This offbeat image is a jumble of shapes and color that all seemed to coalesce into an interesting photograph when a car outside the frame to the left double-parked and its headlights lit up the street in front of it. This image is the result of a rare case of a spontaneous reaction to a changing environment.

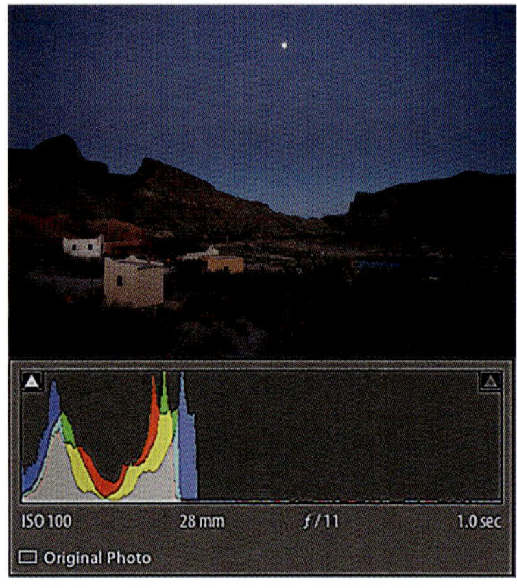
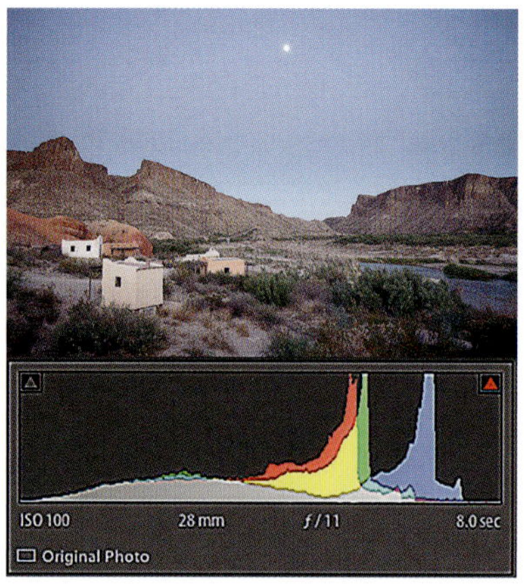
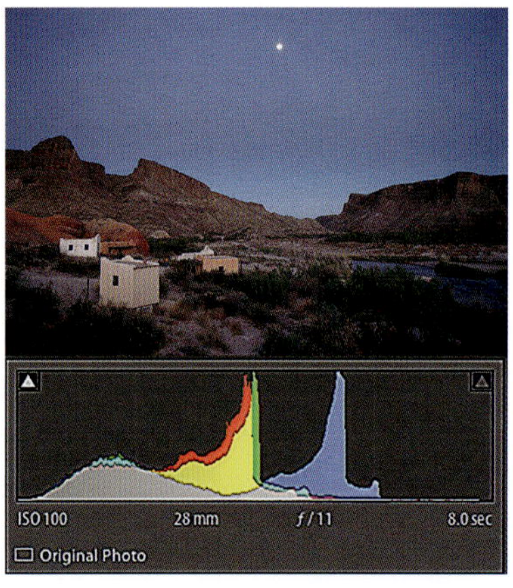
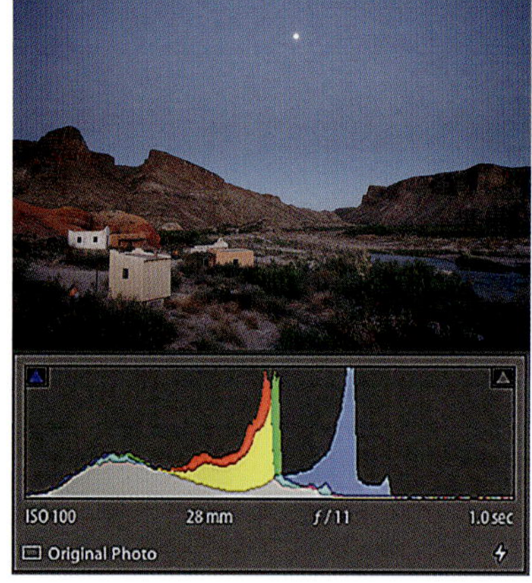
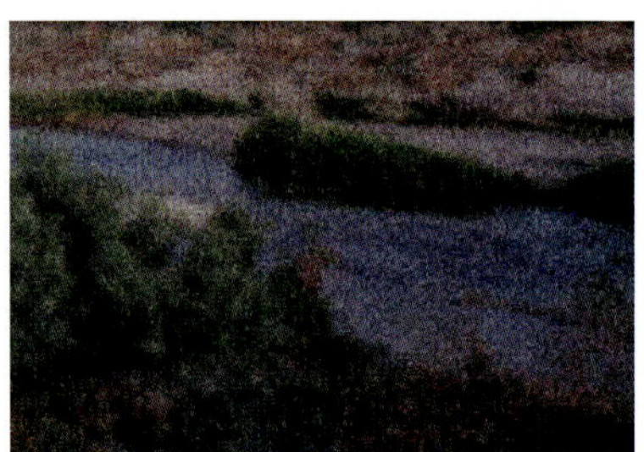
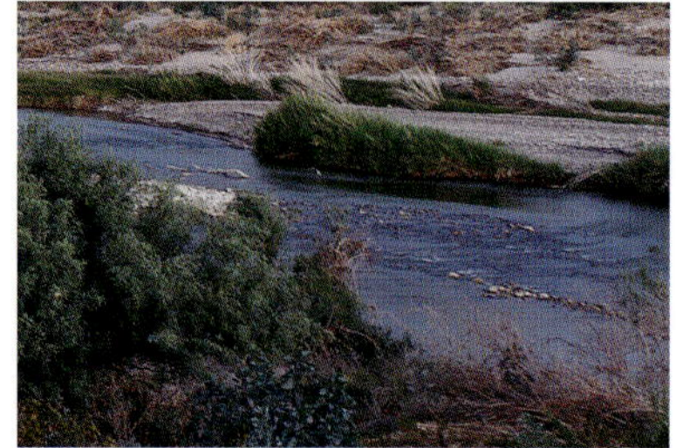

"Contrabando Movie Set," Lajitas, TX, Scott Martin

This illustration shows how increasing the exposure for a right-biased histogram improves image quality. The image on the left looked good in-camera. The image on the right was exposed by an additional three stops and looked too bright. The two images developed to look the same show similar histograms, but are not the same. This full magnification section shows that the image on the right with more exposure has more detail and less noise. It will clearly make a superior print. Photographic prints have much higher resolution than offset printing, and the difference would be even more obvious in a large print.

the bulk of the data is on the right side—is more flexible, and apt to make a better quality print. Camera meters provide an exposure reading based on 18 percent reflectance, assuming that all of the tones that make up the image will average out to middle gray. Exposing for middle gray probably yields the best exposure for JPEG shooters, but RAW files benefit from additional exposure. How much? An optimal RAW file is given as much exposure, and the histogram is pushed as far to the right as possible, without clipping important highlights. A good deal of compromise is often required to balance the need for a right-biased histogram with the need to preserve highlights.

THE CAMERA SENSOR

Digital photography is a complex process, and of course it is not necessary to understand how a camera works to use it. However, a basic understanding of how photons of light passing through a lens and falling on a digital sensor are translated into a photograph will clarify the concept of optimal exposure. Your camera's sensor are an array of millions of pixels (1 megapixel = 1 million pixels). Each pixel has a photosite that collects and stores photons of light during an exposure. These photons accumulate during an exposure, and some photosites catch many photons as the exposure builds over time and becomes saturated. These saturated photosites become the highlights of the image. Photosites that become so full that they overflow into surrounding areas cause a phenomenon known as sensor blooming, which is a problem that commonly occurs when light sources are included in an image. Some photosites catch only a few photons of light during the exposure, and these become the shadows. In deep shadow areas, noise can be confused with the signal data. The threshold of shadow detail is the point at which background noise can be distinguished from signal data.

RAW files concentrate information in the highlight values of the images. Half of the total potential brightness levels or tones are located in the brightest stop of the camera's dynamic range. Half of the remaining potential tones are contained in the next brightest stop of

Linear encoding in digital photography means that the camera sees a very dark image that has to be lightened a great deal for it to look normal to us humans. The effect is that most of the tonal information in a RAW file is concentrated in the highlight values. An image with lots of exposure can be darkened, redistributing some of that information into the shadow areas. This is great for night photography and leads to rich shadow detail and color. Conversely, lightening an underexposed image spreads data that was already thin over a wider area and will lead to poor image quality. The white lines in this image represent linear bit depth in the tonal range.

dynamic range. The pattern repeats until the few remaining tones in the darkest levels become confused with the noise inherent in the sensor and detail is no longer distinguishable.

Larger sensors with fewer megapixels can record a wider dynamic range with less noise than smaller, higher megapixel sensors.

HISTOGRAMS

The histogram feature is a graphic representation of a digital exposure. When reviewing images on the camera monitor, the histogram is enabled to provide additional information about the image and helps to determine if the exposure is adequate. It is an essential tool for the digital photographer, and should be used faithfully if optimal image quality is important. Luminance, or light intensity, is expressed on the X, or horizontal axis of the histogram, and the Y (vertical) axis represents the relative quantity of light at any given intensity: that is, how much of each tone is present in the image. The histogram describes the tonal range of the image. Most cameras can display both a luminosity histogram that shows overall brightness, and an RGB histogram that provides different mapping for each color channel. Both are useful, but in different ways. The luminosity histogram gives a better indication of overall exposure, and whether or not there is any significant clipping in either shadows or highlights. The RGB histogram shows if there is color clipping in any of the red, green, or blue color channels. In most lighting situations, the luminosity histogram gives reliable exposure guidance, but at night when there are a variety of different light sources with very strong color casts, the RGB histogram is invaluable. It will indicate clipping in a single color channel that may go unnoticed with the luminosity histogram alone.

In addition to showing the tonal range of an image, a histogram can describe dynamic range. A high-key image will have most of the information on the right side, while a low-key image will be bunched up to the left. A high-contrast image without many midtones will be shaped like a bowl, and a moderate contrast image with no bright highlights or deep shadows might show a histogram that has a hump in the center, or a bell shape. An image where the distribution of shadows, midtones, and highlights is relatively even will display a histogram without many sharp peaks. When the histogram is touching, or pushed up against the left side of the graph, this indicates underexposure and shadow clipping. When it is bunched up against the right side, there is highlight clipping. Both are problematic and should be avoided whenever possible. Shadow clipping means there is not enough detail present in the shadows, and highlight clipping means that pixels have become pure white, hold no detail, and cannot be recovered. Highlight clipping can be especially hard to detect in the histogram because it may be represented by a very narrow spike against the right-hand wall of the histogram. Shadow clipping is usually more obvious because there are usually larger volumes of dark tones to form a more distinct peak in the histogram. The histogram and image preview should always be

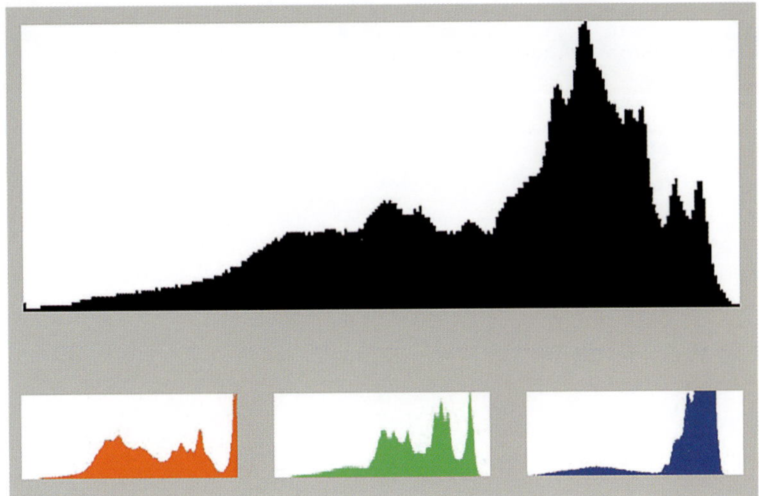

considered together in the context of the scene being photographed, because together they provide more information than either one alone.

> The histogram is especially useful when photographing scenes of limited dynamic range, such as photography by moonlight, or in a studio where the light can be well controlled. In such instances, it is relatively easy to expose far enough to the right to avoid shadow clipping without risking blown highlights. By contrast, when photographing environments with a wide dynamic range, such as street scenes at night, it may not be possible to push the exposure histogram far enough to the right to avoid shadow clipping without also sacrificing important highlight detail. The best option is usually to expose the scene as much as you can without clipping important highlight detail. The challenge becomes how to distinguish between important and unimportant highlight detail, and how to determine if it has been clipped or not. Therefore, in situations with a wide dynamic range, it is better to base the exposure primarily on the flashing highlight indicator.

THE FLASHING HIGHLIGHT INDICATOR AND ZEBRA PATTERNING

The histogram does not show *where* the image is clipping. The flashing highlight indicator function, also known as "the blinkies," serves as a warning that highlights are being clipped and shows where they are. This feature should be enabled and used as an additional indication that there is highlight clipping somewhere in the image. The blinkies are overlaid on top of the image preview after the image has been taken, and show exactly which part of the image has been clipped. Typically in night photographs, highlight clipping occurs when light sources are included in the scene. In this case, clipping is usually unavoidable. Highlight detail in light bulbs is not particularly important, but the blinkies will show if there is also clipping in the areas *surrounding*

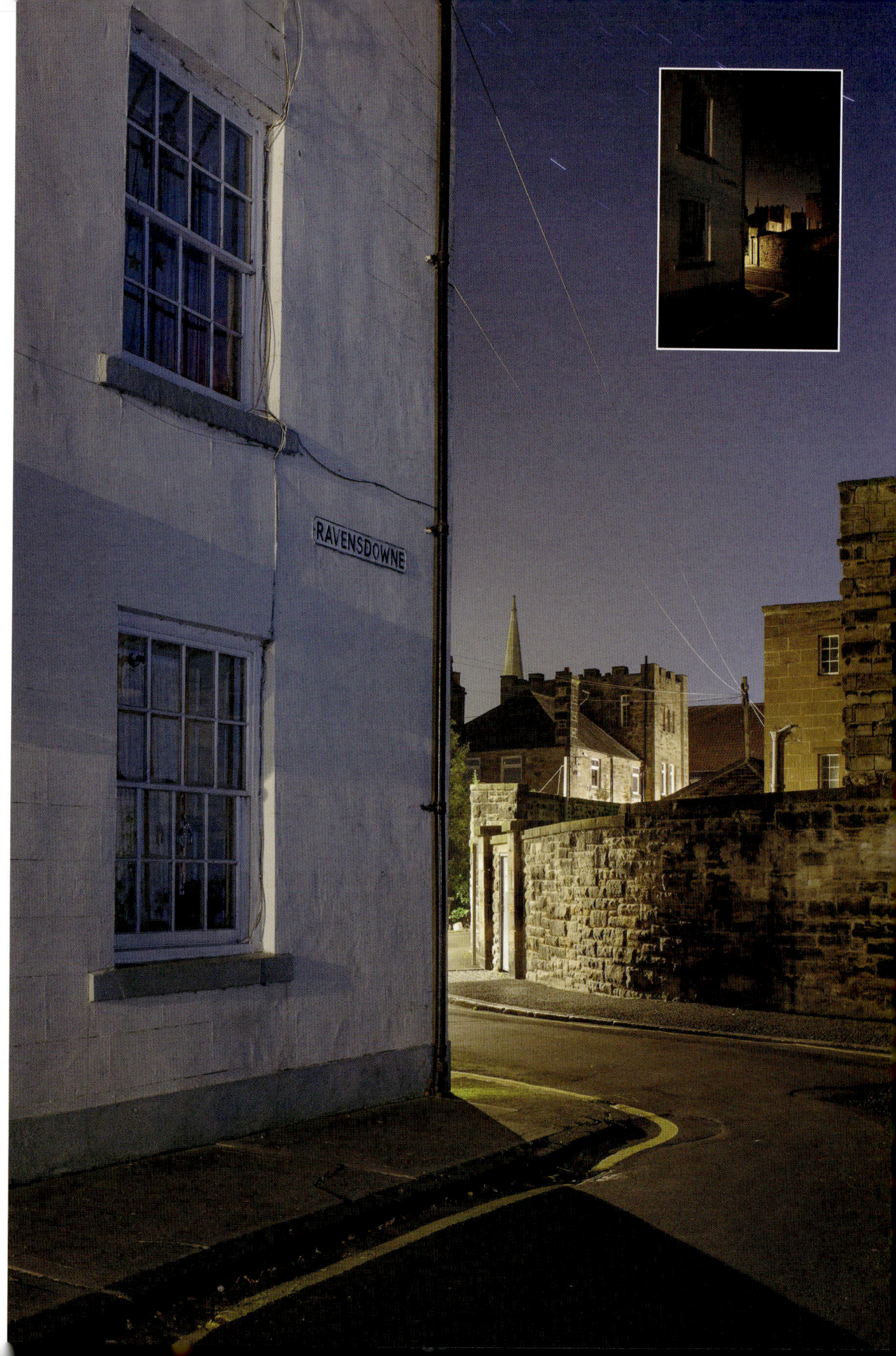
RAVENSDOWNE

the light sources. If there is, you will probably want to reduce the exposure to preserve detail in this part of the image. Differentiating between important and unimportant highlight detail is the key factor in determining optimal exposure in dynamic or high-contrast environments.

> It is up to you to decide if the highlights are important or not. Do you wish to see detail in a highlight area? If so, those highlights are important, and exposure should be reduced until those areas are not blinking. If you don't mind that this part of the image will be pure white with no detail, then ignore the blinkies in this area, and look for other parts of the image that may be clipped.

Zebra patterning is a function that overlays a striped pattern on the image in live view. Unlike the blinkies, zebra patterning is applied in real time before the image is exposed. It is a feature more common to video than still cameras, but some Sony and a few other cameras offer this useful feature for highlight and shadow clipping with both still and video photography. It is likely that zebra patterning will be increasingly common on future camera models.

The histograms and flashing highlight indicators are based on the JPEG preview of the image displayed on the monitor, not the RAW data itself. They are fairly low resolution, and not 100 percent accurate, but still provide the best gauge of exposure that we have. The preview image and histograms are modified by picture styles and any custom functions that may be enabled, while the RAW files generally are not if you use a third-party RAW converter like ACR (Adobe Camera Raw) or Lightroom. When shooting in RAW mode, setting the picture style to neutral and disabling custom functions that affect the image *other* than long-exposure noise reduction (LENR) will provide more accurate preview data. The picture style parameters include settings for sharpness, contrast, saturation, and tone and offer a way to customize the look of JPEG images in-camera. In the case of Canon's Digital Photo Professional and Nikon's Capture NX, they do recognize the actions of custom function settings, which are applied to the RAW files as metadata and executed when the file is opened on the computer.

"Ravensdowne," Berwick Upon Tweed, England

4 minutes, f8 at ISO 160. Canon 5D MK II, Nikkor 28 mm f3.5 PC lens. This image had to be underexposed by about two stops to prevent important highlights from clipping on the stone wall. The small image shows the image straight out of camera.

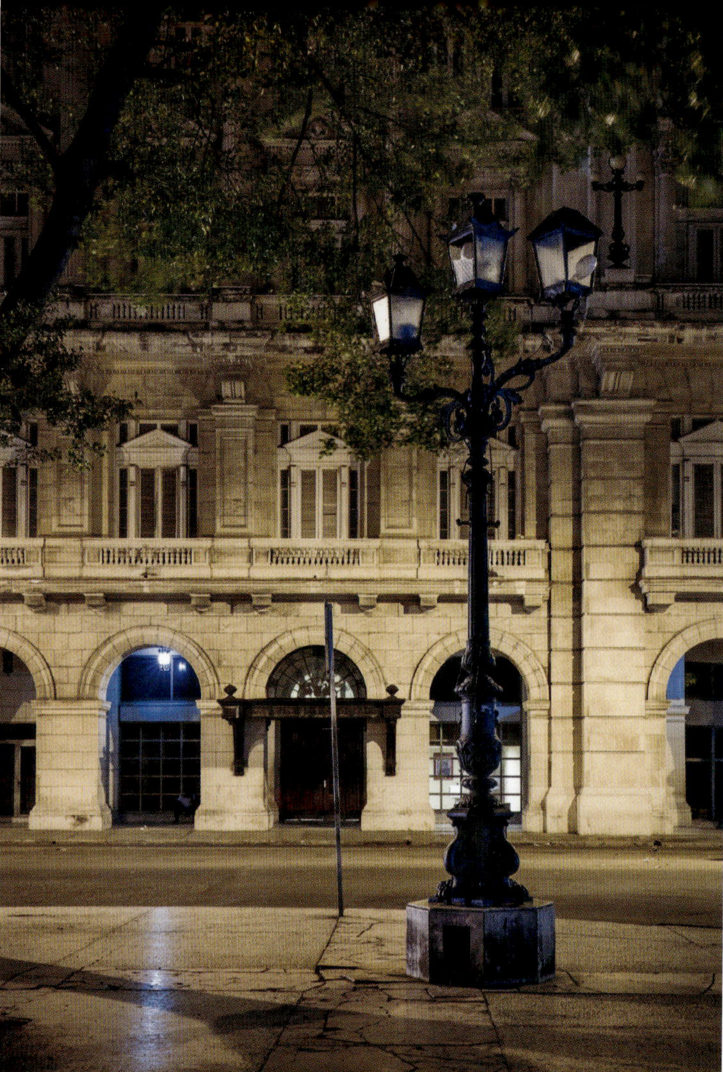

"Broken Streetlight," Havana, Cuba. Canon G1X MK II. 6 seconds, f8 at ISO 320. This elegant streetlight with its sad broken bulbs and the strongly contrasting mixed lighting caught my attention while strolling the boulevard one night in old Havana. The limited dynamic range of the compact camera was just enough to capture this scene. Only the lightbulb across the street is clipped.

DYNAMIC RANGE

Dynamic range is the ratio between the brightest and darkest tones, and can describe a scene, a capture device such as a camera or scanner, or a display such as a computer monitor or a print. Tonal range describes the number of tones within the dynamic range. There could be many tones within a narrow dynamic range or relatively few tones within a wide dynamic range. A greater tonal range means smoother color transitions, and a greater dynamic range means there is a greater difference between the brightest and darkest tones.

A camera's dynamic range spans the range of tones that a sensor can capture between saturation—when a pixel becomes pure white, and when texture is indistinguishable from background noise—which is almost but not quite black. Scene dynamic range often exceeds the capability of the camera to record it, especially in artificially lit environments at night. Any time there are lights or specular highlights in the scene, it will have a large dynamic range.

Making the determination of which highlights are important to preserve is critical to optimal exposure. If a scene that includes light sources is exposed to prevent any clipping, the remainder of the image will be so underexposed that there will be significant shadow clipping in the rest of the image. Underexposure and shadow clipping can dramatically increase noise and lower the signal to noise ratio. In this situation, it is better to allow the light sources to clip, and restrict the exposure just enough to prevent extensive sensor blooming around the clipped highlights. Sometimes the dynamic range of a scene can be reduced by recomposing to eliminate lights from the scene, as was discussed in Chapter 3. Another option for controlling extremely contrasty situations is high dynamic range (HDR) photography that combines multiple exposures of the same scene in postprocessing. Options for HDR include software like

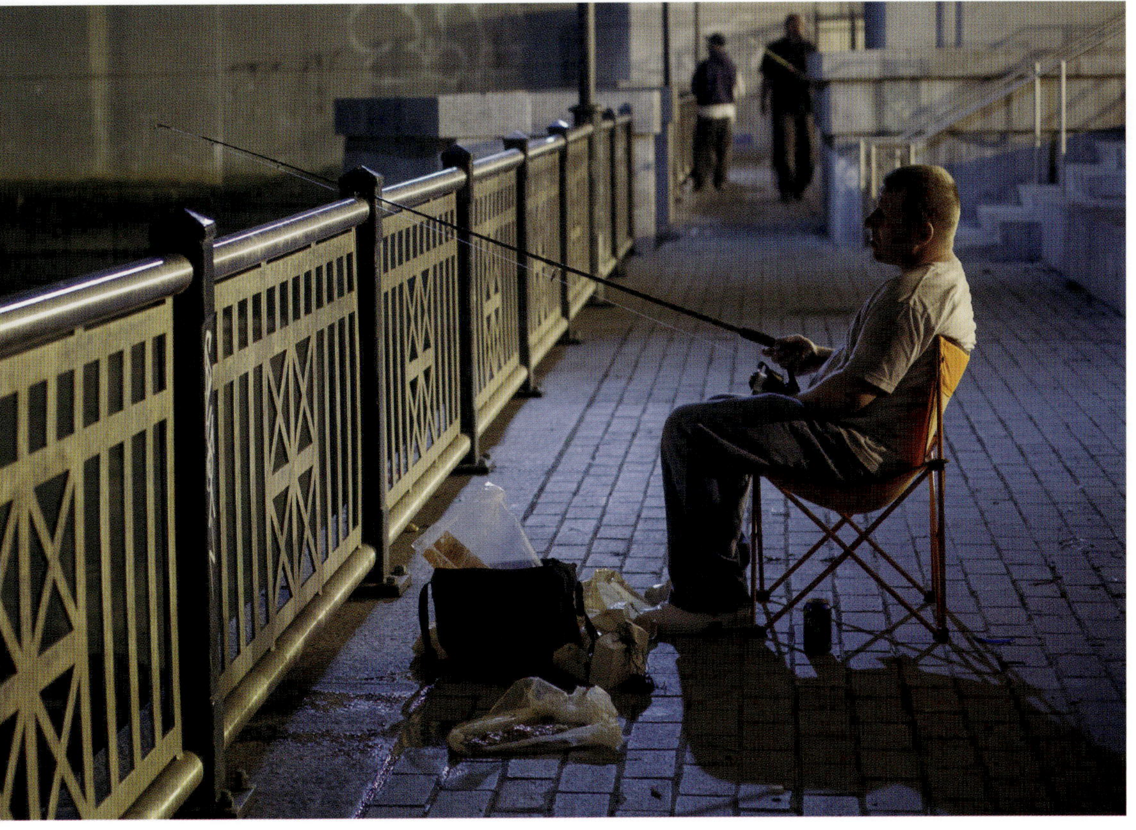

"Friday Night Fishing," Providence, RI. One-quarter of a second, f4 at ISO 1250. Canon 5D MK II, 35 mm f2.8 Zuiko Shift lens. The expression and gesture of this guy was too good to pass up. He'd obviously had a rough week, and I didn't want to bother him—or miss the shot. Ordinarily, I would have waited for the two guys in the background to walk out of the frame, but I didn't want to chance losing the moment. As it happened, he looked up at me after I made the exposure, and the opportunity for another shot was gone. To minimize the risk of blurring because of movement, I chose to raise the ISO and keep the shutter speed as short as possible.

Photomatix that automate the process. Beware though: Photomatix and other HDR applications can be difficult to control, and results often have a distinctive look that is not very realistic. The gimmicky "HDR look" that was popular in the early 2000s can be seductive at first, but it is probably best left to the dustbin of forgotten photo trends. HDR software does not perform very well in situations where light sources are included in the scene, which is precisely when most night photographers want to use it. Most HDR software does a poor job of interpreting *sensor bloom*—areas of extreme overexposure surrounding light sources that are common in night photos.

One of the simplest and most elegant HDR options is an open source application called Enfuse GUI. Enfuse works in conjunction with Timothy Armes' LR/Enfuse plugin for Lightroom to incorporate HDR directly into a Lightroom workflow. LR/Enfuse does not work for images with starry skies, but for urban scenes of relatively modest dynamic range it does a great job blending images without creating unrealistic looking results. It is available as donationware from www.photographers-toolbox.com, and Enfuse can be downloaded for free from www.software.bergmark.com.

SET IMAGE QUALITY TO RAW

To produce the highest quality images possible, you'll need to set your camera to save RAW files rather than JPEGs for optimal image quality. RAW files preserve all of the image data that the camera records. When an exposure is made, light falling on individual pixels, or photosites, is registered as a voltage level, which is then converted to either a 12- or 14-bit digital signal, depending on the camera circuitry. Cameras that record 14-bit files can express 2^{14} (16,384) potential tones, or brightness levels, per pixel. If the camera is set to save JPEG files, each pixel can represent 2^8 (256) different tones. The 14 bits of data in the capture file are compressed into 8 bits in the JPEG file. Having 16,384 brightness levels available to work with in an image is certainly preferable to 256, because it allows for more flexibility when the image is processed. It is a misnomer to say that a camera is set to shoot JPEGs because the camera always shoots, or captures, RAW image data. The difference lies in what happens to the data after is is captured. A camera set to RAW mode creates a tag for each image with camera settings (like white balance) and the picture style settings (contrast, sharpening, and saturation). This metadata does not actually change the image, but it is like a set of instructions for the software used to open the RAW file.

Camera manufacturers' RAW converters, such as Nikon's Capture NX or Canon's Digital Photo Professional, will apply the picture style settings to the RAW file when it is opened. Third-party applications like Adobe Camera Raw or Lightroom will apply the white balance setting but ignore the picture styles. With RAW files, these settings are temporary until the image is saved as a TIFF, JPEG, PSD, or other type of rendered file. A camera set to JPEG mode applies these settings in-camera, permanently embedding them in the file. JPEG files are developed in-camera and compressed to save storage space, and provide a ready to print file directly from the camera. The compression method used by the JPEG compression algorithm is lossy, meaning that some original image information (typically 25–40 percent of the RAW data captured by the camera) is lost and cannot be restored. In some situations, like news photos image content takes priority to image quality, and JPEG files might be preferable to larger RAW files that must be processed before being printed. A RAW file can be compared to the latent image on a piece of film that has yet to be developed. Unlike a piece of film, a RAW file can always be preserved in its original form. Simply put, RAW files contain more data, are more malleable, and provide the photographer with more flexibility, especially to bring out shadow detail.

NATIVE ISO SETTINGS

Every camera has a native ISO setting that will produce the best images. For Canon, and many other cameras, 100 is the native ISO. Nikons have a native ISO of 100 or 200, and Leica cameras have a native ISO of 160. Increasing the camera's ISO setting has a detrimental effect on image quality, by lowering the ratio of image information relative to background noise. When a digital exposure is made, photons of light fall on the individual pixel sites or light wells in the sensor and are converted to an electrical voltage by an amplifier. This analog voltage is then converted to a digital equivalent in the form of a number that represents a specific brightness level. At the native ISO setting, the analog input is directly converted to digital output. When the ISO setting is raised, the sensor does not become more light sensitive. Instead, the analog signal is amplified, resulting in a brighter picture and more noise. Perhaps surprisingly, lowering the ISO below the native setting can also negatively impact image quality. The brightness values from the signal input are digitally reduced—halved in the case of switching from 200 to 100 or 100 to 50—and this permanent loss of information reduces the dynamic range of the sensor. Continually improving technology has brought significant improvements in image quality from higher ISO settings, but for optimal image quality it is best to use the camera's native ISO setting. Testing to determine the highest ISO that will yield images of acceptable quality is a worthwhile endeavor. Of course, acceptable quality is purely subjective and dependent on the final usage of your photos. Images to be viewed on-screen or in small print form will have a higher threshold for noise than those intended for large prints. Making test exposures at varying ISOs and comparing them at full magnification, and in final form, is a great way to learn about the capabilities and limitations of your camera.

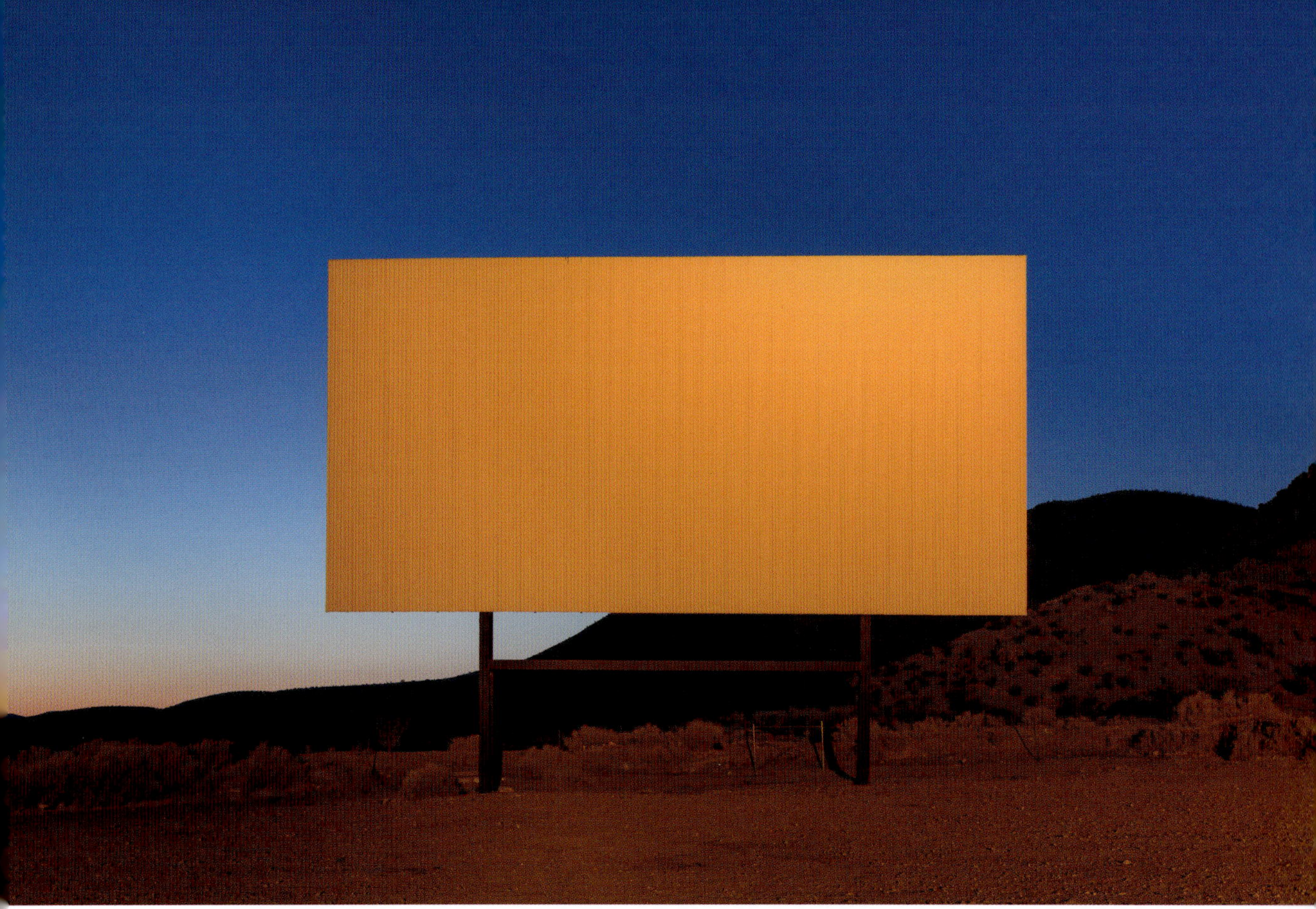

Sodium vapor dreams

3 seconds, f8 at ISO 100. Canon 6D, Sigma 35 mm f1.4 lens. The title is taken from a Flickr group dedicated to images made by sodium vapor light. The intense yellow light of a just turned on sodium fixture contrasted against the rapidly darkening blue twilight was obvious, but fun. What's the correct white balance here? Whatever looks good.

WHITE BALANCE

White Balance is the camera function that corrects for color variations in photographs due to varying types of light. Our eyes do a remarkable job accommodating different light sources, and we normally perceive white-colored objects as white regardless of the lighting. DSLRs have a selection of white balance settings that include an automatic selection (AWB), a setting that allows the user to set the color temperature on the Kelvin scale (K), and a custom setting that adjusts the white balance based on a white or gray card placed in front of the camera. There is a tungsten and generic fluorescent setting that adjusts white balance both on the yellow–blue color temperature scale and a second axis that ranges from green to magenta. The remaining white balance settings include daylight, flash, cloudy, and shade. The AWB setting works well in most natural and artificial light situations, and has been greatly improved in recent cameras. When multiple light sources are present, the AWB setting averages all of the light in a scene, which does not truly correct for any of the light sources. In situations where the multiple sources are separated in different parts of the image, it may be preferable to balance for one of them rather than use an average setting that does not fully correct for any of them.

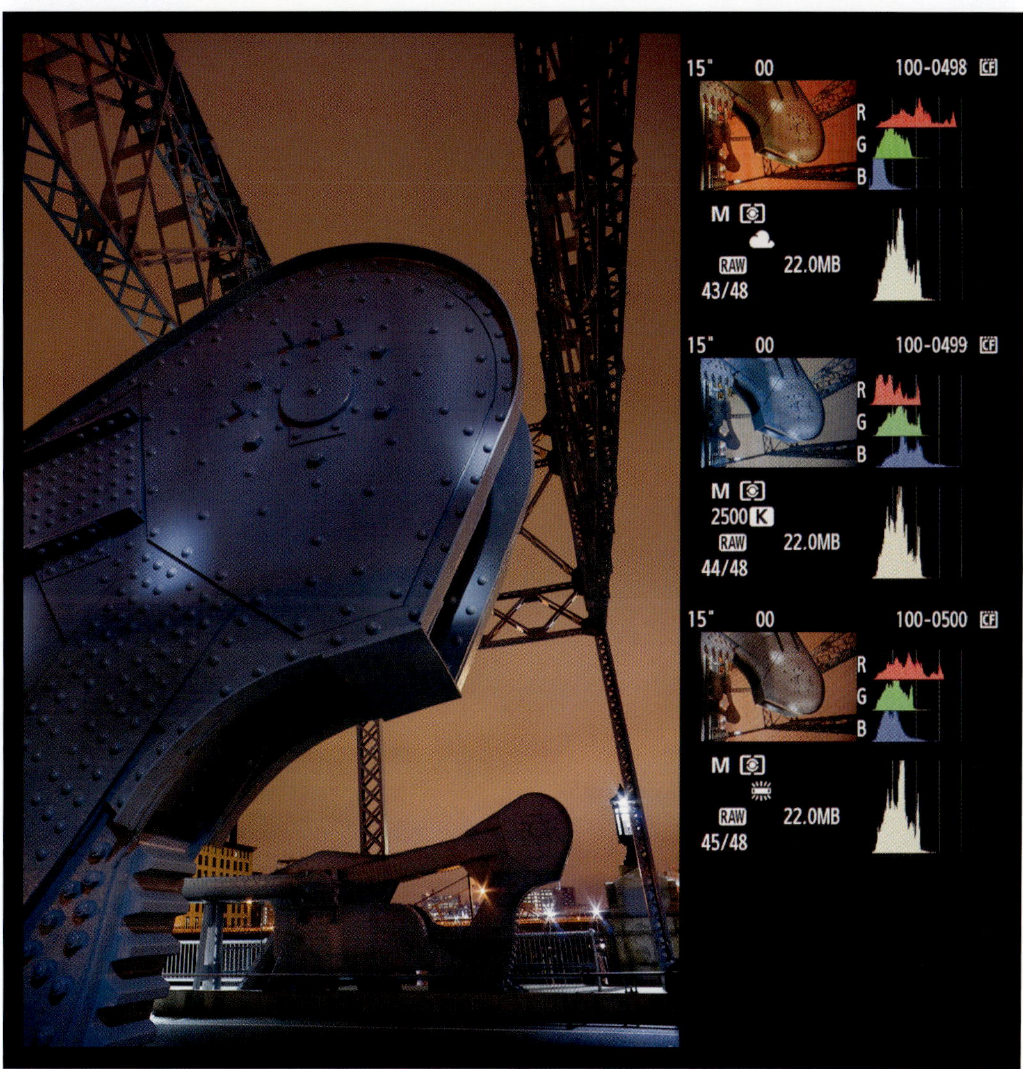

Congress Street Bridge, Boston, MA. Lance Keimig, 2009

The white balance setting affects the appearance of the histogram. The Congress Street Bridge in Boston was shot on a cloudy night with three different white balances to show the effect of white balance on the histogram. The top image shows an image taken with the white balance set to shade, the middle exposure had the white balance set to 2500 K, and the bottom image was shot on the fluorescent white balance setting. The final image utilized the fluorescent exposure with hue, saturation, and luminance (HSL) adjustments to bring out the blue. Notice in the histograms that the green stays relatively unchanged, but the blue, and red in particular, change dramatically with the white balance shift.

It is true that the white balance can be easily adjusted in any RAW conversion software, but setting the white balance in-camera as close as possible to what you think it should be can provide useful information in the histogram. Light sources with strong color shifts will produce quite different RGB histograms at different white balance settings, although the luminosity histogram will not change significantly. This is important because there may be unrecognized single-channel color clipping with some white balance settings, but not with others, even with the same exposure. For example, a street scene illuminated with sodium vapor lights will clip in the red channel first, and then the green channel, but rarely the blue unless there is massive overexposure. In these circumstances, there may be a good deal of clipping if the white balance is set to daylight, but none if it is set to tungsten. Because of the unusual lighting conditions encountered at night, it is often informative to do several test exposures with different white balance settings simply to get a sense of what the scene will look like.

White balance can be a subjective choice in night photography. Removing all color casts may not be the ideal solution for a photograph, and in the case of mixed lighting situations it may not be practical. Having the flexibility to tweak the white balance in postprocessing reiterates the need to shoot RAW images. Changing the white balance setting can completely change the mood of an image. Most of the time, there isn't a right or wrong white balance, but there is a wide range that will give varying effects.

CONSIDERATIONS FOR NIGHT PHOTOGRAPHY IN URBAN ENVIRONMENTS.
Photographing in urban or artificially lit environments presents unique challenges, primarily due to multiple light sources. Scene dynamic range can be extreme, and the many lights in or just outside of the frame can cause significant flare. The following checklist will help to avoid these problems.

1. Set the white balance as close as possible to how you would like your images to look in final form. Use the color temperature chart in Chapter 3 for guidelines.
2. Use the maximum exposure that does not clip important highlight detail. Make the exposure determination primarily with the blinking highlight indicator, but also review the RGB histogram.
3. Make several different exposures for review when you load images onto your computer as the low resolution screen on your camera is not always sufficient to make the best exposure determination. Having options to choose from for postprocessing is always a good thing.
4. Do not use any filters on your lens unless you are prone to accidents. Most filters are not made from the same quality glass as camera lenses. Make sure both the lens and any filters are completely clean. Dust and fingerprints are major contributors to flare in night photos.
5. Always use a lens hood and, ideally, a black card to shade the lens when the hood fails.
6. Avoid light source or bright objects near the edge of the frame.
7. Always review your images carefully and at full magnification. Look for flare that might not be obvious. Look for objects in the frame that escaped your notice when composing.

MINIMIZING NOISE AT THE SOURCE

Noise is unwanted information. It is a by-product of electrical processes that receive or transmit signals. Noise can have several sources, and is present in all images to some degree. It can be independent of the image, and therefore relatively easy to separate and remove, or integral to the image, which makes it harder to deal with. Noise generally detracts from the image quality, but a small amount of noise can enhance apparent sharpness in a photograph. The best way to minimize noise is to eliminate it at the source. There are five key ways to minimize noise in night photographs. In the real world, you won't be able to use all of them, but if you are aware of the sources of noise, you can take measures to minimize it.

The main contributors to noise are:

Small sensors: A full-frame sensor adds considerably to the cost of a DSLR, but offers several distinct advantages, including noticeably less noise than "cropped" APSC sensors. Although full-frame sensor cameras are beyond the budget of most amateur photographers, professionals and anyone intent on making large-scale prints should seriously consider a full-frame DSLR.

High ISOs: Shooting at your camera's native ISO setting will probably have the greatest impact on noise levels. There are times when higher ISOs are called for, but the native setting should be used whenever possible.

High ambient temperatures: Ambient temperature also has a definite influence on noise levels. The impact of temperature will vary from one camera model to the next, but the hotter it is, the more noise you will encounter in your images. For the most part, 75–80 F seems to be the point when many cameras start to get noisy with long exposures, especially at high ISOs.

Long exposures: Results vary widely by generational and price point differences in cameras, but regardless of which model you use, the longer the exposure, the more noise you'll see. It is probable that the length of the exposure itself is not the cause; it is more likely to be the heat buildup during the exposure that causes the noise in long exposures.

Underexposure: Inadequate exposure will also increase noise levels, especially in the shadow areas: the least exposed part of the image. Noise stands out more in the shadows because there is less image detail to obscure it. Along with using native ISO, exposing for a right-biased histogram is the other controllable factor that will dramatically reduce noise levels in your images.

Most cameras seem to perform noticeably better at temperatures below about 50°F (10°C), but for best results, you should test your camera to determine the longest exposure your camera will tolerate at different temperatures. When factors like ISO and exposure length are combined with high temperatures, the noise gets exponentially worse. Most late model DSLRs perform very well in below freezing temperatures, and exposures of 30–40 minutes are usually quite clean. The tradeoff is that battery life is greatly reduced in low temperatures.

One of the best but most overlooked ways to avoid noise with night photography is to utilize image stacking. Not only are the base frames cleaner due to their shorter exposures, but applying noise reduction to each of the frames, and possibly to the final combined image, can be quite effective. Image stacking leads to a far cleaner final product and can be worth the extra effort. There is no fixed exposure length when stacking becomes the best solution, and it won't work in every situation. In general, stacking is mostly used in very dark environments when exposure lengths are quite long. Only images produced with the earliest DSLR models will benefit from stacking exposures of less than five to ten minutes. Because newer, high-end models should produce clean images at 30 minutes or longer, stacking is usually unnecessary with these cameras.

There are several sources of noise. Photon noise is the result of sampling error when the photons of light are converted to digital information. Photon noise is generally limited to the deep shadows and tends not to be a significant problem unless the shadow levels are greatly increased in postprocessing. Amplifier or readout noise is largely the result of higher ISO settings, and is fairly predictable. Higher ISO settings artificially boost both the input signal and the inherent noise in an image, which is the trade-off in image quality for using higher ISOs. Random noise has many variables, and is electrical in nature. Because it is unpredictable, random noise is the most difficult to remove. Fixed pattern noise, also known as hot pixel noise, is largely a factor of sensor imperfections, long exposures, and heat. Fixed pattern noise is relatively easy to remove from images because it is consistent from one photograph to the next if the exposure length and environmental conditions remain the same. Fixed pattern noise is specific to each individual camera and thus in-camera long-exposure noise reduction (LENR) does a great job at reducing fixed pattern noise. LENR also helps minimize random noise generated by long exposures.

Noise manifests itself as chrominance noise (think colorful pixels) or as luminance noise (think black and white film grain). Although color noise is universally considered to be a bad thing, luminance noise in modest quantities is not nearly as detrimental to an image. Chrominance noise is fairly easy to eliminate in postprocessing, but luminance noise can be harder to reduce because images tend to lose sharpness when it is removed. In postproduction, noise reduction

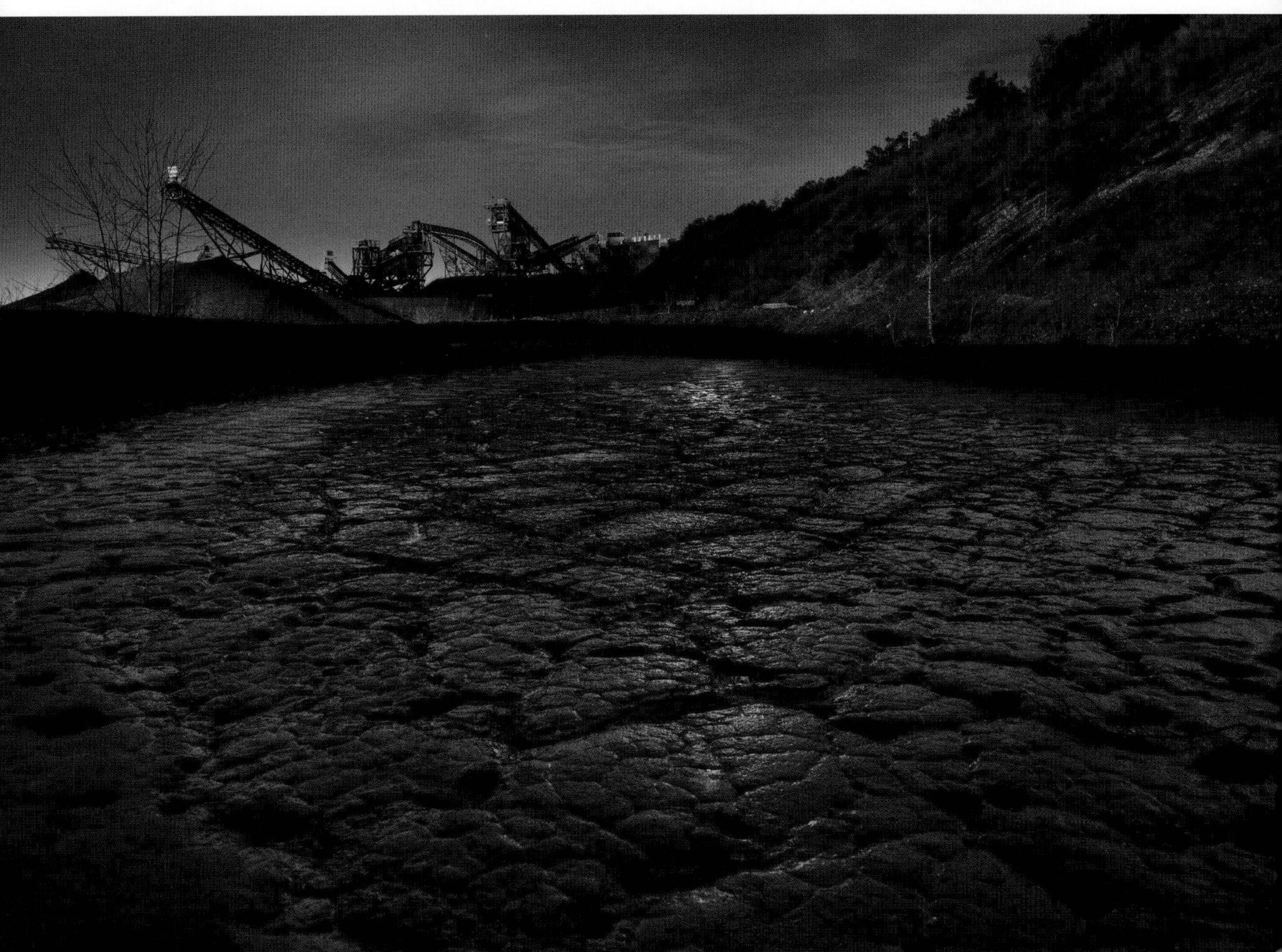

"Mud Pit," Plymouth, MA. Canon 5D MK II, 24 mm f3.5 Zuiko Shift lens. 30 seconds, f5.6 at ISO 1600. Deep shadows and a high ISO meant a likelihood of noise in this image. Auto LENR did the work, and the image is relatively clean, unlike my boots after this night. The high ISO was chosen out of fear of the tripod sinking into the mud during the exposure.

can be applied during RAW file development and to final rendered files. We discuss these options further in Chapter 6.

LONG-EXPOSURE NOISE REDUCTION (LENR)

Long exposures can generate substantial noise that is exaggerated by high temperatures. Most of this noise is fixed pattern noise, and it is consistent from one exposure to the next in images of the same length taken in the same atmospheric conditions. Because the noise pattern is reproducible, it is relatively easy to separate from the image. In-camera LENR uses a technique known as dark frame subtraction to remove noise. When it is enabled, LENR creates a "dark frame" after each exposure, which is essentially a second exposure of equal length, except that the shutter is not opened. The dark frame contains the same noise as the original exposure. The two frames are combined together, and the noise is subtracted from the image. This process results in a doubling of the exposure time, which can cut down on productivity in the field. With LENR enabled, a 10-minute exposure means that the camera is inoperable for about 20 minutes. LENR also has features that help to minimize random noise.

Most cameras have either an on or off option, but Canon cameras have a third auto setting that analyzes the image on the fly and determines whether or not LENR is needed. It can be left on all of the time, and it will be applied only when noise is detected. The performance of in-camera LENR varies from camera to camera, and whether or not to use it involves an evaluation of the trade-off between shooting time lost and improvements in the image. There is considerable debate about whether noise reduction is best achieved in-camera, in postproduction, or a combination of the two. Testing your camera can help you to decide which approach to take. To do this, make a series of exposures of varying lengths from 1 to 30 minutes, with and without LENR, both in summer and winter. When you process the images in your RAW conversion software, you may find that you only need to use LENR over a certain temperature or exposure length, and that postcapture software is adequate most of the time.

HIGH-ISO NOISE REDUCTION

Newer cameras have an adjustable high-ISO noise reduction feature with several levels of noise reduction. RAW files are tagged with the high-ISO noise reduction data from the camera, but only the camera manufacturer's proprietary software will recognize the tags. This metadata will be applied as a default setting when you open an image in Capture NX or Digital Photo Professional, but can be overridden by utilizing the adjustment sliders. Those using third-party applications like ACR or Lightroom will not notice any difference in RAW files shot with high-ISO noise reduction. ACR, Lightroom, or other RAW converters will apply their own defaults regardless of camera metadata.

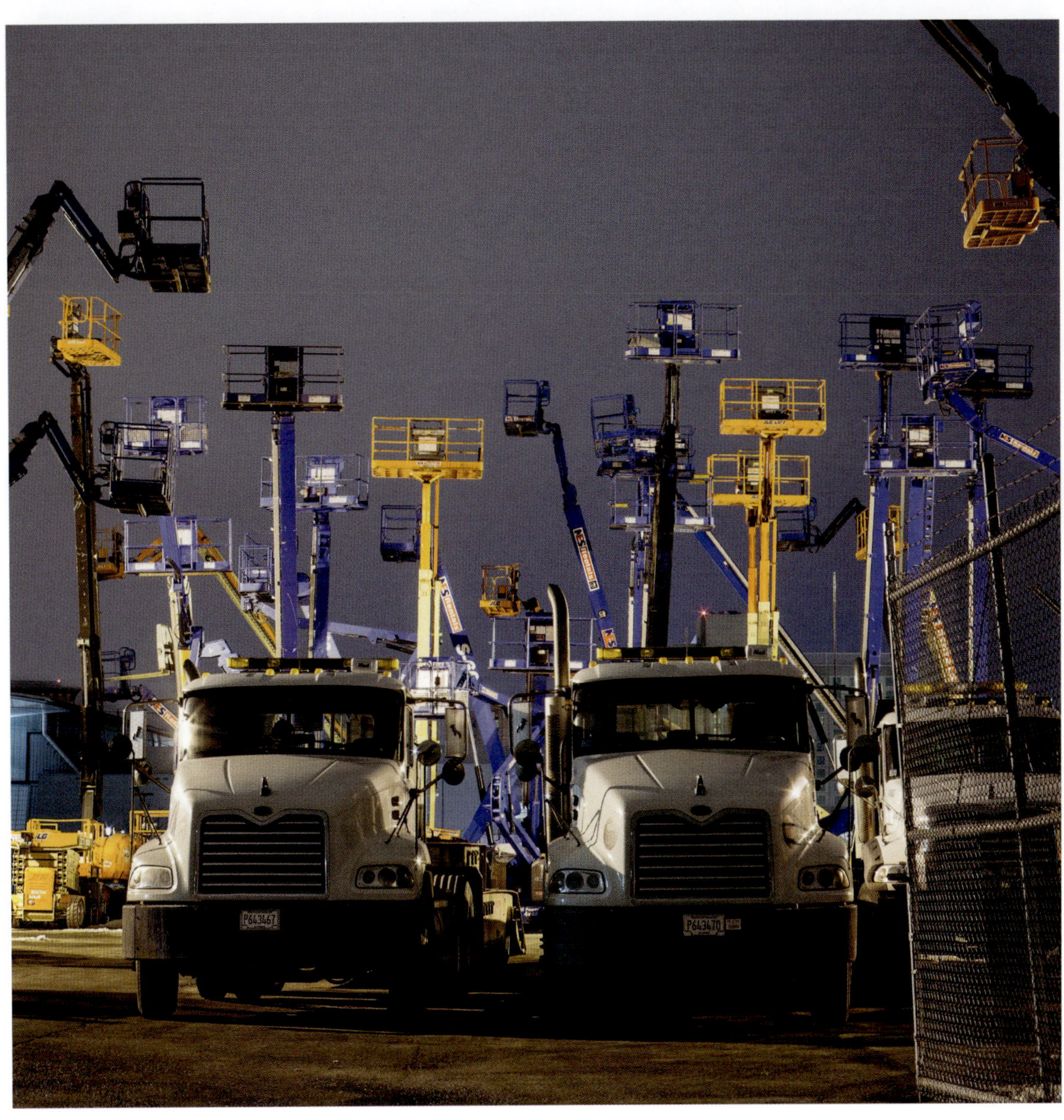

"Cherry Pickers," South Boston, MA

30 seconds, f9.5 at ISO 100. Canon 5D MK II, 50 mm f2.5 compact Macro lens. This fantastic collection of cherry pickers made for a great shot, but trying to organize them into a workable composition was virtually impossible. The square crop was the only way that I could get the image to look close to the way I envisioned it. Just after the image was made, a security guard came by and rousted me and the group of students who were with me at the time.

HIGHLIGHT TONE PRIORITY/AUTO LIGHTING OPTIMIZER/D-LIGHTING PICTURE STYLES

These Canon and Nikon features aim to expand dynamic range with a combination of exposure modification and in-camera processing. Canon's Auto Lighting Optimizer function and Nikon's D-Lighting are designed to boost underexposed areas in backlit images with a wide dynamic range. Canon's Highlight Tone Priority restricts exposure to preserve highlight detail, and applies processing to enhance the image further. If you have a Canon camera, and have been unable to access ISO 100 in the menu, it is because Highlight Tone Priority (HTP) is enabled. Many a student has sworn to me that their Canon camera's native ISO is 200 for this reason. Turn off HTP and 100 becomes an option in the menu.

These features are useful primarily for JPEG shooters—not for night photographers who *always* shoot RAW files. As with high-ISO noise reduction, RAW files are tagged, but only the camera manufacturers' software will recognize the tags. One thing that may not be obvious is that the image preview on the back of the camera does not represent the RAW data. It is a processed JPEG, with all activated camera settings reflected in the image. If you have D-Lighting or Highlight Tone Priority activated, you'll see the effect in the preview image, but not necessarily the RAW file.

OTHER CAMERA SETTINGS

Exposure mode is normally set to either manual (for exposures up to 30 seconds) or bulb (for exposures longer than 30 seconds). Unfortunately, camera manufacturers do not program shutter speeds longer than 30 seconds, and auxiliary timed releases, or intervalometers, are required for long exposures. Manual and bulb modes give full control over both aperture and shutter speed to the photographer, and are simpler and more efficient than aperture or shutter priority modes that often need to be overridden with exposure compensation. Many midrange and almost all professional cameras offer at least one custom exposure mode that allows the user to program frequently used combinations of settings. Custom modes are extremely useful because they allow you to save and quickly switch to your night photography settings. It is especially helpful to have multiple custom modes, as one can be set for high-ISO testing, one for moonlight conditions, and one for urban nighttime environments. The main difference between moonlight and urban settings would be the white balance, and perhaps manual exposure mode would be used for urban where exposures tend to be shorter, and bulb exposure mode would be used for moonlight.

Live view is the most accurate way to focus, as discussed in Chapter 3, and should be employed for critical focusing when possible. It does consume considerable battery power, so it is best to turn it on only when focusing rather than leave it on continuously.

Mirror lockup is one of the few features that has carried over from film cameras, and is occasionally useful in low-light photography, but is generally not necessary at night. When mirror lockup is enabled, the mirror used to reflect the image through the prism and into the viewfinder is flipped up out of the image pathway in advance of the shutter. This reduces vibrations from the movement of the mirror, which can result in a loss of image sharpness. Mirror lockup is useful for exposures ranging from about 1/15 of a second to 2 seconds, especially with telephoto lenses or images focused at macro distances. It is unnecessary for exposures longer than 1 or 2 seconds.

LCD brightness is set to medium on most cameras by default. In low-light conditions, it is best to turn LCD brightness down one to three levels. Though you will be judging your exposures primarily by reading the camera's histogram, it is easy to be fooled by an overly bright image preview. The appearance of the image on the LCD is relative to ambient illumination. An image that looks well exposed in-camera in the moonlight may turn out to be grossly underexposed when loaded into a RAW converter. Turning down the LCD brightness also saves the battery power for more exposures. The LCD screen is the single largest consumer of battery power, and turning down the brightness makes a big difference in how long the battery will last.

CAMERA SETTINGS FOR NIGHT PHOTOGRAPHY

1. Set quality to RAW.
2. Use your camera's native ISO setting when possible: 200 for some Nikons, 100 for most cameras.
3. Set white balance to auto, or try ~ 2500–2800 K for sodium vapor streetlight situations, or ~ 3700K–4100 K for moonlight. Try to approximate the desired look in-camera.
4. Set your camera's LENR to auto (if available). If your camera doesn't have auto as an option, testing will be required to determine when it is needed. In general, the newer the camera, the less likely you will need it. All cameras need LENR in high temperatures.
5. Enable your camera's RGB histogram—the primary exposure determinant in moonlight.
6. Enable the blinking highlight indicator—the primary exposure determinant in artificial light.
7. Set the LCD brightness to "auto" or reduce it manually two or three levels below middle setting.
8. Set exposure mode to manual or bulb, depending on your camera.
9. Set focus to manual.
10. Turn off IS/VR lens functions.
11. Use flashlight-assisted magnified live view for focusing.
12. Learn to use camera info rear screen controls and buttons. You won't be able to see them at night (unless you have a D4)!
13. Once you become an advanced night shooter, consider programming your camera's custom functions for high-ISO testing and final exposure starting points.
14. Set picture style to neutral for the sake of histograms and image previews.
15. Auto lighting optimizer, highlight tone priority, D-lighting, high-ISO noise reduction, and other similar features are designed for JPEG shooters and have no effect on the manually metered RAW exposures that we'll be doing at night— unless you are using your camera manufacturer's software to process your files.

SUMMARY

The guidelines in this chapter are oriented toward producing the best possible quality images. If your images will only be displayed online, or will never be printed larger than 8.5 × 11, you have considerably more leeway with camera settings than those who want to make large prints. ISO, white balance, and LENR are the only settings that are critical for night photographers or anyone who shoots RAW files. An optimal RAW file exposure has a right-biased histogram and no highlight clipping in important details. The camera meter provides a starting point for exposure, which is refined by using a combination of the image histogram, the highlight clipping indicator, and situational analysis based on experience.

White balance settings are set as metadata tags in RAW files, and are recognized by all RAW conversion software. It is useful, but not essential to set the white balance precisely when shooting RAW files. In-camera LENR is useful for removing noise due to long exposures and exaggerated by heat. LENR effectively doubles exposure length (except on Canon cameras with auto LENR turned on, which applies LENR on an as needed basis) which can be an issue with very long exposures. Similar noise reduction can usually be achieved in postprocessing, but if it can be done in-camera without disrupting your shooting, it is best to remove noise in-camera. Most custom function settings do not affect RAW files. You should consult your camera manual to be sure. Finally, having a solid understanding of your camera's settings and functions frees your attention to focus on the creative aspects of night photography.

"Back End, Z3," Charlestown, MA. 20 seconds, f8 at ISO 160, Canon 5D MK II, 35 mm f2.8 Zuiko Shift lens. Quiet scenes like this often go unnoticed, but with careful observation, little details jump out and fall into a natural composition. Sometimes rules have to be broken—like not shooting into a streetlight.

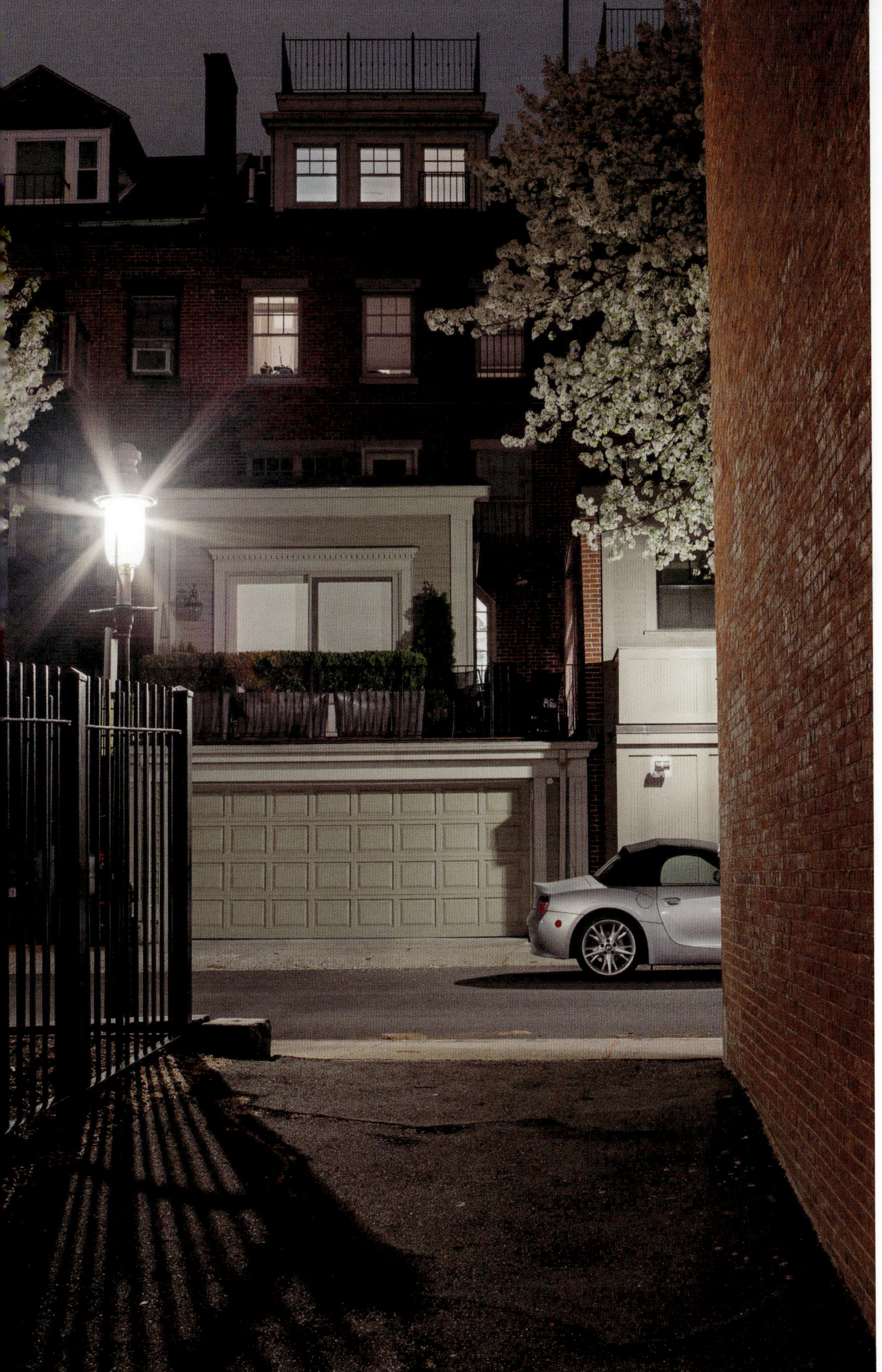

ASTRO-LANDSCAPE PHOTOGRAPHY

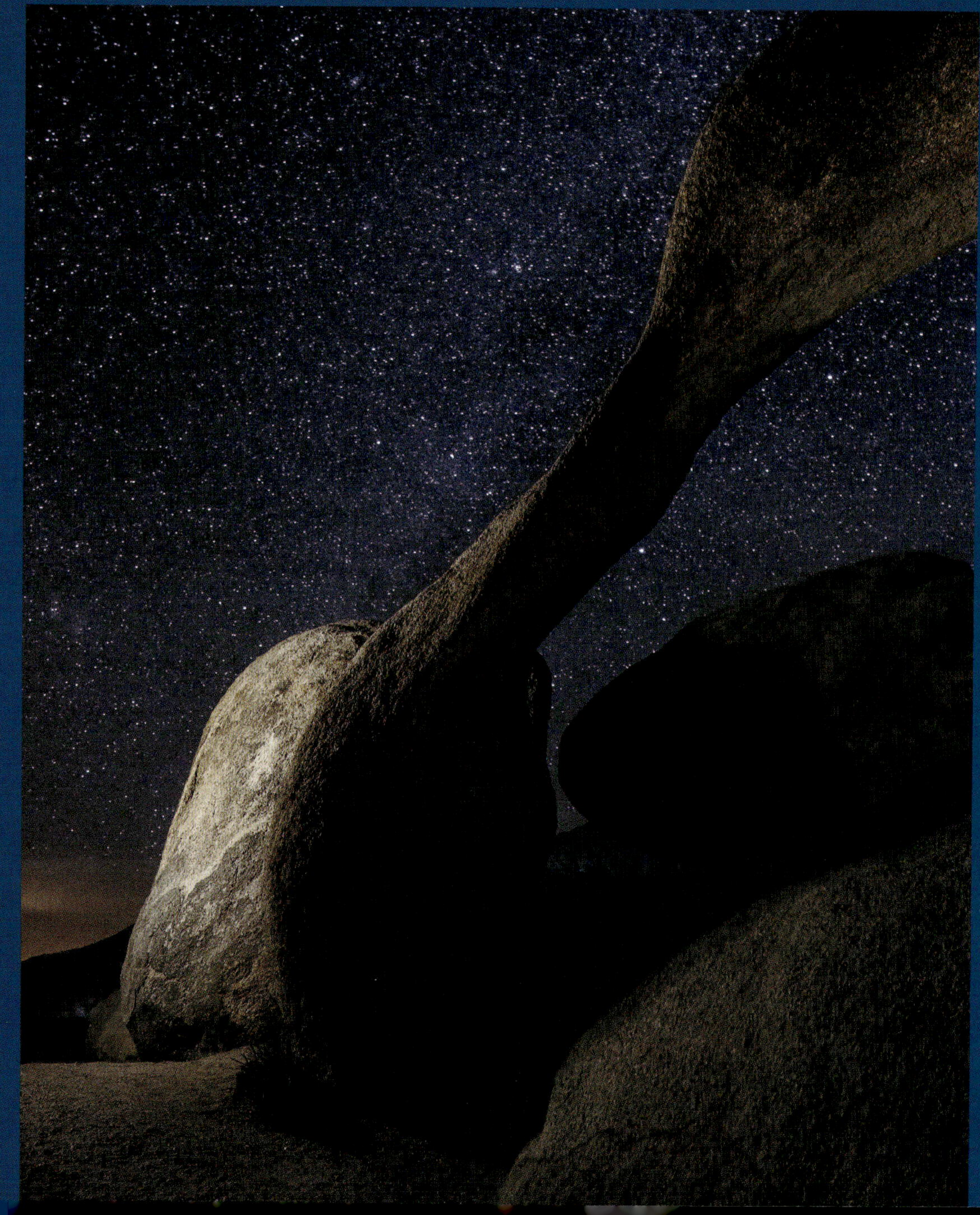

The term "astro-landscape photography" describes short-exposure, high-ISO night photography of the natural landscape. Recent technological advances in digital cameras and the introduction of affordable and fast wide-angle lenses have made this type of photography possible. The short exposures required to register stars as points of light rather than star trails require using wide apertures and very high ISOs. High levels of digital noise in previous generations of cameras—and film grain before that—made this type of photography virtually impossible. The Earth's rotation causes stars to appear as lines in the sky rather than as points of light in long exposures, so shutter speeds need to be kept as short as possible to avoid trailing. This type of photography pushes your equipment to the limit, but once you have the right gear and work out the exposures, making the images is fairly straightforward. Composing in extremely low-light levels, and light painting the foreground if you choose to do it—that is the real challenge. Examples of astro-landscape photography include starry sky and Milky Way images on clear, dark nights, aurora photographs, lunar eclipse photography, and meteor shower photography. This chapter addresses the technical and aesthetic considerations, and the special circumstances required to be successful at astro-landscape photography. The process is mainly about making compromises to favor one thing over another, depending on the situation at hand.

PLANNING AND PREPARATION

Perhaps more than any other type of night photography, astro-landscape photography requires thoughtful planning and preparation because, as the Scottish photographer Alister Benn says in his excellent ebook *Seeing the Unseen*, photographers can be proactive or reactive. You could plan a specific photograph months in advance, waiting until conditions are right and celestial bodies converge to make an image possible, or you might just go out and see what there is to photograph without much forethought. Some degree of preparation is always advisable, but photographing fleeting events like eclipses, meteor showers, and auroras requires more intense planning. For example, you might spontaneously decide to go out with the intention of making Milky Way images in the dead of winter, thinking that the crisp, clear air would make more stars visible. This might well be the case, but in the northern hemisphere, the bulk of the Milky Way never rises above the horizon in winter! Consideration of celestial phenomena, coupled with good location scouting, usually leads to better pictures, although they hardly guarantee success.

To a large extent, astro-landscape photographers are dependent on weather conditions and other unforeseeable events, even after preparing as much as possible for the many variables that might be encountered. There is always some aspect of luck involved, as the following example illustrates. There was a spectacular total lunar eclipse in the early hours of April 15, 2014. I was in Massachusetts at the time, where the forecast was for complete cloud cover with a slight chance of rain. Considering the weather, and that the totality of the eclipse began around 3 am, I didn't feel guilty about not going out to try and photograph it. Much to my surprise, a friend shared his composite sequence of the eclipse the following day, which he shot nearby in coastal

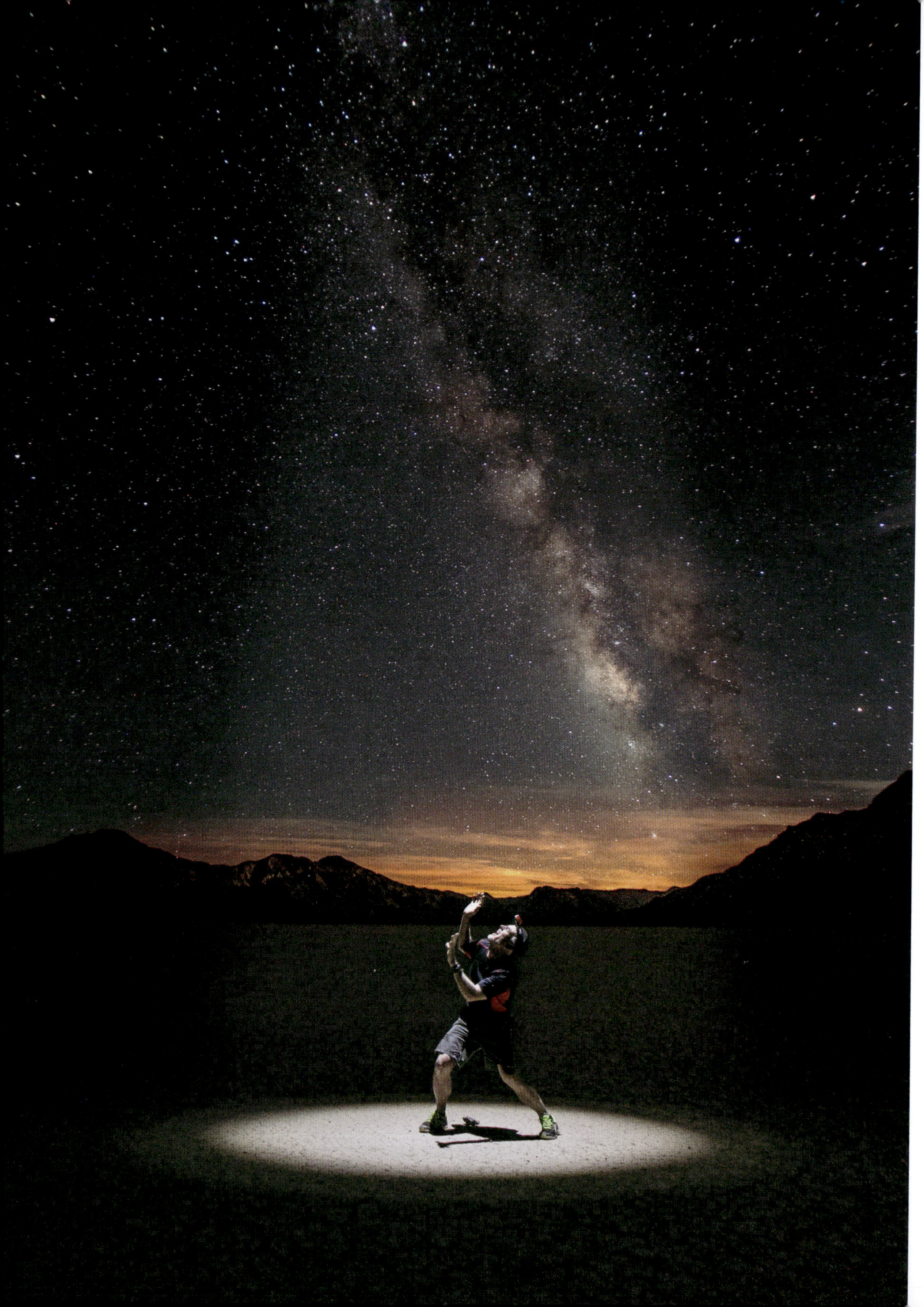

"Alien Encounter," Russell Preston Brown

Russell Brown used two different images to create this composite that was captured with a Canon 5D Mark III on a dry lake bed near Las Vegas, NV. The concept was to create an alien encounter image and he used a quad-copter to lift a high-powered LED flashlight into the sky to light the figure. He then added the overhead-lit image to the Milky Way background images to get the final results. Both images were enhanced and corrected in Adobe Camera Raw. The astro-landscape photograph of the Milky Way and landscape was exposed for 30 seconds, f2.8 at ISO 1600 with a 15 mm fisheye lens. The figure was lit from above by the quad-copter hovering overhead, and exposed for 1/20 second, f2.8 at ISO 800, with a 24 mm lens.

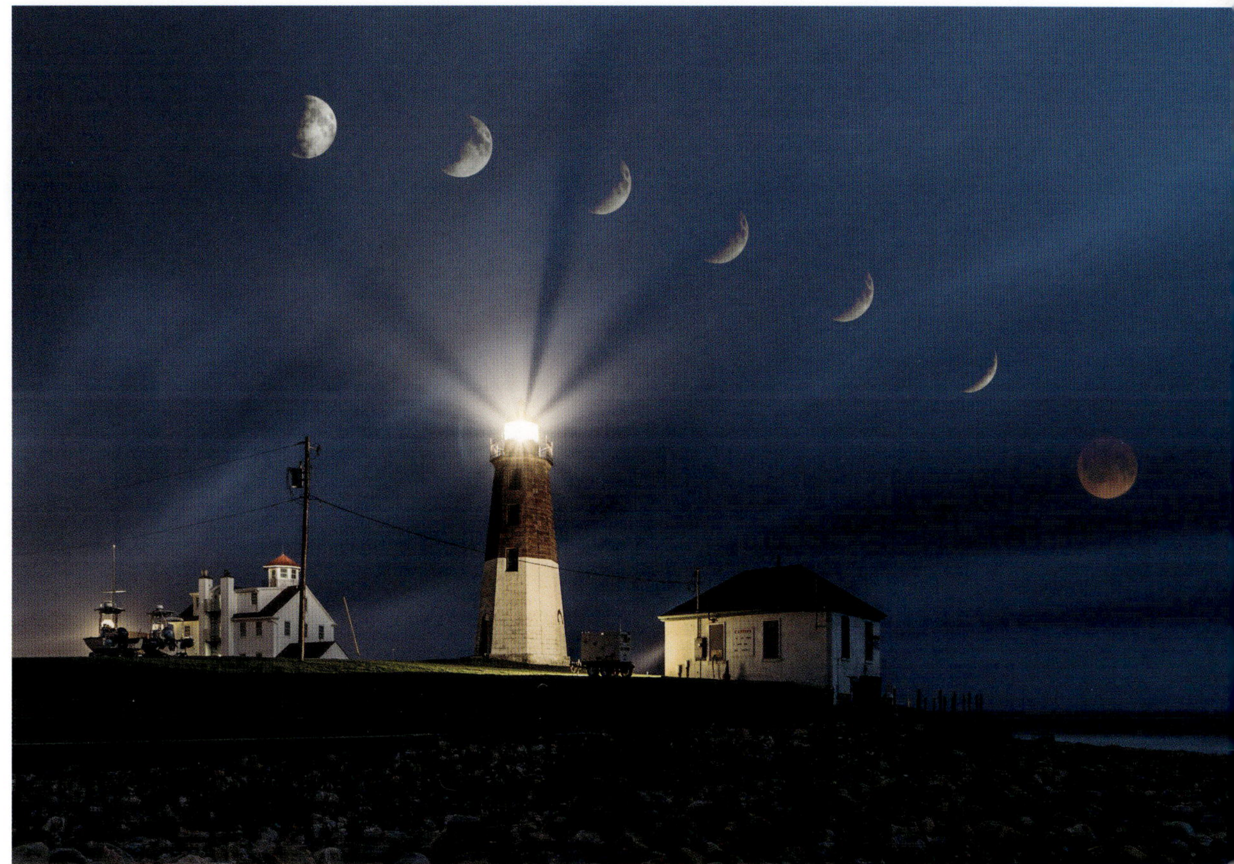

"Blood Moon Over Point Judith Lighthouse," Jürgen Lobert, April, 2014

The base lighthouse image was 2 minutes at f8, ISO 200, with a 24 mm lens on a Nikon D4. The partially eclipsed Moon images were taken with a Sigma 120-400 mm lens and 2× teleconverter set to 500 mm, with exposure times ranging between 1/125 and 1/30 of a second at f8, ISO 400. The fully eclipsed "blood" Moon was exposed for a quarter of a second at f6.3 and ISO 3200. After processing in Lightroom, the images were composited in Photoshop. These images were not made at evenly spaced intervals, because it was cloudy during most of the eclipse, and there were only a few opportunities to make exposures when the Moon was visible.

Rhode Island. He described how the sky was indeed cloudy for most of the night, but for a few brief moments the clouds opened up, and he was able to make about 10 exposures during different phases of the eclipse, which he composited to make a single, stunning image.

ASTRO-LANDSCAPE PHOTOGRAPHY TECHNIQUES

As long as people have photographed at night, there have been star trail photographs. Due to the Earth's rotation, exposures longer than just a few seconds show stars as lines in the sky rather than as points of light. Often these star trails are desirable and can add interest to night imagery, but sometimes it is nice to have a more natural looking sky that shows the stars as points of light the way that we see them when we look up at the night sky. Until very recently, this has been extremely difficult to achieve because the need for short exposure times has necessitated not only wide apertures, but also the use of extreme ISOs that yielded images that were so noisy they were virtually unusable. The most recent middle- to high-end digital cameras—especially full-frame sensor cameras released in 2012 or later—are capable of excellent image quality up to 6400 ISO or even higher. No doubt future generations of digital cameras will be capable of print quality images at even higher ISOs. (In April 2014, Sony announced the A7s, a mirrorless camera that features ISO speeds of up to "an astronomical" 409,600 on a full-frame sensor!)

Astro-landscape photographs look very different at different phases of the lunar cycle because moonlight greatly diminishes the number of stars visible both to the eye and camera. If you are primarily interested in recording the Milky Way as the main subject of your images, you should photograph during the last quarter of the lunar cycle when the waning crescent moon rises very late or near dawn, and there is little moonlight to reduce the visible stars in the sky. Working without any moonlight at all means not only that you will need a flashlight or headlight to get around, but also that you will not record much of the landscape in your images due to the lack of light at ground level. Most likely, the only evidence of the landscape will be a horizon line or vague silhouettes of the topography. The options for having a better exposed foreground include blending a second, longer exposure (with or without added light) in Photoshop, or light painting the foreground. Both methods have their own unique challenges. The multi-exposure technique requires rendering your RAW files in Photoshop or another program to merge the exposures, and more work in postprocessing. The single exposure with light painting method is difficult because the lighting must be executed within the short exposure time, which is usually limited to 30 seconds or less. Because of the wide aperture and high ISO, the added light must also be quite dim to avoid overexposure. Using a brighter light source and moving it extremely quickly across the scene is possible, but very difficult to control.

A wide-aperture, high-ISO, short exposure focused at infinity for the sky blended with a refocused, longer, low-ISO exposure that may or may not include light painting for emphasis

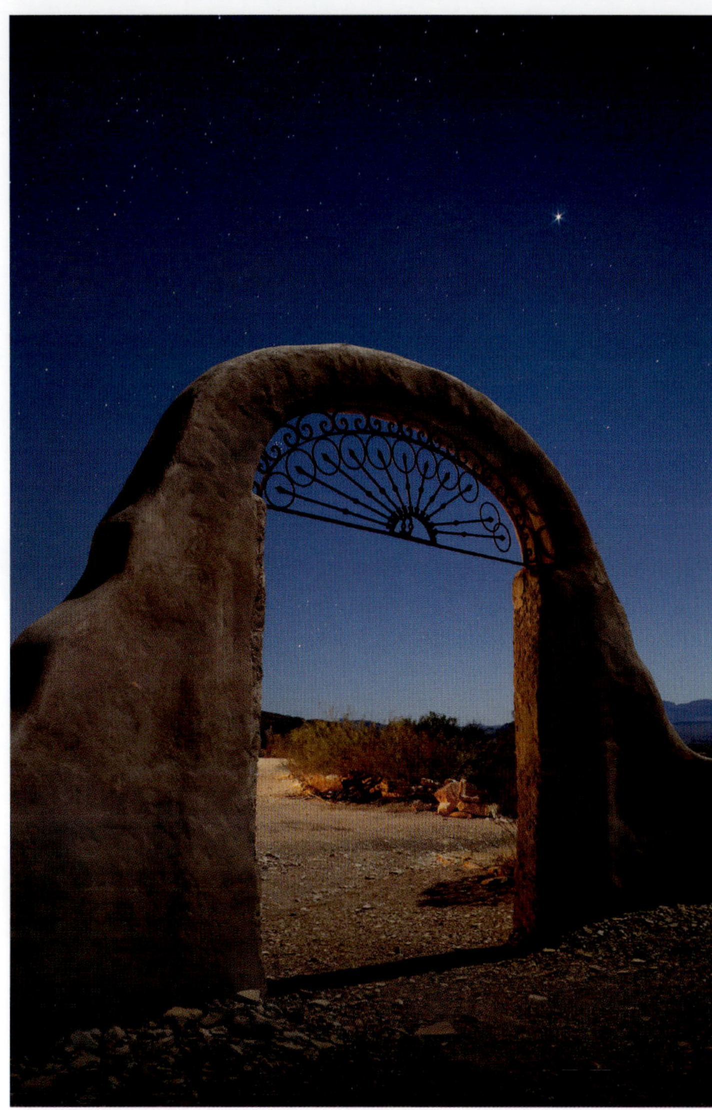

Jupiter rising, Terlingua, TX.
20 seconds, f11 at ISO 6400

Canon 5D MK II, 24 mm f2.8 Zuiko lens. This exposure was made near the full moon and as a result only the brightest stars show in the sky. Additionally, the moonlight provides much more illumination for the landscape, balancing nicely with the artificial light from a nearby building.

gives you the most control over the image, and best image quality. Great care must be taken not to move the camera during refocusing, and this is one place where a weighted, sturdy tripod is especially helpful. The scope of this book does not allow for detailed explanations of layer blending techniques, but this information is widely available, and does not differ significantly from layer blending in daytime imagery. A layer mask is applied to hide the sky of the foreground exposure, and this is easily accomplished with a simple horizon. If there are foreground elements such as leafless trees that extend into the sky, the masking is obviously more complex. Light painting is discussed in great detail in Chapter 8.

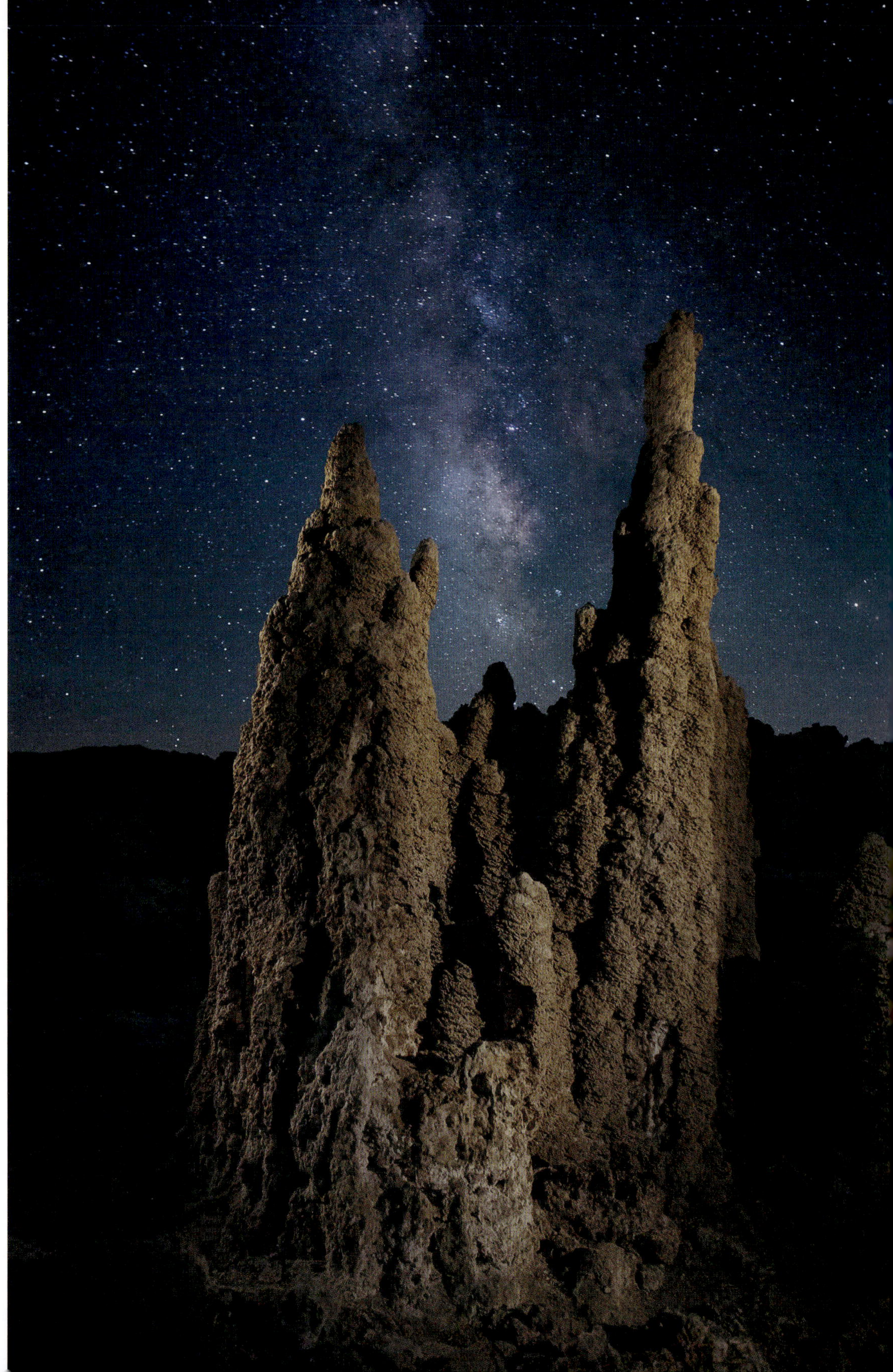

Guardian Tufas, Mono Lake, CA

20 seconds, f4 at ISO 12,800. Canon 6D, Rokinon 24 mm f1.4 lens. It is very difficult to light paint at such high ISOs and with such short exposures, especially with no Moon on very uneven ground. I enjoy the challenge, and it makes the resulting photographs that much more satisfying.

It is also possible to blend multiple high-ISO exposures, one for the sky and one or more for light painting. There really aren't any practical reasons for doing your light painting in separate high-ISO exposures rather than one long native ISO exposure, but it can be a fun challenge to light paint a complex scene at 6400 ISO! Keep in mind that the final image may not be as high quality as one with a foreground exposure shot at native ISO. Some light painters follow the code of SOOC (Straight Out Of Camera) shooting JPGs and not employing any postprocessing at all. Their motivation is to demonstrate image integrity by assuring that the final image was achieved entirely in-camera rather than as a result of postprocessing wizardry. My own philosophy is that in art there are no rules and we should use whatever techniques we like to achieve our desired results. That said, I most definitely try to create as much of the final image as possible in-camera rather than in postprocessing, because I'd rather be out photographing than sitting at the computer, and because less image processing leads to higher image quality. Both layer blending of multiple exposures and light painting at high ISO require lots of trial and error, experimentation, and practice to master.

Another option worth considering, especially if the foreground is important, is to photograph when there is just a little moonlight. Even the small amount of moonlight between the crescent and gibbous phases will help to illuminate the landscape, but it may not eliminate the need for light painting entirely. In addition to adding light to the sky, moonlight reduces the number of visible stars in your photographs. Fewer stars are not necessarily a bad thing. One example would be when photographing constellations. With the dimmer stars rendered invisible by moonlight, the brighter stars in the constellations stand apart more and this therefore makes them easier to read. Of course, the more moonlight, the fewer stars you will see, with only the very brightest stars and the planets showing themselves on or near the full moon. The densest part of the Milky Way is not visible at all near the full moon. Finding just the right balance between enough moonlight to illuminate the landscape without obliterating the Milky Way can be a challenge. There's no fixed rule because any light pollution will also factor into the images.

Whenever we look up into the sky, all of the stars we see are part of the Milky Way galaxy. The Milky Way has a central disc with spiral arms extending out from it. The Earth is located on one of the arms, 27,000 light years away from a massive black hole in the galactic center. In the summer, the Earth faces toward the center of the galaxy, and is in between the Sun and the center. We see the central part of the Milky Way as a dense band of stars that looks more like a

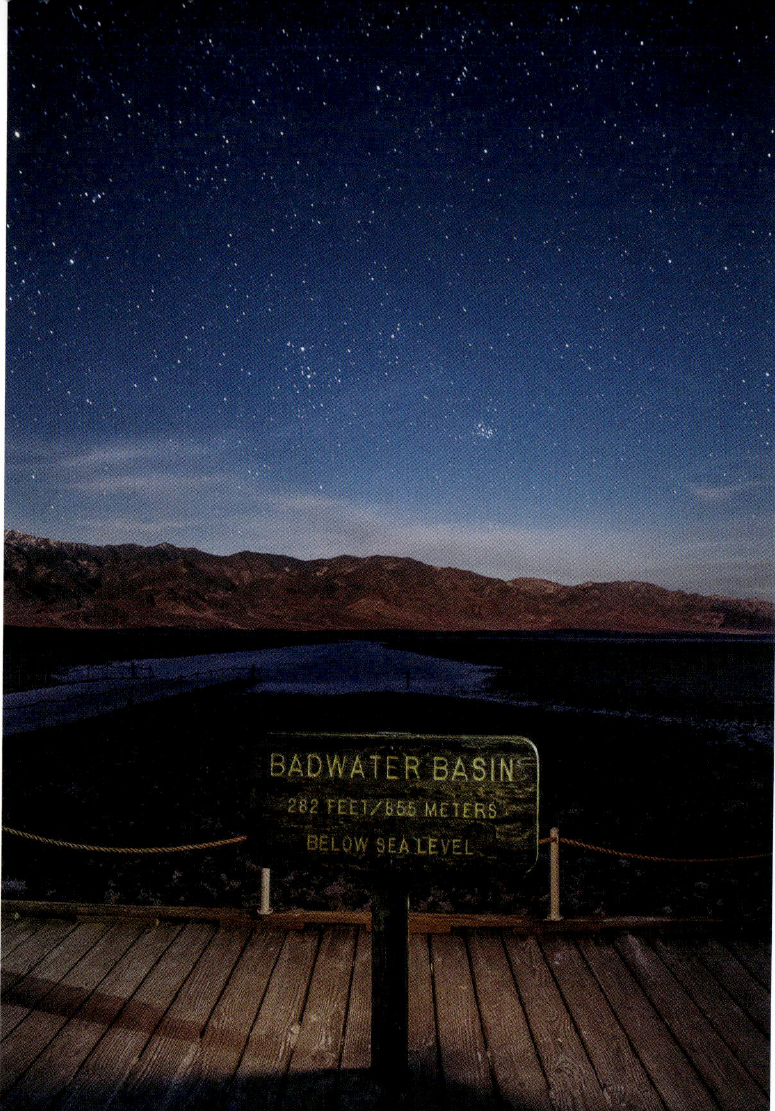

Badwater Basin with moonlight on the distant hills. Death Valley National Park

30 seconds, f4, ISO 6400. Canon 6D, Rokinon 24 mm f1.4 lens. Low-power LED flashlight from 75 degrees to camera right on the front of the sign; LED glow stick hung on the back of the sign. The Moon was rising over the mountains behind the camera, but the fore- and middle ground were still in shadow.

mottled cloud stretching in an arch from the horizon in the south, across the eastern sky to the North. In wintertime, the Sun is between Earth and the center of the galaxy, and the Earth is facing away from it, so we do not see the richest part of the sky in winter.

The variable relationship of the Earth to our galaxy also impacts the appearance of the night sky. As mentioned at the beginning of the chapter, the densest concentration of stars in the Milky Way is not visible in the night sky from about October to February. The Milky Way is visible about 2 hours before sunrise from March to May, from about 10 pm to 2 am from June to August, and as soon as it is dark from September to October. The central core, or galactic center of the Milky Way galaxy, can be seen between the constellations of Sagittarius on the left and Scorpius to the right.

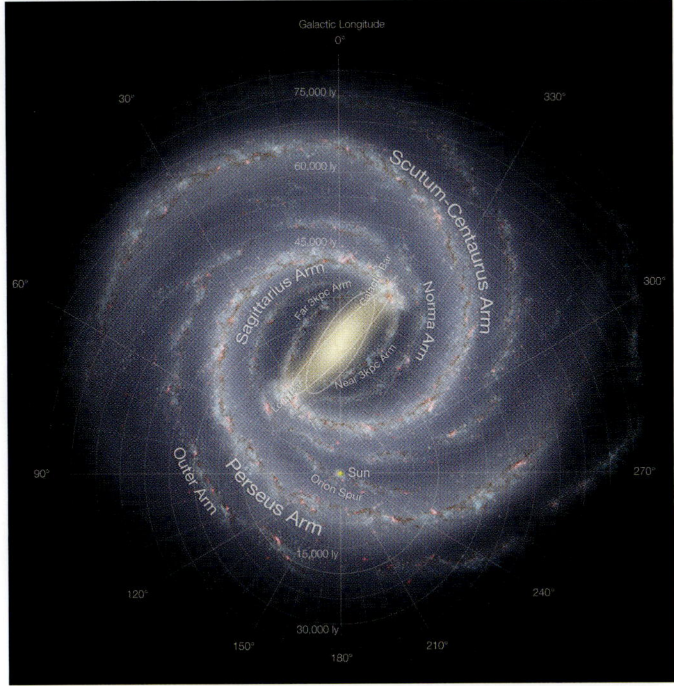

Created by NASA/JPL-Caltech/ESO/R. Hurt

The Milky Way galaxy, and relative position of our solar system. This illustration was commissioned by NASA and helps to give a slightly better understanding of the enormity of our galaxy.

CAMERAS FOR ASTRO-LANDSCAPE PHOTOGRAPHY

Let's look briefly at the specific camera and lens requirements for this type of photography. As we have already established, astro-landscape photography requires the use of high ISOs and wide maximum apertures. The range of cameras capable of delivering quality images at ISO 3200 and above is rapidly expanding. In 2012, I would have recommended using only recent model DSLRs with full-frame sensors for astro-landscape photography. By mid-2014, several mid-level APSC sensor cameras and a few high-end mirrorless compact cameras perform well enough to use for this type of work. No doubt more models are on the way. Other than high-ISO performance, most considerations are the same as for other types of night photography. Usable live view for focusing, ease of feature access, simple button layout, and navigable menus all facilitate working in very low-light levels. Being able to focus on a bright star using magnified live view is advantageous, but not essential, as there are multiple ways to achieve infinity focus. Currently, only the Nikon D4 and D4s have illuminated rear buttons, eliminating the need to memorize which buttons are where, or hunting around until you find the right one, which is what most people seem to do. Whenever choosing a new camera, I recommend carefully considering what your intended uses of the camera are, researching various models under consideration thoroughly, and finally renting the top contenders, and then trying them out under the various conditions you expect to encounter on a regular basis. The website DPReview.com has in-depth reviews on all aspects of digital cameras, and DXOMark.com does extensive testing on camera sensors to determine which models have the best image quality based on specific parameters. Using both sites together gives a well-rounded assessment of what to expect with different models. BorrowLenses.com and LensRentals.com both offer reasonably priced rentals of a wide selection of cameras and lenses.

LENSES FOR ASTRO-LANDSCAPE PHOTOGRAPHY

Lens choices for astro-landscape photography are quite specific. The primary considerations are focal length, maximum aperture, aperture area, and comatic aberration. The ideal lens has a wide angle of view, a very low f number, physically large aperture, and well-corrected chromatic, and especially comatic, aberration.

Wide-angle lenses are preferred for astro-landscape photography because they allow for a large area of sky to be included in the images (the Milky Way is immense after all), they allow for longer exposures without trailing, and they have a greater depth of field relative to longer lenses at equivalent f stops. Being able to shoot wide open, or as close to it as possible, is key, as there is little wiggle room for exposure adjustment. Wide to short telephoto prime lenses are the only ones with genuinely wide maximum apertures, and ideally those with an f number of less than 2.0 are ideal. Aperture area is a factor of focal length relative to f number that determines light-gathering potential—longer lenses generally have larger aperture area than shorter ones at the same f number. For example f1.4 on a 24 mm lens has an area of about 230 mm^2, while f1.4 on a 50 mm^2 lens has an area of about 1000 mm^2. The larger area of glass has a greater light-gathering potential, but this is offset by the shorter maximum exposure length before stars begin to show movement.

Comatic aberration (examples in Chapter 2) is a lens artifact that appears primarily in the corners of astro images shot at or near wide open. It is well corrected in most lenses by stopping down one to two stops, but we need to shoot as close to wide open as possible for this type of work. This is where the Korean Rokinon/Bower/Samyang lenses really shine, as they show considerably less coma than their name brand counterparts. Chromatic aberration can usually be easily corrected in postprocessing, so it is less of an issue than coma.

Photographer Ian Norman has created a detailed chart available on his website lonelyspeck.com comparing lenses on the basis of maximum aperture, aperture area, and longest usable shutter speed. It is intended for use with full-frame sensor cameras, and does not take into account aberration, brand, or image quality, but it does provide a useful comparison of focal lengths for astro-landscape photography. Ian has concluded, and I concur, that the 24 mm f1.4 lens is the overall most useful lens for this type of work with full-frame cameras. Many photographers use 14 mm f2.8 lenses too, but this is such a wide lens on full-frame that it is rarely used in other applications. If you intend to make a regular habit out of wide field Milky Way images, a Rokinon

14 mm lens is a good investment for about $300. Most people will never get their money's worth from a Canon or Nikon 14 mm lens, as they cost over $2000. The Rokinon 12 mm f2.0 is probably the best choice for a camera with an APSC sensor for astro-landscape photography. The 14 mm f2.8 is also a good choice, but at one stop slower and a bit less wide the 12 mm is a clear choice.

If you prefer to stick with zoom lenses, the ones mentioned in Chapter 2 are still the best choices. For full-frame cameras, the Nikon 14–24 mm f2.8 is the best zoom lens for any camera, although you lose autofocus when adapting to non-Nikon bodies. The Canon 16–35 mm II f2.8 is the best option for Canon lenses. For APSC cameras, the Tokina AT-X116 PRO DX-II 11–16 mm f2.8 or Sigma 18–35 mm f1.8 DC HSM lenses are the preferred options. The Sigma is one stop faster but not nearly as wide, and slightly more money.

Recommended lenses for astro-landscape photography

Full-frame sensor cameras	APSC sensor cameras	Smaller than APSC sensors
Rokinon/Bower/Samyang 14 mm f2.8	Rokinon/Bower/Samyang 10 mm f2.8	Rokinon/Bower/Samyang 8 mm f2.8
Rokinon/Bower/Samyang 24 mm f1.4	Rokinon/Bower/Samyang 12 mm f2.0	Rokinon/Bower/Samyang 10 mm f2.8
Sigma 35 mm f1.4 (autofocus)	Rokinon/Bower/Samyang 14 mm f2.8	Rokinon/Bower/Samyang 12 mm f2.0
Rokinon/Bower/Samyang 35 mm f1.4	Rokinon/Bower/Samyang 16 mm f2.0	Rokinon/Bower/Samyang 14 mm f2.8
	Rokinon/Bower/Samyang 24 mm f1.4	Rokinon/Bower/Samyang 16 mm f2.0

Exposure

Shutter speed is the determining factor in astro-landscape photography, as successful images are dependent on the stars appearing as points of light rather than trails. The longest shutter speed that can be used without showing signs of star trailing is the starting point for every exposure. Of course, the degree of acceptable trailing is subjective, and to a large extent dependent on the size and viewing conditions of the final form of the image. Pixel peepers who scrutinize every detail of an image at 100 percent magnification will be more critical of trailing than the casual photographer who mainly posts images on Facebook or Flickr. Large prints will show trailing much more than smaller ones from the same image. In essence, the longest shutter speed that doesn't cause star trailing offensive to your aesthetic sensibilities is the one you should use, and then build the rest of your exposure around that. The noise produced in high-ISO images, sharpness falloff, and shallow depth of field from wide open apertures will

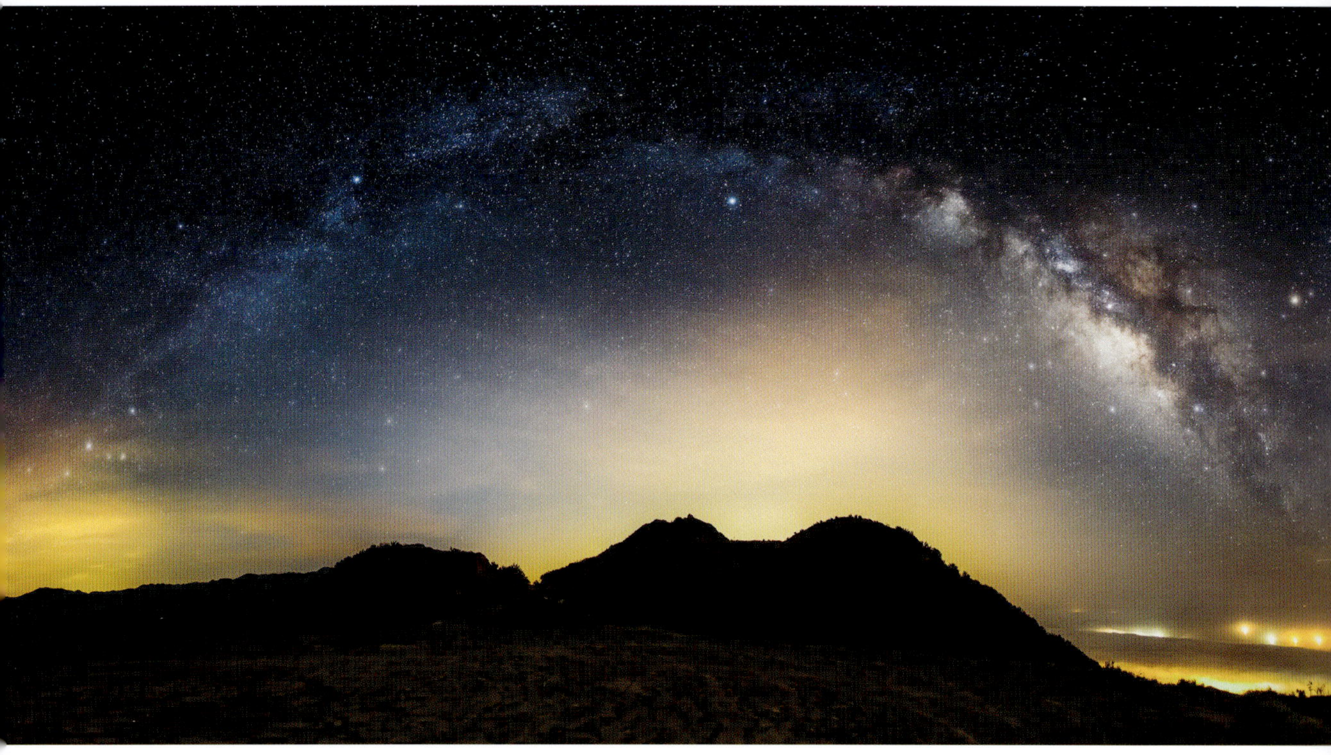

Alchemy, a 14-frame panoramic image by Michael Shainblum, who says: "I visualize where the Milky Way arch will be in the landscape. Panoramas require anywhere from 10–40 shots depending on how high the Milky Way is in the sky. Panoramas work best when the Milky Way is a low in the sky, the arch looks nicer and shots are easier to compose. I work from left to right, making vertical photos and manually move the ball head, making sure I overlap each photo. Sometimes it takes two rows of images. I use Merge to Panorama in Photoshop to stitch the images."

also be more apparent in print than on a screen, and increasingly apparent as the size of the print goes up, just as star trailing becomes more obvious with print size. It is easy to see how astro-landscape photography really pushes the limits of our cameras.

Astro photographers use a device known as the "500 rule" to determine the longest shutter speed that will render sharp stars in images. Divide 500 by the focal length of your lens (with a full-frame camera) and you get a number that equals the approximate number of seconds of the longest usable shutter speed for that particular lens. Some people use 600, and some people use 400 depending on their tolerance for movement, but for the most part 500 works well. For example, with a 24 mm lens on a full-frame camera, you get 500/24 = 20.833 seconds. Rounding down to 20 seconds gives a pretty good measure of the longest usable shutter speed for that lens. If you are using a camera with a smaller sensor, you need to use the 35 mm focal length equivalent when making the exposure calculation.

The 500 Rule—longest usable shutter speeds for astro-landscape photography with various lenses

Focal length	Full frame	1.5x crop factor (most APSC)	1.6x crop factor (Canon APSC)	2x crop factor (micro 4/3)
10 mm	50 seconds	33 seconds	31 seconds	25 seconds
14 mm	36 seconds	24 seconds	22 seconds	18 seconds
20 mm	25 seconds	17 seconds	16 seconds	13 seconds
24 mm	21 seconds	14 seconds	13 seconds	10 seconds
28 mm	18 seconds	12 seconds	11 seconds	9 seconds
35 mm	14 seconds	10 seconds	9 seconds	7 seconds
50 mm	10 seconds	7 seconds	6 seconds	5 seconds
85 mm	6 seconds	4 seconds	4 seconds	3 seconds

Note: To determine the longest usable shutter speed that maintains stars as sharp points of light, divide the focal length equivalent for your camera by 500, and the result is the number of seconds for your exposure.

Let's put that same 24 mm lens onto a 1.5 factor crop sensor camera, and the effective focal length becomes 36 mm. Then 500/36 = 13.888 seconds, so 14 seconds is the longest usable shutter speed with this camera lens combination. If you were to use a 24 mm lens on a micro 4/3 sensor camera, which has a crop factor of 2, the effective focal length becomes 48 mm, and the longest usable shutter speed would be 10 seconds. As we have seen though, nothing is that simple or straightforward in night photography, so it is also necessary to take into account the direction your camera is pointing, as polar-facing exposures can generally be a bit longer than those taken in other directions. We'll look more closely at the length and direction of star movement in the next chapter, but for now know that north-facing exposures in the northern hemisphere, and south-facing exposures in the southern hemisphere yield shorter star trails at equivalent exposure lengths. In short, you should do some testing with each of your lenses and decide for yourself what shutter speeds give you results you can live with based on your final image size. It is all relative! Take comfort in knowing that once you figure out a time for a particular lens, it never changes. Twenty seconds will always be your shutter speed for astro-landscape photography with a 24 mm lens. There are very few constants in night photography, but the longest usable shutter speed with a particular lens is one of them— providing you allow for variation due to the direction your camera is pointed!

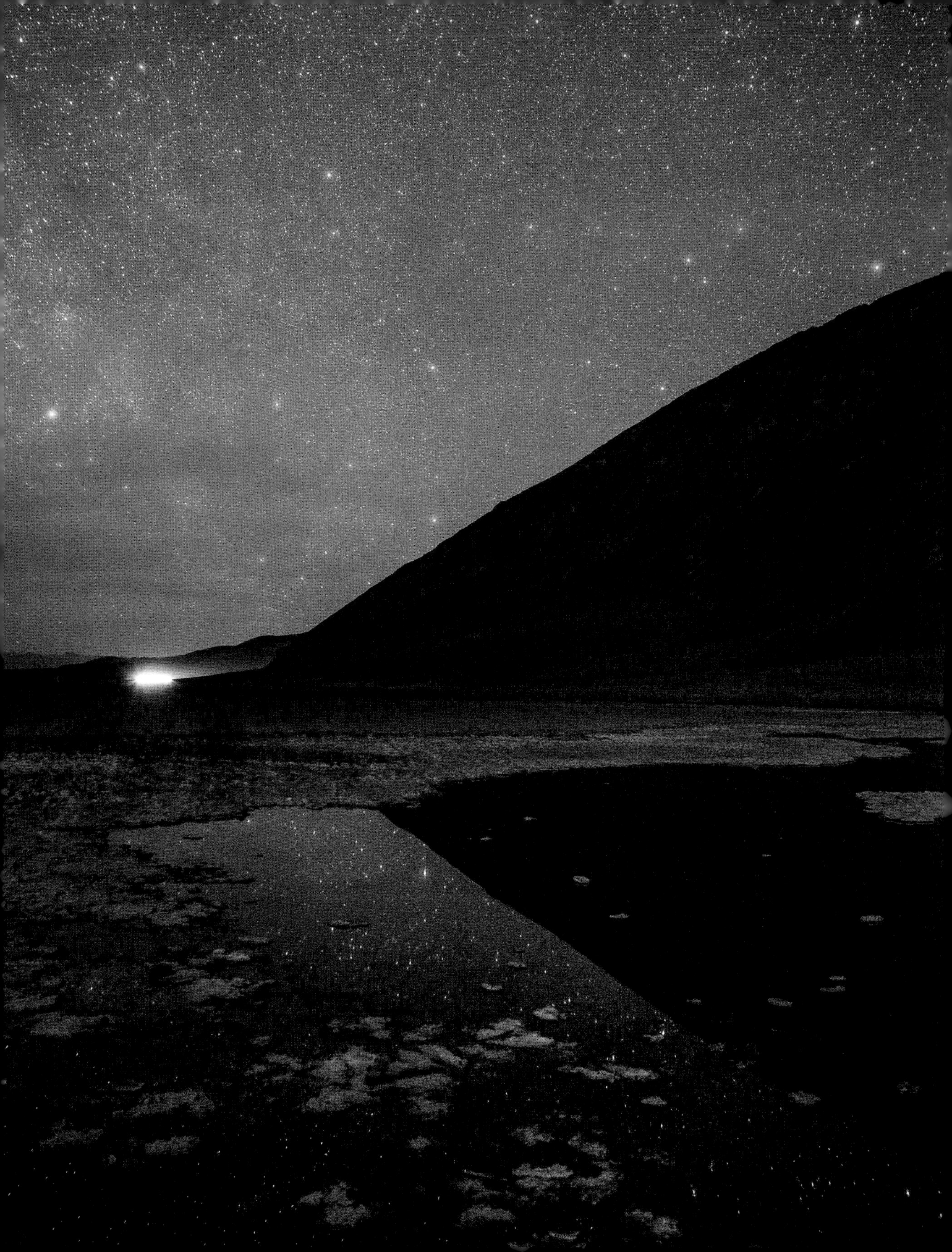

Badwater, good light, Death Valley National Park, California

30 seconds, f4 at ISO 6400. Canon 6D, Rokinon 24 mm f1.4 lens. Car headlights from several miles away compete with brake lights from the opposite direction to make this surreal scene look even stranger than it did without the human presence. The image is underexposed by about one and a half stops, but the 6D performs admirably even in these challenging conditions.

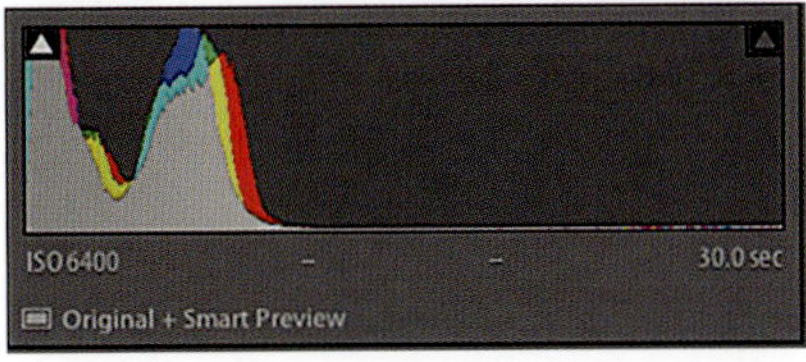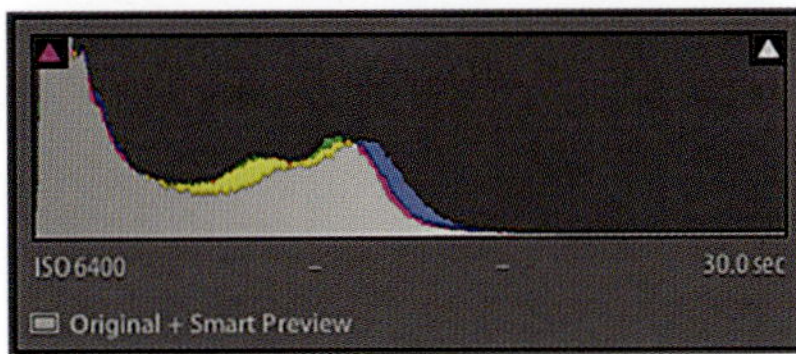

Badwater, good light—histograms before and after development

It is generally best to avoid lightening an underexposed image in postprocessing, as the noise will be increased. In this case, I'll accept the noise to save the image.

Now that we have determined the shutter speed for your astro-landscape image, we need to decide on the aperture and ISO settings. We'll use the histogram combined with our own experiences to make the decision, but it is unlikely that you will ever overexpose this type of image because of the technical limitations previously described. A good starting point for any astro-landscape photography in truly dark environments made on a moonless night is 20 seconds at f2.8 at ISO 3200, or an equivalent exposure. Start here, and make modifications to the settings as needed based on the longest usable shutter speed, the widest available aperture that gives you the sharpness and depth of field that you need, and the highest usable ISO on your camera. See the sidebar on determining the highest usable ISO for your camera. Interpreting histograms for astro-landscape photography is slightly different than for other types of night photography. It is unlikely that you will ever have a truly right-biased histogram without star movement or extreme noise in your images, so if you are able to achieve a centered histogram without any shadow clipping, that's likely to be as good as you will get without lighting the foreground. It is possible to move the histogram toward the right with light painting, but high-ISO light painting is not easy to do well, especially when limited to 20–30 seconds.

You may find that this starting point exposure gives a good result for the sky, but that the foreground is considerably underexposed. If that's the case, you can consider blending a separate foreground exposure, lighting the foreground, or both. If depth of field is inadequate, you might also consider using a second image that has been refocused on the foreground, and masking out the sky.

PHOTOGRAPHING CELESTIAL PHENOMENA

Now let's look at the various celestial phenomena that you may encounter in your nocturnal wanderings. Each of these occurrences, regardless of whether they are naturally occurring or the result of human activity in space, are interesting, fun to seek out, and rewarding to photograph.

Photographing the Aurora Borealis or Aurora Australis

The Aurora Borealis, as the Northern Lights are also known, occurs when electrically charged particles from the Sun are carried by solar wind toward the Earth, and collide with gases in the upper atmosphere. Those gas particles, which are usually oxygen (green aurora) and nitrogen (pink aurora), are "excited" by the collisions, and release photons of light. The Earth's magnetic field deflects most of the solar particles, but the field is weakest at the poles. This is why the aurora is mainly seen near the polar regions. Solar activity peaks and falls on an 11-year cycle, and the winter of 2023–2024 will be the next peak of the cycle, and the best opportunity to view and photograph the aurora in the next decade. Auroral activity is unpredictable, and it can still be viewed under the right conditions at any point in the 11-year cycle. In general the chances of viewing the aurora are best at latitudes above 55°N, and between the months of October and March, which are historically the best months for aurora viewing. The frequency of clear skies is a big factor in seeing the aurora as well, but broken cloud cover can add a lot of visual interest in aurora photographs. The aurora can appear at any time it is dark, but the best viewing times are typically 10 pm to 2 am. Iceland lies between 64 and 66°N, and is ideally suited for viewing and photographing the aurora in the northern hemisphere. Despite being so far north, its position on the gulf stream keeps the winters relatively mild compared to other good aurora viewing places like Scandinavia and Alaska. In the southern hemisphere, the Aurora Australis is visible in Antarctica, New Zealand, and Australia, and parts of South America.

Equipment considerations for aurora photography

The best cameras and lenses for astro-landscape photography are also the best ones for aurora photography, and other than making accommodations for the cold, you won't need any additional equipment. You should keep your extra camera batteries close to your body in an inner pocket, as they will not last as long in the cold. Have at least one fully charged extra battery. Remove any filters from your lenses, and be sure to use your lens hood, which will help minimize frost or condensation buildup on your lens. Using rubber bands to attach

Aurora Borealis in Iceland

20 seconds, f5.6 at ISO 3200. Canon 5D MK II, Zuiko 24 mm f2.8 lens. The light from a last quarter moon helped to illuminate the landscape, and barely dimmed this spectacular display of Aurora Borealis. The light coming from the window is actually my incandescent flashlight bounced off of the ceiling through a different window.

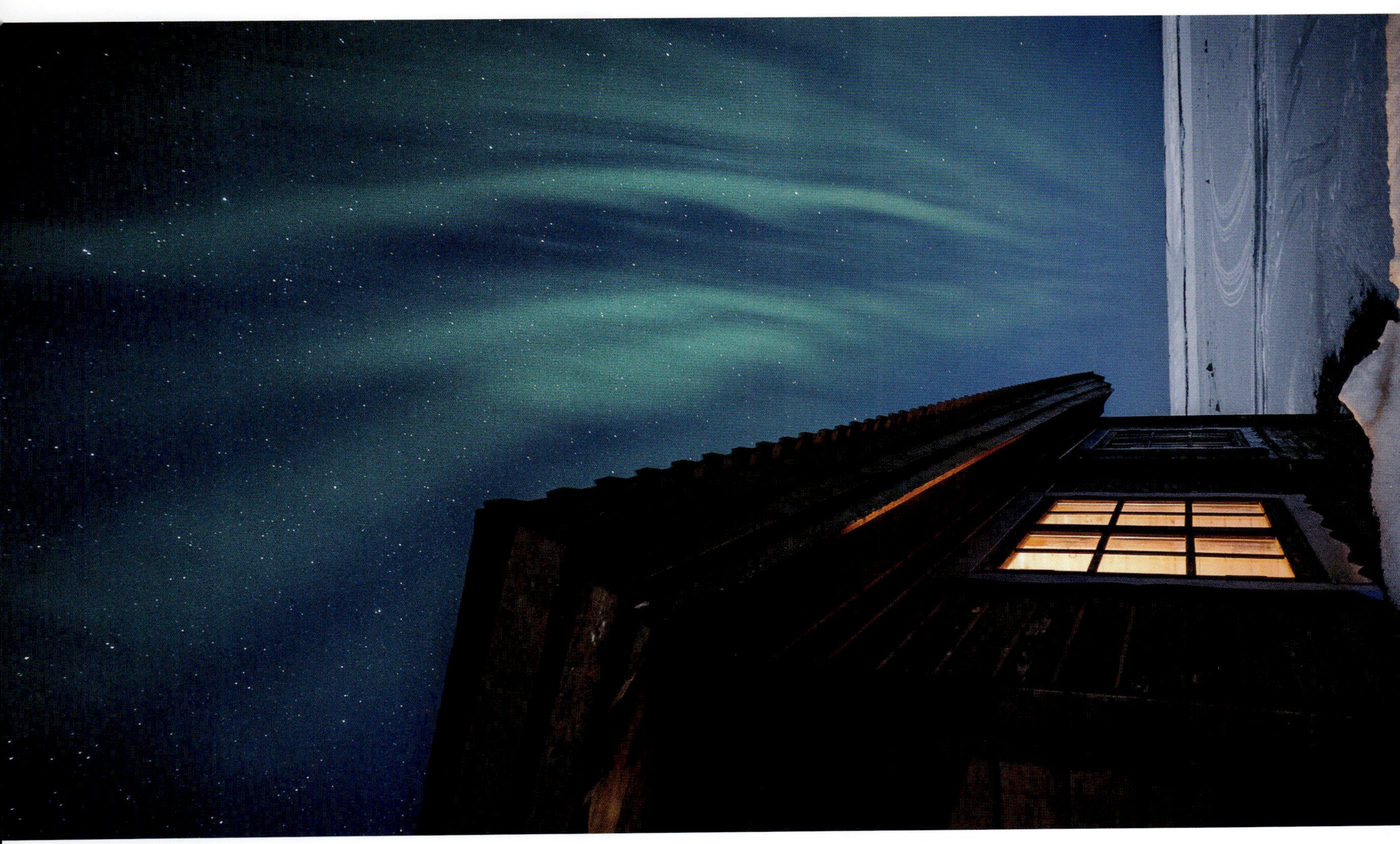

hand warmers to the barrel of your lens can help to prevent condensation or frost on your lens, although in sub-zero weather conditions more specialized insulation may be required. Insulated tripod leg sections are easier to handle, especially on aluminum tripods. Carbon fiber tripods may not feel as cold to the touch, but they do become brittle in extreme temperatures. Ball heads are better suited for this work than traditional pan-tilt heads, because they can be adjusted quickly to track quickly changing aurora. Since exposures are generally 30 seconds or less, a remote release or intervalometer is not required, but helpful. The cables can freeze and break in extremely cold weather, so if the temperature is below 0°F, you're better off without one. If you are working without a remote release of some sort, be sure to use the 2-second delay on the self-timer to avoid camera movement when depressing the shutter button. The only other equipment you'll need are flashlights—a dim, or preferably red, one for finding things in your camera bag or adjusting your camera, and a very bright flashlight to use as a focusing aid.

Ambient light and aurora photography

Ambient light from towns and cities will obscure all but the brightest aurora displays, so make sure you are well away from urban areas. That said, the distant glow from streetlights and the last glow of a fading sunset on the horizon can add another element of color to your photographs. Sodium vapor streetlights reflecting off of low clouds is another possibility to add contrasting color to aurora photos. Lunar phase and lunar elevation in the sky both have a profound impact on night photography in general, and aurora photography in particular. Photographing without any moonlight will mean primarily silhouetted foregrounds and longer exposures at higher ISOs. Photographing under a full moon will mean much brighter foregrounds, especially if there is snow on the ground, shorter exposures at lower ISOs, and fainter aurora in your photographs.

You can photograph the aurora at all phases of the lunar cycle, and the results will vary fairly dramatically. It is just a matter of what kind of images you are looking for. My own personal preference is to photograph near the first quarter phase as there is sufficient moonlight to illuminate the landscape without overpowering the aurora. The first quarter moon rises around noon, and sets around midnight, and then rises about 45 minutes later each day until it is full, when it rises about sunset and sets about sunrise. If you include interesting foreground elements, you may want to add light painting to your foreground, especially when there is

---

Aurora Borealis in Iceland with ambient light from nearby Reykjavik. Canon 5D MK II

20 seconds, f5.6 at ISO 2500. Canon 5D MK II, 24 mm f2.8 Zuiko lens. The sodium vapor glow combined with broken clouds and the aurora make for an unusual photograph. Most people try to avoid any trace of artificial light or manmade objects in their aurora images, but my preference for mixed lighting got the best of me. I lit the foreground with an incandescent flashlight, while Scott Martin shone a light through a window in the back of the little house.

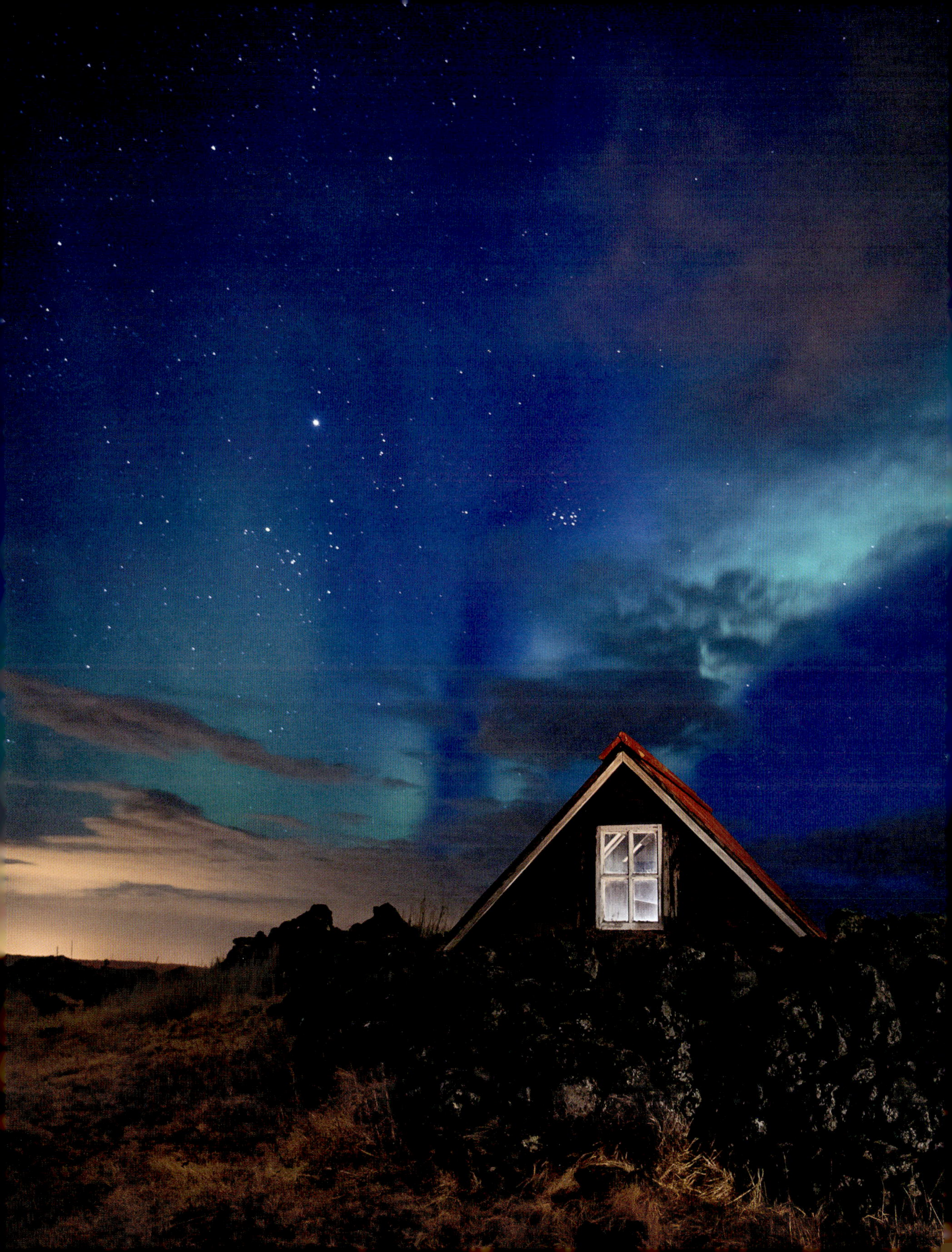

little or no moonlight present. The Moon during last quarter provides the same amount of moonlight as first quarter, but doesn't rise until midnight or later.

Camera settings and exposure for aurora photography

Camera settings for aurora photography are the same as for astro-landscape photography, except rather than star trailing, the goal is to freeze the aurora before it loses definition and becomes just a solid color field, or even simply overexposed highlights. The difference is that the behavior of the aurora is not nearly as predictable as star trails resulting from the Earth's rotation, and therefore success is due to a combination of luck and a quick reaction to changing circumstances. Exposures for aurora photography range from approximately 30 seconds at f2.8, ISO 6400 for faint to average aurora on a moonless night, to 4 seconds at f4, ISO 400 for bright coronal aurora on a full moon night. The intensity of the aurora can vary dramatically; sometimes it is barely visible to the naked eye, but shows up nicely in photographs, and sometimes the aurora can be so bright as to illuminate the landscape itself. Determining exposure is accomplished by a combination of the RGB histogram and the blinking highlight indicator. At a minimum, you should have a histogram that shows no shadow clipping—it may be a left-biased histogram, but the histogram should not be touching the left edge of the graph. Images with more exposure will have cleaner shadows with less noise. Ideally, you should not have to lighten your image in postprocessing. Use the highlight indicator to make sure that you are not overexposing the aurora itself or any highlights created by light painting. Use the LCD image preview primarily for confirming composition and focus.

As with any type of photography, you'll get better results with experience and practice. It is very helpful to have some experience with astro-landscape photography and to be completely familiar with your equipment before departing for northern skies. Simply working in the cold and darkness complicates photography exponentially, so do your homework and be prepared. Don't expect to get perfect results on your first attempt. Photographing the Northern Lights can be like photographing a close friend or family member's wedding: you're so focused on the task at hand that, before you know it, the event is over and you've completely missed out on the experience! Make sure that you take some time to simply step back, look up, and enjoy the magnificence of this special phenomenon.

Zodiacal light and Gegenschein

Two seldom experienced and fascinating types of celestial phenomena, Zodiacal light and Gegenschein, can be observed and photographed in very dark locations near the spring and fall

Zodiacal light in the Western sky in Death Valley National Park, March, 2014

15 seconds, f2.8 at ISO 6400. Canon 6D, Rokinon 24 mm f1.4 lens. Zodiacal light appears in the sky near the equinoxes—just after dark in the spring, and just before dawn in the fall.

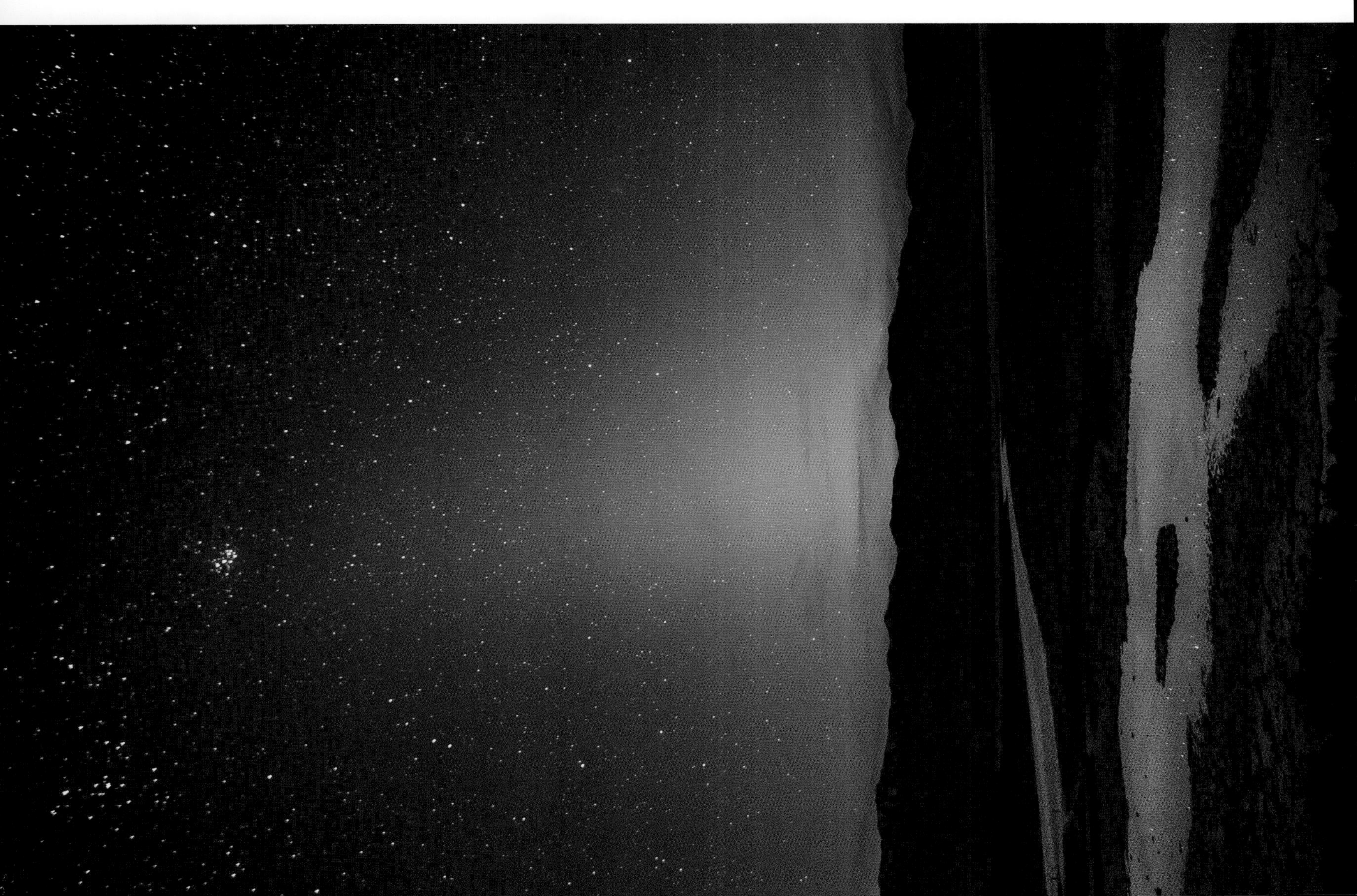

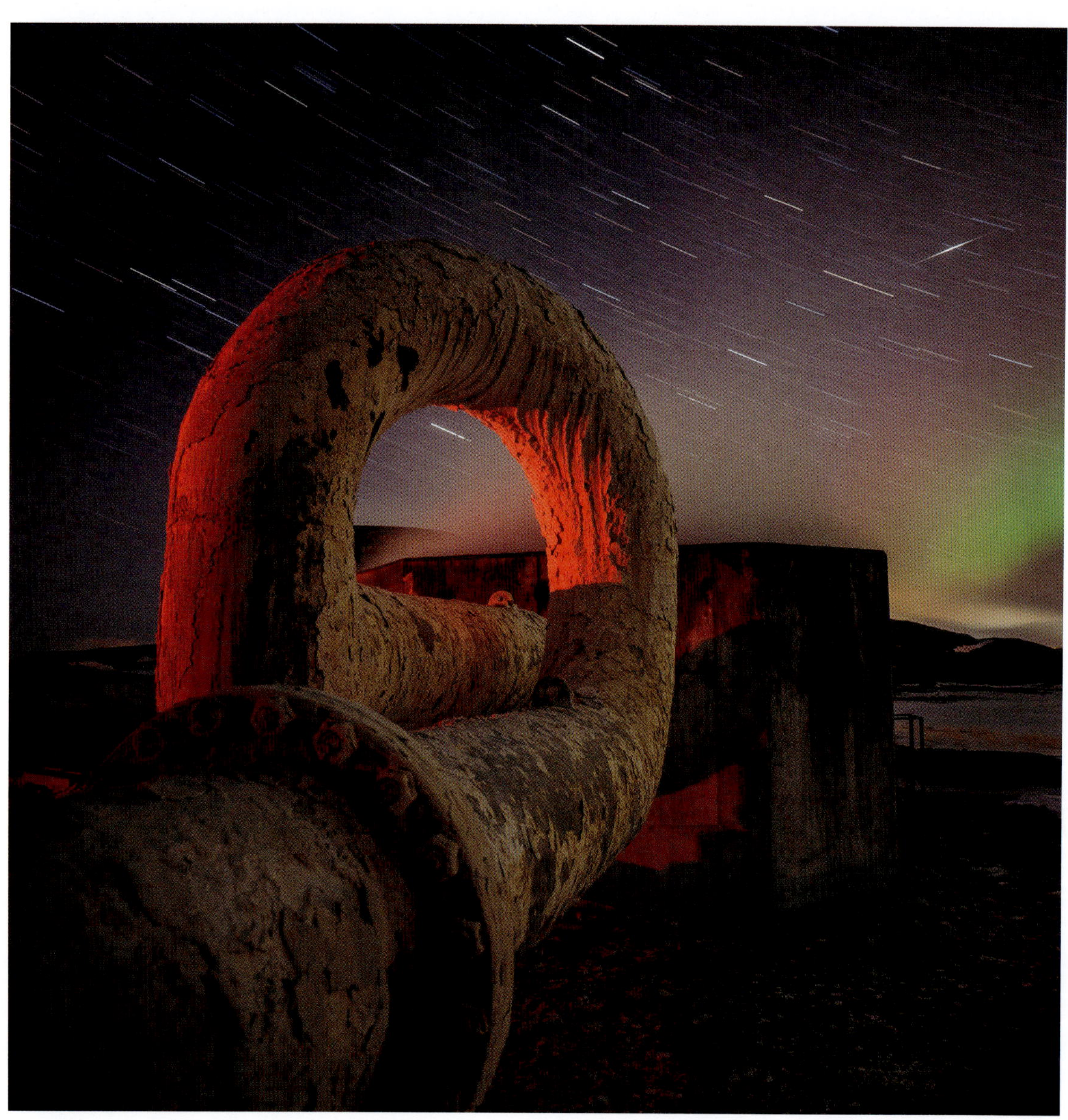

Iridium flare over geothermal energy plant, Myvatn, Iceland

10 minutes, f8 at ISO 640. Canon 5D MK II, 24 mm f2.8 Zuiko lens. This image has so many different things going on, but adding a little color seemed like the right thing to do. Red LED from camera left for about 15 seconds. Steam from the geothermal area, Northern Lights, star trails, a well-placed momentary flare from an iridium satellite all somehow come together with the corroded pipe in the foreground, and the shot worked.

equinoxes. Both can be found along the ecliptic or apparent path of the Sun across the sky, and are the result of sunlight reflected off of interplanetary dust—the microscopic remnants of asteroid collisions and cometary debris. Zodiacal light may be observed about 2 hours after sunset or 2 hours before sunrise above the horizon where the Sun has set or will rise, and extending in a conical pattern along the path of the ecliptic. The best viewing conditions for Zodiacal light are in very dark remote areas between 30°N and 30°S of the equator. The dust cloud is actually uniform along the ecliptic, stretching across the entire sky, but is generally only visible when viewed at a small angle with the Sun. Under ideal conditions, Zodiacal light might be observed along the ecliptic all the way to the point in the sky midway between the point of sunset and sunrise, and this is where the Gegenschein may be observed as a luminous band of light, also near the equinoxes, but primarily in the exact middle of the night rather than just after or before twilight.

Airplanes, ISS, iridium flares

Manmade objects in the sky are also often part of night photographs, often unintentionally, and frequently unwanted. Dotted lines from the blinking lights on the wing tips of airliners are the bane of many a night photographer, as air traffic can be an unwelcome reminder of human activity in the remotest of locations. Long-exposure photographs might contain the trails of a dozen or more airplanes, and cloning them out of images can be a time-consuming endeavor if they are unwanted. On occasion though, the graceful arcing path of an airplane through the sky in an image might be just the thing the image needs to create movement in an otherwise quiet part of the frame. It is thrilling to be able to see the ISS as it orbits the Earth, but in photographs it is easily confused with just another airplane in scratching a line across the sky. Iridium communications satellites, with their large antennae, reflect sunlight back to Earth at night and create an effect that looks somewhat like meteorites in night photographs. As they rotate in space, the Sun reflecting off of their antennae momentarily renders them as bright as any star or planet in the sky.

STEPS TO SUCCESSFUL ASTRO-LANDSCAPE PHOTOGRAPHY

1. Do some pre-planning to learn about the area where you will be photographing, and study up on celestial conditions in the time and place where you will photograph. What is the lunar phase? Rise and set times? Where will the Milky Way core be in the sky? How about light pollution? Use an app like Photo Pills or The Photographer's Ephemeris if you like. Use Google Maps.
2. Allow at least 20–30 minutes for your eyes to dark adapt without using a flashlight when you arrive on location.

3. Take some test shots at maximum ISO and maximum aperture to find your composition. Don't worry about exposure or focus at this time, just get the composition. Make sure you are happy with the framing, and that there are no unintended objects in your frame. Once you work out a shot, lock down your tripod.

4. Focus your shot. Assuming that you want the stars to be tack sharp, consider any foreground elements, and determine what aperture you need to use to get an adequate depth of field. If there is no foreground, focus on the stars or Moon if possible, or a distant light source. If you need depth of field, use a depth of field or hyperfocal distance (HFD) calculator such as Tack Sharp to determine where to focus. Measure that distance, put your flashlight down there, return to the camera, and focus on the light. Use magnified live view. Use the toggle on the camera to move the red or white box over the section of the image where you want to focus before you magnify the image. Do not move the camera or zoom the lens after you have established your shot. Consider taping the focus ring on the lens, especially if using HFD. That way, you do not need to refocus in between shots as long as you use that aperture or a smaller one. (You can also prefocus during the daytime to the HFD, and tape it down then.) Confirm your focus at full resolution in one of your test frames.

5. Calculate your ambient exposure. In a moonless landscape start with 20 seconds, f2.8, ISO 6400 or equivalent. You have picked the aperture based on required depth of field. Next choose the longest usable shutter speed for your lens based on the 500 rule. Now select the ISO that will give you the best balance between a workable histogram and manageable noise levels. Accept that you may not be able to achieve a right-biased histogram with ambient light. Go for one that minimizes shadow clipping. You can push the histogram to the right with light painting if you plan to light the foreground.

6. Decide if you will use light painting, and then try several different ways of lighting the foreground until you find what looks best. After you think you have nailed it, do at least one more insurance shot—it is only 20–30 seconds! Alternatively, lower the ISO, and do a longer, lower ISO shot for the foreground to be blended later in postprocessing.

RICK WHITACRE: PHOTOGRAPHING METEORS

Meteors are one of the more challenging subjects in night photography. With a lot of preparation and a little luck, however, you can come away with some amazing images. Meteors are random, fast, and appear relatively faint to our camera sensors. The key to meteor night photography is to cover as much of the sky as possible while maximizing the amount of light received by your camera sensor. This means shooting at high ISOs with a very fast, wide-angle lens. Many of the techniques for photographing meteors are the same as photographing the Milky Way.

When shooting meteors, you want your shutter to be open as much as possible during the night. This means shooting back-to-back images as quickly as possible using an intervalometer. An added advantage to shooting back-to-back images as quickly as possible is that you will be able to create photographs of single fireballs, composites of all the meteors, time-lapse video, and star trails all from the same set of exposures.

Preparation

Meteor showers occur roughly the same time each year as the Earth plows through the debris fields of comets that are orbiting the Sun. Each meteor shower appears to radiate from the same portion of the sky each year and they have been named for the constellations from which they originate. For instance, the Perseid Meteor Shower's radiant is located in the constellation Perseus.

The larger meteor showers each year are the Perseids, Leonids, and Geminids occurring in August, November, and December, respectively. A quick internet search will give you the peak dates and times for each shower.

Since the meteors are fairly faint, you need very dark skies to photograph as many as possible. This means being in an area with very little light pollution from city lights and paying particular attention to the phase of the Moon. To find areas with the darkest skies, I recommend the Dark Sky Finder website: http://www.jshine.net/astronomy/dark_sky/. There are many online tools for predicting the Moon phase, rise, and set times. Knowing when the Moon will rise and when it will set can help determine the best times to be capturing images. If you have a nearly full moon that has risen for most of the night, it will severely limit the number of meteors that will be visible in your images.

As in many types of night photography, you will need a stable tripod, a camera with good high-ISO performance, an intervalometer, a large memory card, and fully charged batteries. Because you may be out for many hours at night, particular attention is required to having warm clothing (layers), sufficient water, flashlights (several), spare batteries, snacks, and maybe even a chair or sleeping bag to stay warm and comfortable. Make sure you tell people exactly where you are going and take a buddy along if possible.

CAMERA SETUP FOR METEORS

1. Set the ISO to 3200 or 6400.
2. Set the quality to RAW.
3. Use a memory card that will hold 120–180 images for every hour you plan to be out.
4. Set the exposure mode to bulb.
5. Use a 14–24 mm (full-frame equivalent) lens to capture more of the sky.
6. Use an aperture of f1.4 to f2.8.

7. Use an intervalometer with 1 second between exposures.
8. Set a shutter duration of 20–30 seconds to avoid clipping meteors while not streaking stars.
9. Focus manually on stars, or use hyperfocal or infinity points on your lens.
10. Use a white balance of 3500–4000 K.
11. Use a lens hood for dew reduction.
12. Turn off LENR for fast sequencing.
13. Remove any lens filters to reduce stray light.
14. Turn off the image stabilization on IS or VR lenses.
15. Turn off mirror lockup.

Composition

As in most photography, composition is the most important aspect. Compose your scene with a strong, interesting foreground and as much sky as possible. While meteors can be seen in all portions of the sky, those associated with a meteor shower originate from a single point in the sky, known as the radiant. If you want to create a composite image with several meteors aligned to the radiant (see image), you will want to include the radiant in your composition. Because the radiant will appear to move during the night due to the Earth's rotation, you will need to visualize where the radiant will arc through your chosen composition and make sure it stays in or near your field of view the entire time. There are many desktop and smart phone apps that can help you with this. Additionally, to help with aligning the meteors around the radiant in postprocessing, try to include the North Star (Polaris) in your composition if possible. The North Star will not move significantly during the night. Both vertical and horizontal orientations can be used. Your foreground, movement of the radiant, and location of the North Star are important considerations when selecting the camera orientation.

Because the camera settings for meteors are very similar to those used to capture Milky Way images, you can combine the Milky Way with meteors very effectively. The Perseids, for example, originate in the northern arm of the summer Milky Way that can show both the radiant and a portion of the Milky Way in one shot.

Technique

Once a composition has been determined, take a test shot to confirm. Make sure your camera is level and the tripod stable. Focus on the brightest stars using 10× live view, or set the focus manually on the lens at the predetermined infinity or hyperfocal locations. Confirm sharp star focus on a test image. Zoom in and use a hoodman or magnifier if available.

Set your intervalometer to take an infinite (or very large) number of shots of 20–30-second duration (500/FL rule) with 1 second between exposures. Ensure your camera is in bulb mode.

Put a fresh, full battery in the camera or hook up an external battery pack for all-night power. Ensure that you have an empty, large memory card in your camera.

Start the intervalometer and ensure that the camera is functioning and taking successive images. Check the lens periodically for dew buildup and gently wipe it off if it appears. Lie back and enjoy the show!

Postprocessing for composite image
Download the images into your favorite image handling software (such as Lightroom). Edit a representative (middle of the night) image to tune the white balance, add contrast, vibrance, clarity, and improve the shadows if desired. Noise reduction can also be added at this point. Copy these settings to all the other images.

Go through every image and flag those that have meteors in them. Select only the images with meteors in them and load them into Photoshop as Layers. From Lightroom, this is done by selecting all the images that have meteors and going to Photo > Edit In > Open as Layers in Photoshop.

Once in Photoshop, each of the images with meteors should be seen as layers in a single Photoshop file. Change the Blend Mode for each layer to «Lighten.» Take a look at your (messy) image and try to determine if there is any particular meteor that works best in your composition, such as a long or bright meteor that points to a foreground object or creates a strong diagonal. If so, you will want to identify the layer that has this meteor. This will be the Base Layer that you time-shift all the other meteor layers to. Change this layer title to "Base Layer" so you can find it easily again. It usually works best if this Base Layer is near the middle of your set of images.

If your composition includes the North Star, locate it. This will be the reference for time-shifting all the other layers to match the Base Layer. If the North Star does not appear in your composition, estimate where it is and use that side or corner as a rough approximation. If you are comfortable with adding more canvas to your image, you can add enough canvas to include a virtual north star for reference and use that.

Turn off all of the layers except for the Base Layer and the first layer that you want to time-shift into place. With the first layer highlighted in the Layer Palate, go to menu Edit / Free Transform (shortcut Ctrl/Cmd-T). In the middle of the layer is a rotation mark. Move that mark to the North Star and drop it there. Now, when you rotate this layer, it will rotate around the North Star, which is just what happened during the meteor shower. Rotate the layer until the star pattern lines up with the star pattern of the Base Layer. It won't be exact due to lens distortion, but you should be able to get close. Double-check by seeing that the meteor on the layer you are rotating points to the same area as the one on the Base Layer. When happy with the alignment, click the check mark symbol near the top to complete the Transform.

With this first layer still selected, click the Add Mask icon or go to menu Layer > Layer Mask > Reveal All. Get a small, medium-edge brush, and using black ink paint over the meteor in this layer mask until it disappears. With the layer mask still selected, do an Image > Adjustments > Invert (Cntr/Cmd-I) to invert the layer mask to reveal only the meteor.

Depending on what time of night or what portion of sky the meteor came from, you may need to adjust it to get it to blend into the Base Layer properly. The biggest problem you might

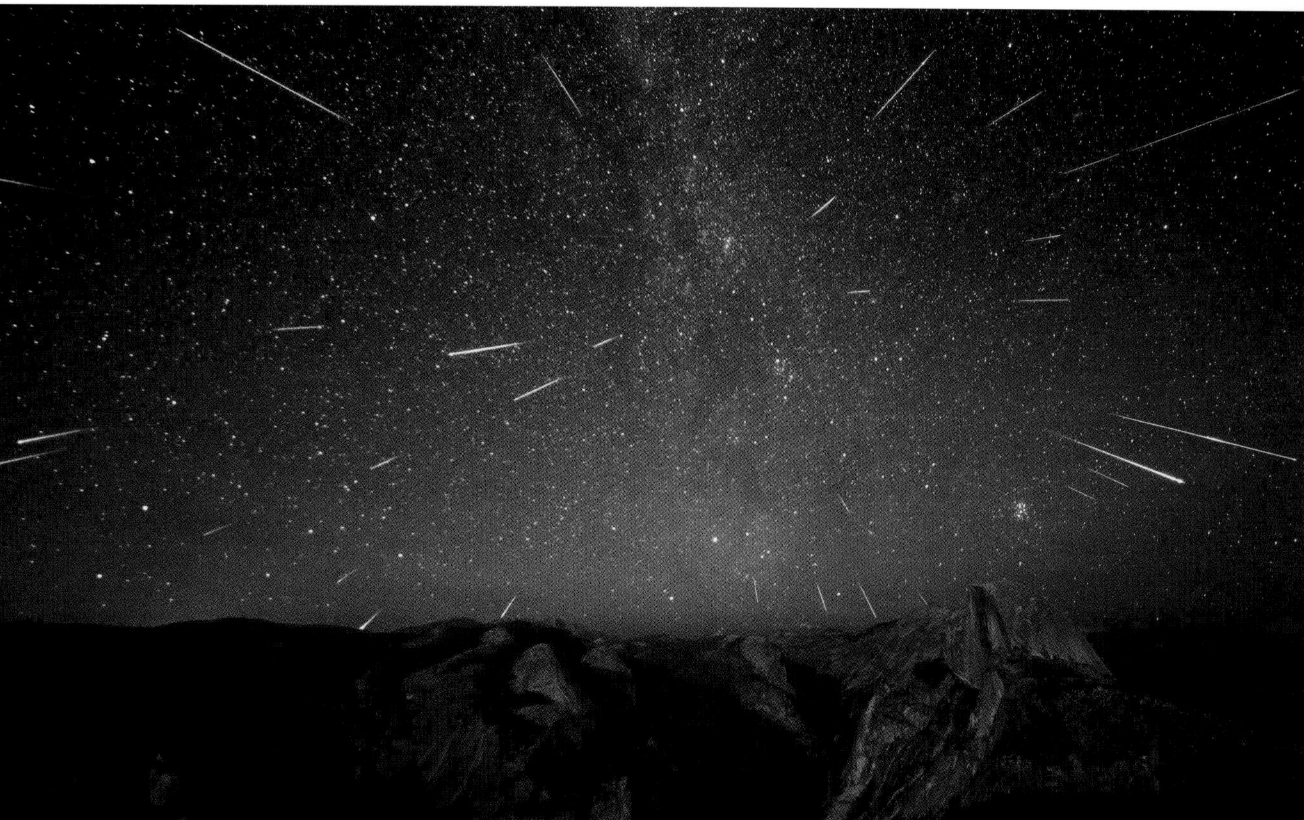

Rick Whitacre, "Warp Factor 9," August 10/11, 2013

Composite of 30 images stacked in Photoshop
Settings: Each one 15 seconds, f2.8, ISO 12,800
Canon EOS IDx, Samyang 14 mm f.2.8 lens

encounter is usually a bright halo around the meteor. To fix this, add a Curves Adjustment Layer as a Clipping Mask to the layer and adjust the black point on the curve until the halo disappears. Once happy with the first meteor, make the next meteor layer visible and repeat the Transform process to time-shift it into place. Mask out the meteor, invert the layer mask so that only the meteor shows, and use a Curves Clipping Mask to blend if necessary. Repeat for all the rest of the meteor layers.

It is not uncommon to have meteors that get time-shifted right off the edge or get placed on top of mountains and trees. Unfortunately, you will have to delete these layers and move on to the next one. If you find that you are throwing too many meteors away, you may want to start over and pick a new Base Layer to align all the other meteors to. This is the reason it usually works best to pick a middle image as your Base Layer if possible.

When you have finished with all the layers and happy with the blending you can flatten your image. Make sure all the meteors are where you want them and blended nicely before you do so! At this point, you can dodge, burn, add contrast, etc. to finish and save your image. If you are not concerned with taking up too much storage space on your hard drive, consider saving the layered file to make further adjustments in the future.

MICHAEL FRYE: PHOTOGRAPHING LUNAR ECLIPSES
Lunar eclipses are spectacular events to view and photograph. They're more common than solar eclipses, and easier to photograph too—though capturing a lunar eclipse still presents challenges. Lunar eclipses only happen when the Moon is full. You'll most likely be combining multiple exposures, either for the Moon and landscape, or multiple images of the Moon at different phases during the eclipse.

Predicting the eclipse
First, you'll need to find out when and where an eclipse will occur. A simple Google search is a good starting point, or you can just go directly to the NASA lunar eclipse page: http://eclipse.gsfc.nasa.gov/lunar.html.

Of course you'll want to move away from city lights to photograph an eclipse. To calculate the Moon's position accurately—if you want to line it up with a building or mountain for example—there are several excellent apps available. The Photographer's Ephemeris and PhotoPills are two of the best, and PhotoPills even has an augmented reality feature for visualizing the path of the Moon against a live picture of the scene in front of you.

Equipment

There are no special equipment requirements other than what you would normally use for astro-landscape photography. You'll be using high ISOs, so a camera that performs well at 1600 or higher is best.

Focusing

The most accurate way to focus is to use magnified live view and focus manually. It may help to temporarily crank up the ISO for this, depending on your camera's live view settings. Autofocusing on the Moon should also work if the Moon is bright enough (before the total eclipse begins), but be sure to then turn autofocus off so that the camera doesn't accidentally try to focus on something else when you depress the shutter.

Exposure

When the partial eclipse begins the Moon will become a smaller and smaller crescent as the Earth's shadow seems to take a bite out of the Moon. During the total eclipse the Moon will look much dimmer and turn orange, or even red–orange in color. Just after the total eclipse the Moon will return to a slender crescent and then get larger and larger, until the eclipse ends and the Moon becomes completely full again. (You may only be able to see part of this sequence, depending on your location and the timing of the eclipse.)

Light meters are useless for getting good exposures of the Moon, because even a 1-degree spot meter can't read just the Moon, but will also include some of the surrounding dark sky. So here are some suggestions based on past experience, including those used in the photograph on page 121. You'll need to use manual exposure mode, and check your camera's highlight alert (the blinkies) to make sure you're not overexposing the Moon:

Full moon, or moon more than half visible: 1/60 seconds at f11, 200 ISO

Half to one-quarter of the moon visible: 1/30 seconds at f11, 200 ISO

Less than one-quarter of the moon visible: 1/15 seconds at f11, 200 ISO

Just the edge of the moon lit: 1 second at f11, 200 ISO

Fully eclipsed at the beginning and end of totality: 8 seconds at f11, 800 ISO

Fully eclipsed, deepest totality: 8 seconds at f11, 1600 ISO

In these examples I've kept the aperture constant at f11, but you could use any aperture that will give you adequate depth of field. It is a good idea to vary the shutter speed and/or ISO rather than the aperture for consistently sharp images. You want to keep the exposures relatively short, otherwise the Moon will move and blur. You can get away with 8 or maybe even

15 seconds with a wide-angle lens, but with a telephoto lens you need to use shutter speeds of 4 seconds or less. To find the maximum exposure time for your lens before movement appears, divide the focal length into 400. So 400 ÷ 25 mm = 16 seconds, or 400 ÷ 100 mm = 4 seconds. Bracketing exposures is a good idea.

Eclipse strategies

Trying to include a foreground makes things more complicated, so the simplest way to photograph a lunar eclipse is to take a long lens and zoom in on the Moon. A good exposure for the Moon is not also likely to be a good exposure for the surrounding landscape; typically the landscape requires at least several stops more exposure than the Moon, even when fully eclipsed. If you photograph a sequence of the Moon during different phases of the eclipse you can use Photoshop to assemble your images into a montage.

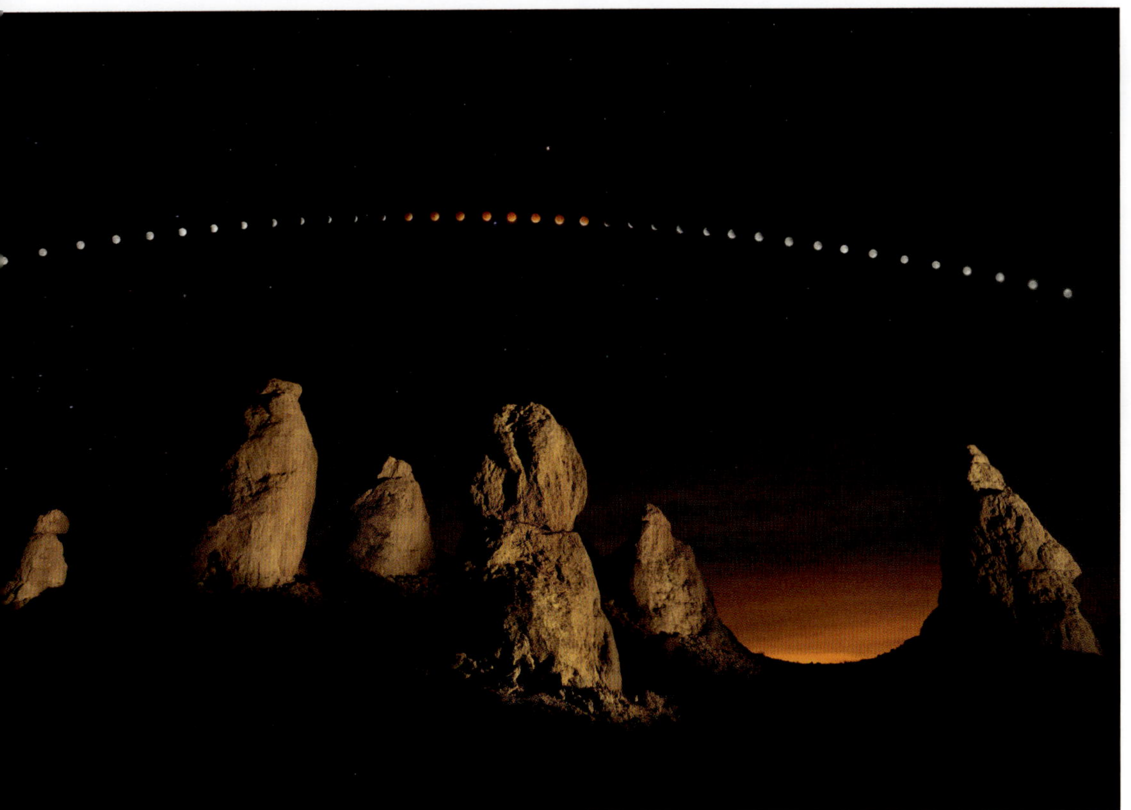

Michael Fry, "Lunar Eclipse Sequence" April 14/15, 2014. Composite of 44 images stacked in Photoshop

Location: Trona Pinnacles, Mojave Desert, California
Settings: 20 seconds to 1/60 seconds, f5.6–f11, 200–6400 ISO
Sony A7s, Canon 17–40 mm f4 lens

A more evocative approach—but a more complicated one—is to capture the eclipse sequence with a foreground as I did in the photograph of the Trona Pinnacles. This means making a series of exposures for the Moon, plus at least one frame to add some ambient light, and possibly another frame (or frames) to light-paint something in the foreground—and then blending these different images together in Photoshop.

You'll first need to figure out the exact path the Moon will take so you can compose your photograph accordingly. The apps I mentioned above, PhotoPills and The Photographer's Ephemeris, are invaluable for this.

Once you've composed your photograph, make sure your tripod is solidly planted and locked tightly. You'll want to focus on the foreground, not the Moon, or use hyperfocal focusing with a small enough aperture to get both the foreground and the Moon in focus. (A bright flashlight and live view are helpful for focusing on the foreground.)

Then make a series of exposures to capture the eclipse sequence. In the Trona Pinnacles photograph the interval was 10 minutes between each Moon capture, but you could make it 15 or 20 minutes if you want to space the moons farther apart in the frame. Just make sure you keep the interval the same throughout the sequence. You can use an interval timer for this, or just use a watch and trip the shutter manually (using a remote or cable release, of course). You'll need to adjust the exposure times (and possibly the ISO as well) as the Moon's brightness changes during the eclipse.

You'll also want to capture a frame for ambient light that you can blend in with the eclipse sequence. This could be an exposure of the moonlit landscape made before or after the eclipse (make sure the Moon is out of the frame, and shade the lens to prevent flare). It could also be an image of the dawn or dusk sky. But my favorite way of adding some ambient light is to make an exposure of the stars when the Moon is fully eclipsed. Do this in between taking frames of the Moon for your sequence. To show lots of stars you'll have to overexpose the Moon (even though it is fully eclipsed, it is still a lot brighter than the stars), which means you'll need to clone out the Moon from this frame before blending it with the other images in the sequence.

To make things more interesting—and yet again more complicated—you can light-paint something in the foreground. In the Trona Pinnacles photograph I used a tungsten-balanced, battery-powered spotlight to light the pinnacles, but for other eclipse sequences I've used flash or smaller flashlights, depending on the situation and the size of the objects being lit. Light-painting techniques are covered elsewhere in this book, but for an eclipse sequence like this I'd recommend making separate frames for each object you're lighting (in between exposures for the Moon), so you can adjust the exposure for each frame independently.

Assembling a sequence

For a sequence, the final step is to assemble the images in Photoshop. From Lightroom you can select the images and choose Photo > Edit In > Open as Layers in Photoshop, and Photoshop will stack the images into one document as separate layers. You can do this by hand in Photoshop by using the Move tool to drag one image on top of another; just make sure you hold down the shift key while dragging so that the images align properly. Russell Brown's Stack-a-Matic script (described in detail in the next chapter) is yet another way to combine eclipse images, and is especially helpful if you have a lot of images to combine, or need to mask out parts of the images.

Then change the blending mode of every layer except the bottom one to lighten. This makes light areas override dark areas, so the Moon from one frame will override dark sky from another frame. As you do this you'll see all the moons magically appear and complete your sequence. If you light-painted a tree or other object, that too will appear when you change the blending mode for that layer. And if you used a telephoto lens to capture the whole eclipse sequence, you can use the Move tool to drag each layer around and arrange the moons on your canvas.

ASTRO-LANDSCAPE PHOTOGRAPHY CHECKLIST

Now you are ready to venture out on the darkest of nights to photograph using astro-landscape photography techniques to capture images of the Milky Way and other celestial phenomena in all their glory. These techniques, thanks in large part to recent advances in digital technology, make astro-landscape photography accessible and fun. It is a great way to reconnect with nature, and to gain a real appreciation for the night sky and its beauty. This chapter ends with a checklist of camera settings and basic astro-landscape photography procedures. In the next chapter, we explore the possibilities of low-ISO, long-exposures that show the stars as trails rather than as points of light.

ASTRO-LANDSCAPE PHOTOGRAPHY CHECKLIST

1. Set Quality to RAW.
2. Use your camera's highest usable ISO setting, ideally at least 1600, preferably 6400. Note that the highest usable ISO will vary depending on ambient temperature.
3. Set white balance to auto, and use that if you like the results. Otherwise, set the white balance to approximate the desired look in-camera.
4. Set your camera's long-exposure noise reduction (LENR) to auto (if available). If your camera doesn't have Auto as an option, testing will be required to determine when LENR is needed.
5. Enable your camera's RGB histogram—primary exposure determinant in natural light.

LONG EXPOSURES IN NATURAL LIGHT —MOONLIGHT AND STAR TRAILS

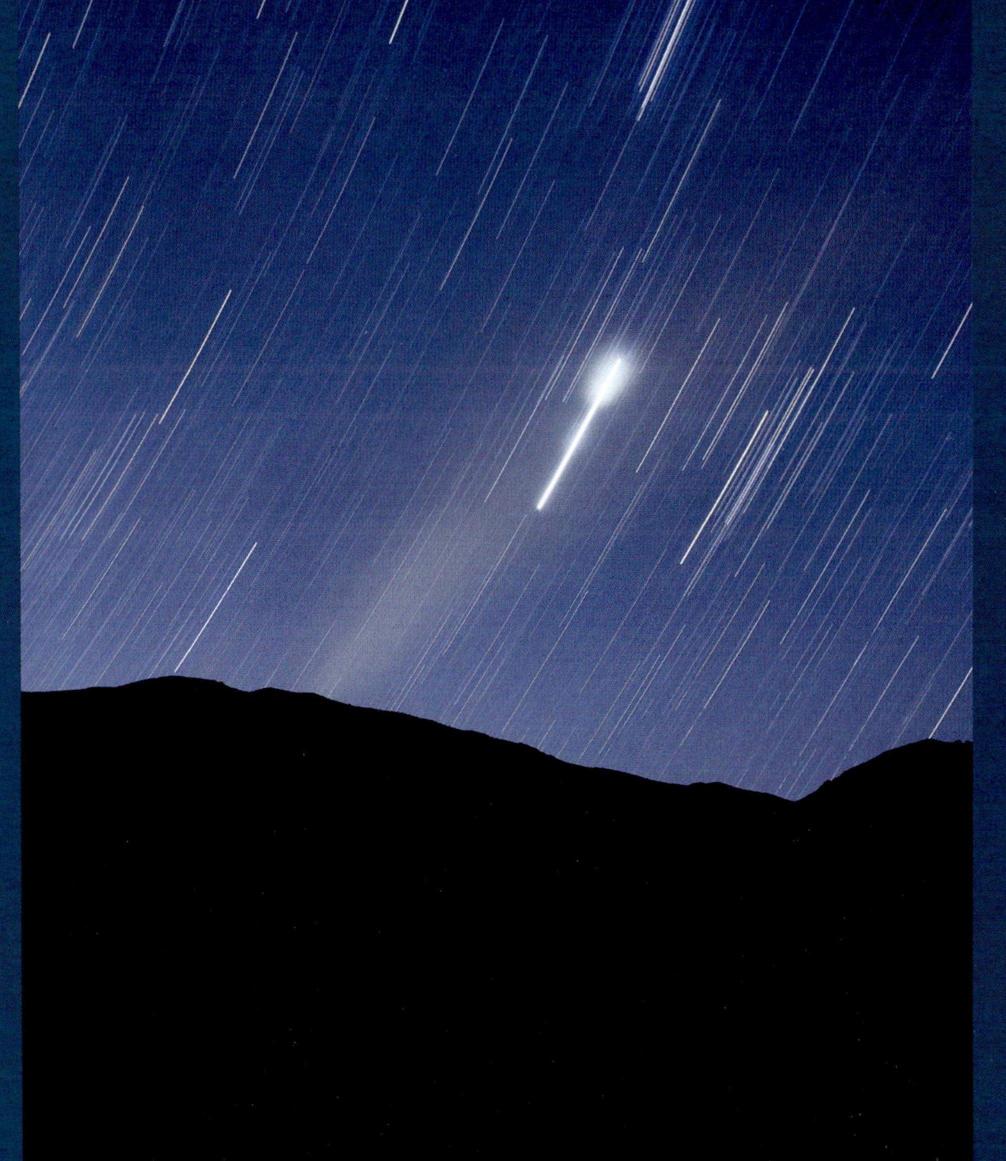

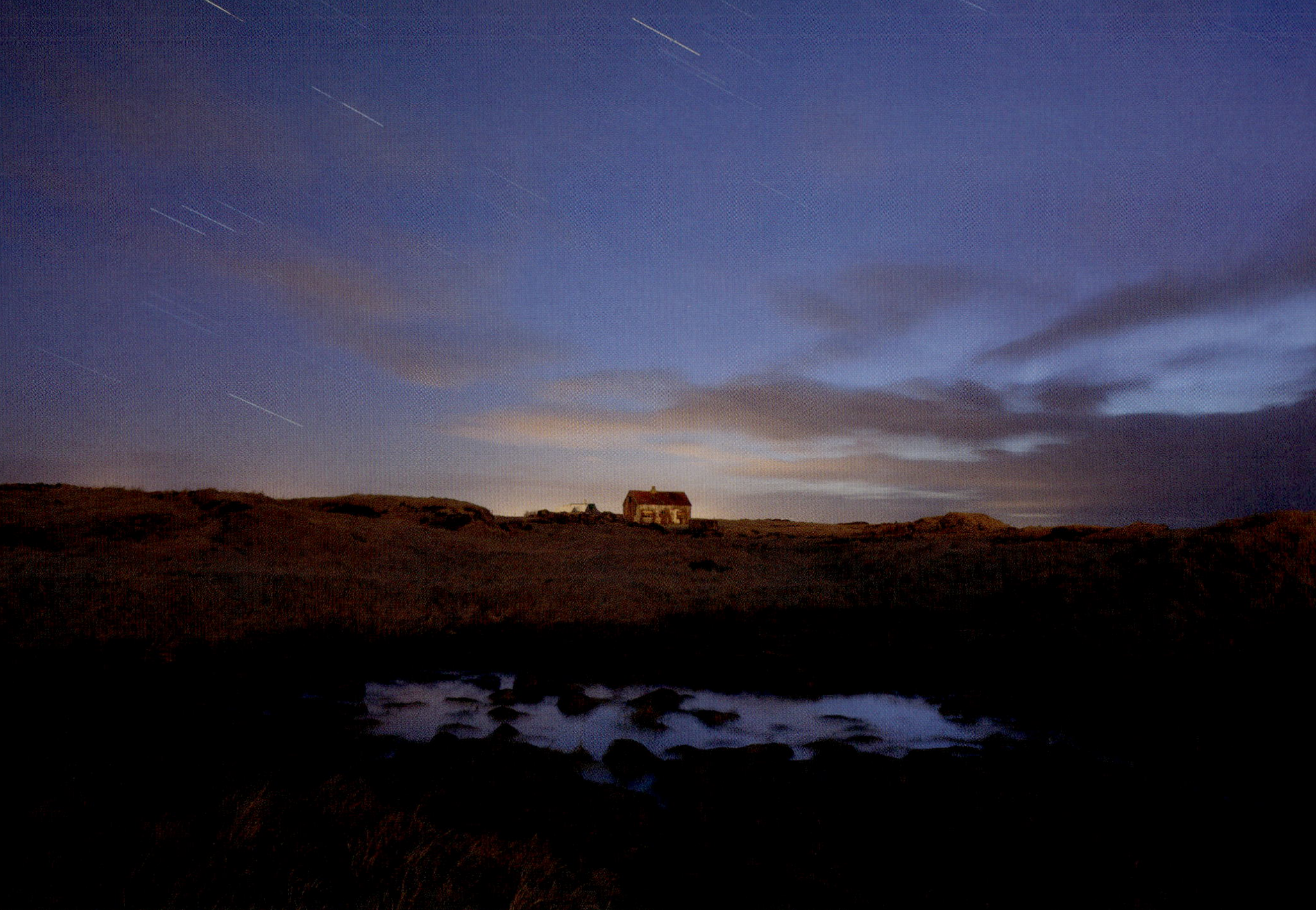

6

A lonely barn under a huge sky outside Reykjavik, Iceland

15 minutes, f8 at ISO 200, Canon 5D MK II, 28 mm f3.5 PC Nikkor lens. Waning gibbous moon. The landscape is lit by a combination of moonlight and the glow of distant city lights, and a small pool of water reflects the blue sky.

"Mission San Juan Bautista," California. 20 minutes, f5.6 at ISO 200, Canon 5D MK II, 28 mm f3.5 PC Nikkor lens. The light level was very low, as is indicated by the exposure, but there was distant ambient light falling on the mission and trees in addition to the light from the waxing gibbous moon. Fortunately, the lighting ratio of artificial to moonlight was just right.

Photographing by moonlight can be a sublime experience. Rarely do we find ourselves alone in nature with the time and attitude to reconnect with the natural world in a very real way. It only takes a little while for our senses to open up to the night, for stress to melt away, and for creative juices to begin to flow. For many people, night photography, especially under a full moon, is as much about the experience of being in a place and creating the image as it is about the final product. The peace and solitude afforded by a night of full moon photography bring ample opportunities to ponder the great mysteries of the universe.

After a few minutes for our eyes to adapt to the dark, it is fairly easy to see well enough to navigate the landscape, to see to compose images, and to connect with the Earth as well as

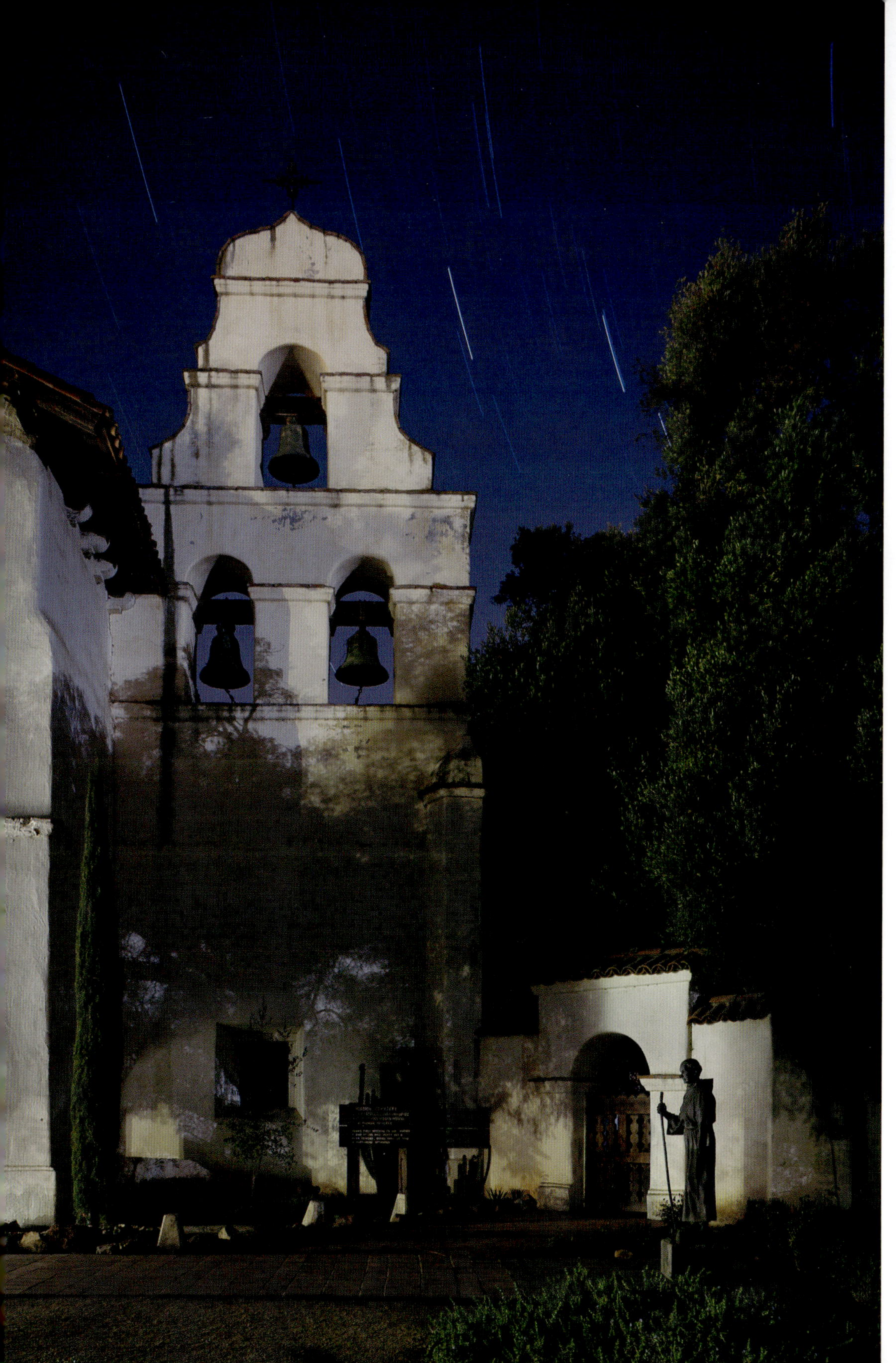

the heavens. Because of the light in the sky, only the brightest stars are visible, and recorded in photographs taken by moonlight. For the photographer, the greatest difference between astro-landscape photography and full moon photography is time. There is time to carefully consider the scene before the camera, how to show it, and whether or not to add our own light. Usually, photographers working with moonlight are less concerned with stopping the movement of the stars in the sky than with the potential for time—in the form of long exposures—to transform the landscape. Full moon photography generally involves long exposures at native ISOs and star trails rather than star points. Full moon photography is very different from astro-landscape photography but there's no reason not to use high ISOs and short exposures if you want to.

THE CHANGING NATURE OF MOONLIGHT

The Moon rises in the east and sets in the west every day, just like the Sun. The times depend on the phase of the Moon. It rises about 50 minutes later each day in the lunar cycle, and is present in the daytime sky as often as it is at night. Throughout the lunar cycle, the new moon waxes to become a crescent moon, a half moon, and a gibbous moon, and finally a full moon. It takes another 2 weeks to wane back to a new moon, completing the cycle every 28 days.

As the lunar cycle progresses, the Moon rises later each day during daytime, and it sets later and later each night. At the full moon, the Moon rises close to sunset, and it sets at about the same time that the Sun rises. As the Moon wanes, it rises during the night after sunset, rising later each night. It then sets in the daytime, after the Sun rises. The new moon rises and sets with the Sun. At first quarter the Moon rises about noon, and at last quarter it rises about midnight.

The position of the Moon in the sky is approximately inverse to that of the Sun. In other words, in the summer time when the midday Sun is high overhead, the Moon tracks a lower arc across the nighttime sky. In winter, when the midday Sun never gets very high, the Moon is directly overhead at night. Just as with sunlight, the angle of the Moon relative to the Earth will affect the length of shadows. Shadows from moonlight will always appear softer than shadows in sunlight in photographs because of the Moon's movement in the sky during extended exposures.

The Moon moves about its own diameter in the sky every 2 minutes, so a 2-minute exposure would show an elongated Moon that is twice as tall as it is wide. Long exposures that include the Moon in the frame will eventually render the Moon as a very bright and wide white line in the sky. An exposure of an hour or more begun at moonrise may show the Moon traveling entirely through the image and out of the frame, depending on the angle of view and the position of the horizon.

Most moonlight photography is done within a few days of the full moon because that is when there is the most light. Calculating precise moonlight exposures is somewhat difficult because of the complexity of the numerous variables and difficulty in achieving accurate measurements of those variables. There is considerable variation in the brightness of light from the full moon from month to month, but it is straightforward to determine the optimal exposure by performing a test exposure at high ISO, checking the histogram, and adjusting as needed.

DETERMINING EXPOSURE

There are very few light meters that are sensitive enough to measure moonlight, so metering is not usually an option when ambient light levels are so low. In September 2014, Nikon announced the D750, which has a light meter that reads light levels as low as −3 EV, which is essentially the light of the full moon at 40 degrees of elevation or higher. I have not had the opportunity to test the camera yet to see if it will measure moonlight in real-world situations. Those with a keen interest in mathematics and astronomy might enjoy calculating lunar luminance levels, but it is time consuming and not particularly necessary.

The amount of moonlight when the Moon is full will never vary by more than two stops (and usually considerably less) after it is well above the horizon. However, two stops represents a significant increase or decrease in brightness and needs to be accounted for in an exposure. There are several factors that cause moonlight brightness to vary. The phase of the Moon has the greatest and most obvious effect on lunar brightness, and fortunately it is relatively easy to compensate for. Simply adding a half stop of exposure to your baseline full moon exposure either 1 day before or after the full moon, and adding one stop of exposure 2 days before or after the full moon, will usually be sufficient to account for phasic variation in lunar brightness.

The brightness of moonlight varies by approximately three and a half stops of light between first or last quarter and full moon, based on the relative positions of the Earth, Sun, and Moon. Also, due to the elliptical orbits of the Moon around the Earth, and the Earth around the Sun, lunar brightness can vary by as much as 30 percent, or another one-third of a stop. The point when the Moon is farthest away from the Earth is called apogee, and perigee is when the Moon is at the closest point in its orbit. When the Moon is full at perigee, it is called a "Super Moon" because it appears larger and brighter in the sky.

The opposition effect, which is caused by retroreflective properties (think cat's eyes) of the Moon's surface, may account for an increase in lunar brightness of another one-third to two-thirds of a stop when the Sun is almost directly behind the Earth, or in opposition to the Moon. Determining whether the Moon is near its apogee or perigee of its orbit and the angle of incidence of the Earth and Sun relative to the Moon is relatively easy to accomplish with smartphone apps or from the internet, but I find it unnecessary and distracting from the enjoyment of photographing the moonlit landscape.

A more important consideration when photographing by moonlight is the Moon's angle of elevation above the horizon. In general, the higher the Moon in the sky, the more illumination it will provide to the landscape. The Moon becomes a useful light source when it reaches about 30 degrees above the horizon; the quality of moonlight is less appealing when it is directly overhead. Atmospheric conditions on the Earth can dramatically affect the intensity of

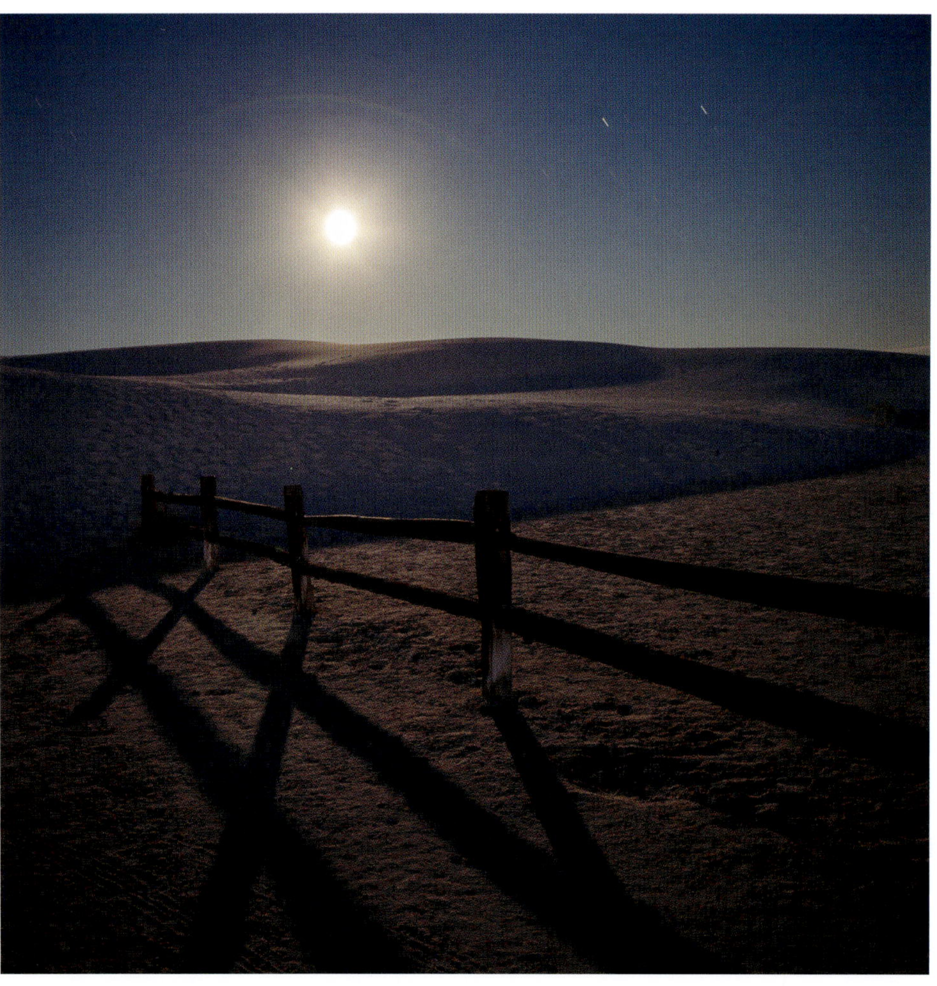

"Just Before Moonset and Dawn," White Sands National Monument, NM. 2 minutes, f8, 100 ISO, Canon 5D MK II, 28 mm f3.5 PC Nikkor lens. Full moon, predawn light. The light of predawn makes this image possible. Ordinarily, shooting directly into the Moon is little different from shooting into the Sun, but this shot was timed to manage the scene contrast.

moonlight reaching the surface of the Earth. It is fairly obvious that moonlight diffused by cloud cover will not only be dimmer than direct moonlight, but also softer and shadowless. It is less obvious that particles in the atmosphere, such as smog, dust, moisture, and even the air itself, can reduce moonlight intensity, especially when the Moon is near the horizon and the light must travel through considerably more atmosphere before it reaches the Earth. The difference in exposure when the Moon is directly overhead and when it is just above the horizon is about seven stops in clear, dry air, and considerably more in moist or dusty air. This is because moonlight travels through 40 times more atmosphere when the Moon has just risen than when it is directly overhead. A simple illustration of this effect is that it is possible to observe the sunset by looking directly at the Sun, but you cannot look directly at the midday Sun without damaging your retinas. Also for this reason, higher altitudes and clear winter skies may lead to slightly shorter exposure times.

PHOTOGRAPHING THE FULL MOON

When most people think of full moon photography, they understandably imagine taking pictures of the full moon. To the seasoned night photographer, however, full moon photography means photographing by the light of the Moon, which is a different thing altogether. If you want to include the Moon in your night photographs and record detail in the surface of the Moon while having a balanced overall exposure, you are generally limited to photographing on the actual day of the full moon, near moonrise and moonset, or by combining multiple exposures. This is the only time in the lunar cycle when the exposure for the Moon and surrounding landscape is approximately the same. It is very rare for the sunset and moonrise to occur at the exact same moment, and the two times can vary by as much as 30 or 40 minutes, even on the night of the full moon. The ideal photographic situation would be for the Sun to set about 10 minutes before the moonrise.

Latitude and season will determine how long conditions will be favorable to photograph the moonrise. Darkness always comes quickly near the equator, regardless of the season. At equatorial latitudes, it may be possible to photograph the moonrise successfully only a few nights of the year, depending on the congruence of sunset and moonrise times. In far northern or southern latitudes, twilight lasts much longer, and this increases the opportunities to photograph the moonrise. The following table illustrates differences in the length of twilight at different latitudes at different times of year.

	Twilight at summer solstice	Twilight at winter solstice	Twilight at equinox
Singapore Latitude 1°N	+/– 20 minutes	+/– 20 minutes	+/– 20 minutes
Boston Latitude 42°N	+/– 35 minutes	+/– 25 minutes	+/– 30 minutes
Helsinki Latitude 60°N	+/– 110 minutes	+/– 60 minutes	+/– 40 minutes

Because the difference between sunset and moonrise times change from month to month and year to year, you can see from the table how your chances of finding the Moon rising during twilight is greater the farther away from the equator you are. Once again, the reason to photograph the moonrise during twilight is because the exposures for the landscape and the Moon are the same for just a few minutes. When the full moon is high in the sky, it will be dark, and the difference in exposure for the Moon and landscape will be extreme, necessitating a compromise favoring exposure for one or the other. You'll either end up with a well-exposed landscape and a blown-out, overexposed Moon, or a very dark landscape with no details and a properly exposed Moon. For this reason, capturing detail on the Moon is for low-light twilight photography. True night photography tends to show the Moon as a streak, or, more commonly, does not include the Moon in the frame at all.

Because moonlight is reflected sunlight, and the surface of the Moon is approximately equal to middle grey in tonality, the exposure for a full moon that is high in the sky is roughly equal to a midday landscape exposure in full sunlight. This is also known as the Sunny 16 rule, which is expressed as $1 \div \text{ISO}$ at f16, where $1 \div \text{ISO}$ is used for the shutter speed. The exposure will vary within a stop or two depending on atmospheric conditions, the distance from the Moon to the Earth (which varies with the Moon's orbit), the angle of lunar opposition to the Sun, and, most importantly, the elevation of the Moon relative to the horizon. The Moon will always require considerably more exposure just after it has risen than when it is high in the sky. These are the same factors that affect the length of exposures when photographing the Moon itself, as well as by the light of the Moon. As with all night photography, the best results are achieved by shooting in the RAW mode and confirming the exposure with the histogram and flashing highlight functions.

Another way to include the Moon in the landscape is to take two separate exposures and combine them later in Photoshop or other software. The usual technique for this method is to first make an exposure of just the Moon surrounded by dark sky with the camera mounted on a tripod, using the longest available lens. Using your longest lens provides the most flexibility when pasting the Moon into another image because you will not have to increase the resolution of the image of the Moon to have it appear fairly large in the frame. After you have an image of the Moon, and because the same side of the Moon always faces the Earth due to their synchronous orbits, there's no reason not to use the same Moon image any time you want to use this technique. Although some purists will cringe at the thought, your Moon can now be incorporated into any photograph you like. It is very easy to select the Moon from the image and paste it into another frame, but it does take some skill to apply this technique without it being fairly obvious. For example, a wide-angle night view of a city skyline with a gigantic Moon filling the sky would not be very believable.

It is interesting to note that the Moon only appears much larger when it is near the horizon than when it is fully risen. This is an illusion due to the frame of reference provided by the Earth when the Moon is low in the sky. An easy way to confirm that the relative size of the Moon is constant in the sky is to hold a coin at arm's length in front of the Moon just after it has risen, and again after it is high in the sky. You may be surprised to see that the size of the Moon relative to the coin is unchanged, although to your mind the Moon seems much larger near the horizon. Additionally, the reason that the Moon sometimes appears pink, yellow, or orange when it is low in the sky is because of the greater amount of atmospheric particles the light must pass through at low angles.

PHOTOGRAPHING BY THE LIGHT OF THE MOON

Full moon night photography is quite different from shooting in urban areas for several reasons. First, to use moonlight as a primary light source, it is necessary to find a location that is away from streetlights and other artificial lights. Ambient light levels are much lower, which necessitates considerably longer exposures. Second, that same lack of artificial light sources makes for much less contrasty lighting situations than are typically found in urban and suburban areas. Finally, longer exposures and lower light levels provide the opportunity to add light—referred to as light painting in your photographs. Light painting is discussed in depth in Chapter 8.

A primary consideration for photographing by moonlight should be to establish a baseline exposure for a landscape lit by the light of the full moon. There are several rules of thumb you can use to make this determination, such as the Loony 16 rule, which assumes that the Moon is about 250,000 times dimmer than the Sun, or 18 stops less than the Sunny 16 rule discussed earlier in this chapter. Using the Loony 16 rule gives us an exposure of 44 minutes at f16, ISO 100, or 11 minutes at f8, ISO 100.

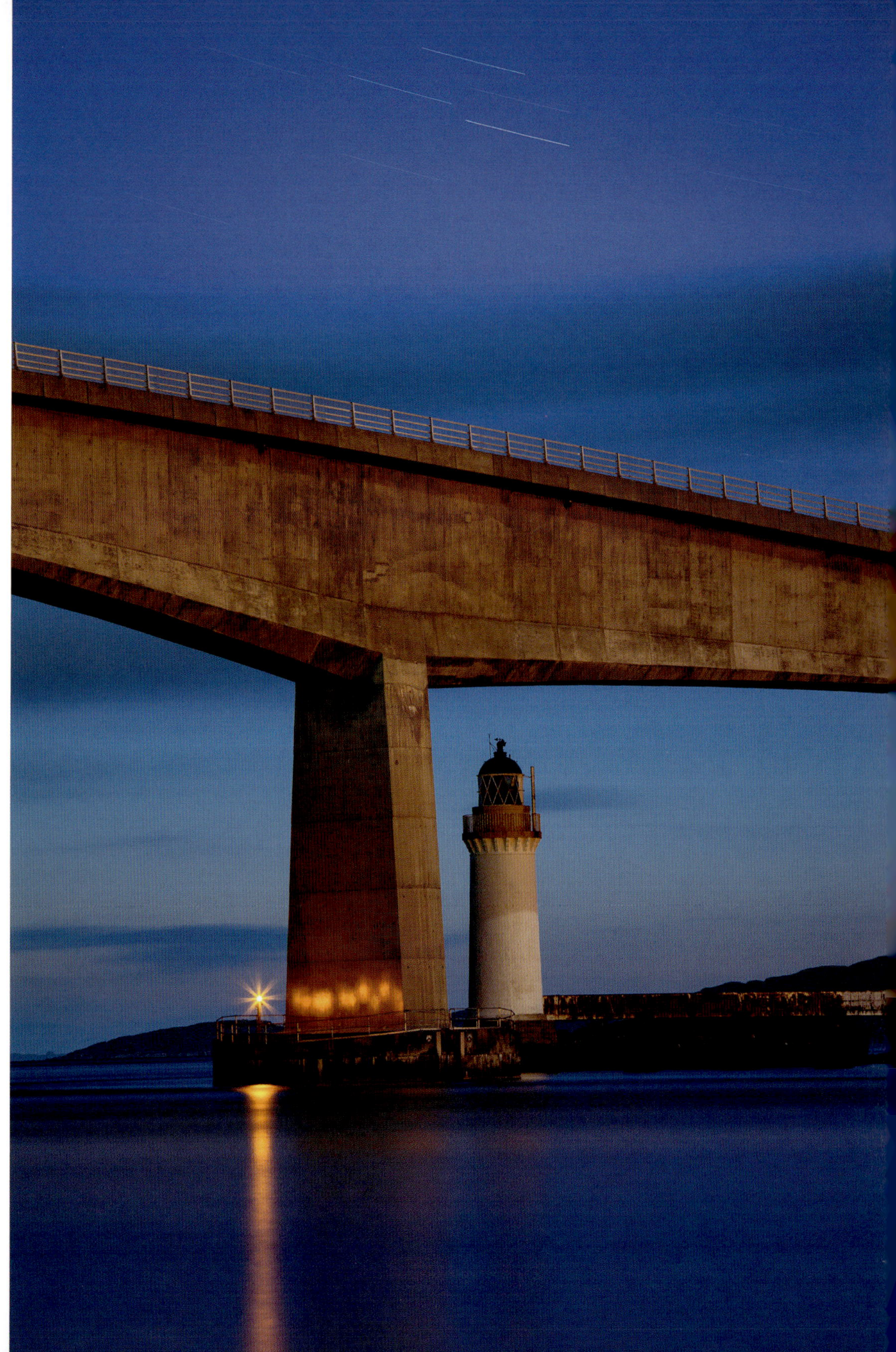

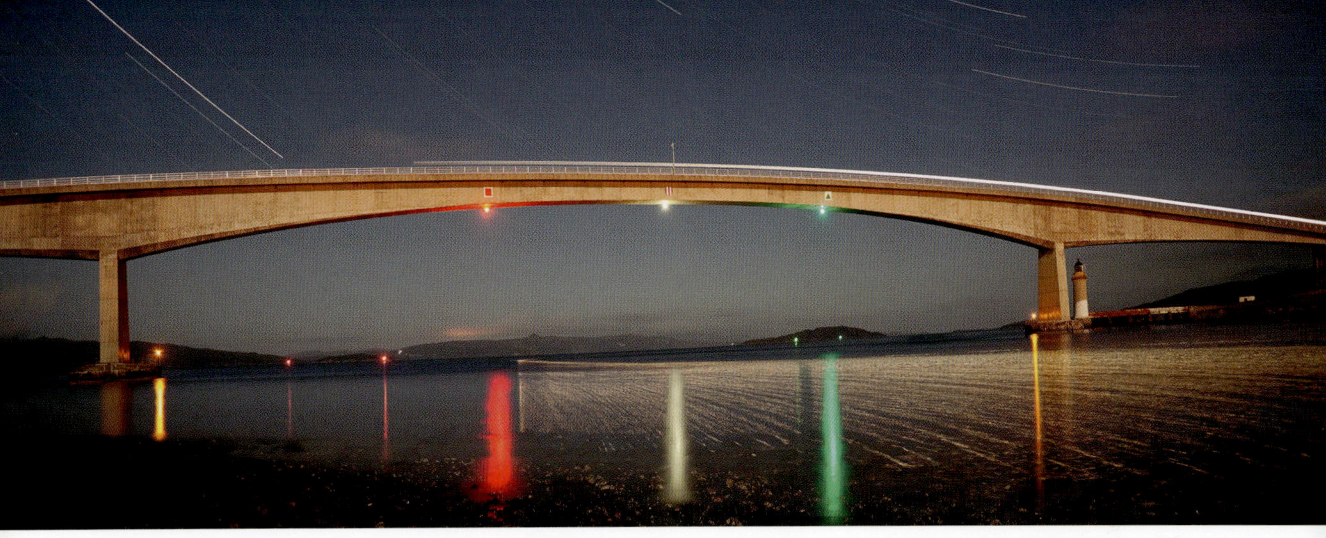

"The Skye Bridge," Isle of Skye, Scotland. 9 minutes (×10) f8, ISO 160. Last quarter moon. This image of the bridge that connects Skye to the mainland is a combination of 10 9-minute exposures, assembled using a technique called stacking to get longer star trails than you could achieve in a single exposure. Stacking is explained later in this chapter.

None of the various rules for moonlight exposures take into account all of the variables, whether it is cloud cover that varies during the exposure, changes in the altitude of the Moon over the course of a long exposure, the elevation above sea level and corresponding variance in atmosphere, or the influence of distance sources of artificial illumination. It is also important to consider the desired effect in the final photograph. Do you want a realistic nighttime appearance with deep, dark shadows, a brightly illuminated scene with full detail everywhere, or something in between? The histogram is the key exposure determinant for moonlight photography. Remember that when shooting RAW files, it is best to expose for a right-biased histogram. This will yield an image that almost looks like daylight, but exposing to the right will ensure clean and detailed shadows when the raw file is developed, especially with older or consumer-level cameras. For newer DSLRs, especially full-frame sensor cameras, simply providing enough exposure so that the histogram is not touching the left-hand edge of the frame is adequate. As a general rule, plan not to lighten your image in postprocessing, as this will exaggerate noise in the shadow areas of your images. Darkening an image by developing it down moves more exposure information into the shadows, which makes for cleaner images. If

"Skye Bridge and Lighthouse" by moonlight, Isle of Skye, Scotland. 6 minutes, f8, at ISO 320. Canon 5D MK II, 85 mm lens, last quarter moon. There's no rule about how bright or dark to make a moonlight image. Go for full on brightness, or make it look as dark as it was when you were there—it is up to you.

you are adding light, you will probably want to reduce the ambient exposure to make your light painting stand out more. Any light that you add to an image "counts" toward building a right-biased histogram. Ambient to added light ratios is discussed in detail in Chapter 8 on light painting.

Moonlight is sunlight reflected off of the gray surface of the Moon. The color of moonlight is about 4100 K, slightly warmer than daylight, but our eyes are more sensitive to blue in low light. The ability to adjust the white balance in camera and refine it even further is a great advantage for digital shooters. For the sake of consistency, it is a good idea to pick a color temperature between 3400 K and 4200 K, and use that setting for all of your moonlight photography. Most DSLRs have a Kelvin setting in the white balance options, and this can be set to the desired temperature. Older or less expensive models may not have this feature, in which case you'll have to decide between the preset white balance settings, usually either tungsten or daylight. As long as you are shooting RAW files, the white balance can be adjusted in postprocessing, but it is good practice to try to get the white balance as close to the way you want it to look in-camera. Changing the white balance will change the appearance of the histogram, which can influence the way you determine exposure.

HIGH-ISO EXPOSURE TESTING

When photographing in very dark environments, the camera's light meter is usually unable to suggest a starting exposure. It can be a tedious exercise of trial and error to determine the best exposure to use. Waiting 15 or 20 minutes for an exposure to finish, and then an additional 15 or 20 minutes for long-exposure noise reduction (LENR), can be very frustrating if the end result is an image that is considerably under- or over-exposed. Waiting that long for an image only to find out that the shot was not properly focused, or that the camera was not level, isn't any better. To take some of the guesswork out of calculating long exposures, and to save time in doing so, there is a simple method for testing exposures at high ISOs.

The aim of high-ISO test exposures is twofold. The first purpose is to confirm focus, composition, camera alignment, and to make sure there are no unintended distractions in the frame. The second purpose is to quickly determine the correct exposure in moonlight or other very dark situations. High-ISO testing is only useful in situations where the exposure will be more than 2 or 3 minutes. Using this procedure will save you a lot of time and minimize frustration in the field.

By increasing your digital camera's ISO to the maximum setting, and opening your lens to the widest aperture, you can take a well-exposed moonlight photograph in just a few seconds. This flexibility is enormously liberating, and provides the opportunity to get a feel for a location by doing a series of quick handheld shots to assess the exposure, lighting, and framing of a shot without investing too much time. Most people can handhold a 2- or 3-second exposure steady enough to evaluate whether or not the scene merits a full-length exposure. When working in moonlight, or other very low-light-level environments, temporarily raising the ISO and doing a short exposure, and then translating it into a longer exposure at optimum ISO, will save you a lot of time.

Efficiency can be further increased by choosing test exposure settings that allow for second to minute translations. In other words, you'll want to use the exposure settings that enable you to have the same number of minutes at your native ISO as you have seconds at your testing ISO. This greatly simplifies exposure calculation in situations with very low-light levels.

Testing is performed by raising the ISO six stops above your camera's native ISO. This is because there are six stops of exposure between one second and one minute, and using this formula allows for a direct translation from testing exposure in seconds to final exposure in minutes. Some older cameras may not have a six-stop range in ISOs, and an aperture adjustment is required to compensate. If this is the case, you must open the aperture during the test by one stop for every stop less than six in the ISO range of the camera.

To access the highest ISO settings on some cameras, you may need to activate ISO Expansion in the camera's menu. Also, the highest ISO may be indicated by something like H2. If this is the case, you may need to refer to your camera's manual to figure out which numerical ISO the H settings correspond to. Generally, H3, H7, and H1 refer to one-third, two-thirds, and one full stop of additional sensitivity above the highest ISO without expansion enabled, and if your camera menu says only H1 and H2, that means the expanded range is in increments of full stops only.

For example, cameras that have a native ISO setting of 100 can test at ISO 6400, and cameras with a native ISO of 200 can test at ISO 12,800. This means that if you determine that the correct exposure during testing is 8 seconds at ISO 6400, the final exposure would be 8 minutes at ISO 100, using the same aperture for both shots. If you have a native 200 ISO camera, and you determine that the correct testing exposure is 20 seconds at ISO 12,800, the native ISO exposure would be 20 minutes. Of course, it is possible to use other ISOs than your native 100 or 200; you'll just need to do an extra calculation if you wish to shoot at 400 or 800.

This leaves the question of where to begin with a testing exposure. As a general rule, 10 seconds, ISO 6400, f8 or 5 seconds, ISO 12,800, f8 is a good starting point for full moon conditions. On moonless nights, 20 seconds, ISO 6400, f2.8 or 10 seconds, ISO 12,800, f2.8 is a reasonable starting point. Exposures during other lunar phases fall somewhere in between the full moon and new moon exposures. Keep in mind that there is no one correct exposure,

"Kathy's Kosmic Kowgirl Kafe," Terlingua, TX.
4 minutes, f8, ISO 100 final; 4 seconds, f8, ISO 6400
test shot. Full moon. High-ISO test shots allowed me
to fine-tune the composition and exposure before
committing to a long exposure. This trailer was part of
a compound that served a tolerable breakfast alongside
the road in Terlingua—a place with very limited
options. The ambient exposure was purposefully left
underexposed so that the light painting would stand
out more.

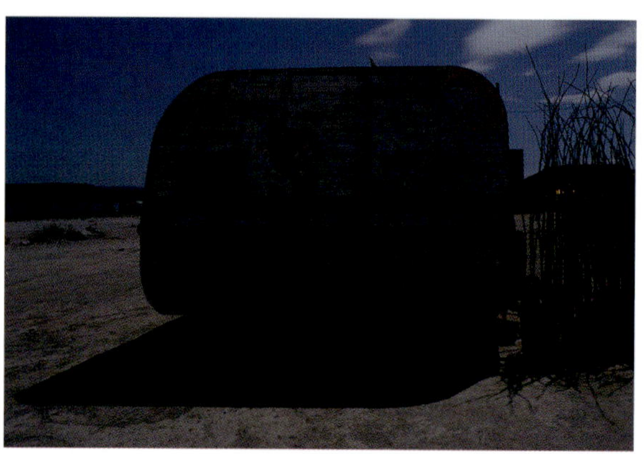

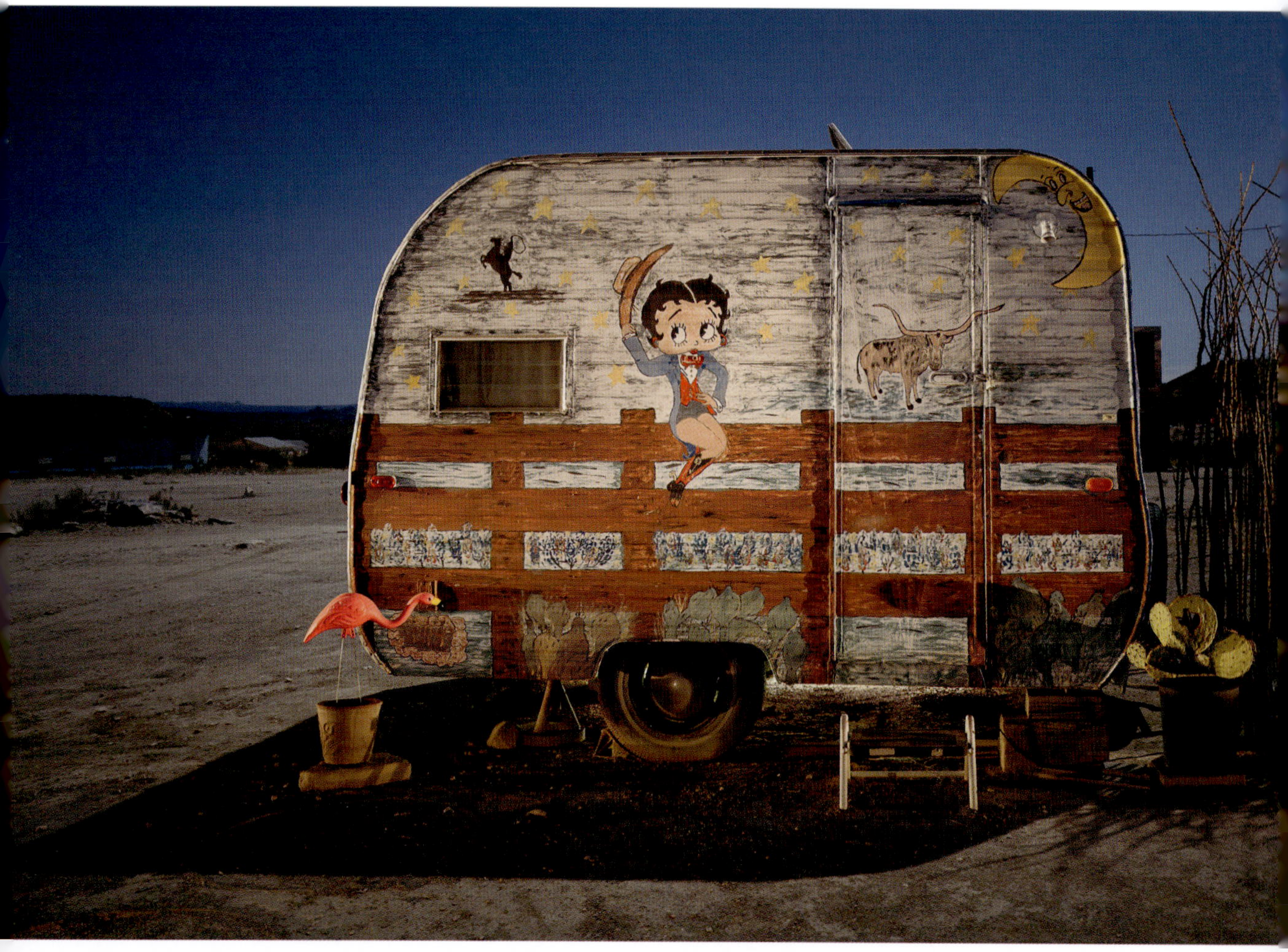

but many possibilities that will all yield different results. Use the exposure that best meets your needs based on your intended appearance for the final shot.

In a moonlight only image, a full, right-biased histogram may be best for optimal image quality, but might also yield an image that looks too bright in the field. It is almost always better to darken an image rather than lighten it in postprocessing providing you do not have any clipped highlights.

If you will be adding light to the shot, a better ambient exposure might be one that is just enough to avoid shadow clipping. In this case, the highlights will be provided by the added light, which will also push the histogram to the right. Simply increase or decrease the exposure until the desired histogram is achieved, and remember that the important axis of the histogram is the horizontal one—don't be concerned if the highlight section of the histogram is short and the shadows are tall. You still have a right-biased histogram and a good exposure if the tail of the histogram extends far to the right.

It is important to be aware that this technique only works for ambient light exposure testing, and not for light painting. If you will be adding light painting to the shot, do the high-ISO testing first for the ambient light only. Trying to calculate the lighting with a six-stop difference between exposures can be challenging with strobe, and is impossible with flashlights, especially if you need to change apertures to compensate for inadequate ISO range in your camera. Once the ambient exposure has been determined, set your camera at the final shooting ISO and aperture, and then begin to experiment with the lighting. Because the ambient exposure has been predetermined, there is no need to wait for the full exposure to evaluate the lighting. Once you have finished lighting, end the exposure and check the lighting, disregarding the areas where no light was added. Modify the light as needed until the desired result has been achieved, making mental or written notes as you go along if the lighting is complex.

When you are satisfied with the lighting, then go back and combine the full ambient exposure with the lighting to complete the final image. Keep in mind that once you see the combined results, you may wish to either increase or decrease the ambient exposure to change the ratio of ambient to added light. Of course it is possible to combine separate ambient and lighting exposures in postprocessing, but I find real satisfaction in being able to complete the shot in-camera rather than using Photoshop to finish the job.

You might want to begin by shooting a few frames at your camera's maximum ISO and lens' maximum aperture before high-ISO testing or even before putting the camera on your tripod. These handheld shots will be blurry from camera movement, but it is a great way to get a rough idea of how the scene might look, and whether or not it merits investing the time required to complete the shot. If your camera has customizable shooting modes that allow you to preprogram exposure settings, programming one of those custom modes to your high-ISO testing settings and another to your native ISO low-light settings is a convenient way to quickly and easily switch back and forth between testing and native shooting settings.

One final thought is that high-ISO testing comes with a catch—and that is, forgetting to reset your ISO to the camera's native ISO setting after testing. Almost every night photographer has stories about the best photograph they ever took being inadvertently exposed for 20 minutes at ISO 6400!

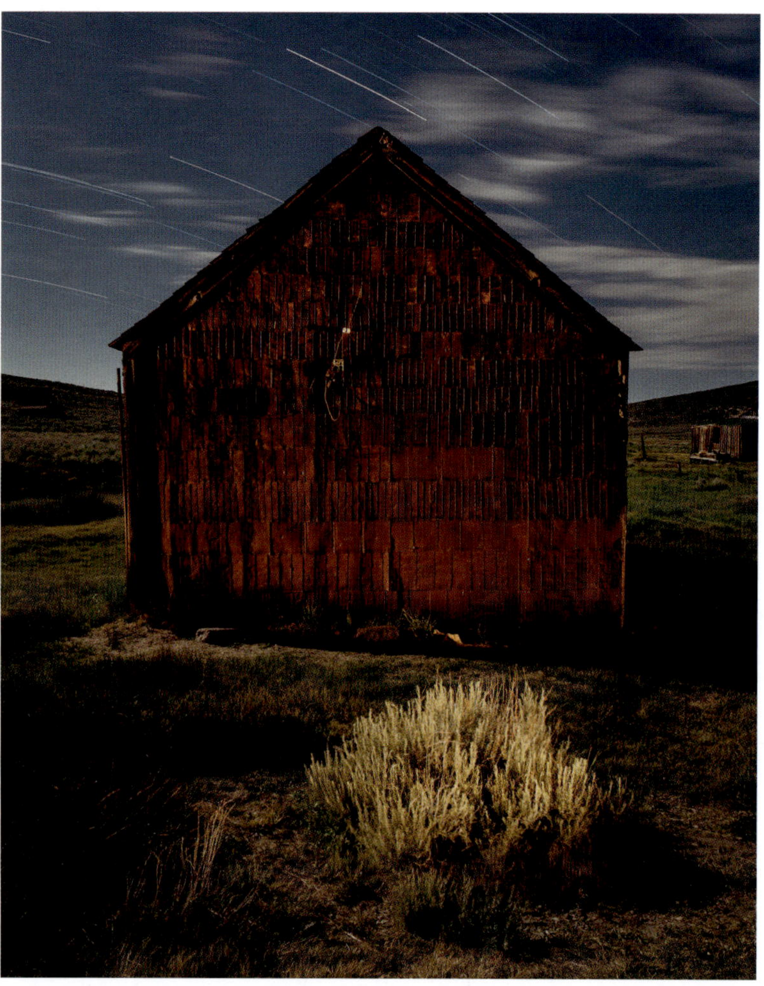

"Bodie Ghost Town State Park," California. 8 exposures, 5 minutes each, f8 at ISO 400, Canon 5D MK II, PC Nikkor 28 mm f3.5 lens. A stacked composite of eight 5-minute exposures, with light painting in the first exposure. Bodie Ghost Town State Park, California.

MOONLIGHT AND LIGHT POLLUTION

Unless your shooting location is far from any urban area, even a small town, your full moon exposures are likely to be influenced by artificial lights. Along the east coast of the United States, for example, there's so much light pollution that it is virtually impossible to avoid all artificial light. In some cases there may be only a faint glow on the horizon from a distant town, which won't affect your exposure, but it will register in the image. Sometimes nearby streetlights may be bright enough to influence your exposure, and the white balance of the scene. Adjusting for the exposure is simple enough, but it is important to be aware that stray light can be a factor. Nearby streetlights will affect the color of the foreground, while distant lights can influence the color of the sky, especially on cloudy nights, and especially near the horizon. Unless the artificial light sources are overpowering the moonlight, it is probably best to use your normal moonlight white balance and tweak the images during development as

"Kingsland Point Light and the Tappan Zee Bridge," Sleepy Hollow, NY

90 seconds, f8 at 160 ISO. Canon 5D MK II, 35 mm f2.8 Zuiko Shift lens. Full moon and light pollution. A myriad of artificial light blends with the light of the full moon to dramatically cut down on exposure times, and adds color to the scene.

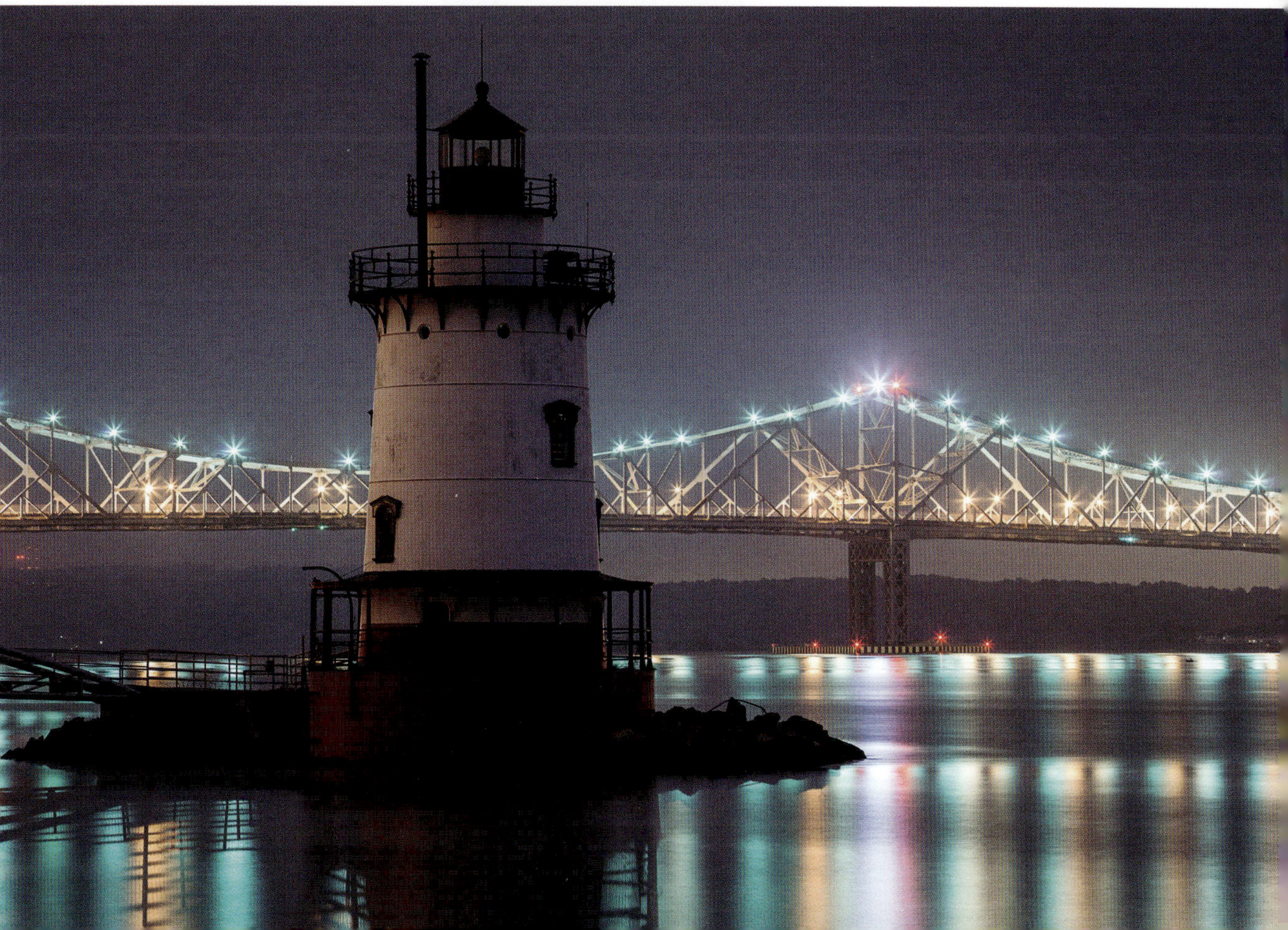

needed. Shooting toward the Moon can create dramatic images, but it also increases the likelihood of lens flare, increases overall contrast, and changes the exposure. More than likely, you'll use a shorter exposure in backlit situations, and may need or want to fill in the shadows with some added light of your own. Chapter 8 discusses adding light, or light painting.

STAR TRAILS VERSUS STAR POINTS

Although the movement of both the Earth and the Moon affects the Moon's appearance in night photographs, it is primarily the rotation of the Earth that causes stars to appear as trails in the sky in night photographs. All of the heavenly bodies in the universe are indeed moving through space, but the relative distance of Earth to stars makes the movement of the stars

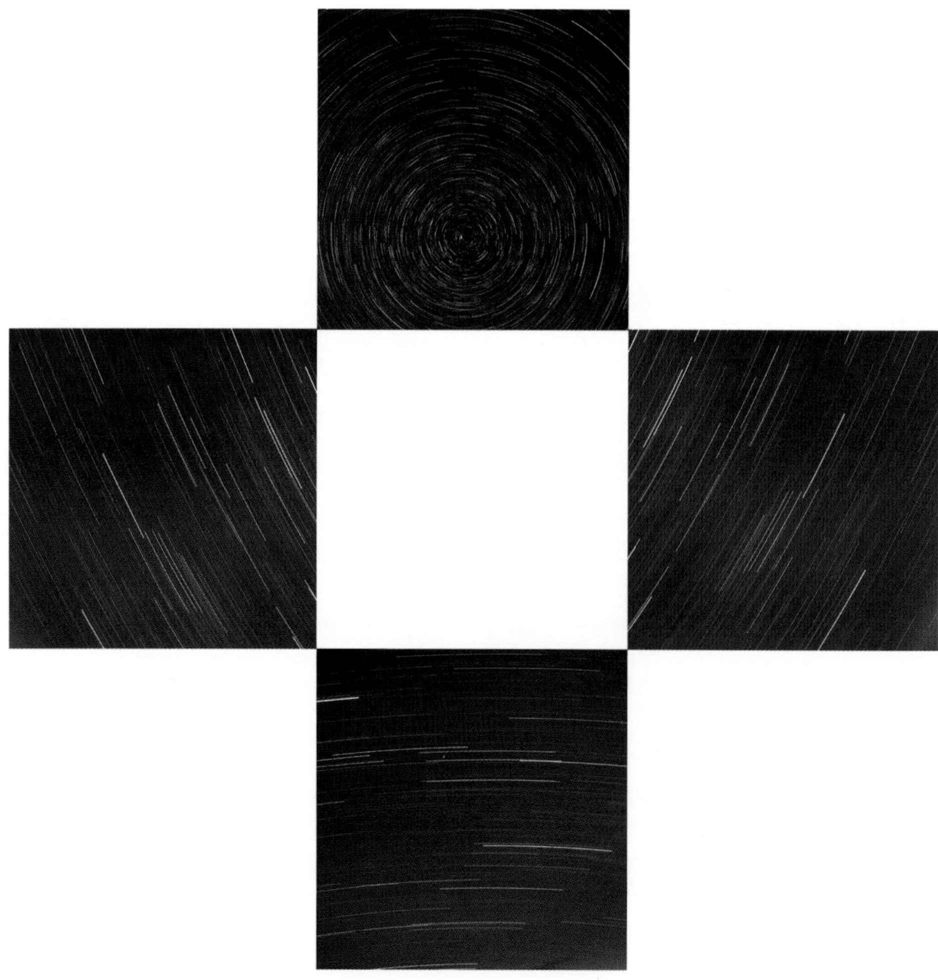

Star trails in cardinal directions. The stars form trails at different angles depending on the direction that the camera is pointed.

insignificant during the length of an exposure. To illustrate this phenomenon, imagine a car traveling at 60 miles an hour passing directly in front of you versus the same car a mile away. The near car would pass through your entire field of vision in less than a second, and the distant car would remain in your field of vision for quite some time. Multiply this effect by light years, and you can see how the stars are so far away that their movement relative to their distance doesn't matter.

On the other hand, the Earth's rotation causes stars in night photographs to appear as lines in as little as 10 seconds, depending on camera format, lens focal length, and which direction the camera is pointed. In the northern hemisphere, all of the stars in the sky appear to revolve around Polaris, also known as the North Star. This is because Polaris is the closest star to alignment with the northern polar axis of the Earth. As a result, pictures including the northern sky will show relatively short star trails circling the North Star. Photographs of the eastern sky will show star trails that resemble a slightly curved forward slash, and photographs of the western sky will have star trails that look like slightly curved back slashes. Photographs taken with the camera pointed due south will show long star trails that appear relatively parallel to the horizon.

STAR TRAIL FACTS
Here are a few generalizations about star trails:

- The further away from the North Star your camera is pointed, the longer star trails will appear in your photograph. A star trail from a 5-minute exposure in the northern sky will be much shorter than one from a 5-minute exposure in the southern sky.
- The wider an aperture and higher the ISO, the more stars will be recorded in the image.
- Longer focal length lenses will yield longer, brighter star trails than shorter lenses at equivalent apertures.
- The less ambient illumination at ground level, and in space, the more stars will register in the image. You will not see many star trails on full moon nights or in the city.
- Broken cloud cover will cause star trails to appear as irregular dotted lines rather than lines. Chances are that if you can't see the stars, your camera can't either.
- Star trails will have slightly different colors depending on the age or type of the star. Younger, hotter burning stars will be cooler or bluish in color. Older, dying stars will be warmer or reddish in color.
- The lights of airplanes, or light reflected from satellites, and even the International Space Station, may appear in your photographs of the night sky.

STACKING IMAGES FOR LONGER STAR TRAILS

Camera settings

Ironically, another challenge of incorporating stars into your night photographs is that it can be difficult to get an exposure long enough for significant star trails. With many cameras, it is difficult to make digital exposures longer than about 15 or 20 minutes without generating a lot of noise, especially in warm conditions. It is also difficult to do long exposures if there is too much ambient light or moonlight without stopping down to a small aperture, which in turn minimizes the number of stars that appear in the image. Long star trails can enhance an image, especially if the direction of the trails works in conjunction with the rest of the composition. Very long exposures of the northern sky can be quite dramatic, because the stars appear to revolve around the North Star, creating a circular pattern in the sky.

Stacking, or combining a series of relatively short exposures, is a great way to create longer star trails with digital cameras. Shooting images for stacking is straightforward, but there are many different ways to combine the images after you have captured them. The concept of stacking

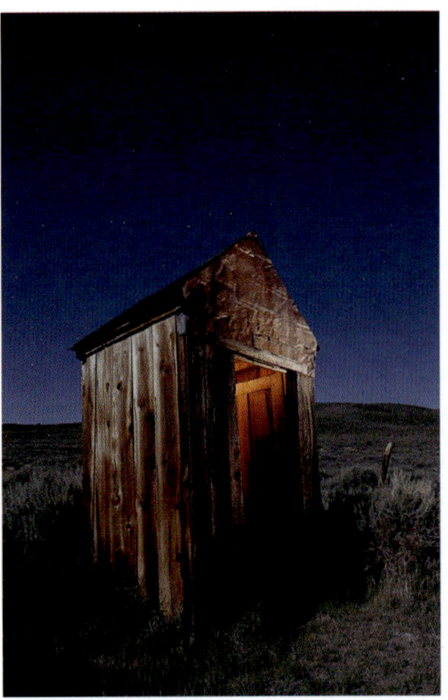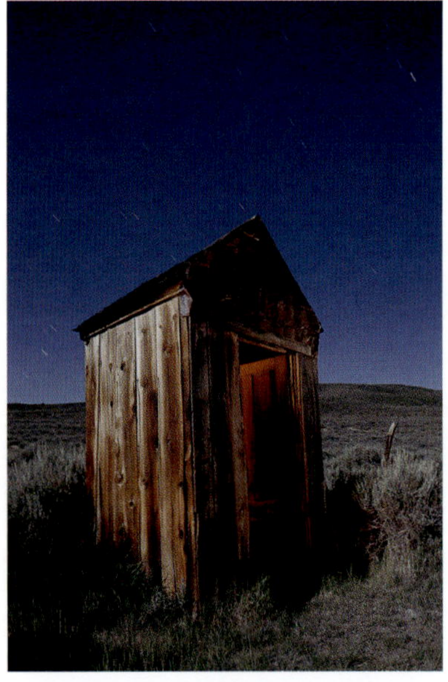

"Outhouse," Bodie Ghost Town State Park, California. Star point and short star trail images. 15 seconds, f5 at ISO 1600, and 4 minutes, f6.3 at ISO 200. Canon 5D MK II, Canon 24 mm f3.5 TS-E lens.

16 × 4 minutes, f6.3 at ISO 200, Canon 5D MK II, Canon 24 mm f3.5 TS-E lens. The three variations of this image by Scott Martin show three different ways of photographing a subject. The high-ISO short exposure is unsatisfactory because relatively few stars are showing due to the full moon in the sky out of the frame. The single frame long exposure is also not very satisfying because the star trails are rather short. By combining a series of exposures using Stack-A-Matic, Scott was able to achieve a much better image with longer trails than he could have achieved in a single image that would have been time limited due to overexposure.

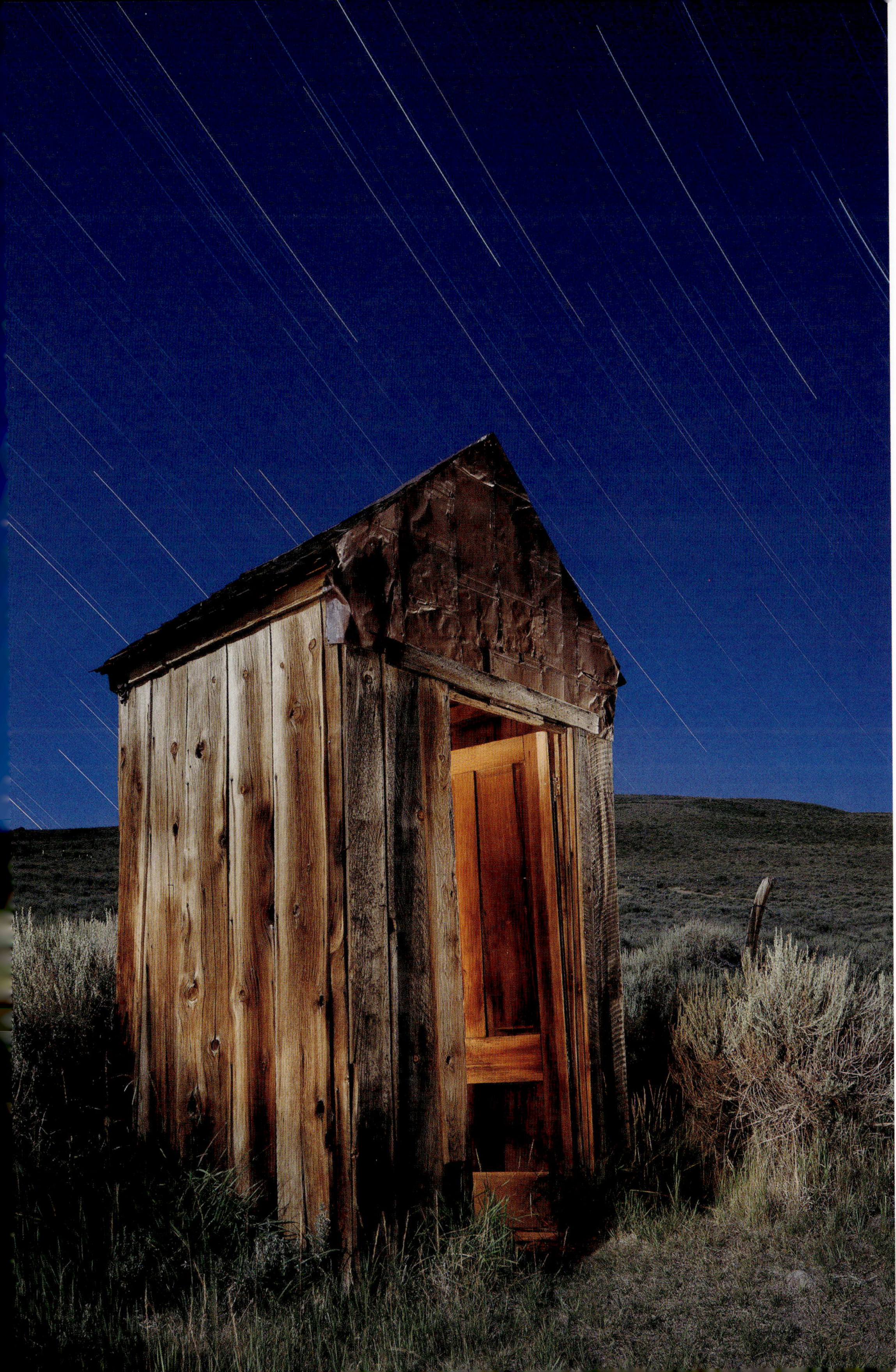

is simple: by shooting a sequence of exposures and blending them in postprocessing, it is possible to minimize noise and achieve exposure times not possible with a single frame. There's no special equipment required to create stacks of images for long star trails, but an intervalometer is immensely helpful. There are numerous ways to stack images, but I'm presenting only what I consider to be the best option in this book: Dr. Brown's Stack-A-Matic. Scott Martin and Russell Brown collaborated in 2011 to create this free Photoshop script specifically designed for stacking images for star trails. You can download it at russellbrown.com. No other stacking method (other than manually recreating Stack-A-Matic in Photoshop) leaves you with a layered Photoshop file, which allows for working on individual images—after the stacking is completed.

Say, for example, an airplane flew past in the sky during one of the exposures, or some other source of stray light appeared in a single frame of your stack sequence. The unwanted parts of individual images can easily be masked out, and the other layers can be used to fill in the empty space. With a flattened file, there is much less flexibility in correcting any errors.

Let's look at the procedure for exposing, processing, and stacking images to create long star trails with digital cameras. The first step is to set up the camera. The basic settings are the same as for most night photography: native ISO, RAW quality, bulb exposure mode, turn off IS or VR lens functions, manual focus. Make sure your battery is fully charged. External grips that contain a second battery are useful for this type of work because the combination of long exposures and cold can drain a battery quickly. It is essential to turn LENR off. LENR works by creating a second exposure without opening the shutter immediately after the initial exposure is completed. The result is that most cameras will not be able to take another exposure until the LENR is finished. The Canon 5D/6D/7D family of cameras does allow continued shooting for a few frames while holding the exposures in the camera buffer, but after about 45 minutes the buffer fills, and no further images can be captured until the processing is completed and space

CAMERA SETUP FOR STACKING

- Exposure mode set to bulb.
- LENR should be turned off.
- Quality set to RAW.
- Use your camera's native ISO.
- Turn off the image stabilizer on IS or VR lenses.
- Use an aperture between f2.8 and f8.
- Focus manually using hyperfocal, live view, or infinity focus, and confirm that the stars are sharp.
- Use an intervalometer programmed with 1-second intervals between exposures.
- Perform a high-ISO test to confirm composition, focus, and exposure.

is cleared in the buffer memory. Wide-angle lenses allow for greater depth of field if you have a foreground element that needs to be in focus.

Capturing the images

Now it is time to compose the shot. Choose a location that is far from artificial light sources, and has something of visual interest in the foreground. Even the lights from a distant town on the horizon can have a negative impact on your image by obscuring dimmer stars that are low on the horizon. Make sure that the closest object in your foreground is not too close to the camera because you will be shooting at a fairly wide aperture, albeit with a wide lens. If you want to create a star circle, you'll need to locate the North Star (Polaris). The North Star can be located with the aid of the Big Dipper. After finding the Big Dipper in the sky, locate the two stars on the right-hand edge of its cup. Extend an imaginary line through these two stars until it intersects with another bright star, and you've found the North Star. There is no polar star in the southern hemisphere, but the Southern Cross points toward the South Pole. The stars in the southern hemisphere will also form a circle over the South Pole, but it is more difficult to establish your camera position without the aid of a polar star. The North Star does not have to be placed in the center of the frame to create the circular star pattern in the sky. It can even be cropped just outside of the frame to make a semicircle of star trails.

Select the widest aperture that enables you to focus on your foreground, preferably f8 or larger. The larger the aperture you use, the more stars will appear in the image because dimmer stars will not be recorded with small apertures. If you choose to include foreground elements in your shot, focus using the hyperfocal distance for one f stop larger than your actual aperture setting. In other words, if you are shooting at f8, set the hyperfocal distance for f5.6. This will ensure that the stars are truly sharp and crisply in focus in the image. You could also focus on the foreground for the first frame, and then refocus at infinity for the remaining frames where only the sky will be used in the stack. The sky can be masked out of the foreground layer to hide any gaps in the star trails that appear during the time it takes to refocus. If there is nothing of importance in your foreground, perhaps only the horizon, focus at infinity and use the aperture setting one stop down from maximum. You should check foreground focus using live view and a flashlight, with the lens stopped down to your shooting aperture. Live view can also be used to focus at infinity on the stars, and to assist in composing the shot by establishing the four corners of the image. You may wish to do high-ISO test shots to help you establish the composition and position the foreground elements and stars in relation to each other. However, it is a good idea to do a full-length exposure to test the direction of star trail movement in your shot. The stars will not move enough during a high-ISO shot to clearly establish the pattern and direction of movement.

If you plan to do any light painting in the foreground, you should test the lighting at your working ISO to determine the best way to illuminate the shot and how much light is needed. Because you'll be investing a long period of time in this procedure, you'll want to make sure everything is perfect.

The length of your exposures is determined by a combination of factors. All of the shots should be the same exposure. It is not absolutely critical that the times are exact, but the aperture must remain constant in order to stack the images. You'll need enough exposure to get a reasonably good histogram—there should be no shadow clipping at the very least, but as usual, a right-biased histogram is best. If you are shooting when there is little or no Moon present, it may be difficult to have the perfect histogram without significantly raising your ISO, which should be avoided if possible. Open up the lens instead. The quality of your camera and the ambient temperature are a factor in determining your exposure times. Shorter exposures should be encouraged for entry-level cameras and warm temperatures, which both tend to create noise. Professional, full-frame sensor cameras and cold temperatures allow longer exposures with less noise. In suboptimal conditions, exposures of a few minutes may be the longest you can do without introducing noise. Mid-level prosumer cameras on cool nights might allow for 10–15-minute exposures, while the best cameras can get away with 30–40-minute exposures on cold nights. Battery technology has improved along with camera technology, and newer batteries are remarkably long lasting. Still, you should begin this process with a freshly charged battery, especially on cold nights, which drain battery power faster. Experience will guide you as to how much time you can get out of a single battery.

There is no rule on the number of shots or total length of time, but you'll probably want to have an hour and a half or more of total time for shots of the northern sky. Star trails get longer the further they are from Polaris. Star trails will be shorter in images of the northern sky and longest in the southern sky. It is easy to see why if you take a photograph of the night sky that includes Polaris and other stars, and then extend two lines from Polaris to the beginning and end of any star trail in the image, you would end up with two lines that intersect at Polaris, and extend infinitely outwards at a constant angle. The distance between the two lines near Polaris is very short, and increases the further away from it you go. The measurement of that angle is a representation of the length of the exposure, measured in degrees of a circle. There are 360 degrees in a full circle, which represents a full revolution of the Earth, or a 24-hour day. Accordingly, a 180-degree angle would indicate a 12-hour exposure, a 90-degree angle would

"Star Spinning Tufa," Mono Lake State Preserve, Lee Vining, CA

12 × 10 minutes, f4.5, ISO 200. Canon 6D, 24 mm f1.4 Rokinon lens. This stack of 12 images was made during a night photography workshop at Mono Lake in California's Eastern Sierra. There were photographers all around, and each frame contained someone else's light painting somewhere in the image. Fortunately, Stack-A-Matic adds an empty layer mask to each image, so it was relatively quick to mask out the parts of each layer that I did not want to use. The only other stacking method where that would be possible is to manually combine the layers in Photoshop, which is essentially the same thing—only far more time consuming.

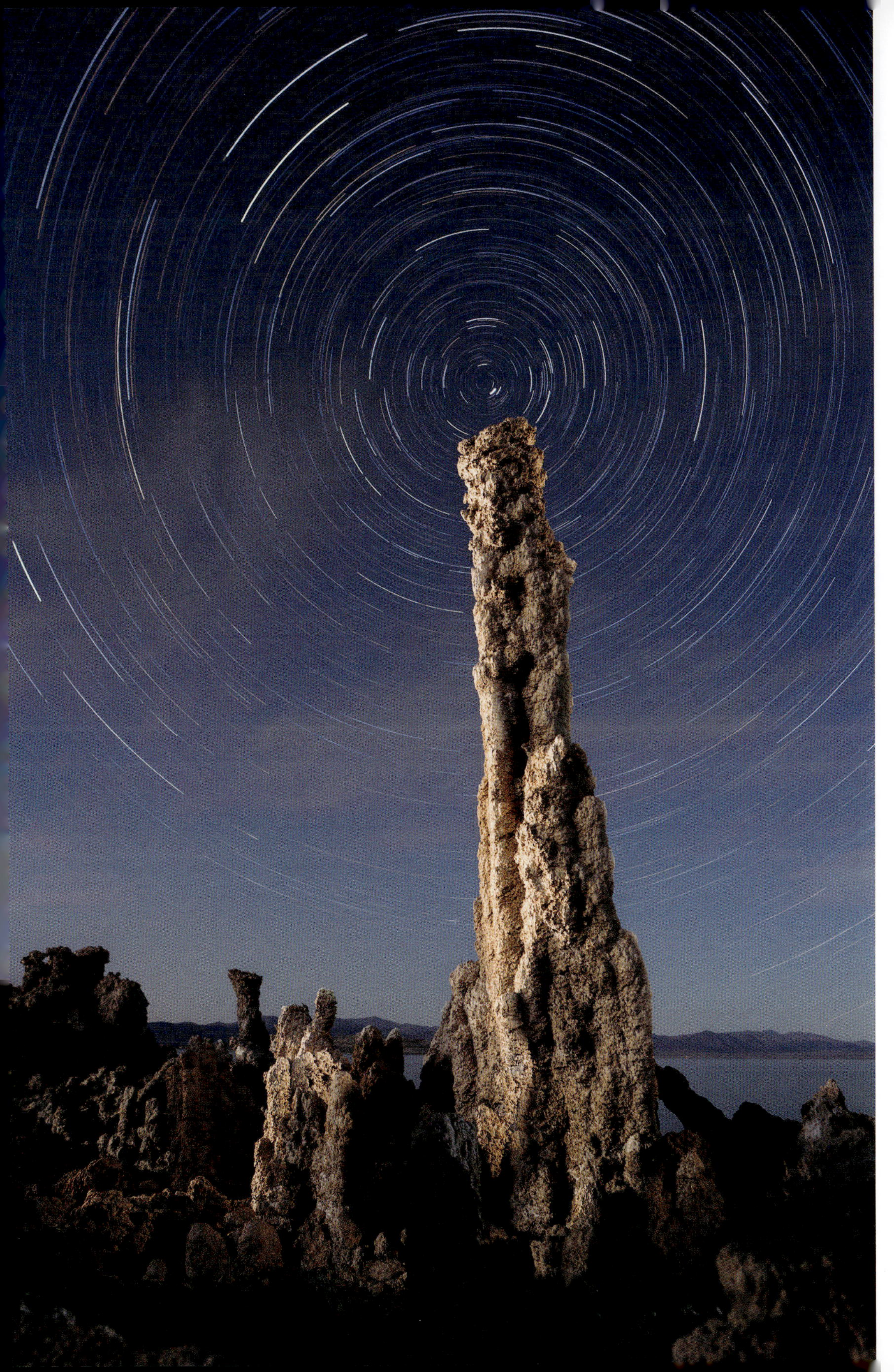

represent a 6-hour exposure, and a 15-degree angle is equivalent to a 1-hour exposure. You can determine the length of any exposure that includes Polaris using a measurement of the angle formed by connecting the beginning and end of a star trail to Polaris, and applying the following formula: $> \div 360 \times 24$ = exposure length, where $>$ = angle. For example, let's say you measure a 24-degree angle then $24 \div 360 = 0.0666 \times 24 = 1.6$. This number indicates an exposure of 1.6 hours, which can be further multiplied by 60 to get the number of minutes: $1.6 \times 60 = 96$ minutes. Whew! That's probably more math than you are looking for, but it is interesting to be able to determine exposure length simply by looking at a photograph. Back to the procedure.

Program your intervalometer to take a series of consecutive shots with a 1-second interval to ensure minimal gaps in the trails. Longer intervals will show obvious gaps in the star trails, making them appear as dotted lines. It is not possible to set a zero interval. If you do not have an intervalometer, set the camera shutter speed to 30 seconds, the camera drive to continuous, and lock the release open to force the camera to take continuous exposures until you close the release, the memory card is full, or the battery dies. You will end up with many more frames and a huge file on your computer, but it can be done this way. Any lighting should be done during the first and last exposures because if you mess up and have to eliminate a frame, you don't want it to be in the middle of your sequence. If you were to remove one of the middle exposures, it would leave unsightly gaps in the star trails. By lighting the first and last frames, you have the freedom to choose whichever frame you like better, and discard the other.

CAPTURING IMAGES FOR STACKING

- Expose for a right-balanced histogram or at least no shadow clipping.
- Base exposure length on your past experience with your camera's noise levels and the ambient temperature.
- Base the total time on desired length of star trails.
- Without a timed release, use 30-second exposures with camera on continuous drive and a locking release.
- Add light painting if desired on the first and last exposures only.
- Take an extra identical exposure at the end of the sequence with the lens cap on and the eyepiece covered. This can be used for a manual dark frame subtraction if excessive fixed pattern noise cannot be removed by other means.

Processing and combining the images

There are many ways to stack images; you can combine images as layers in Photoshop or use a specialized application created just for this purpose. In the pages that follow, we'll go through the steps to combine them as layers in Photoshop using Stack-A-Matic. You can stack as many images as the memory in your computer will accommodate. It is great to have star trails that stretch all the way through an image, but it is not so great to crash your computer by trying to stack 100 20 megabyte RAW files. Large image stacks take lots of processing power, and take a long time to render. If you don't have a timed release and are stuck using 30-second exposures, you will undoubtedly have many frames to stack. At some point, it might make sense to create two or three stacks, flatten them, and then combine the flattened stacks together in another stack. Establishing the longest noise-free exposure length your camera can handle, given the ambient temperature at the time of capture, will speed up and simplify your postprocessing workflow.

IMAGE STACKING WITH STACK-A-MATIC

1. Begin by importing your images into your RAW file converter application of choice.
2. If you did light painting on more than one frame, choose which frame you will use, and discard the others.
3. Develop this image as you normally would, setting the white balance and other adjustments. Apply chromatic aberration adjustments as needed, and noise reduction, taking care that the star trails are not obscured by overly aggressive noise reduction. If necessary, you'll be able to reduce the noise further in the final, flattened image.
4. Synchronize the image developments with the other images to be stacked.
5. It is probably best to hold off on local adjustments until after stacking is completed.
6. Unfortunately, Stack-A-Matic cannot be accessed directly from Lightroom. In Adobe Bridge, select the images that you want to stack.
7. Choose Tools>DrBrown'sServices>Stack-A-Matic.
8. Use the following settings in the pop-up dialog box: Create layers / Set Blend Mode: Lighten / Auto Align (optional) / Add Layer Mask To Each Layer / Mask Reveals Layer.
9. Once completed, all of the images will be stacked together as layers in one Photoshop file.
10. If there are any airplane trails or other artifacts you wish to remove, now is the time. If there are elements to specific layers you not wish to have in your final image, use the empty layer mask created by Stack-A-Matic for those layers and brush out the unwanted portions with black foreground ink. After carefully reviewing the combined image for problems, flatten and save. You may also wish to save the layered document, but it will be quite a large file. It is unlikely that a stacked image will have much noise at this point, but if there is you can implement noise reduction in Lightroom or Photoshop.

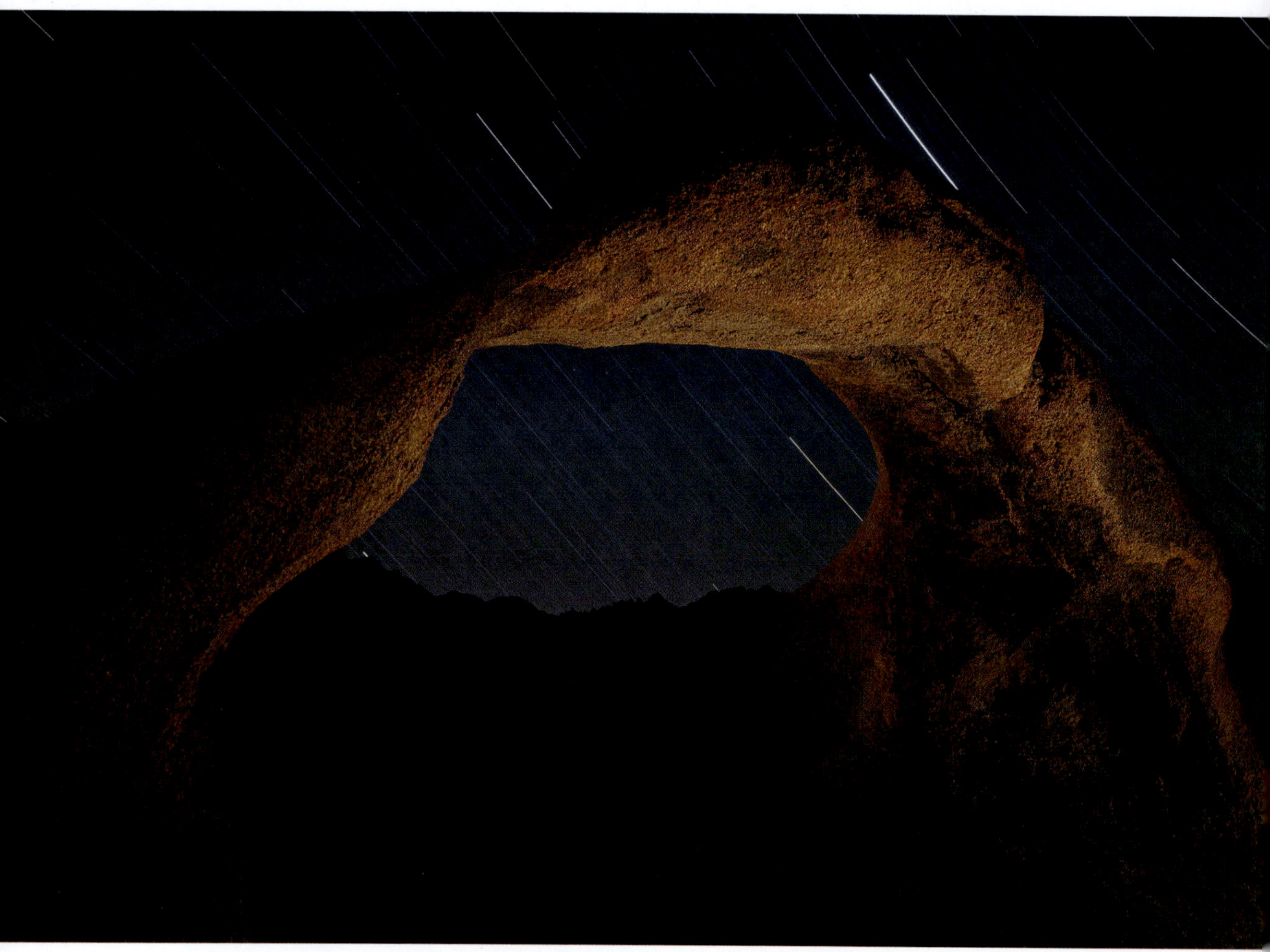

"Mobius Arch," Alabama Hills, Lone Pine, California by Scott Martin

Light painting exposure: 84 seconds, f7.1, at ISO 100. Star trail exposure: 2804 seconds, f7.1 at ISO 100. Canon 5D MK II, Canon 24 mm f3.5 TS-E lens. Scott combined two exposures for this dramatic image—pushing the limits of his camera with a 47-minute exposure for star trails. He didn't want to risk ruining his time investment with poor light painting, so he decided to add his lighting in a second, separate exposure. He still used Stack-A-Matic, even though the final image was created from only two frames. Keeping the light painting separate was a way of ensuring that the time invested in the long exposure would not be ruined by bad light painting.

7

POSTPROCESSING FOR NIGHT PHOTOGRAPHY

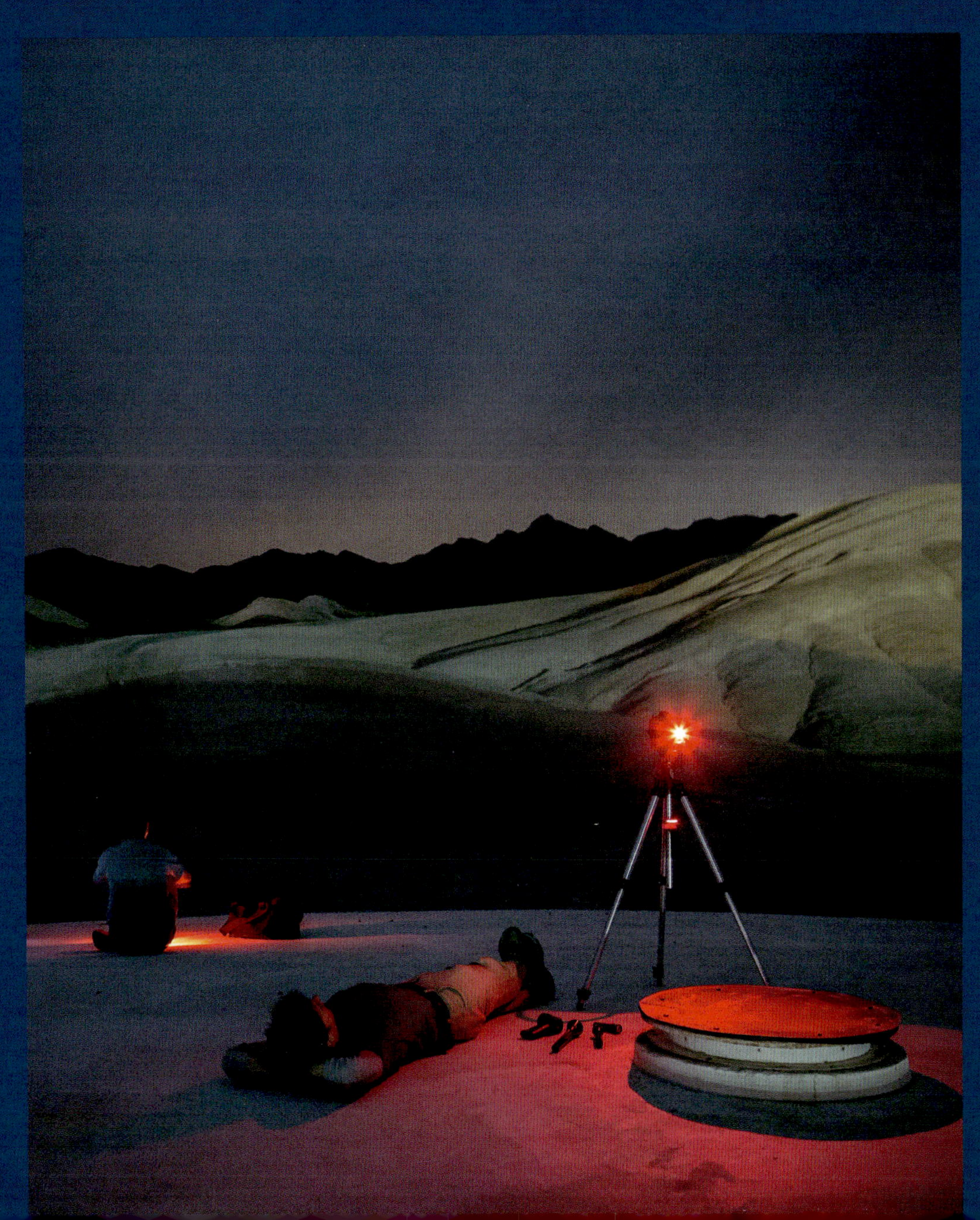

There are many different software choices to develop your images, and lots of differing opinions on the best way to do it. For some light painters, the choice of whether or not to develop images at all is a valid question. Others choose to compile layer after layer of different exposures to achieve the look they want. There is no right or wrong way to do it—you should do what works for you. In this chapter, I present a description and examples of my own postprocessing techniques. I do not make any claim that mine is the right way or even the best way. I have developed a workflow that works for me based on my own experiences in working with digital imaging technology and from what I have learned from my workshop partner Scott Martin, a digital imaging and color management professional who has been working with digital imaging since 1990. This chapter is intended to provide a general overview of using Lightroom to process RAW night photography images.

In short, my workflow philosophy is to make sure that I get as much right as possible in-camera, and to use the most elegant and simple postprocessing techniques that preserve as much of the image data of the original RAW file as possible. The pervasive attitude of, "you can fix it later in Photoshop," does not appeal to me. I'd rather spend my time under the stars than in front of a computer—but that's just me, and it is the approach to photography that I try to impress on my students.

I process all of my images in Adobe Lightroom. A small percentage of images are then opened in Photoshop, primarily when stacking images to create long star trails, to combine images into a panorama, or occasionally to blend different exposures of the foreground and sky. If I am blending multiple exposures, it is to compensate for either extreme luminance differences in foreground and sky or to increase depth of field using focus stacking. On very rare occasions, I'll blend several exposures together where parts of each frame have been lit separately. I try to do all of my lighting in a single frame, but that's not always possible. One good example would be an astro-landscape photograph with a 20-second exposure that needed to have three to four different elements lit from different positions. I have been known to run around waving lights like a madman, but I can't cover the ground as quickly as I used to—at least not with the grace and style I'd like to be remembered for. I'd rather get the shot in several frames than not at all. After the work in Photoshop is completed, the PSD files are then saved back into my Lightroom catalog next to the original RAW files. On occasion, I use the Lightroom Enfuse plugin for exposure blending. This is a great option as it can be initiated directly from within Lightroom, and the enfused files are automatically brought back into the catalog. It is fast, simple, and clean— but it is not for every image. It doesn't work with starry skies because you would end up with double stars, and no layer mask to obscure one set of them. There is no single solution that works in every situation, or for every person for that matter. Just as with every other chapter in this book, I present what I have learned in my 30 years of photographing at night in the hope that you will take my recommendations as a starting point for your own photography, not as the definitive solution to everything.

WHY LIGHTROOM?

There are two main reasons to use Lightroom as your primary photo software rather than a combination of Bridge and Photoshop—Digital Asset Management (DAM) and Parametric Image Editing (PIE). DAM means importing, annotating, cataloging, storing, retrieving, and distributing digital files: in our case, digital photographs. Adobe Bridge is merely an image browser, it does not create a database or a catalog that keeps track of our files, and it cannot automate the tasks of DAM. Lightroom does just that.

Lightroom facilitates instant retrieval of images through a wide variety of search parameters. Say, for example, that you wanted to find all of the night photographs you had ever taken. In a folder-based system using Bridge, you'd have to manually search through all of your folders, and either move or make copies of them to gather them in one place. With Lightroom, you can instantly find them (provided you had key-worded them with the term "night") and create a virtual folder called a Collection that includes all of those images. Now let's say that you wanted to find all of your night photographs of windmills or lighthouses or bridges, taken anywhere in the world under a full moon with a wide-angle lens. How long would that take you? With Lightroom, it would be less than 30 seconds.

With a traditional folder-based system, it is easy to run into trouble because most images could be placed in a number of different folders—night, bridges, ocean, full moon, summer, 2015, trip to California, etc. So where do you store a night photo of a bridge under the full moon shot on a trip to California in 2015? Do you make copies for several different folders? That could get you into a world of trouble in very short order, and it has done just that for many, many people. I see it all of the time on my workshop students' computers. With a database system like Lightroom's catalog, all of your images are permanently stored in unprocessed RAW format in a location assigned by Lightroom; but you can instantly find them by entering a single or multiple search terms. Lightroom uses Collections to point you to groups of images that share common characteristics that you specify—without moving or duplicating them. You can easily find all of your night photographs of bridges under a full moon for example. You can even keep multiple versions of your photos without filling up terabytes of hard drive space because the copies are virtual. This brings us back to PIE.

A RAW file is designed to preserve all of the unprocessed data captured by a camera sensor. When you open a RAW image in Photoshop, your image is processed and converted into a rasterized graphic or bitmap file, which is simply a grid of pixels. Once you save the rendered or processed file, any changes are permanent, and future changes are written over the previous ones, which eventually degrades the image. Rendered bitmap files are considerably larger and far less malleable than RAW files. A typical RAW file from an 18 megapixel camera might be 18–22 megabytes, but once it is rendered and adjusted in Photoshop, it might be three to four times that size, even without creating additional layers. Multiply that by thousands of photographs, and it is easy to see how you would need a lot of storage space for those rendered files.

Unlike Photoshop, Lightroom is a PIE. This means that it does not rasterize the RAW files, and all of the changes you make to the files are saved as metadata, a list of instructions indicating how the file should be rendered when you choose to do so. Here's the beauty of it: the RAW file is always preserved in its original, compact state. Anytime you export a rendered file, it is a temporary, use-specific file for printing, posting online, sending to clients, or emailing to your mum. All that you keep on your hard drive are the RAW files and the metadata that includes the adjustments you have made, the keywords you've assigned, the camera EXIF data, your contact and copyright information, and various other bits of data associated with the Lightroom catalog, like membership in collections and Develop module snapshots. All of that metadata takes up only a few bytes of storage space—less than a one-page Word document.

Photoshop has grown into a huge application with a vast array of capabilities that is used by professionals ranging from neurobiologists to physicists, animators, web designers, and yes, even photographers. Lightroom is an application developed by Adobe just for photographers. One day perhaps there will be Darkroom, just for night photographers, but until then Lightroom works for me. It is not meant to replace Photoshop, but to complement it. I believe it is a better way to manage and develop our digital photographs.

Even though Lightroom is far simpler and easier to learn than Photoshop, it is beyond the scope of a single chapter to provide a comprehensive guide to Lightroom. My intention is to show basic development of typical examples of night photography images, and how the various tools are used specifically for them. I have found that for most people, the format of short video lessons found on lynda.com is a great way to learn software, and Chris Orwig's Lightroom class is very much in line with the way that I use it. If you are more inclined to read a book, I recommend Martin Evening's The Adobe Photoshop Lightroom Book: The Complete Guide for Photographers. This is a huge, comprehensive guide, and not necessarily intended to be read cover to cover, but it has the best information on Lightroom in print.

THE DEVELOP MODULE TOOLS: BASIC

First let's look at the tools in the Develop module, and then some different types of night photography images, and the steps used to develop them and bring them to final form. The tool panels are generally designed to be used from the top down. There's no hard and fast rule, but it is generally a good idea to work your way down from top to bottom. The exception might be the Lens Corrections: Lens Profile and Chromatic Aberration are often applied on import along with Identity And Copyright metadata as part of an import preset. Not every tool needs to be applied to every image—less is more, especially if you already have a well-exposed image.

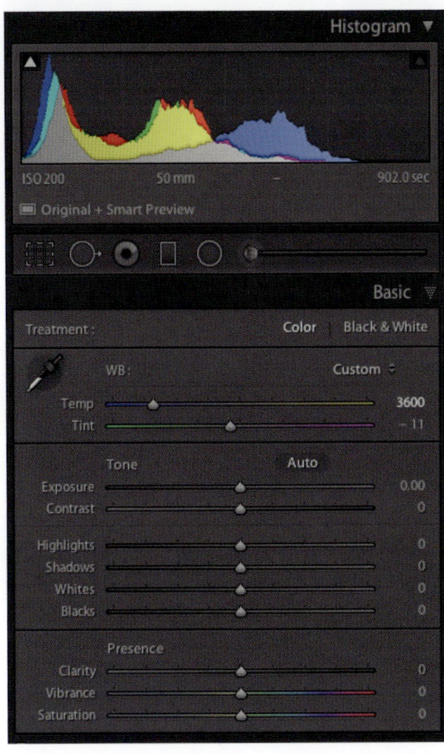

Screenshot of the basic panel. The tools in the basic panel should be used before moving on to the other adjustments, with the exception of anything applied with an import preset.

At the top of the tools panel on the right-hand side of the Develop module is the Histogram. The two little triangles in the upper corners can be toggled on and off to hide and reveal clipping in the highlights and shadows. Red indicates highlight clipping and blue for shadow clipping. Visualizing the clipping is helpful when using the tools in the Tone panel. Below the histogram, the image exposure data is displayed: ISO, focal length, aperture, and exposure time. Below that are the Local Adjustment Tools, which we discuss later.

Next comes the Basic panel. White Balance is the first thing you should adjust. Using the eyedropper tool neutralizes color wherever it is applied in the image. I often use the eyedropper in several different spots in the image that are more or less neutral in actual color—clouds, sidewalks or other concrete objects, asphalt pavement. This quickly gives you an idea of the potential color palette of the image. In most night images, especially if there are multiple light sources illuminating the scene, White Balance is subjective. If you click on a spot and like the results, use that for your White Balance. Frequently, I make minor adjustments with the temperature and tint sliders after using the eyedropper, usually warming the image slightly, but White Balance should be your first adjustment.

Next are the Tone adjustments: Exposure, Contrast, Highlights, Shadows, Whites, and Blacks. These tools were reworked and greatly improved with the 2012 process version that was first implemented with LR4. If you are using version LR3 or earlier, you will have a different set of tools, therefore I strongly recommend upgrading your software. It will be the best $79 that you ever spent on photography.

The Exposure slider does what you would expect, it increases or decreases the overall exposure with emphasis on midtone brightness, but it also sets the white clipping point. In general, set the exposure slider until the image brightness looks good. If you feel that there may be highlight clipping, toggle on the triangle in the upper right corner of the histogram, or for a more precise clipping indicator, hold down the Option/Alt key while using any of the

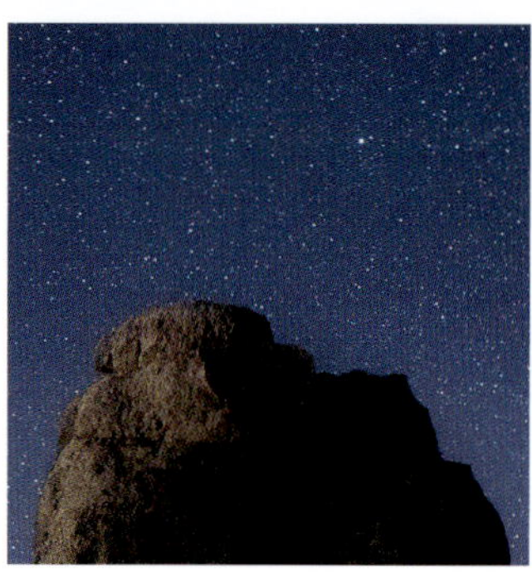 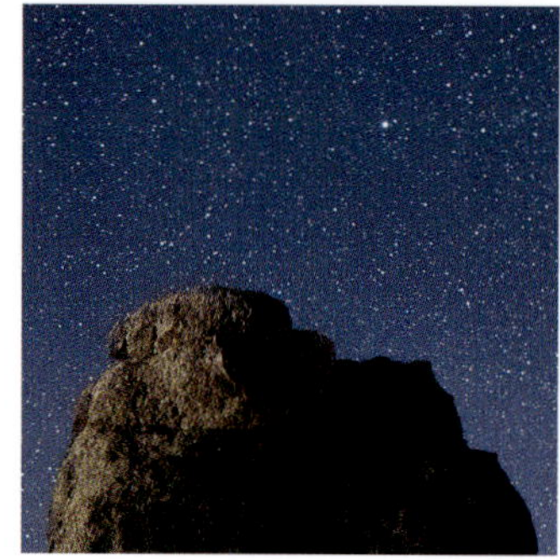 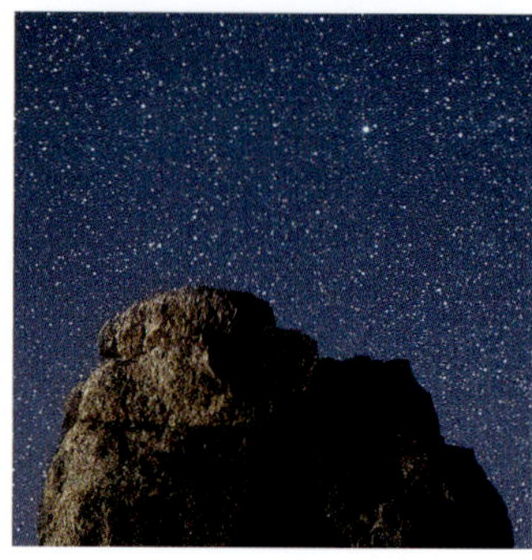

Image detail showing negative clarity, neutral, and positive clarity applied to show the effect on the stars. Negative clarity is a softer look. Positive clarity makes the stars stand out more. It is a matter of personal choice.

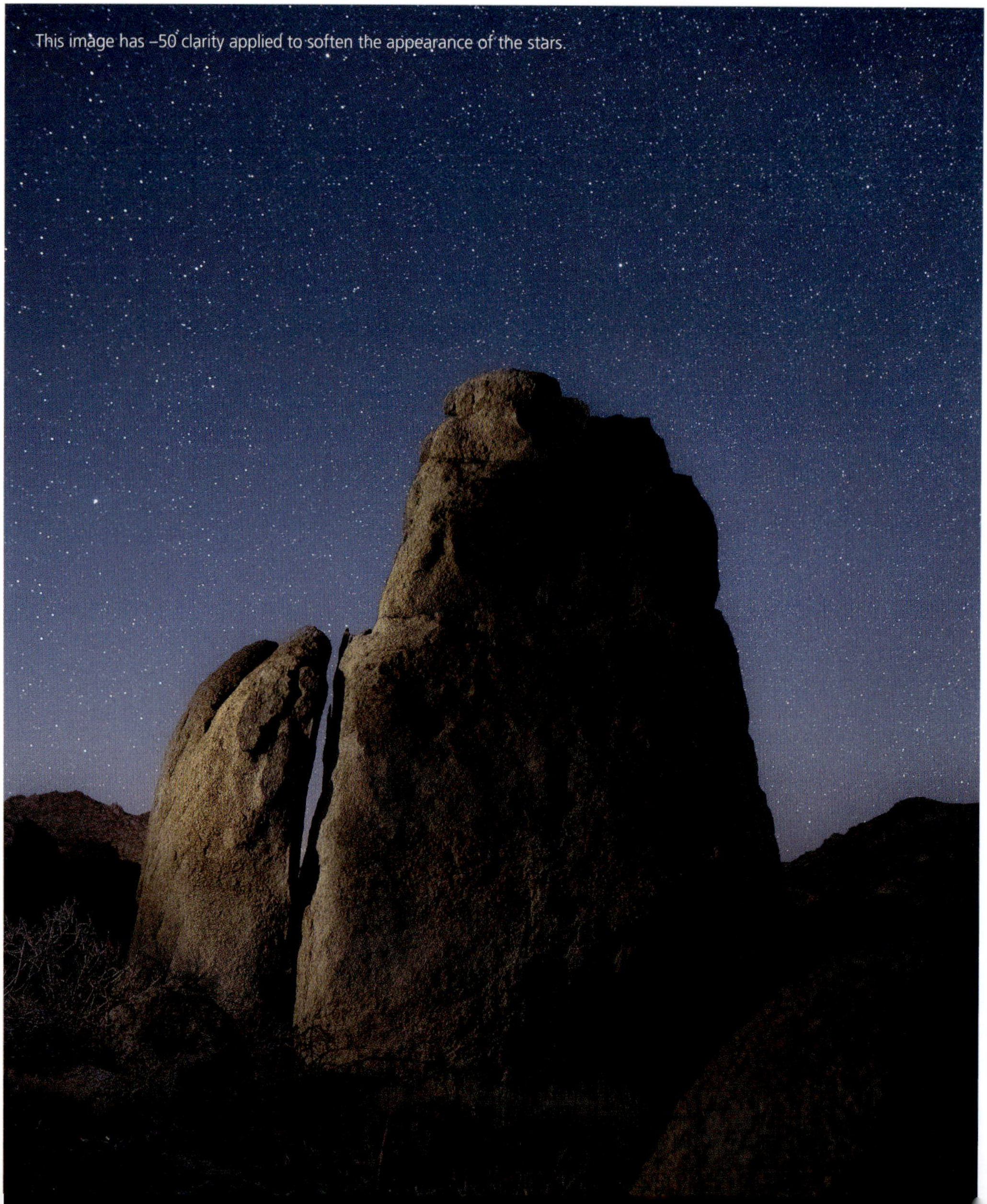

sliders in this panel to show clipping in individual colors. If all you see is black with the Option/ Alt key enabled, there is no clipping. Every tool in this panel will be altering image contrast in some way. The Contrast slider either expands or compresses the tonal range of the image. Increasing the contrast makes the highlights lighter and shadows darker, and decreasing the contrast makes the shadows lighter and highlights darker. Advanced users may wish to explore the Tone Curve panel, which allows for more precise and localized contrast control, but I find it unnecessary for most images with LR4 and later. The Highlights and Shadows sliders are next.

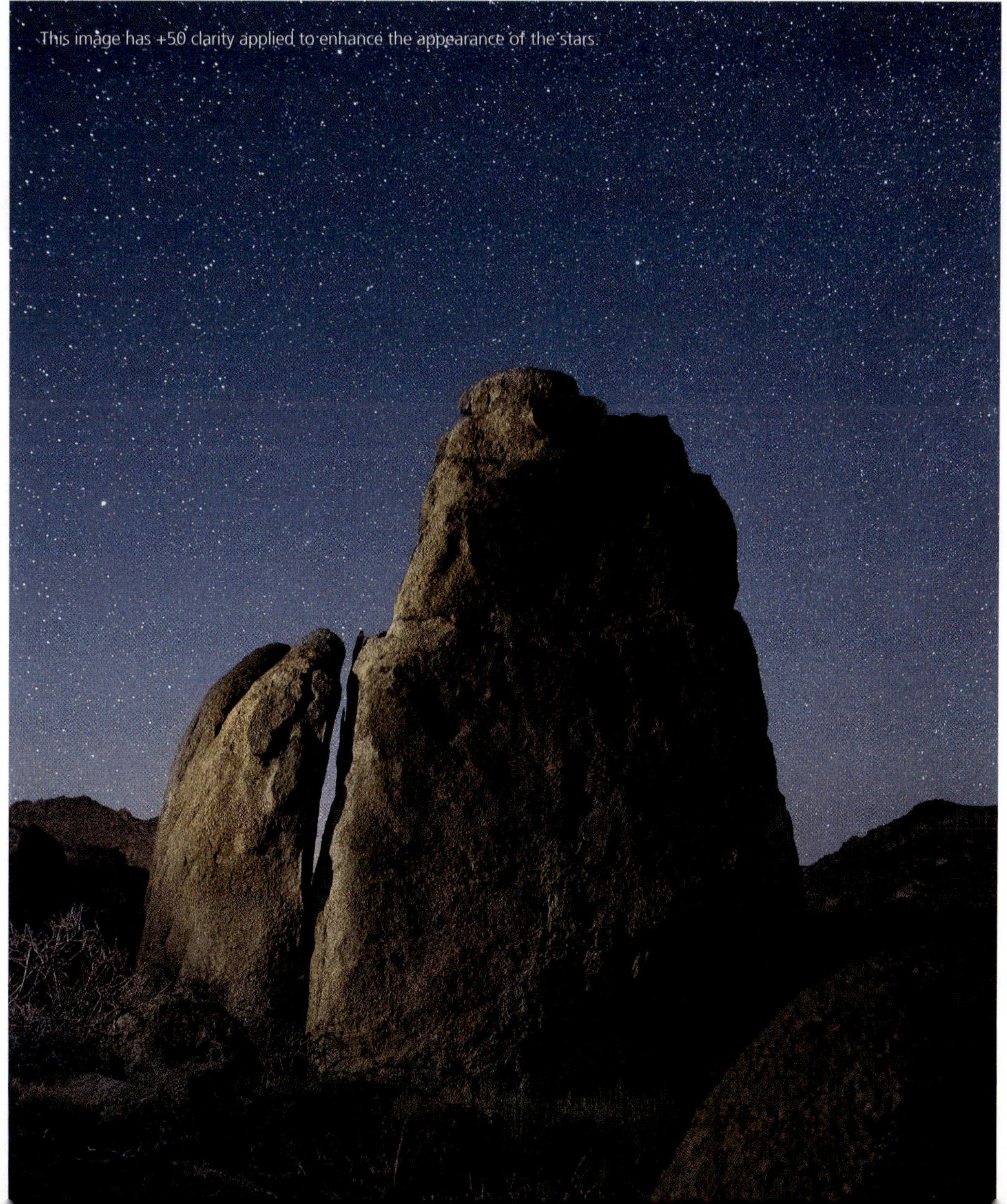

The two sliders increase or decrease only the very brightest and darkest tones in the image. The Whites and Blacks adjustment sliders affect a wider range of tones than the Highlights and Shadows, and can be used to fine-tune the white and black points in the image. Again holding down the Option/Alt key while using these adjustments will reveal the clipping points on both ends of the tonal scale. I do not use the Whites and Blacks adjustments on many of my images, but almost always use the Highlights and Shadows, frequently increasing shadows and decreasing highlights, in conjunction with an increase in Contrast. The net result is a higher contrast image without clipping on either end of the tonal spectrum.

Next, we come to the Presence panel as we work our way down through the tools. All three tools here should be used with caution. Clarity is for adjusting localized or midtone contrast. Clarity works by creating a halo around the edge detail in an image, and has the effect of increasing the contrast in the midtones without increasing overall contrast. This is similar in both appearance and method to sharpening. So when would you adjust Clarity? It is especially useful to open up midtones that have been compressed by a global contrast adjustment. When you increase overall contrast with the Contrast slider, you're pushing the light and dark tones away from the middle—moving them further toward Highlights and Shadows. Judicious use of the Clarity slider can help to bring back definition in blocked-up areas, but excessive use can make an image look chunky or over-sharpened. What's excessive? That varies from one image to the next, but in most cases levels of 10–25 are appropriate. You have to decide what looks best on a case-by-case basis by looking at the image at the final viewing size. It is easy to be seduced by lots of clarity, but it can also be overwhelming. Negative Clarity has a sort of soft focus or diffusion effect. It is useful for minimizing wrinkles and blemishes in portraits, as well as softening the look of stars in the sky, if that's the look you're going for. Some people like to add clarity to starry skies to make the stars stand out more, especially dimmer ones. Clarity is perhaps best used with the local adjustment tools rather than globally; which we return to later.

Vibrance and Saturation both control color saturation but in different ways. The Saturation slider increases or decreases the saturation of all colors equally, while the Vibrance slider increases the less saturated colors or decreases the more saturated colors, depending on which direction you move it. Vibrance is a more subtle tool and the one you'll probably use more often. Dramatic increases in Saturation can lead to lost detail and color clipping, but that is unlikely with Vibrance no matter how hard you push it. In practice, I have found that the Vibrance slider often affects blue tones more than any other color regardless of blue saturation levels in the image. I have not found a satisfactory answer to why that might be. Sometimes partially desaturating an image with either slider can make for quite a beautiful effect. It is also possible to adjust Saturation (but not Vibrance) with the Local Adjustment Tools, and in the HSL / Color / B&W panel that we will look at next you can adjust Saturation of individual colors separately.

I'm bypassing the Tone Curve panel because the Contrast slider is all that's needed for most images, and to keep the workflow simple and straightforward.

THE DEVELOP MODULE TOOLS: HSL / COLOR / B&W

The HSL / Color / B&W panel is where we can fine-tune color adjustments. Rather than make global color changes, you can target specific colors. This comes in handy especially with saturated, monochromatic light sources like low pressure sodium vapor or mercury vapor lights. Let's look at the HSL and B&W tabs of the panel. The HSL tab contains the Targeted Adjustment Tool (TAT), a handy feature that allows you to specify exactly what color or colors you wish to modify based on their true values. When using the TAT, you'll often notice that multiple sliders move as you make the adjustment. This happens because the place where you have placed the TAT contains more than one color. You are simultaneously adjusting whatever colors are directly under the TAT. There are also eight sliders where you can make HSL changes. Adobe added orange and purple to the traditional six additive and subtractive primaries for added subtlety and refinement. HSL stands for Hue, Saturation, and Luminance, the three characteristics that differentiate colors from each other. The Hue sliders are for making color balance adjustments in individual colors. For example, moving the red slider to the right makes the reds in an image more orange. Moving it to the left makes the reds more magenta. Saturation works the same way—it is useful for reducing overly saturated color casts from artificial lights, unless the color is clipped or 100 percent saturated. The Luminance adjustment modifies the tone or brightness of a color.

A real-world night photography situation when you might use these adjustments would be to use the TAT to reduce the saturation and luminance of the orange glow surrounding a sodium vapor streetlight. Bear in mind that when you use the TAT, everything in the image that is that color will change, not just the spot directly under it. The Luminance slider can also recover detail obscured by gamut clipping, which occurs when the color gamut of a RAW file is greater than a monitor or printer can display. If you have an image with a very saturated area that has less detail than you

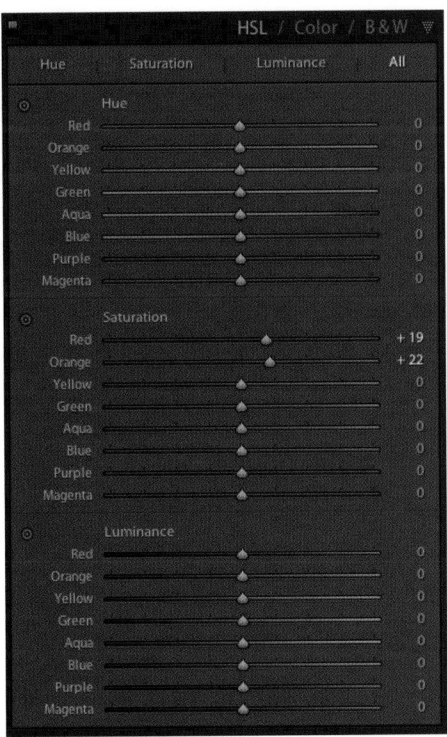

Screenshot of the HSL / Color / B&W panel showing HSL sliders.

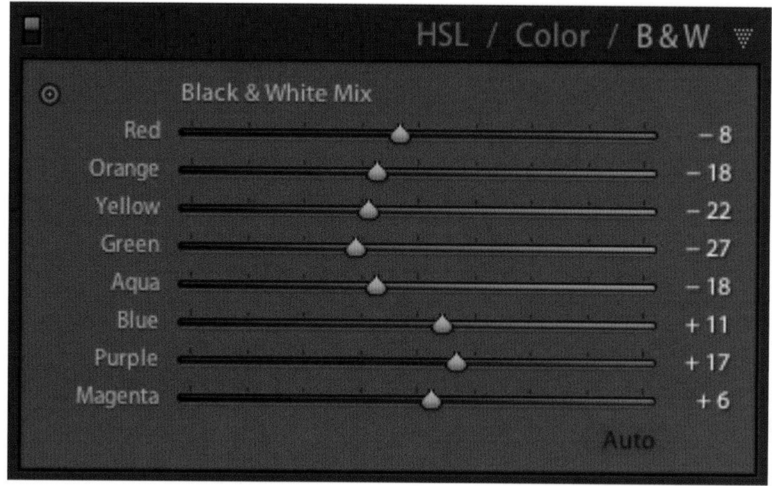

Screenshot of the HSL / Color / B&W panel showing B&W sliders.

expected to see, use the TAT to reduce Luminance in that area, and you may well be able to recover some image detail.

There are several ways to convert to black and white in Lightroom, and the most straightforward is by clicking on Black and White in the Basic panel (or using the V keyboard shortcut), and then tweaking the tones with the White Balance and Tint sliders. However, you'll have more control over the image tonality if you click on B&W in the HSL / Color / B&W panel, and then use the eight color sliders or the TAT to adjust the tones. Simply move the various sliders back and forth until you find a result that looks right for that image. There is an Auto tone button in the panel, but most people find the results to be either unsatisfactory or just a starting point. The Auto tone settings are dependent on the White Balance, so if you change the white balance significantly, try clicking the Auto tone button again. Either way this instantly converts the image to black and white. Lightroom comes with a number of B&W presets, and you can also make your own if you have a formula for conversions that you would like to be able to easily repeat. All of these are better options than simply setting your camera to save black and white JPEGs because the camera processor makes all of the tonality decisions on the fly and discards the color information, leaving you with very little flexibility to go back and modify the image later.

The Split Toning panel is used for adding color tones to black and white (or occasionally color) images. To create a classic sepia-toned look with Split Toning, set the Hue adjustments in both the highlights and shadows to 45, and the Saturation of both to 15. In most instances, using different hues for highlights and shadows does not look good, but you can experiment with this panel in all sorts of ways for interesting effects. Subtlety is usually better.

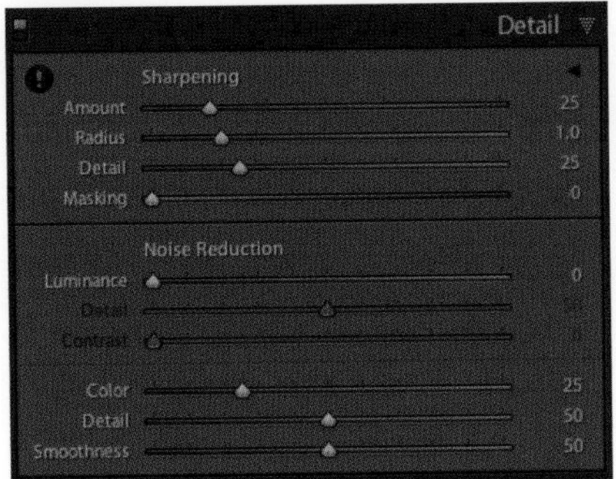

Detail Panel Default Settings

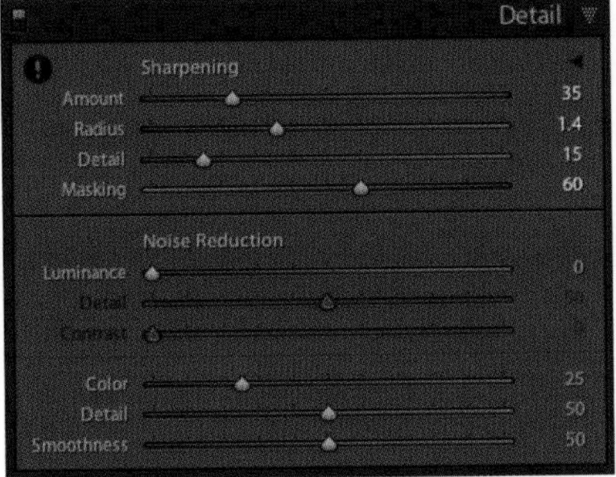

Detail Panel Faces Preset

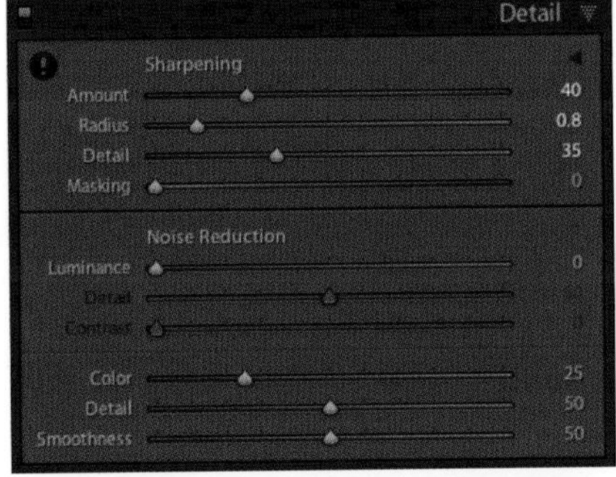

Detail Panel Scenic Preset

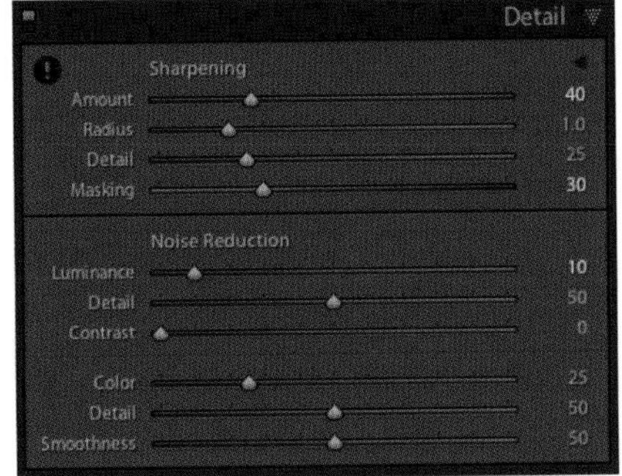

Detail Panel Custom Preset for high-ISO shots with starry skies.

THE DEVELOP MODULE TOOLS: DETAIL

The next panel is Detail, and includes Sharpening and Noise Reduction. Both of these have historically been poorly understood and overused. Sharpening and Noise Reduction are closely related and need to be considered together. Over-sharpening can lead to any noise in the image also being sharpened, and therefore exaggerated. Removing too much noise can obscure image detail, which in turn necessitates more sharpening. It can be a vicious cycle that you do not want to get caught up in. The goal is to strike a balance between sharpening that does not increase the noise, and noise reduction that does not reduce the apparent sharpness of your images. Subtlety is always better in this case. Fortunately, with the 2012 process engine that was first introduced with LR4 and the ever-improving image quality from newer cameras, these controversial image adjustments are generally simple to use. Often the default settings in this panel are adequate without significant additional adjustments. Lightroom applies default Sharpening and Noise Reduction only to RAW files. JPEGs are sharpened in-camera and do not need sharpening. Many people are overly concerned with noise, and want to remove any trace of it from their images. Color noise and luminance pattern sensor noise are problematic and should be minimized. Random luminance noise helps to maintain the appearance of image sharpness. Attempts to remove this random noise often results in overly smooth or "mushy"-looking images because most people are too heavy handed with the Luminance noise slider.

Screenshots of the detail panel showing default settings, included presets, and a custom preset the author used for a Canon 6D for shots at 12,800 ISO.

SHARPENING

There are two types of sharpening, Capture (or Pre-Sharpening) and Output Sharpening, and it is important to understand the difference. Digital RAW files are inherently soft, due to the way light is captured and transformed into digital images, so some sharpening is necessary to all RAW files. The Sharpening applied in the Develop module, be it Lightroom's default settings or a user modified adjustment, is Capture or Pre-Sharpening. In order to view the effect of Capture Sharpening properly, the image must be viewed at full 1:1 resolution. Over Sharpening in the Develop module leads to artifacts (visible halos around edge detail) that are likely to be compounded by adjustments in the Tone and Presence panels. This is why it is important to view the image at 1:1 when working in the Detail panel.

Output or Print Sharpening is applied to the file either on export to a rendered file, or as the file is sent to the printer. The need for Output Sharpening is dependent on several factors, including the type of print to be made, print size, image resolution, and paper type. Files intended for screen viewing also receive output sharpening that is calibrated for a display rather than for a print. Output sharpening is not visually rendered in Lightroom, only in the rendered file or print. Output sharpening needs to be evaluated in the sharpened print.

Lightroom comes with two sharpening presets, one intended for portrait or images with broad areas of subtle tonal gradations, and one for landscapes and architecture that emphasizes edge detail. Both of these presets work well for their intended purposes, but neither one addresses a common problem with high-ISO night photography—noise in starry skies. Differentiating between high-ISO noise and stars is a delicate task, and the goal should be to sharpen the stars without sharpening the noise. This can be achieved by using sharpening settings that are a compromise between the two Lightroom presets. The bottom of the image above (Screenshots) shows my recommended settings to try as a starting point. The effectiveness of these settings will vary depending on your lens, camera, ISO setting, and temperature when you made the images you will be sharpening.

I suggest that unless you are an advanced Lightroom or Photoshop user, ignore the Radius and Detail Sharpening sliders, and don't go over about 60 with the Amount slider. Amount levels of between 25 and 50 are best for most images. Keep it simple. The Masking slider creates an image-based mask that prevents sharpening in areas where you don't want or need it. Notice my suggested starry sky settings include moving the Masking slider from the default of zero to 60; this is to prevent the noise in the sky from being sharpened, while still allowing the stars to receive a sharpening effect. If you hold down the Option or Alt key on your keyboard while applying the Masking slider, you'll see the image change to black and white, with the white areas (high contrast edges) being sharpened and the black areas (lower contrast areas) being protected. Move the Masking slider to the right until only the stars are showing as white in the sky and the noise is black. If the masking prevents your image from looking as sharp as you would like, you can go back to the Basic panel and add about 10 points of Clarity. Just beware of the vicious cycle I mentioned earlier. Subtlety is always better. Images made at lower ISOs generally do not require the use of the Masking slider.

NOISE REDUCTION

Many people assume that removing all of the noise from their images is the way to make them look their best, but this is simply not true. Color noise is bad, and is easily removed, usually with the default Color NR setting. If you still see color noise in the image with the default level of 25, feel free to move the Color slider to the right until the color noise disappears completely. This slider has only a modest effect on the image itself. The default values of the Detail and Smoothness sliders under Color NR are fine for most images. The effects of Detail and Smoothness are quite subtle, and I recommend leaving them as they are unless you are an advanced user with a need to geek out on technical minutia. If that's the case, you might be interested in Bruce Fraser and Jeff Schewe's book entitled Real World Image Sharpening with Adobe Photoshop, Camera Raw, and Lightroom.

Pattern sensor noise is also "bad" noise, and should be eliminated as much as possible. As mentioned earlier, random noise—the type of noise that is sometimes compared to film grain—is not inherently undesirable, unless significantly amplified by high ISOs. The Luminance slider is there for the removal of pattern noise and reduction of obtrusive amounts of random noise. Attempts at removing all random noise obscures image detail, which makes it tempting to increase the sharpening further . . . You see where this is going, right? Subtlety. It is good practice to keep the Luminance slider set as low as possible as it can start to degrade image detail with settings as low as 15. Again, the sub-sliders of Detail and Contrast are subtle, primarily for advanced users, and beyond the scope of this book. You won't miss much by ignoring them because both our cameras and Lightroom have become so good.

Another thing to bear in mind is that your images will generally be viewed in low-resolution on-screen images or as prints, both of which are quite forgiving of moderate amounts of noise. It is only when pixel peeping at 100 percent magnification that most noise is really obvious. Providing that you are using a relatively new DSLR, or high-end mirrorless or 4/3 camera, noise won't be a huge problem. It would be advantageous to do some testing to determine what the highest ISO you can use with your camera is and still get acceptable results. To make the determination of what "acceptable results" are, look at the tests in their final form (whether in print or as the images are intended to be seen on-screen), not at 100 percent magnification. It would not be uncommon to have a situation where a very high ISO, say 12,800, was acceptable for web use, but a lower one like 3200 is the highest ISO you would use for prints.

Prior to the 2010 process version that was introduced with LR3, many people favored the use of noise-reducing plugins like Neat Image, De-Noise, or Noise Ninja, but these are no longer necessary. Except in the most extreme cases, the Noise Reduction built into Lightroom should be all you need. DXO Optics Pro is probably the best option if further noise reduction is required. Let's close the Detail panel with a couple of suggestions. When working in the Detail panel (or any of the tool panels) you can toggle the tools on and off with the little switch in the upper left-hand corner of the panel, but that turns off all of the Detail tools, and it is likely that you'll be wanting to look at the effects of your Sharpening or Luminance adjustments without turning off the Color noise adjustment. The best way to do that is by stepping back and forth in the History panel on the left side of the image. Unlike Photoshop, you always have access to develop the history, even after quitting and restarting the program.

Presets can be very useful, but should usually be considered starting points. Most images will benefit from individual refinements. Having said that, making your own Detail panel presets with camera and ISO specific settings can be a time saver. You might make one for your Nikon D810 at 6400, and another for your Nikon 7000 at 3200. That way you can apply the adjustments that have worked well at those settings in the past, and tweak them from there if needed, rather than starting from the default settings.

LENS CORRECTIONS

The Lens Corrections panel was completely overhauled with the introduction of LR5. There are now four tabs across the top of the panel, Basic, Profile, Color, and Manual. The Basic tab

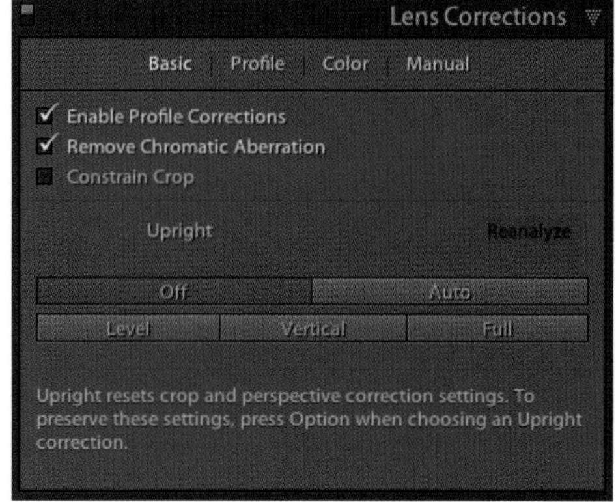

Lens Correction Panel Basic Tab showing the 5 tabs: Off, Auto, Level, Vertical, and Full. Auto works well in most cases.

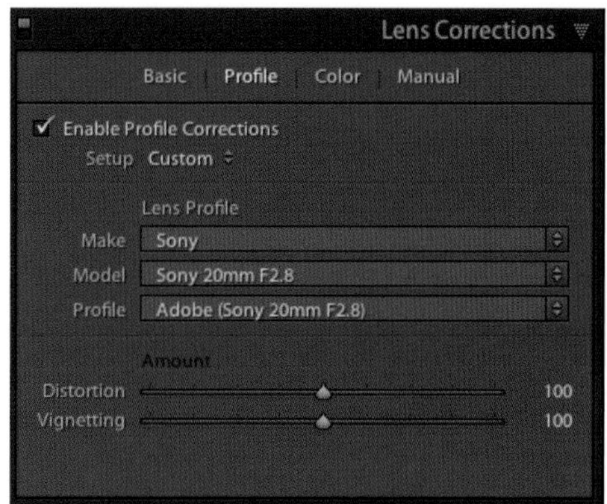

Lens Correcetion Panel Profile Tab showing selected lens. In most cases, the lens is automatically selected.

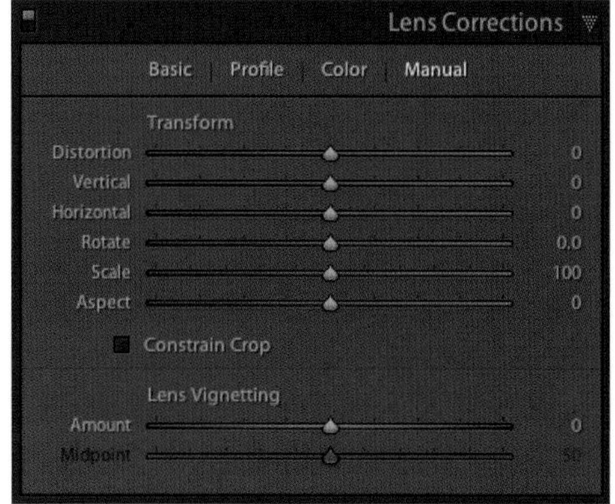

Lens Correction Panel showing manual adjustments for distortion and perspective control. Constrain Crop will crop the image to match the correction.

Screenshots of the Basic, Profile, and Manual tabs of the Lens Corrections panel.

has check boxes for enabling Profile Corrections, Remove Chromatic Aberration, and Constrain Crop. Checking the first two of those boxes negates the need to use either the Profile or Color tabs almost all the time. I recommend enabling Profile Corrections and Removing Chromatic Aberration from all of your photographs upon import into Lightroom by way of a custom Import Preset. The Constrain Crop checkbox eliminates any white space around the borders of an image after distortion or perspective corrections. I prefer to handle this manually to make sure that the image is cropped precisely the way I choose.

Profile Corrections applies distortion correction to your images based on the lens used with the camera. Almost every lens has some characteristic distortion, and this tool corrects for it automatically with a ready-made lens profile. Occasionally, it may choose the wrong profile, so the first time you use it with each new lens, it is good to check and make sure that the right one has been selected. Not all lenses are in the database; for example, you won't find the Rokinon lenses or manual focus film camera lenses. There is a free Lens Profiling tool from Adobe that allows you to make your own, but the process is fairly involved. Each Lightroom update adds a few more lenses to the collection, but it is not envisaged that they will be making profiles for vintage lenses in the foreseeable future.

Chromatic Aberration (CA) occurs because different colors of light do not always converge at the same position on the sensor plane after passing through a lens. CA appears as color fringes along the transition points between light and dark edges in photographs, especially near the edges of the frame. It often manifests near horizon lines, and with tree branches or leaves against a bright sky. CA often appears as complementary bands of color on opposite edges of an object, and while it may not be obvious unless viewed on-screen at 100 percent, it does show up readily in prints. With LR5, CA correction is effortless. In 99 percent of your images, you'll never need to do anything other than check the box in the Basic tab.

Below the three check boxes is a new feature called Upright. Perspective corrections are simple and automatic with Upright—leveling the horizon, correcting for converging vertical lines, and architectural perspective correction is all automated in versions five and beyond. There are five Upright options: Off, Auto, Level, Vertical, and Full. In most instances, the Auto tab yields the best results, giving a natural-looking and realistic perspective adjustment, as well as leveling the horizon and correcting for lens vignetting; it works really well. The Level tab makes the horizon level, nothing more. The Vertical tab corrects for converging vertical lines, and the Full tab renders a more robust perspective correction that is often too extreme to be believable. The Full tab also will frequently stretch an image so much in an effort to correct it that much of the image is stretched outside of the frame. It can be effective in some cases, but it is not for every image. I suggest cycling through the different tabs on several different images to familiarize yourself with how they work. You'll most likely use the Auto correction for architectural images,

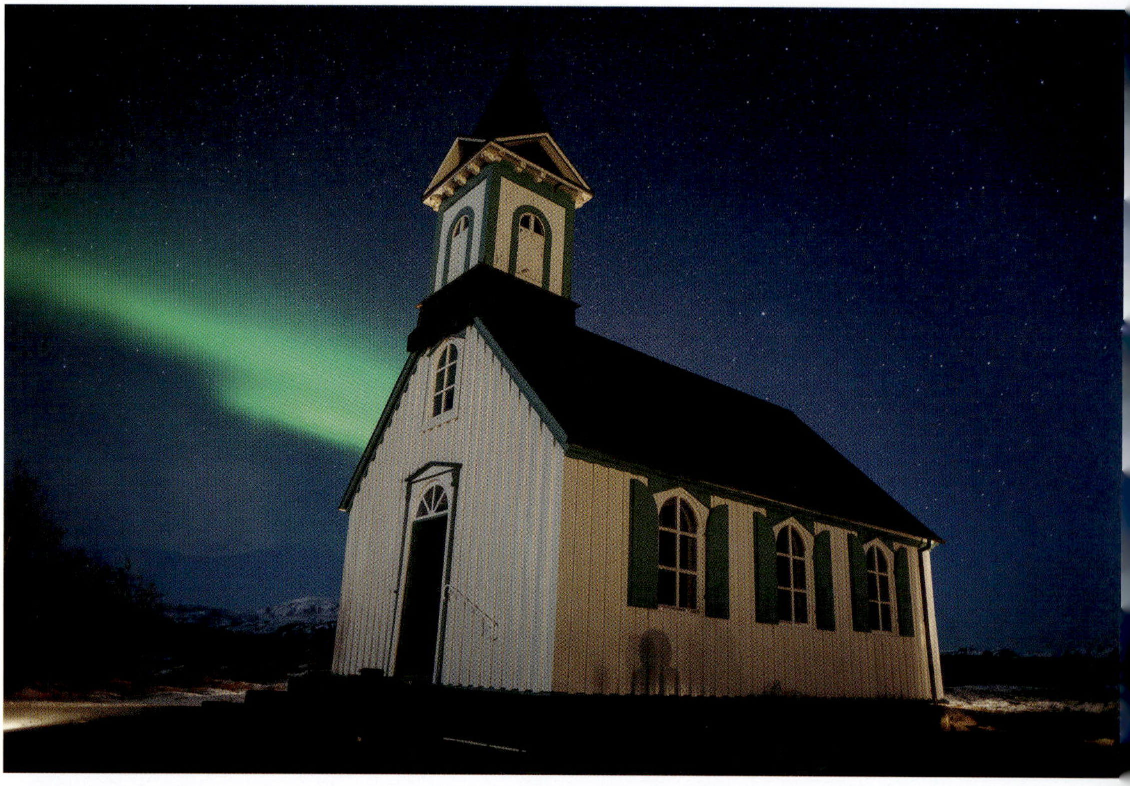

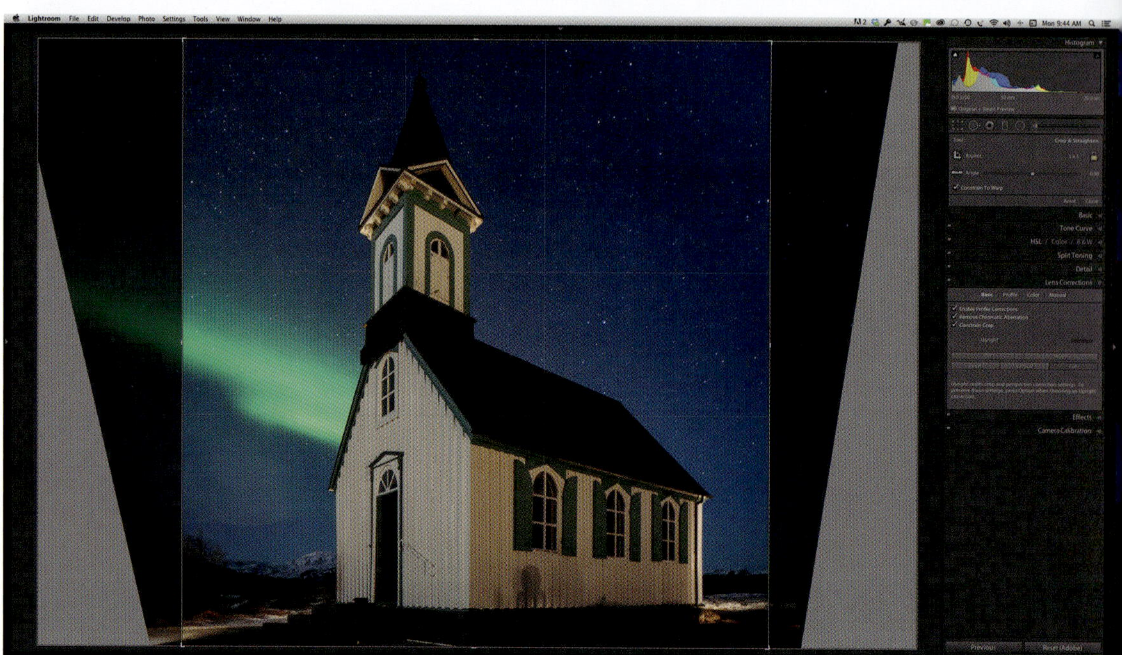

An image of Thingvellir Church in Iceland with aurora, before and after Full Upright correction was applied. To correct for the perspective distortion from the low camera angle, Full Upright was applied. Notice a large portion of the image is lost due to the image being stretched during correction. As a result, the final image is cropped square.

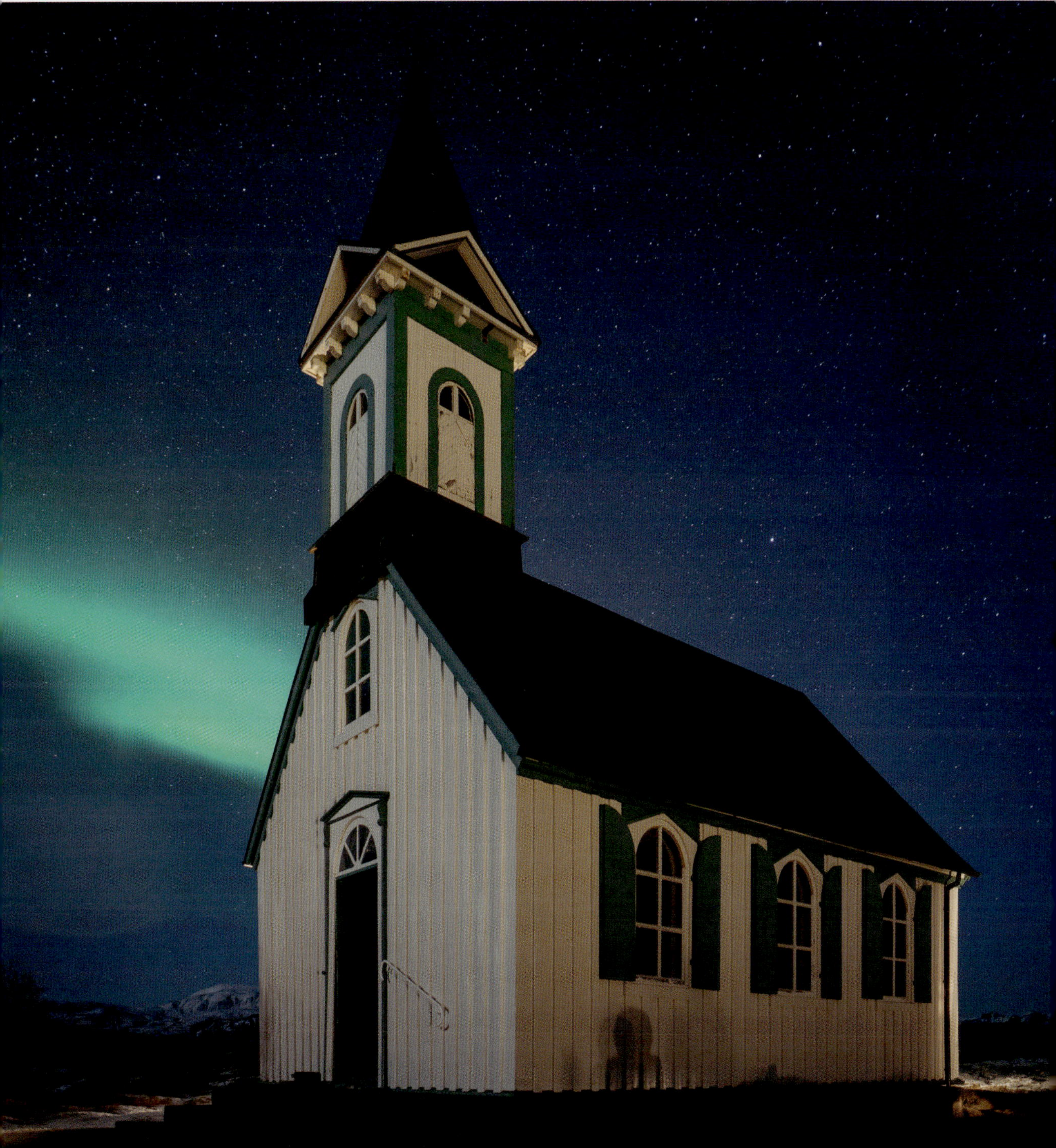

and Level for landscapes. If none of the Upright options are working for you, go up to the Manual tab in the Lens Corrections panel, where you will find six sliders to adjust perspective manually, another Constrain Crop checkbox to use with the Manual tools, and two sliders to manually correct for Lens Vignetting. Amount controls how light or dark the vignette will be. Midpoint determines how far into the image the vignette extends.

The last panel we're going to look at is the Effects panel, which include Post-Crop Vignetting and Grain. Unlike the Vignetting tool in Lens Corrections, which is designed to correct lens flaws, Post-Crop Vignetting is used for artistic effect, and applied to just the part of the image that remains after cropping. When using this tool, you first choose a vignetting style. The default is Highlight Priority, which works best in most instances. It protects highlight contrast at the possible expense of color shifts within the vignette. Color Priority favors preserving color hues, but bright highlight detail within the vignetted area may suffer. Paint Overlay creates a soft effect by blending black or white with the existing colors, but this option also reduces highlight contrast within the vignetted area. The best way to use the Vignette feature is to experiment with different settings and evaluate the effects. A little vignetting will draw attention to the center of the image, but it is easy to get carried away and add too much. It is purely a matter of personal taste.

There are five sliders in Post-Crop Vignetting; Amount, Midpoint, Roundness, Feather, and Highlights. Amount controls how light or dark the vignette will be. Move the slider to the right to darken the corners, or to the left to lighten them. Midpoint determines how far into the image the vignette extends: move the slider to the right to restrict the vignette to the corners, move it to the left to extend it further into the image. Roundness determines the shape of the Vignette: adjust the slider rightwards for a rounder vignette, and leftwards for an oval shape. Feather softens the transition area of the vignette by moving the slider to the right, and hardens it by moving it to the left. Highlights are only available with the Highlight Priority or Color Priority vignette styles when the Amount slider is moved to the left of the default value. Highlights constrains or intensifies the brightness of highlight areas, such as in the glow surrounding a streetlight. In my own night images, I typically use the default Highlight Priority style with the Amount set to between 5 and 20, the midpoint set at about 25, the Roundness left at the default setting, and Feather set to 100, the maximum. This vignetting helps to hold the image together, and looks natural and realistic.

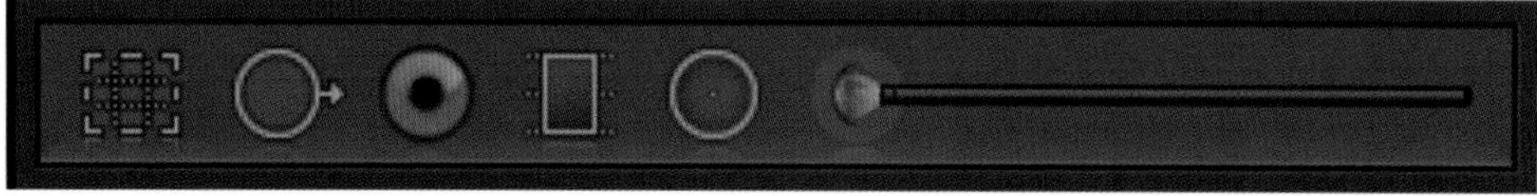

A screenshot of the Local Adjustment Tools in LR5. From left to right, the Crop tool, Spot Removal tool, Red Eye Reduction tool, Graduated Filter, Radial Gradient, and Adjustment Brush.

The Grain tool in the Effects tab simulates film grain for that "retro" look. It can also be used to obscure enlargement artifacts in large prints. The Size and Roughness sliders determine the look of the grain.

Earlier in this chapter, we skipped over the Local Adjustment Tools, which are found sandwiched between the Histogram and Basic panels. These tools allow you to make corrections to selective parts of an image rather than globally. Major advancements in the utility of these tools in LR5 are a key factor in reducing your dependence on Photoshop in your postprocessing workflow.

The Crop Overlay and Straighten tool allows you to crop an image freely, or with constrained proportions, and also rotate the image. Red Eye Reduction is self-explanatory and is rarely used by night photographers. The Spot Removal tool has two modes: Clone and Heal. Clone applies an exact copy of the sampled area to the destination area, and works best with small samples in tight corners where there is other detail nearby. Heal takes the sampled area and then blends it to match the destination area in texture, color, and tone. The Heal mode needs open space to work, as it samples from an area considerably wider than the destination spot being healed. The healing mode is typically preferred over the clone method. Since version LR5, the Spot Removal tool has been available in brush form, which makes it easier to remove telephone wires and the like.

The other tools are the Graduated Filter, Radial Gradient, and Adjustment Brush. These masking tools are customizable, and offer the following adjustments: Color Temperature, Tint, Exposure, Contrast, Highlights, Shadows, Clarity, Saturation, Sharpness, Noise, Moiré, Defringe, and Color. You can apply them one at a time or in any combination with either tool, and the best part about it is that these adjustments are completely non-destructive and remain editable forever. Selecting either of these tools opens the Tool Drawer directly below the tool strip. The Tool Drawer contains sliders or buttons for the various adjustments. A great feature is being able to utilize your develop presets by clicking on the Custom drop-down menu.

The Graduated Filter is commonly used to lighten or darken large areas of an image, but it is much more versatile than that. In the case of night photography, it is often used on the sky portion of an image to add or subtract clarity, depending on the look you want for the stars. It can also be used to darken an overly bright foreground in urban night photography, or to even out a bright or dark corner. After applying the Graduated Filter, you can refine the effect by changing the amounts of the adjustments, or you can change the size and position of the gradient, expanding or collapsing it by dragging the leading or trailing edge. You can rotate the gradient by moving the center line. Holding down the shift key keeps the gradient level, and the H key hides and then reveals the boundary markers, but not the effect. In the center of the gradient is the "Pin," which appears either as a white circle to indicate a deselected gradient position, or a white circle with a black center to indicate an active gradient. You can apply as many gradients as you like to an image, each with its own adjustments.

The Radial Gradient is much like the Graduated Filter, except that it applies effects in a circular or ovoid pattern rather than a linear one. It also has adjustable feathering, and can be inverted to make the effect occur inside rather than outside of the circle. Think of it as Post-Crop Vignetting with a draggable center point, and the ability to apply all of the adjustments of the Graduated Filter.

The Adjustment Brush is a highly manipulable masking tool for applying localized corrections to part of an image. Adjustment Brush selections have the same Pin as gradients. When a local adjustment is active, pressing the O key will reveal the mask, which can then be further refined. You can add to it or remove part of the mask by clicking the Option/Alt key while applying the brush. As with the Graduated Filter, the H key will hide and reveal the adjustment Pins. There is also an erase button in the tool drawer, which works in the same way as the Option/Alt key. In addition to the adjustment sliders in the Tool Drawer, the Adjustment Brush also has controls to regulate the Size, Feather, Flow, and Density of the brush, along with an Auto Mask feature that confines masking areas to adjacent areas with similar tonality. When the Adjustment Brush is active, pressing the O key toggles on and off a colored mask to show you where the effect has been applied. It is extremely helpful if you need to clean up accidental overflow of the effect into an area where you didn't want it. There are two variable presets for brushes, so you can toggle back and forth between two different sizes or styled brushes. As with the Graduated Filter, you can add additional masks, and change them at any time. When a brush stroke or gradient is selected (a black circle appears in the center of the Pin), the delete key will cause that adjustment to disappear.

This concludes our overview of the tools in the Develop module of Lightroom for developing RAW night photography images. There's much more to Lightroom than could be covered here, and one point I'd like to stress is that as important (and fun) as developing our images is, before getting deeply involved with the Develop module, you should learn how the Lightroom catalog is set up and how it functions. Many people jump into Lightroom without knowing what they are doing, and import a mass (mess) of existing folders into Lightroom, which quickly become lost when they start moving files and folders in the catalog around outside of Lightroom. For most people, importing your images by copying them into a date-based folder structure in a single location set up by Lightroom is going to make for a cleaner, neater catalog. Take a class, read Martin Evening's book, or sign up for lynda.com, and learn how the Library module functions before your Lightroom catalog becomes a mirror image of the horrid jumble of folders spread out across your computer that you might be faced with now. One last tip—make sure that you back up both your Catalog and your Library of images on a regular basis. The backup feature in Lightroom only backs up the catalog file, not the actual images. Backing up your images on a second hard drive should be done with another application, such as Windows backup Utility, Time Machine, or my preference, Super Duper, which is available from shirt-pocket.com. Now let's look at some examples of using Lightroom for developing various types of night photographs.

In the following pages, I'll take you through the development of several night photographs. The images have been exposed for optimal quality, and care has been taken to do as much as possible in the field, in-camera, so that as little postprocessing as possible is required to bring the images to final form.

HIGH-CONTRAST AMBIENT ARTIFICIAL LIGHT IMAGE

The image below was taken from a pedestrian bridge over Howard Street in San Francisco's South of Market district; it is all about the tail lights of cars driving away from the camera. The exposure was started when the light turned green, and several different exposure lengths were tried to get the best effect. The lines from the tail lights help create a real sense of depth in the image.

ARTIFICIAL LIGHT IMAGE WITH STRONG MIXED LIGHTING AND PERSPECTIVE DISTORTION

On a recent trip to the Orkney Islands in the north of Scotland, I was testing out a compact camera to see how well it would perform in urban situations at night. The Canon G1X has a much larger sensor than most high-end point and shoot cameras, and is capable of exposure as long as 250 seconds, although the ISO is locked at 80 for any exposures of 30 seconds or longer. The image shown here was taken in the town of Stromness late at night after the pubs had closed. New metal halide streetlights had been installed since my last visit, which completely changed the feeling of the streets at night. The foreground is lit with sodium vapor with the halide lights in the distance. The single illuminated window in the wall that was otherwise in shadow caught my attention, and I wanted to make sure to preserve detail inside the house.

ASTRO-LANDSCAPE PHOTOGRAPH OF STEVE'S ROCK, OLMSTED POINT, YOSEMITE

Steve's Rock was so named by the students of Steve Harper, who took his summer night photography classes from the Academy of Art University to Yosemite and Mono Lake from the late 1970s to early 1990s. The classic view of the rock is looking to the northwest, but this one is oriented toward the south-southwest to include the bright core of the Milky Way. A relatively light touch has been applied to the image for a realistic look. It was taken with a Canon 6D and a Rokinon 24 mm f1.4 lens. The exposure was 25 seconds at f4, and ISO 12,800. The aperture was stopped down to f4 to be able to get both the rock and stars in focus, and the ISO

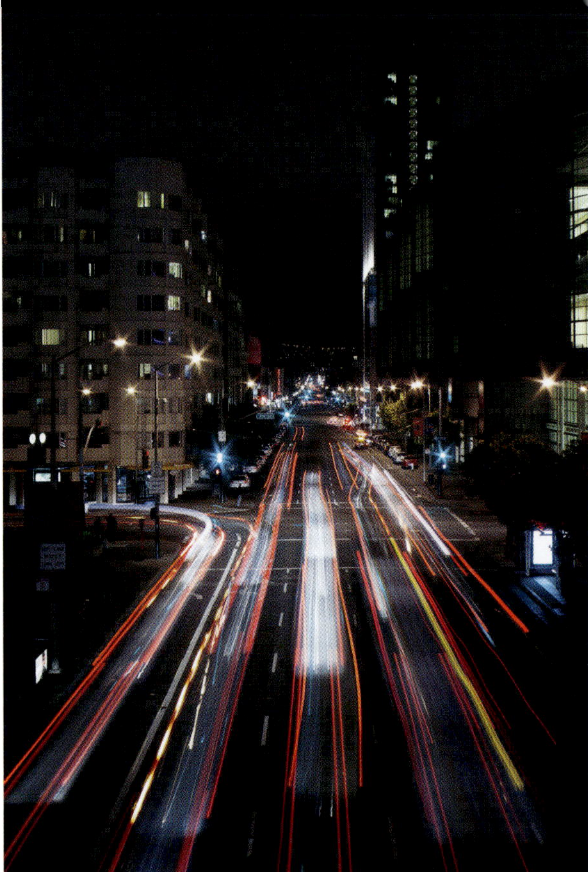

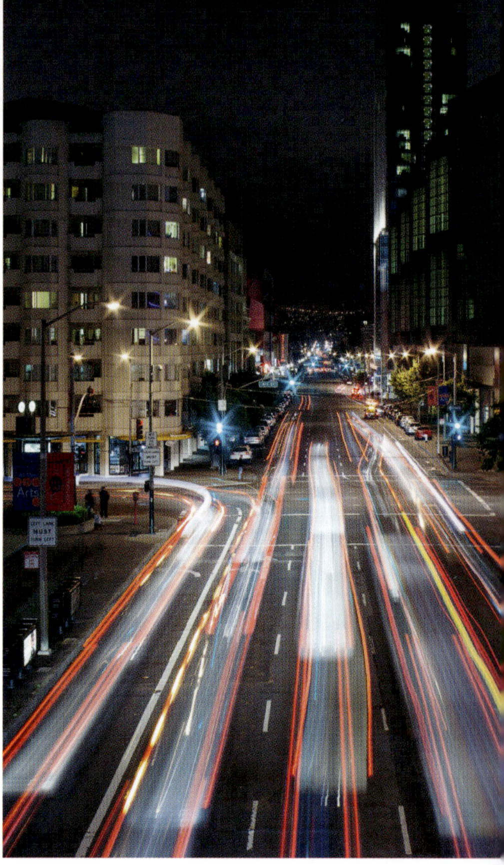

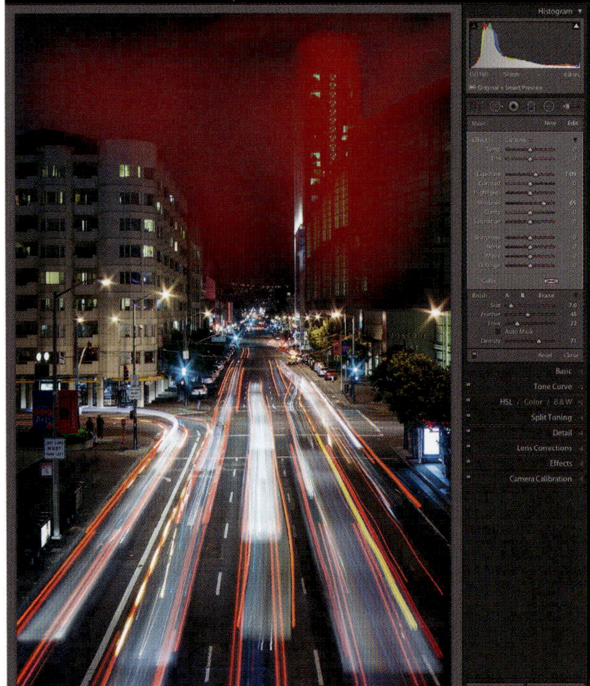

Canon 5D MK II, 28 mm Nikkor PC lens, shifted down. f8, 6 seconds, ISO 160. This image is Straight Out Of Camera (SOOC). It is relatively high contrast, but no so much so that multiple exposures or HDR are required to make it look its best.

The basic panel adjustments and detail, and lens corrections have been applied, with the primary effect being that the shadows have been opened up substantially, and the image has been cropped slightly.

The Adjustment Brush was used to further open dark areas in the frame, particularly in the sky and on the tall building on the right. Several stories off of the ground, it is much darker, and the ambient light is reduced. The red area shows where the mask with the adjustments has been applied.

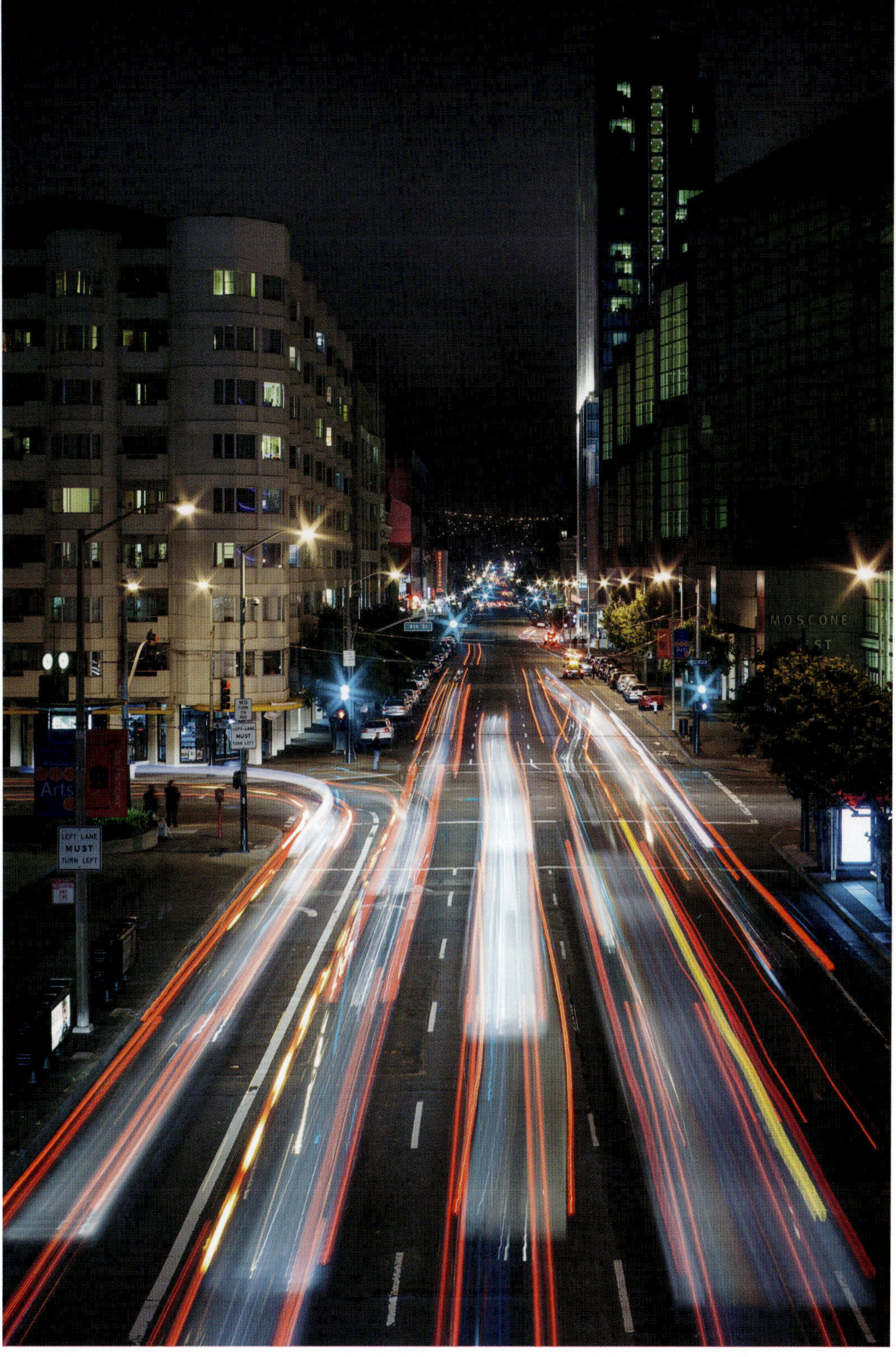

The final image after all adjustments have been applied. The difference between the images is more subtle in print than in the original image on screen, as offset printing is relatively low resolution.

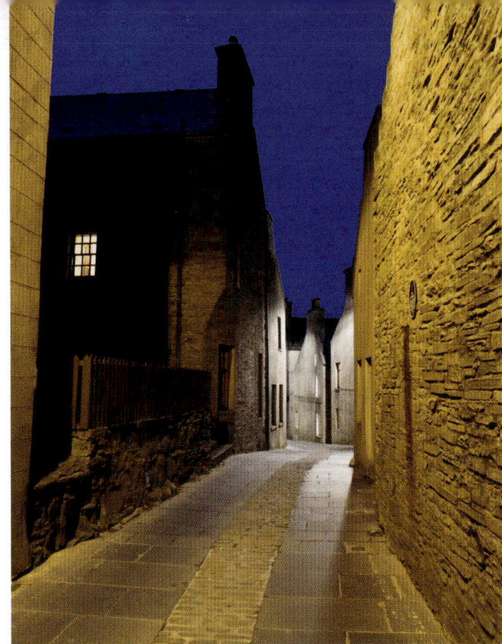 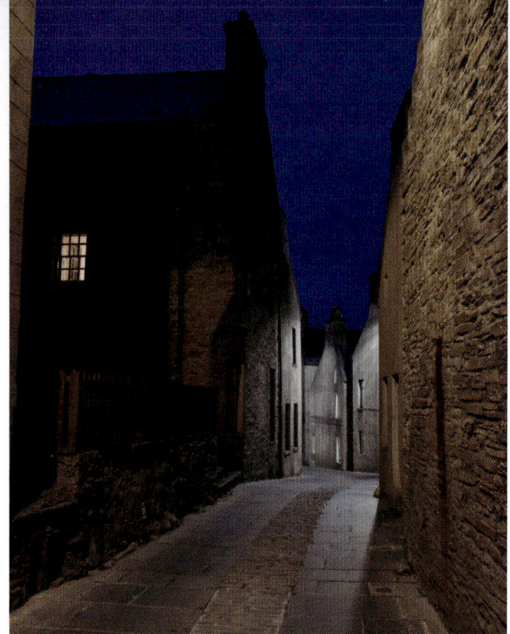

SOOC. Canon G1X, ISO 80, f5, 10 seconds. The image was exposed to preserve the highlights in the illuminated window, and the bright area lit by the halide lights. It is brighter than I wanted the final image to be, but I exposed to get as much detail as possible. There is also some perspective distortion from pointing the camera up.

The image with basic panel adjustments. The White Balance has been lowered from 2750 to 2400, Contrast and Shadows increased, and the Vibrance reduced to tone down the ugly yellow from the sodium lights and the super-saturated blue post-twilight sky. Because there was still a fair amount of daylight in the sky, the contrast was not extreme, and no local adjustments were needed to recover the highlights.

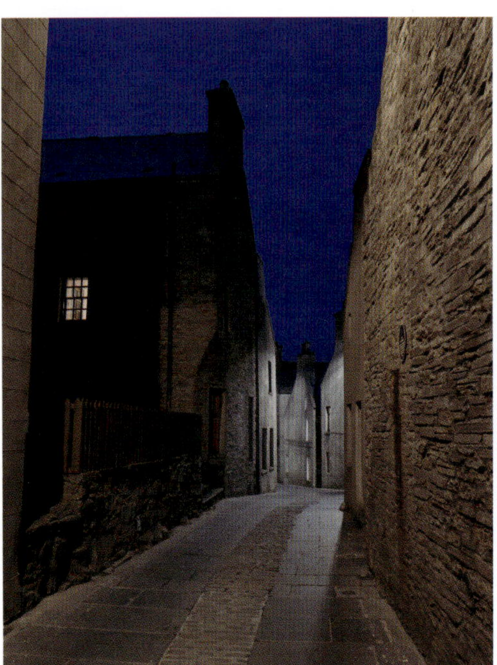 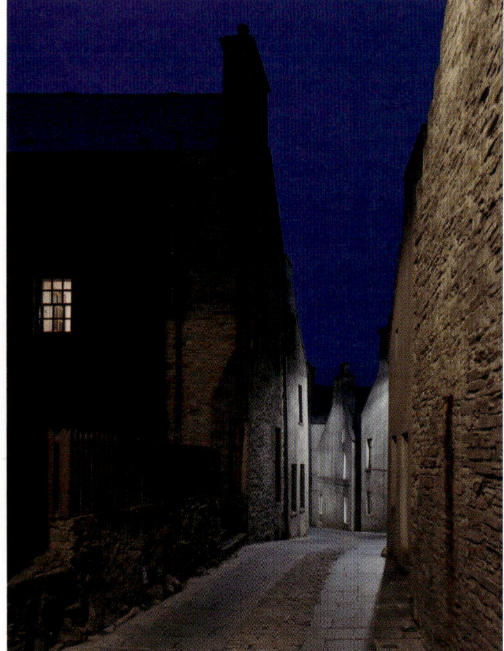

HSL adjustments. The color is still not right despite White Balance and Vibrance adjustments. The yellow was hue shifted toward orange and away from green, and desaturated. The sky, which contains blue and purple, was desaturated, and the luminance was reduced.

Lens Corrections. The Lens Profile and Chromatic Aberration boxes were activated with an import preset. The Upright auto setting was enabled, and then the image was cropped because of the loss of image area during perspective correction. Note the little bit of wall on the left side has been eliminated.

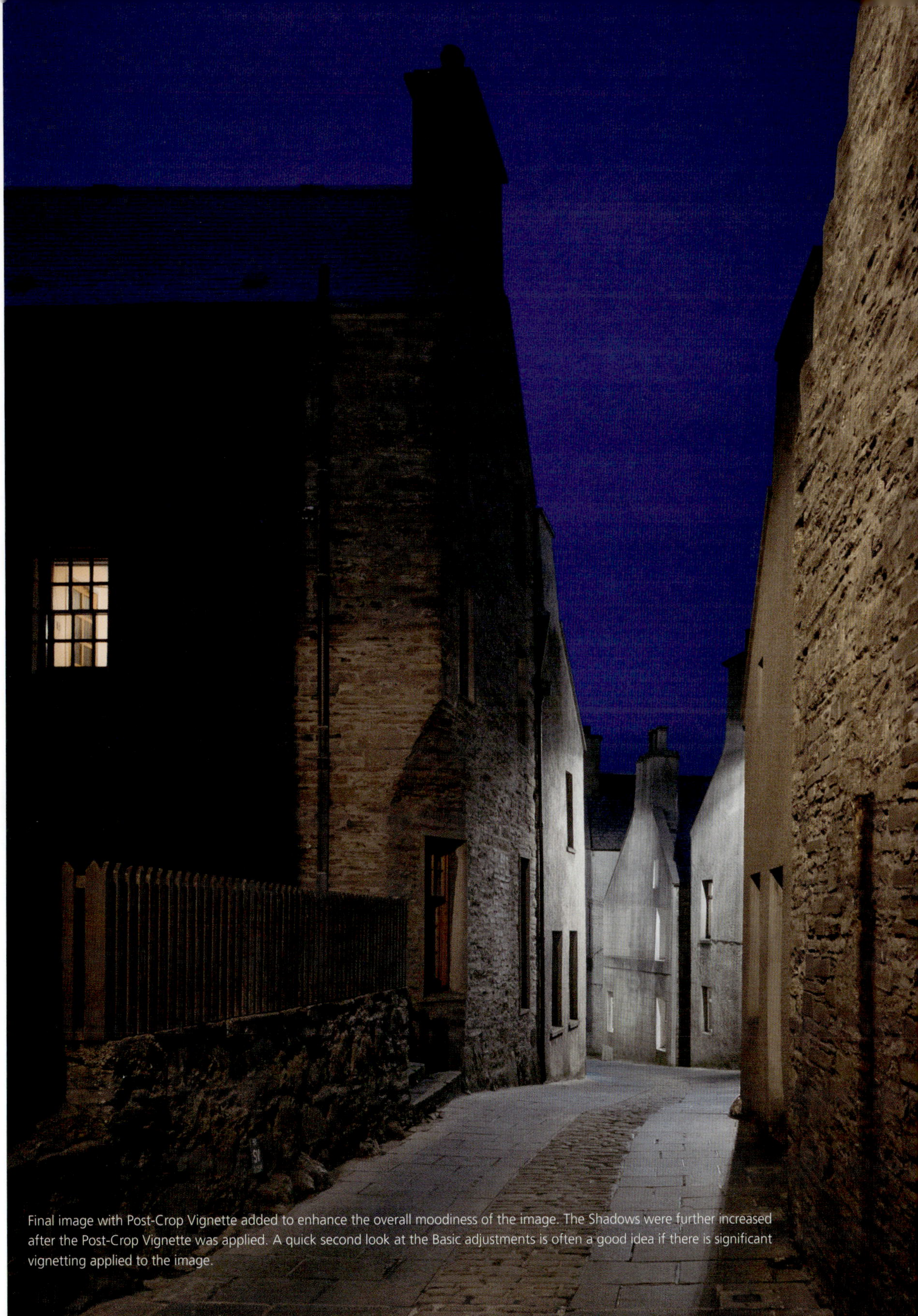

Final image with Post-Crop Vignette added to enhance the overall moodiness of the image. The Shadows were further increased after the Post-Crop Vignette was applied. A quick second look at the Basic adjustments is often a good idea if there is significant vignetting applied to the image.

raised to 12,800 to enable a time that would minimize the apparent movement of the stars. The combination of a 6D and cool night at 10,000 feet of elevation makes for a surprisingly clean image even at this extreme ISO. The rock and and ground around it were lit with a low-powered warm LED flashlight from about 90 degrees to the camera on the left and right sides. The ground was lit from the same positions, but raked across the scene just a few inches above the ground to maximize the texture of the rock. The glow at the horizon is from the city of Fresno, about 60 miles to the west.

ASTRO-LANDSCAPE PANORAMIC PHOTOGRAPH OF OWEN'S DRY LAKE

Owens Dry Lake in California's Eastern Sierra is a great place for panoramas. It has a storied history in California's water saga, and is the site of a commercial salt harvesting operation. The sky is dark, but there are small towns nearby along Highway 395 that add some interesting light to the landscape. The image presented here is a merged file of four vertical shots that were made by rotating the tripod head about 15 degrees between exposures. The first image was developed as usual in Lightroom, and then the other three were synced to the first image in a single click, before creating the panorama in Photoshop.

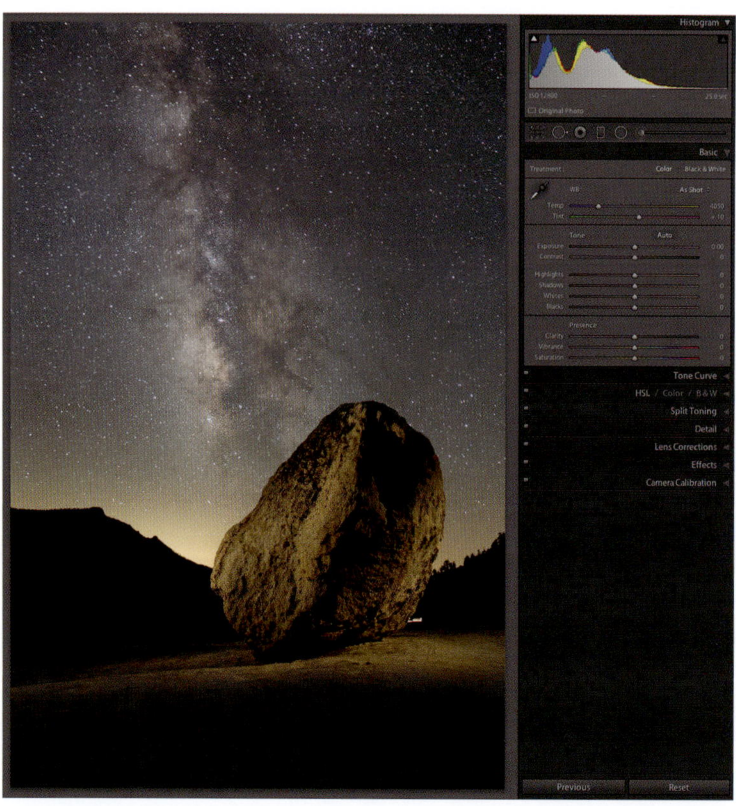

SOOC. Canon 6D, Rokinon 24 mm f1.4 lens. 25 seconds at f4, ISO 12,800.

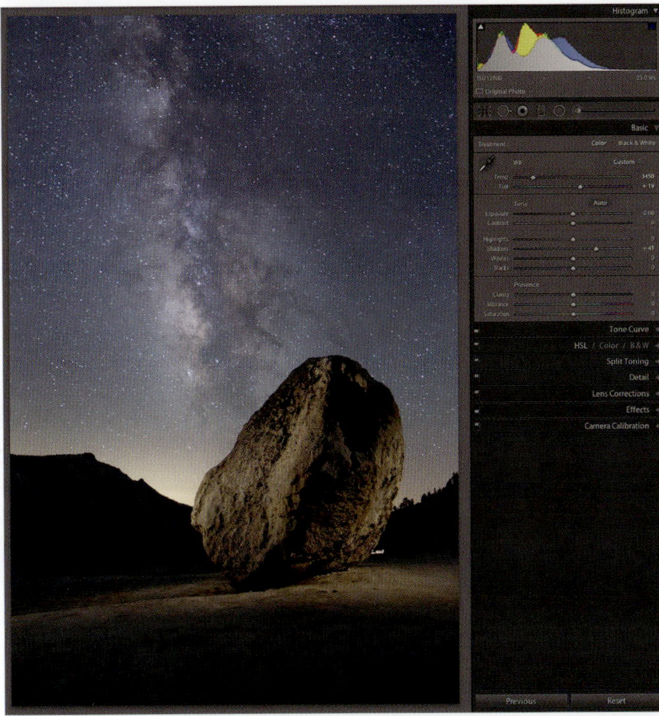

Basic adjustments. The warm LED flashlight confused the Auto White Balance, recording it at a higher color temperature than normal. The White Balance has been lowered from 4050 to 3450, with the tint slider moved from 10 to 19 points to the right to take out some of the green cast from the flashlight. The Shadows were boosted by 41 points.

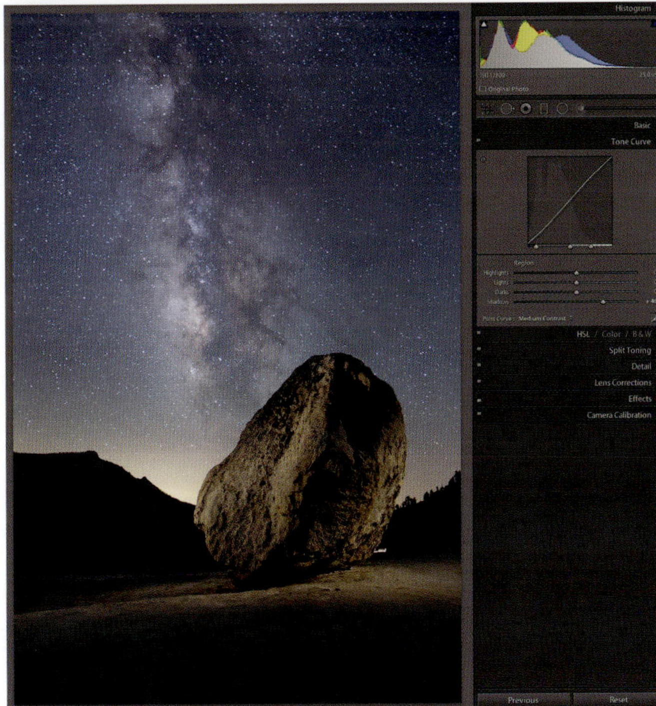

Tone Curve. Rather than simply bumping up the contrast with the slider, the Tone Curve was changed from the default Linear Curve to Medium contrast, and the shadows boosted a further 28 points. The Tone Curve allows for more precise and localized control of contrast.

Local adjustments. The stray light at the base of the rock (from another photographer) on the right side was easily removed with the spot removal tool, and then there were three modifications made with the Adjustment Brush. The glow on the horizon was toned down, and the color shifted from yellow to blue. Next, the dark portion of the rock that did not receive enough light painting was boosted with the Shadows and Exposure sliders. Finally, the Milky Way core was enhanced with Contrast, Highlights, and Clarity. The mask where the adjustments were applied to the Milky Way is revealed in red.

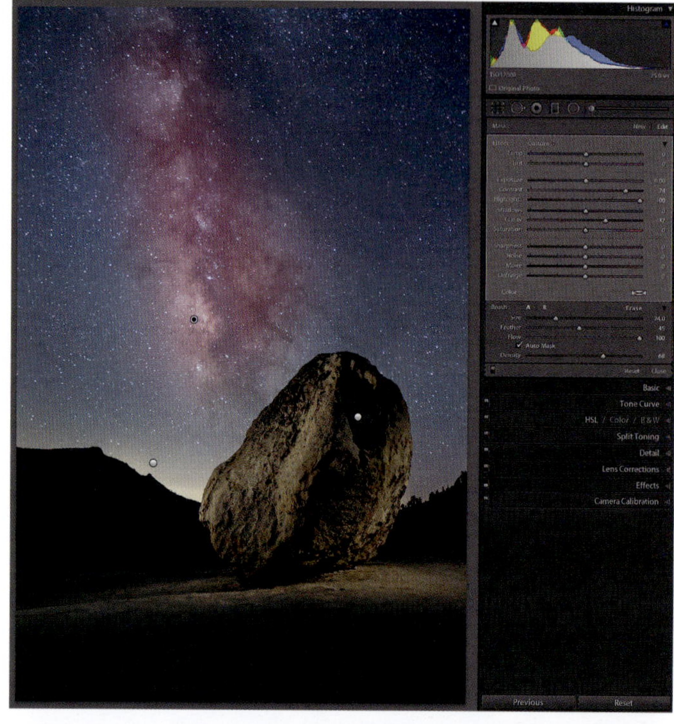

Detail adjustments. The image is remarkably clean considering the ISO, and looks pretty good with just the default Noise Reduction and Sharpening. Still, it can be improved with a modest use of the Luminance slider, and corresponding Sharpening compensation. The Luminance slider is raised to 20, and color is left at the default setting of 25. The Sharpening Amount is raised to 49, and Masking set at 78. The Option/Alt key was held down while the Masking was applied to visualize how it was affecting the image. The aim was to sharpen the image but not the noise.

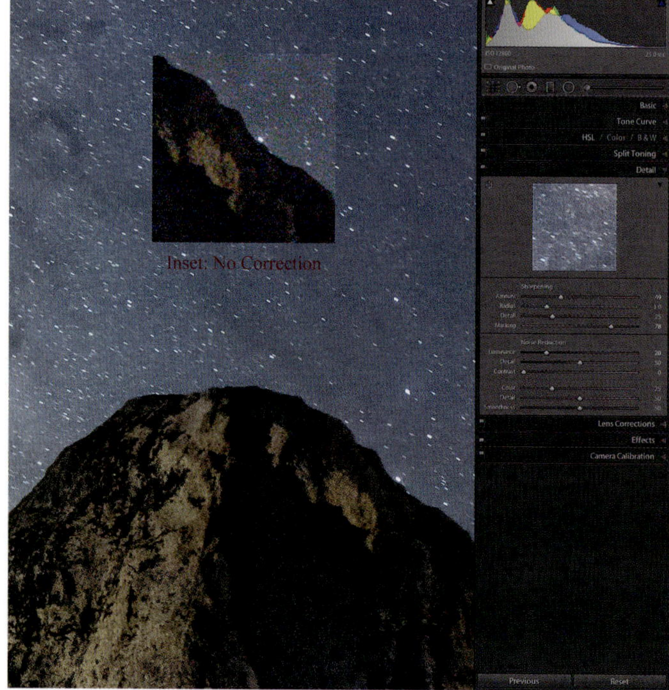

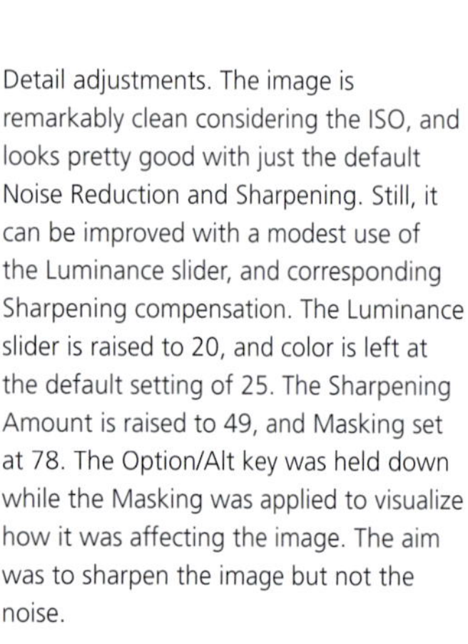

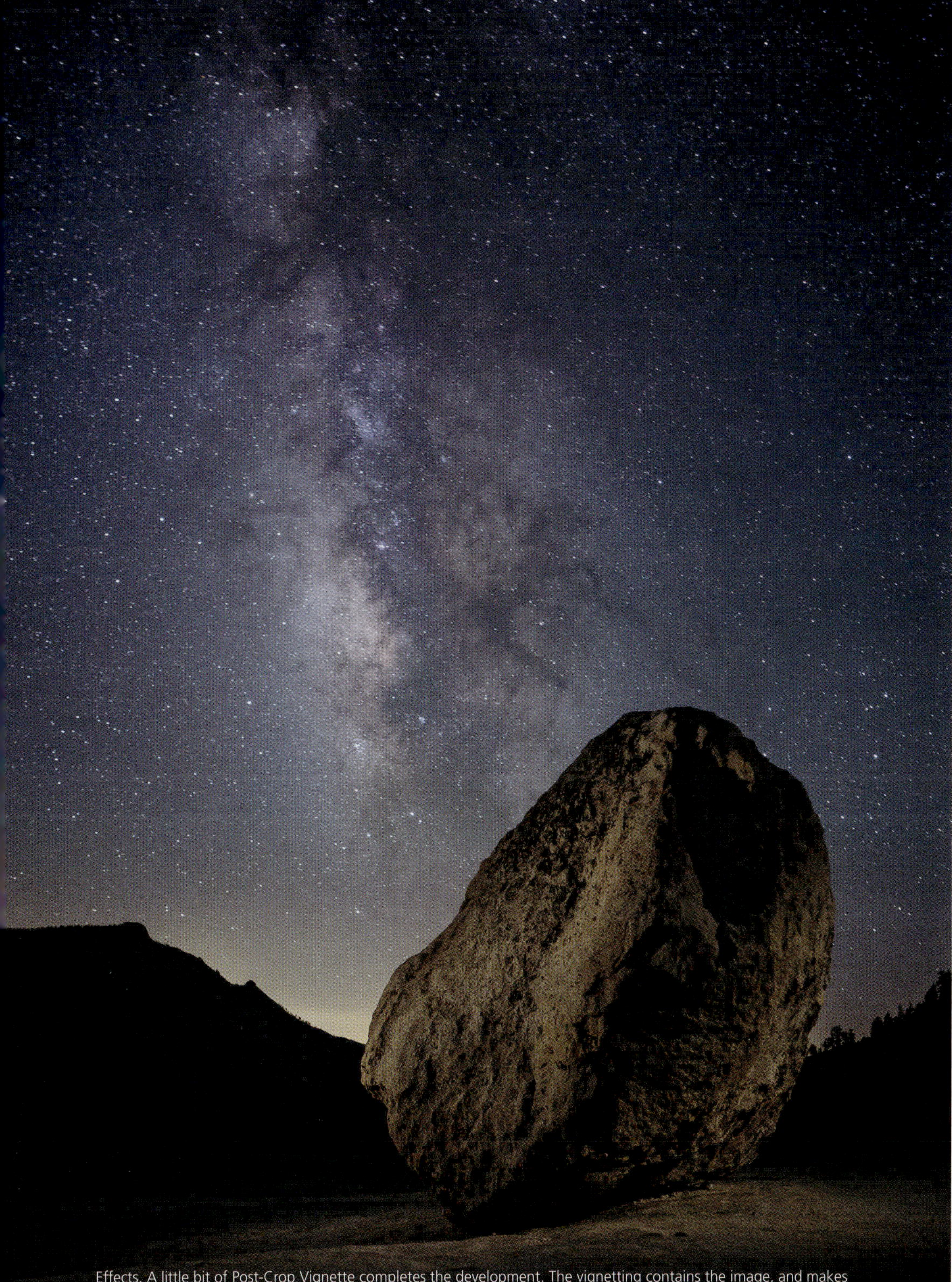

Effects. A little bit of Post-Crop Vignette completes the development. The vignetting contains the image, and makes it seem darker without obscuring detail. The final image is brighter than the scene appeared at the time, although the relative luminosity of the Milky Way core relative to the landscape is similar. It is entirely subjective how to interpret images like this. They can be, but don't have to be, made to look natural.

Canon 6D, Rokinon 24 mm f1.4 lens. 25 seconds
at f4, ISO 12,800. This image was developed
as usual in Lightroom, and then used to sync
the remaining images to the same settings. The
development was typical, except that care was
made to remove lens vignetting in the Lens
Corrections panel. There was no profile available
for the Rokinon lens, so corrections were not
applied automatically by checking the Enable Lens
Profile box in the basic tab.

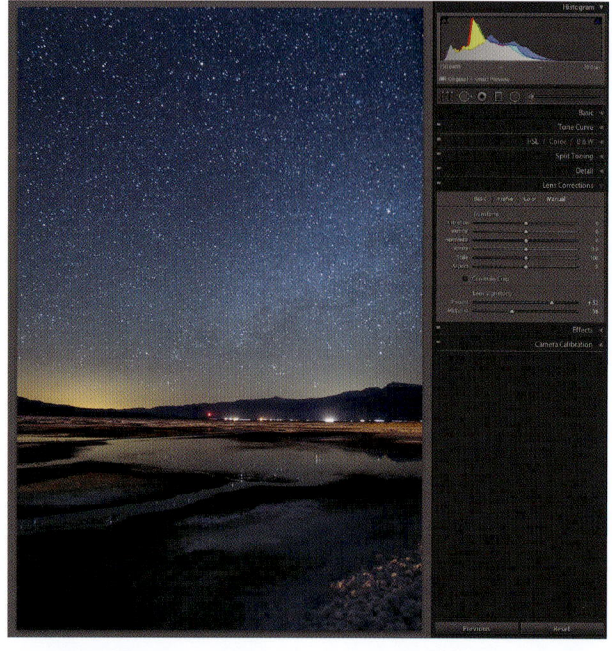

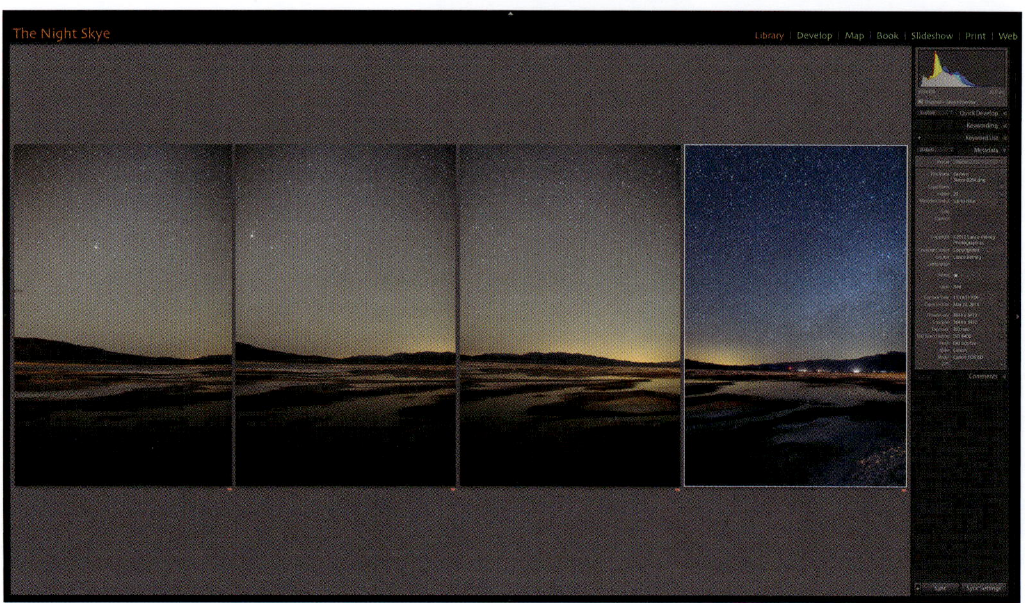

Canon 6D, Rokinon 24 mm f1.4 lens. 25 seconds at f4, ISO 12,800 × 4. Lightroom's survey mode shows the four images that will
be synced and merged. The settings are synced by clicking the Sync Settings button in the lower right corner.

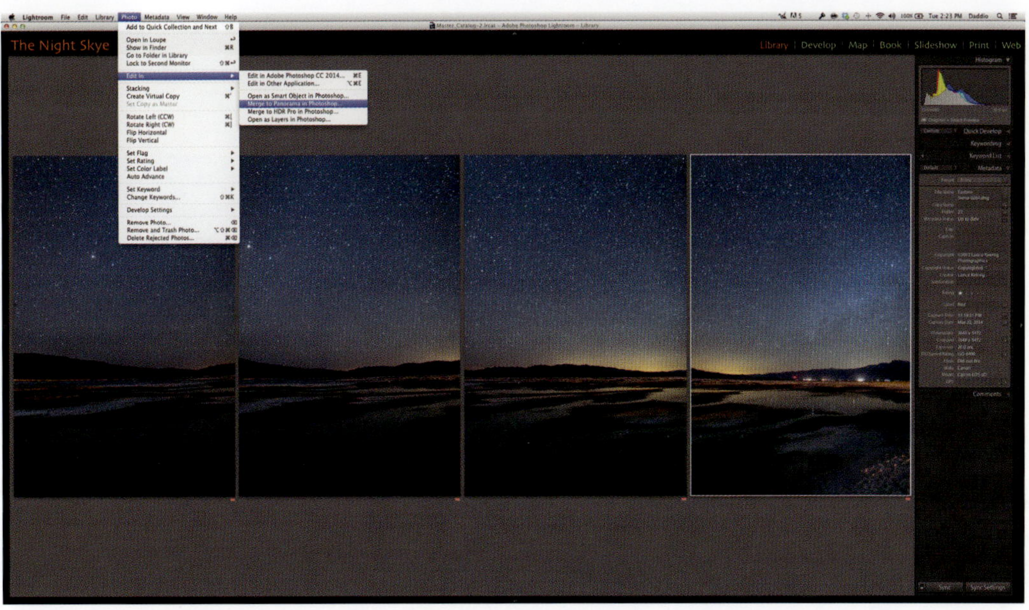

With all four images selected, choose: Photo/Edit in/Merge to Panorama in Photoshop. Photoshop will open and blend the files.

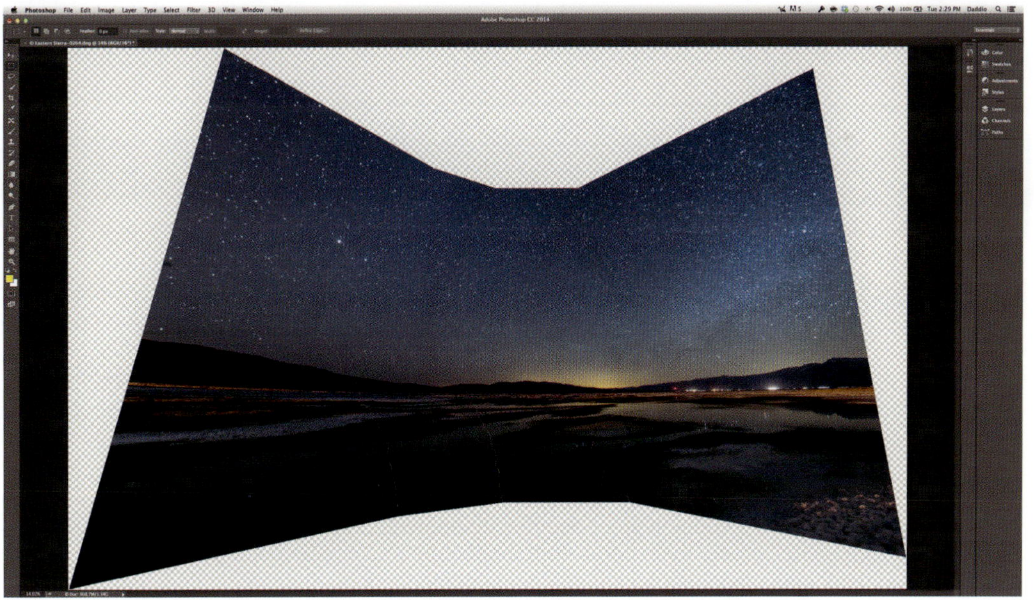

The merged images in Photoshop. The loss of image area is a result of the perspective distortion caused by rotating the lens. Flatten layers, crop, and save. The image appears inside the Lightroom catalog next to the original files as a TIFF file.

The final image. Post-Crop Vignetting is applied to the entire image, and clarity boosted by 10 points once the flattened file is back in Lightroom. This will be a rasterized file, and much larger than the four original DNG files combined. Saving it with layers increases the size even more.

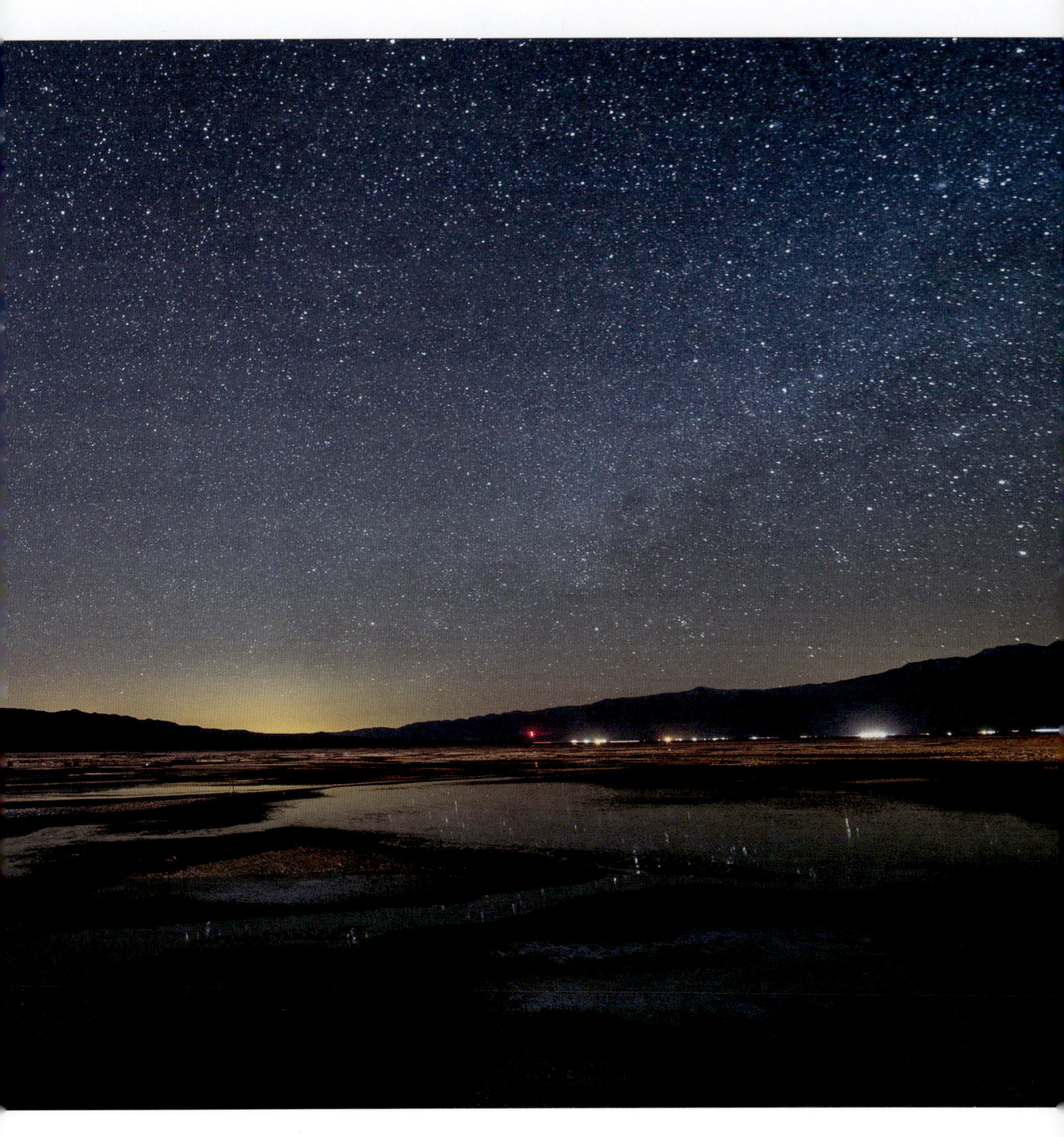

8

PAINTING WITH LIGHT—LIGHTING THE SUBJECT

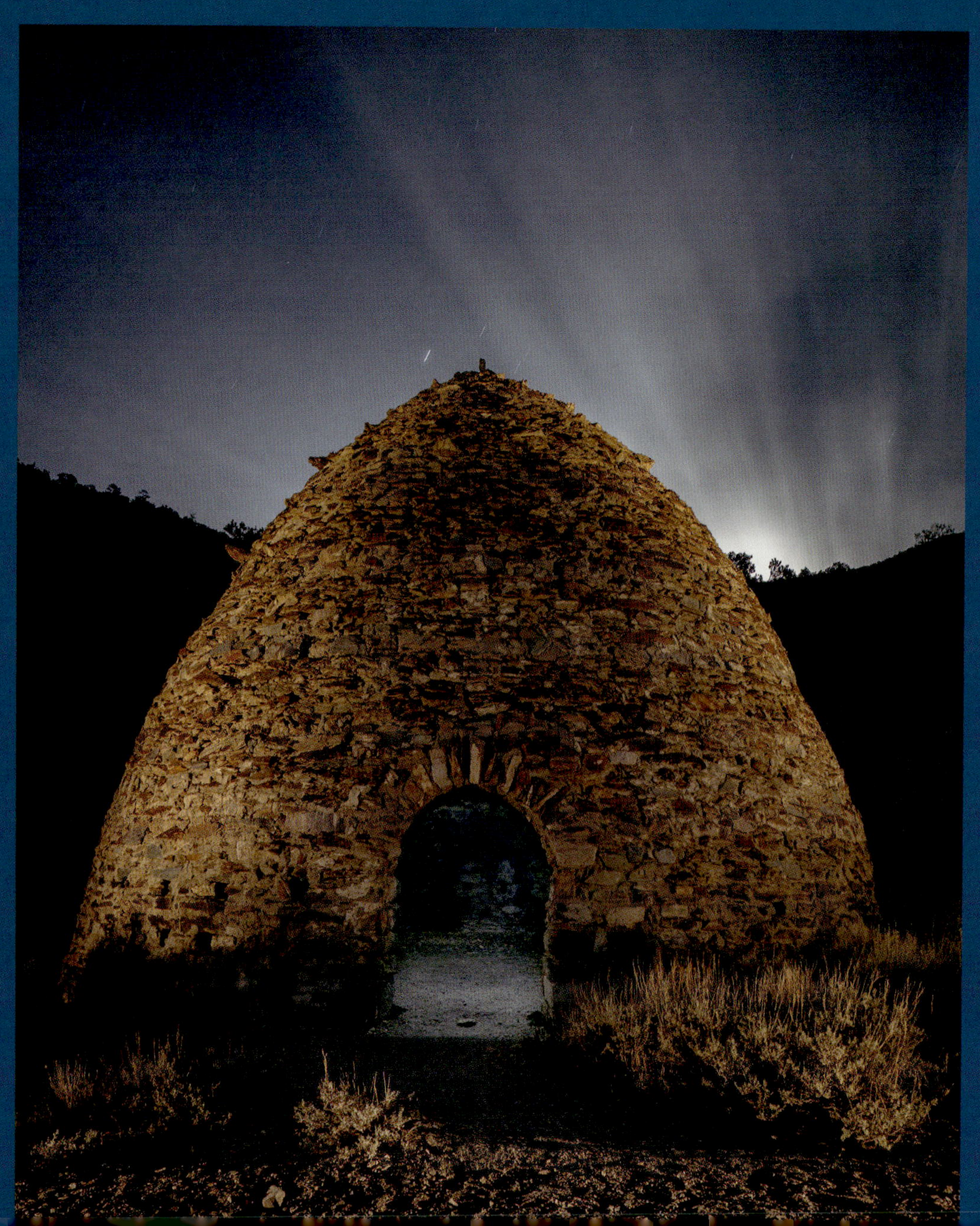

WHAT IS LIGHT PAINTING?

There has been some truly innovative work created in recent years using light painting and light drawing techniques. From simple fill light used to open up foreground shadows, to the use of lights with colored gels, to drawing or writing with light by pointing a flashlight back towards the camera, there are many exciting ways to work with added light. In this chapter, we explore light painting and light drawing with portable, handheld light sources.

The word photography translates literally from the Greek as light writing. For night photographers, the term light painting is often used any time light is added to night photos from a portable source that is not connected to the camera. More specifically, light painting describes situations when light is added to illuminate the subject of a photograph, originating from either inside or outside of the frame, but the source is usually hidden from the camera. Light painting can be supplemental to the ambient light or the primary light source; in some cases it can be the only source of light in the photograph. When flashlights are employed for light painting, they are often kept moving during use. In contrast, light drawing or light writing are the terms that describe when a light is directed back toward the camera from within the image frame. In this case, the light itself becomes the subject. Light can be used to create shapes or lines in the image or even to literally write words, numbers, or symbols. Light painting and drawing techniques can be combined in the same photograph to achieve varied effects.

There are many reasons why you might want to add light to a night photograph. In the simplest and most practical form, light painting can be a form of in-camera contrast control. By adding light to the shadow areas of an image, it is possible to reduce the overall contrast by raising the luminance values of the darkest parts of a scene. Most of the time this technique is used, the goal is to have the lighting so subtle that the photograph appears to have been taken with only existing light.

In many instances, light painting is used to emphasize or draw attention to a particular part of an image. By using supplementary lighting, the photographer has greater control over how the image is interpreted by the viewer. Some well-placed lighting can change the feeling of an image and shift the emphasis to different parts of a scene. The natural landscape can be one of the most challenging subjects to photograph at night because the resulting images have a tendency to look like daylight photographs if they are photographed by the light of the Moon alone. The addition of light from an unexpected direction, especially if it is a different color from the natural light, can completely transform a landscape from ordinary to sublime.

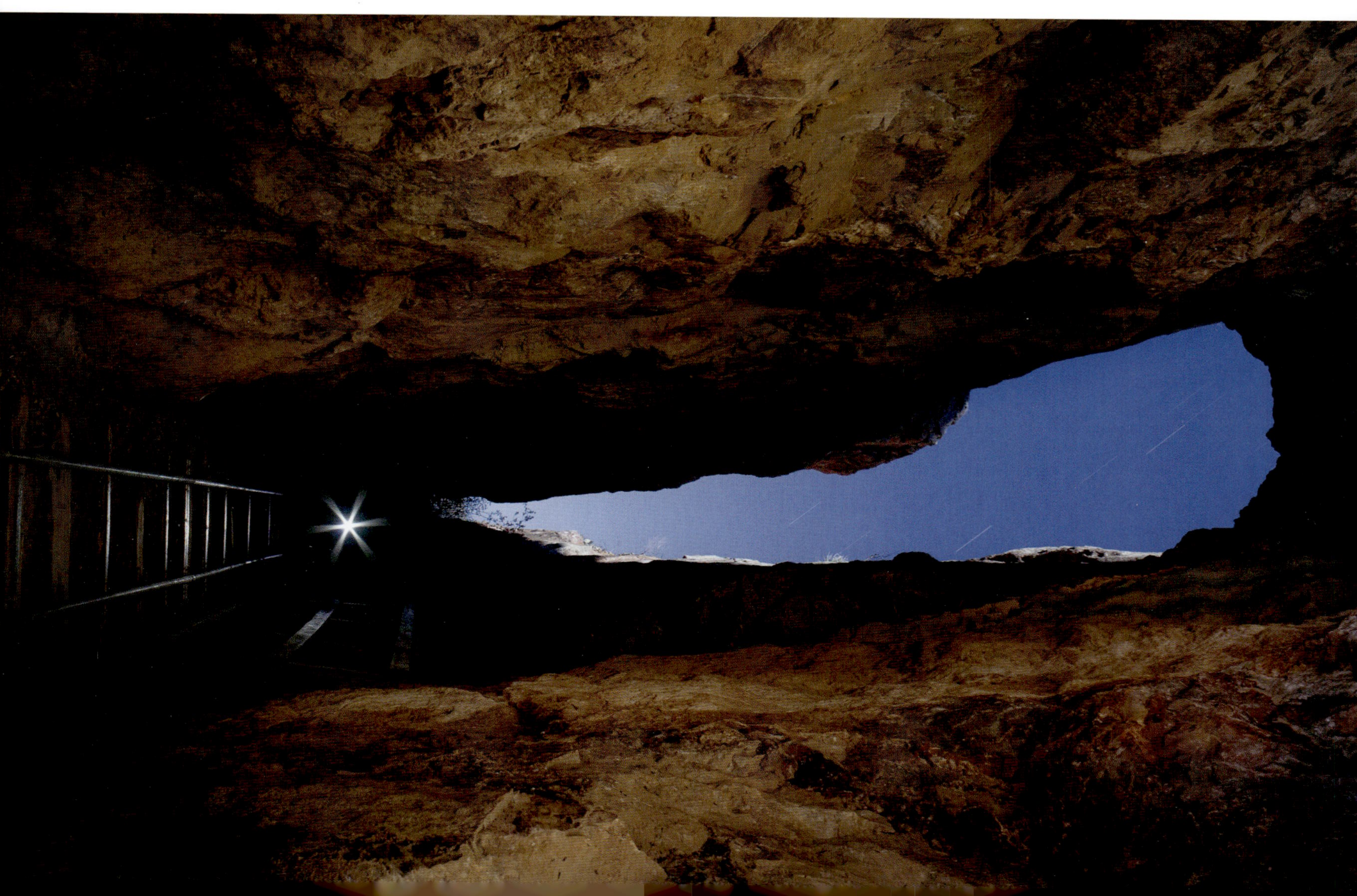

"Villa De La Mina," Terlingua, Texas. 8 minutes, f8 at ISO 320. Canon 5D MK II, 24 mm f3.5 Zuiko Shift lens. It was completely dark inside this mine shaft. Before light painting, the sky was the only thing visible in the frame. For about one-quarter of the total exposure, an incandescent flashlight was bounced off of the top of the shaft, which was about 30 feet high. The "train" was created by pointing the same light back toward the camera, and aiming it slightly below the camera for just a second.

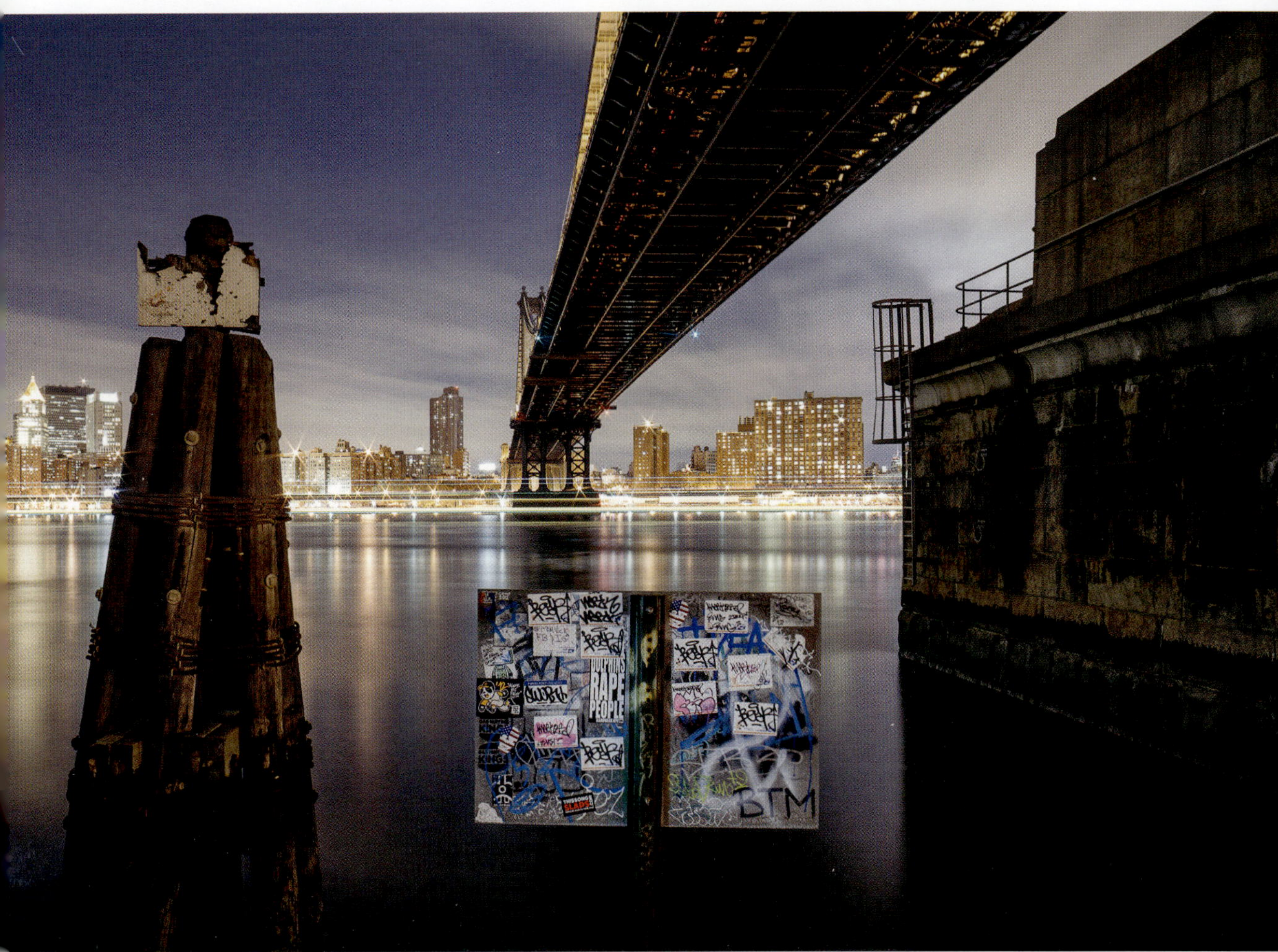

"Sign Of The Times," Brooklyn, NY. 5 minutes, f11, at ISO 100. Canon 5D MK II, 28 mm f3.5 Nikkor PC lens. Underneath the Brooklyn Bridge with some night photographer friends one night, this sticker-covered sign caught my eye. The sign was in shadow, and the first exposure recorded little detail. I wanted to be able to read the stickers and graffiti, but I didn't want any lighting to be obvious. A quick burst of a neutral colored flashlight from camera left gave me just what I needed without looking like the sign had been lit.

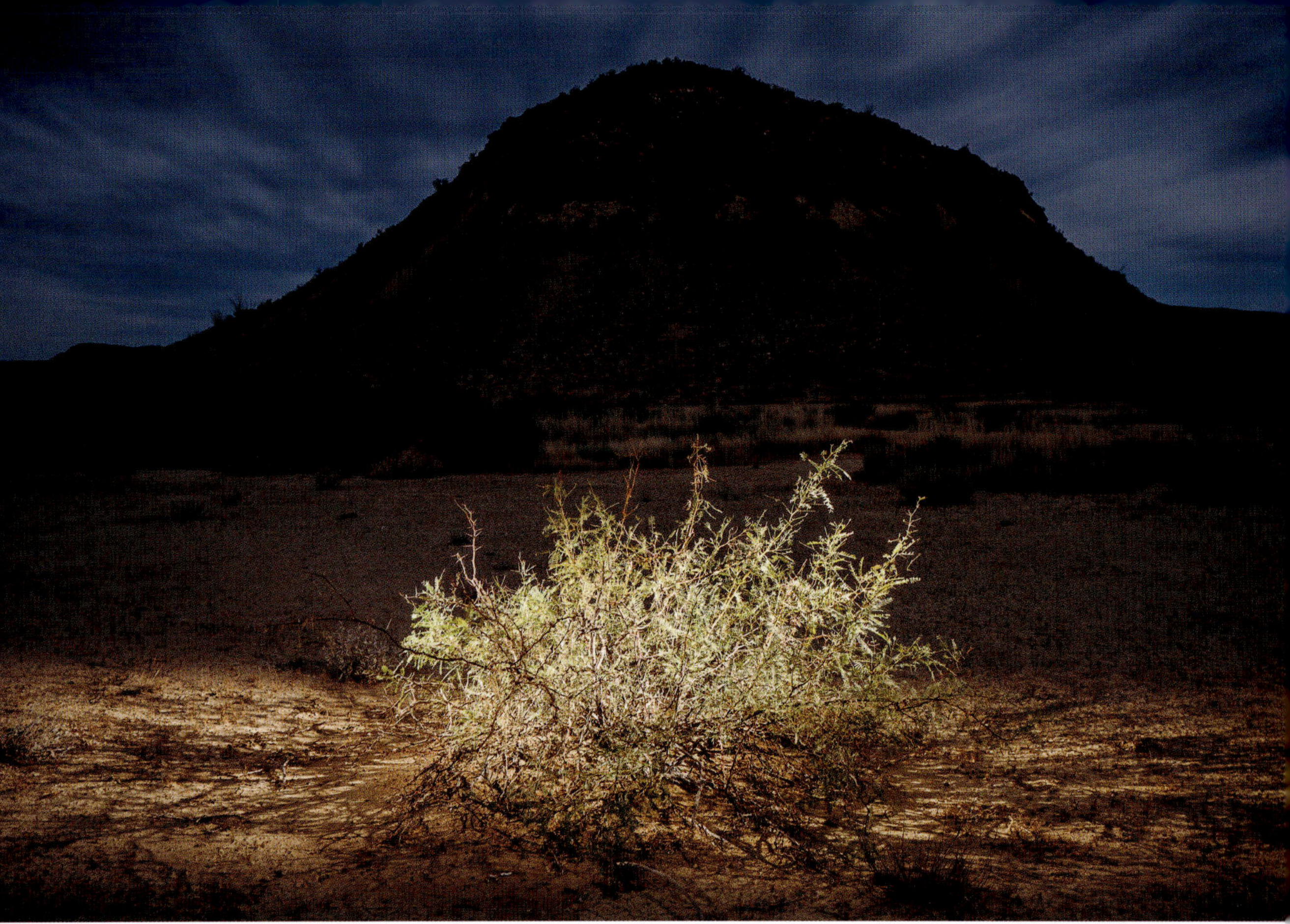

"Burning Bush," Study Butte, Texas. 3 minutes, f8 at 400 ISO. Canon 5D MK II, 35 mm f2.8 Zuiko Shift lens. The exposure was kept relatively short by raising the ISO to favor the movement of the clouds. The bush was illuminated from left and right with an incandescent flashlight.

The ability to make quality images at high ISOs has changed night photography forever. Photographers are no longer limited to long exposures at near native ISOs, but now routinely shoot at 3200, 6400, and even higher to record stars as points of light rather than star trails. I reiterate this here because light painting at high ISO is very different than at native ISO. The wide apertures, short exposures, and high ISOs used for astro-landscape photography mean that light painting needs to be achieved within a narrow time frame, and with very dim light sources. With exposures in the neighborhood of 15–30 seconds, that does not leave much time for lighting. Some light painters work around this problem by doing their lighting and ambient exposures in different frames, and blending them together in postprocessing. Others apply the Straight Out Of Camera (SOOC) approach, and use no postprocessing at all to prove that the shot was created entirely in-camera, without the use of Photoshop. As I've mentioned elsewhere in this book, my own approach is to try to do as much as possible in-camera, in the field, rather than at the computer, but I'm not opposed to using software if the image cannot be created without it. There is no right or wrong way; it is up to each individual to work out techniques that best suit their own particular style.

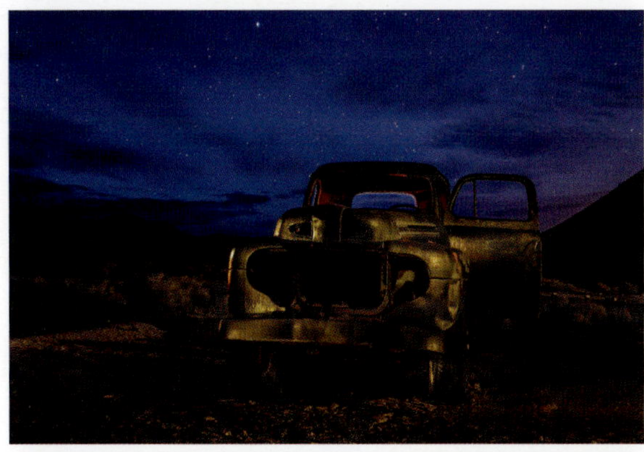

"An Old Truck in Rhyolite," NV. 6 × 30 seconds, f6.7, ISO 6400. Canon 6D, Sigma 35 mm f1.4 lens. In order to preserve the stars as points of light, this image was shot at 6400. The lighting was done in six separate 30-second frames, mainly as an exercise to see how well it would work. The truck was painted matte black, and absorbed most of the light that hit it. This was a fun experiment, but difficult to pull off.

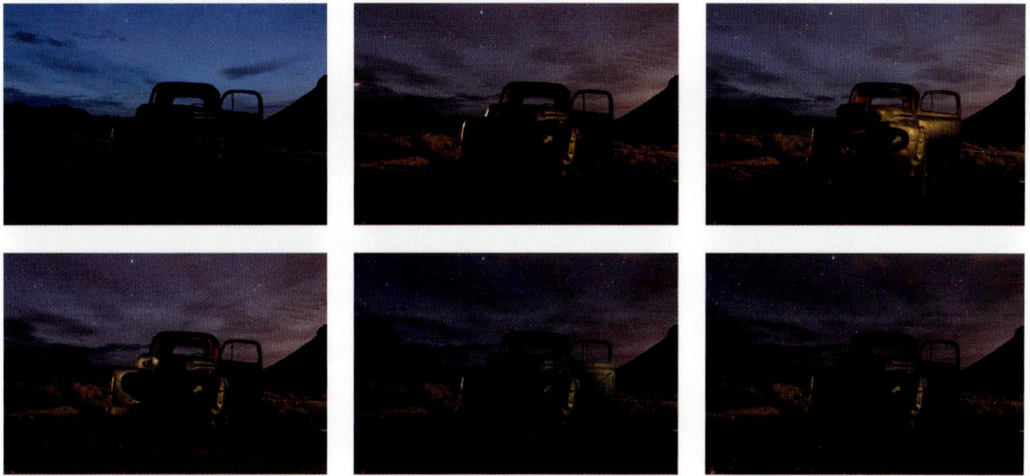

The six frames that make up the previous image, NV. Each was 30 seconds, f6.7, ISO 6400. Canon 6D, Sigma 35 mm f1.4 lens. Only the best parts of each image were used, including the sky from the first image.

Photographer and light painter Eric Curry describes the complex process he uses in his own book on light painting, which involves intensive planning, scouting, and preparation, with many different exposures all combined together in a laborious process involving hours and hours of Photoshop. Many of his images are too complex to be achieved in-camera, in a single exposure, so he developed his own techniques to suit his needs. I encourage you to consider this as your work evolves and to explore the possibilities.

There are many ways to add light to night photographs. Some photographers, like Gregory Crewdson, take a studio approach to lighting. Crewdson's elaborate productions involve truckloads of equipment, a crew of lighting technicians, and the construction of

Hollywood-style sets. Crewdson doesn't really use light painting, but sophisticated location lighting—the difference being that he uses multiple lights mounted on stands. The great train photographer O. Winston Link made his famous railroad images in the 1950s using similar techniques. Most photographers of course don't have access to those types of resources. Even if they did, the majority of night shooters would prefer the intimacy and freedom of working on a smaller scale. It is remarkable what can be achieved with a few simple tools added to the camera bag. Traveling light allows for greater spontaneity and productivity. Most light painting is accomplished either with flashlights or handheld strobes, but there is a dizzying array of lighting tools available today, including a couple of highly specialized light painting tools made just for this purpose. Troy Paiva, whose guest section appears later in this chapter, uses the versatile Protomachines LED2 lighting tool almost exclusively to light his images.

Although both hot shoe-mounted and pop-up flashes provide a ready light source when light levels are too low for handheld exposures, or when a tripod is not an option, the use of an on-camera flash is not recommended for night photography. Night photographers rarely use it because the quality of light from an on-camera flash is not very pleasing. A flash fired from the camera position flattens out shape and texture, and throws hard, unattractive shadows behind the subject. In certain situations, an on-camera flash can be used effectively as a fill light, but it is limited to nearby foreground subjects. Flash is often employed as a creative lighting tool by night photographers, but it is usually handheld and fired manually, well away from the camera.

Just as camera technology has evolved in recent years, there have been major improvements in flashlight and battery technology. There are a wide variety of lighting tools available that all serve a specific purpose. Compact lights with fiber optic tips can be used to add light with pinpoint precision, and high-powered LED lights are capable of illuminating large areas from great distances. Flashlights are available with incandescent, xenon, fluorescent, or LED bulbs, which all have different color temperatures and qualities. There are flashlights with variable width or focusing beams, and light modifiers to control and shape the light. Glow sticks, sparklers, candles, and even car headlights can be used for light painting, and experimentation is the best way to learn to use them effectively.

The camera can even be taken off the tripod, and intentionally moved during the exposure. In this situation, any ambient lights in the scene are recorded as lines or light trails that reveal the movement of the camera. The Hungarian painter and photographer László Moholy Nagy and American Harry Callahan may have been the first to use this form of light writing in the early 1940s by moving the camera up and down and in circles to create abstract patterns of light.

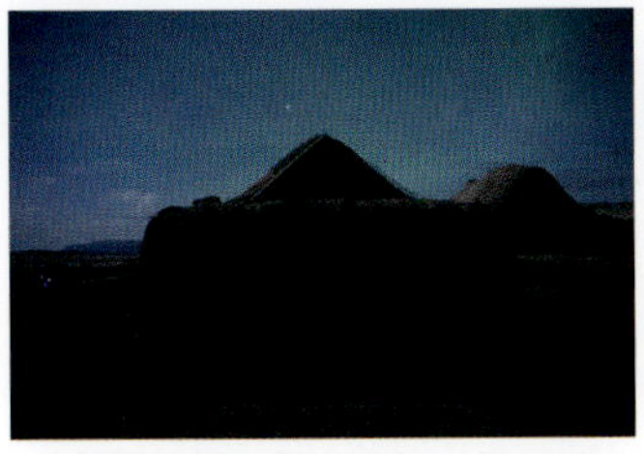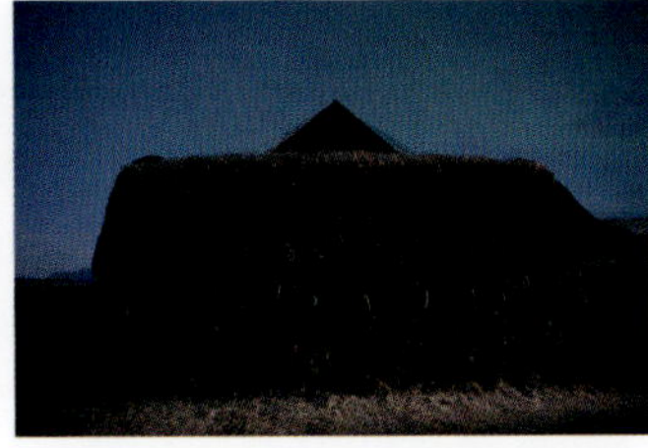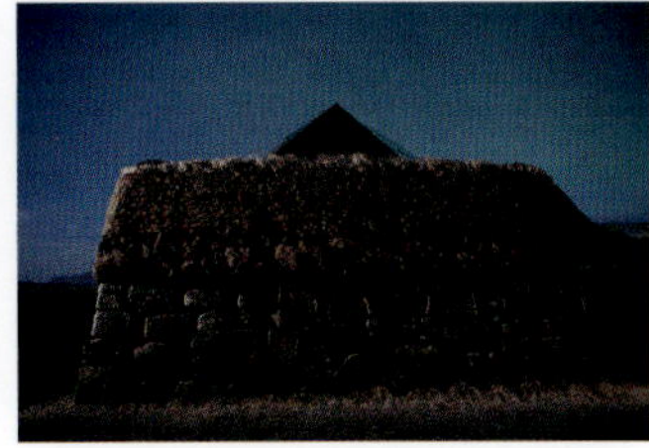

Three test exposures showing ambient light, side lighting from the right, and side lighting from both sides. The side lighting brings out the texture in the rock wall and thatched roof on this building on a farm in Iceland. The green in the sky is the Aurora Borealis.

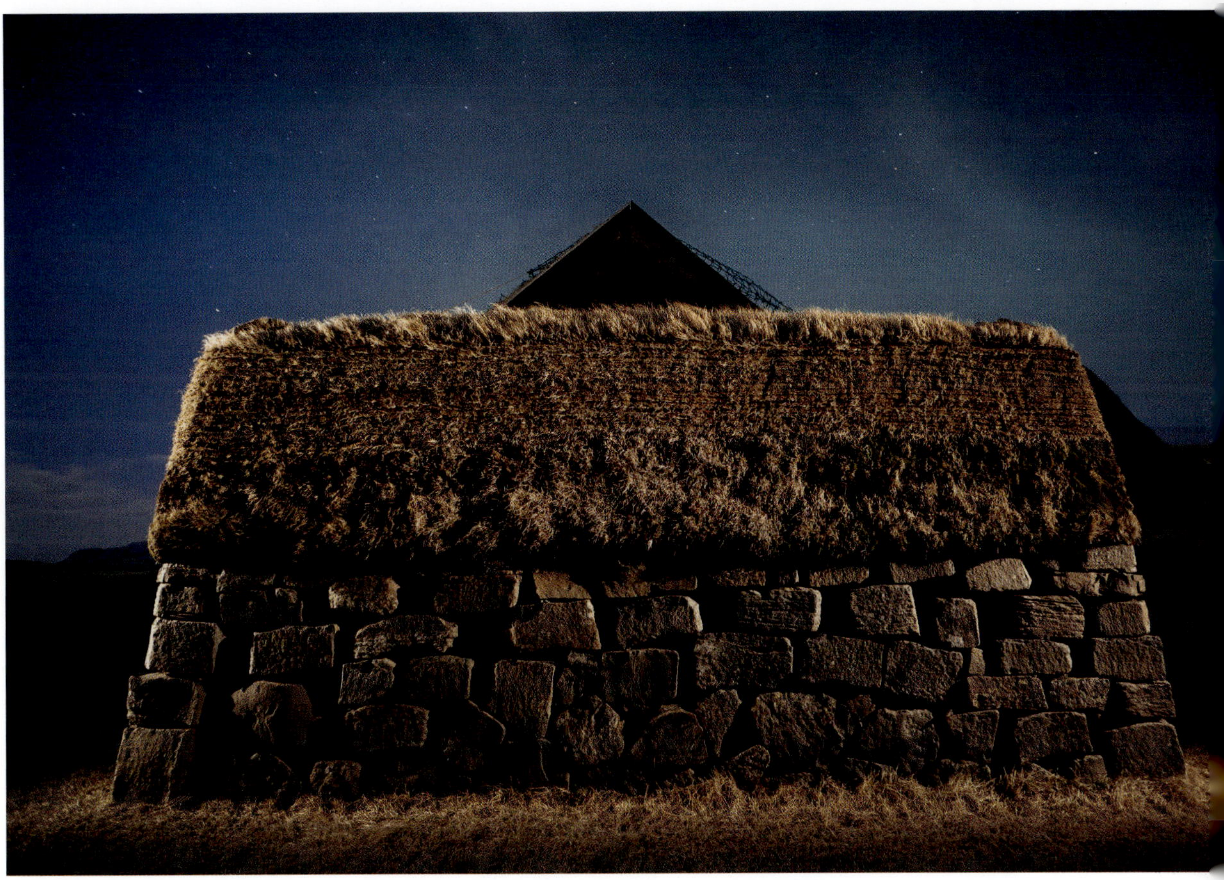

30 seconds, f8 at ISO 800. Moonlight, Aurora, and warm LED flashlight from both sides. A restored 17th-century barn on a farm museum in south Iceland. The dramatic light painting makes up for the bland Northern Lights that night.

LIGHT PAINTING AND EXPOSURE

Light painting and drawing are inexact sciences, and determining the right amount of light to use involves some trial and error. The most important concept to understand when working with added light is that time is used to control the ambient or overall exposure, and the intensity of any added light is largely determined by changing the aperture or ISO. One of the most challenging parts of this type of photography can be finding the right balance between ambient and added light. If your exposure is too long, the background may look like daylight, and the light painting may be washed out or overpowered by the ambient exposure. If your base exposure is too short, you may end up with clipped or underexposed shadows and light painting that stands out too much from the background.

Consider reducing the time of your ambient exposure by one to three stops if you are adding a significant amount of light. The reason for the shorter exposure is not because the light painting will necessarily affect the background brightness but to ensure a better contrast ratio between ambient and added light parts of the image. If the light painting is the only source of illumination in a completely dark environment, the length of the exposure is determined simply by the amount of time required to do the painting. There is no need to hurry to close the shutter, but extending the exposure in this case risks adding noise, more than any useful exposure, to your image.

One instance when you probably would not reduce your overall exposure would be if you were adding light simply to open up dark shadows, and were trying to hide the fact that you had

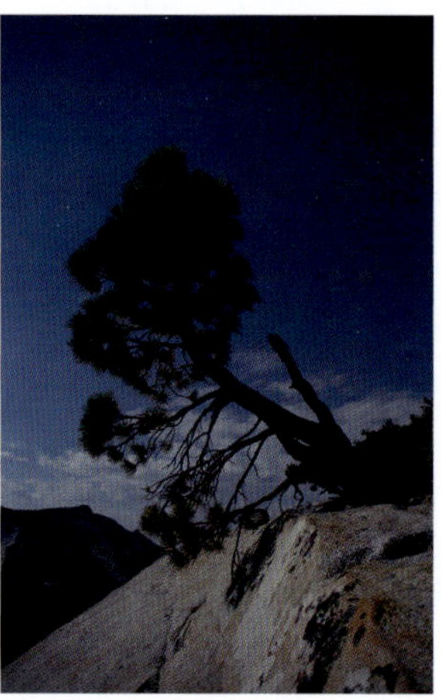 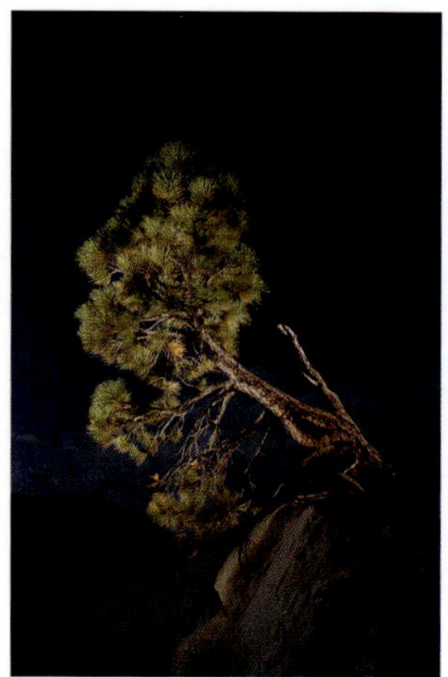 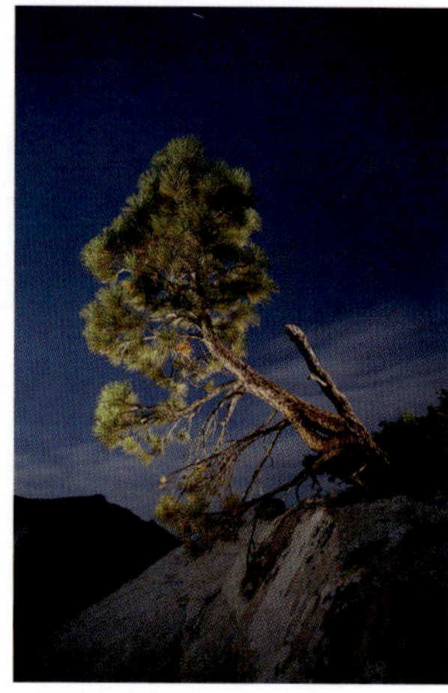

Three variations showing ambient to added light ratios. The image on the left shows a high-ISO ambient-only exposure—8 seconds, f5.6, ISO 6400. The middle exposure is three stops less—1 minute, f5.6, ISO 100. The right-hand image is one stop less than the first image—4 minutes, f5.6, ISO 100. The added light was the same in the second and third images, but the ratio of ambient to added light is two stops different.

added light (see page 189). In this situation, you'll want to make sure that the area with light painting is not brighter than the midtone areas of the image, otherwise the light painting will really stand out. Bouncing the light off of a white card or collapsible reflector is helpful to keep the added light subtle. Be careful not to let the reflector object show up in the image. This has the effect of softening the quality of light, and eliminating, or muting, the shadows. When shooting in color, you'll also want to be mindful of the color of light that you add. We explore the use of color later in the chapter.

HIGH-ISO TESTING AND LIGHT PAINTING

To determine the right exposure length for your chosen aperture and refine the composition, use a high-ISO test as described in Chapter 6. Because changing the ISO will also affect the brightness of any added light, it is difficult to gauge how much added light is needed by a high-ISO test. For this reason, you may be able to use the high-ISO test to analyze the quality and direction of added light, but not the quantity. Technically you could make the calculations, but it is complicated and has lots of opportunities for errors. The only way to accurately work out your light painting using high-ISO tests would be if you had two light sources that were exactly six stops apart in brightness—the difference between testing and shooting ISOs. Even so, this technique would only work if you could successfully achieve all of your lighting in the short duration of the test exposure. Definitely do the high-ISO test to nail down your composition and ambient exposure as well as to check for focus and other potential problems, but don't rely on it to determine your light painting exposure. All testing of light painting should be done at the working aperture and ISO to ensure accurate results.

Flash can be measured with a handheld light meter or by setting the flash power based on distance and guide numbers. If colored gels are used in combination with flash, the power of the flash must be adjusted to account for the light blocked by the gel. It is much more complicated to predetermine precisely how long to use a flashlight because the light is often kept moving during the exposure. Moving the light softens the edges, and makes for interesting effects, but also makes it difficult to ensure even illumination and exposure. Sometimes the photographer will also be moving while painting with a flashlight, which makes it truly impossible to meter the light accurately. There is really no convenient way to predetermine how many seconds of flashlight or how many pops from a flash are required to paint a scene. Fortunately, developing a feel for using lights this way comes fairly easily, and absolute precision is rarely necessary. Digital shooters should review and analyze their images in the field to determine what improvements can be made. Use the RGB histogram to assess ambient exposure, and blinking highlight indicator or zebra stripes, if your camera has them, to determine whether or not you have highlight clipping from too much added light. If you reduce the ambient exposure for a more pronounced light painting effect, try to keep the histogram from moving all the way to the left, which would indicate significant shadow clipping.

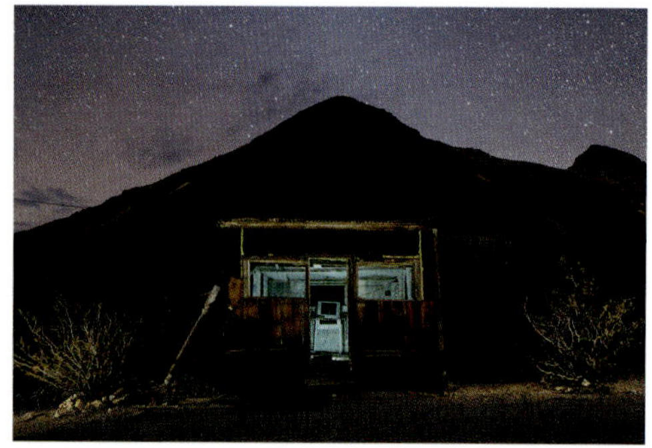 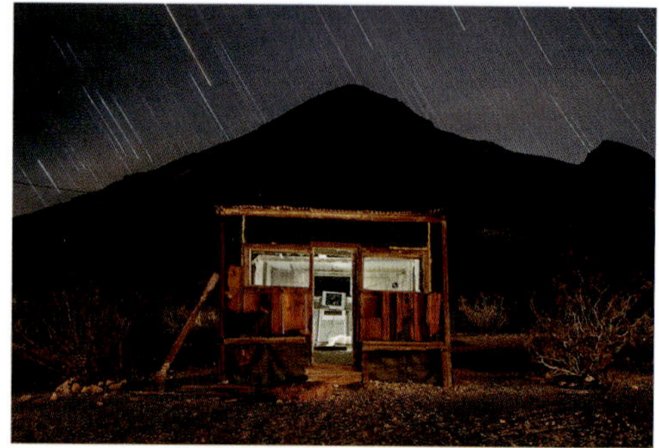

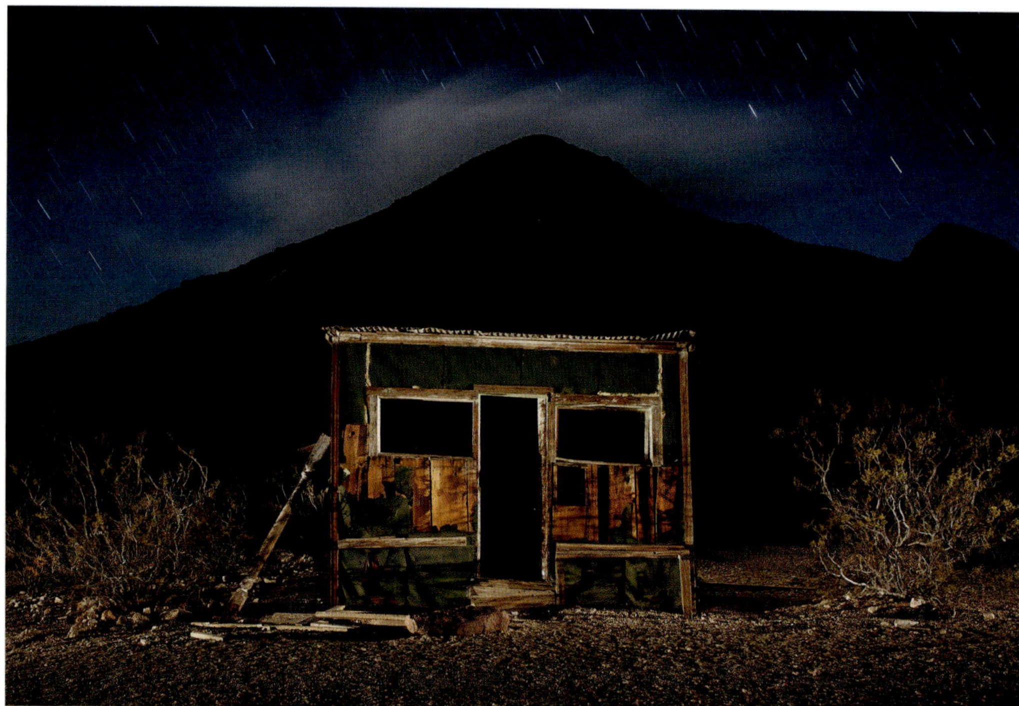

Three variations of the same shot, all taken on the same night within an hour of each other. Top left—30 seconds, f2.8, ISO 12,800. Very dim LED flashlight on the front of the shack and bushes and another weak LED left inside on the floor during the entire exposure. Top right—the other extreme. 54 minutes at f4, ISO 160. Same basic lighting, different white balance. Bottom image—4½ minutes, f4, at ISO 160. Similar side lighting, except with an incandescent light this time, and no light in the interior. A magic cloud appeared above the mountain for this image.

You can still have a right-biased histogram, but be aware that the height of the highlight part of the histogram may not rise much off of the floor if the highlights represent a small overall percentage of the image. The expression of tones across the horizontal axis of the histogram is much more important than the quantity of any one specific tone along the vertical axis.

DETERMINING HOW MUCH LIGHT TO ADD

There are several factors to consider when trying to determine how much and which type of light to add to an image. In addition to the ISO and working aperture, you'll need to consider the brightness of your light source, the distance from the light to the subject, the size of the object(s) to be lit, the reflectivity of your subject, the desired quality of light on the subject, and what color light will help you to achieve the look you want for the photograph.

The intensity of your light source in combination with aperture and ISO probably has the greatest impact on the image. It is fairly obvious that you'll need to paint with a penlight for a much longer time than a big, powerful flashlight, and that a flash set to full power will light a larger area from a farther distance than one set to one-quarter power. Additionally, the same amount of added light will appear brighter with a wider aperture, or higher ISO, than with the lens stopped down, or at native ISO. Flashes will maintain their intensity as batteries begin to wear out, but recharging between flashes takes longer as the batteries get weaker. Most flashlights become dimmer as the batteries are drained, and incandescent lights become warmer in color.

Another consideration is the distance from the light source to the subject. When a light is moved further from an object, the amount of light reaching the object will decrease by the square of the inverse of that distance. For example, doubling the distance from light to subject will result in only 1/4 of the light reaching the subject. This is known as the inverse square law. If the light starts out 6 feet from an object and is then moved to 12 feet from the object, only 1/4 of the light (two stops less) falling on the object at 6 feet will reach it at 12 feet. Tripling the distance results in the light being only 1/9 as bright, quadrupling the distance results in the light being only 1/16 as bright, and so on. The inverse square law applies to any type of light source. Remember that if the light is reduced by half, the exposure will need to be increased by one stop. Camera-to-subject distance has less impact on lighting; it is mainly light-to-subject distance that matters.

The size of the area to be illuminated also needs to be taken into account. A small object can be lit with a single pop from a flash or with a relatively stationary flashlight. If you need to light a large area, you may need to fire a flash repeatedly or use a flashlight for a longer duration, changing positions to cover a wide area. Moving the light back and forth as if painting with a brush can cover a large area with even a modest flashlight given enough time. Remember

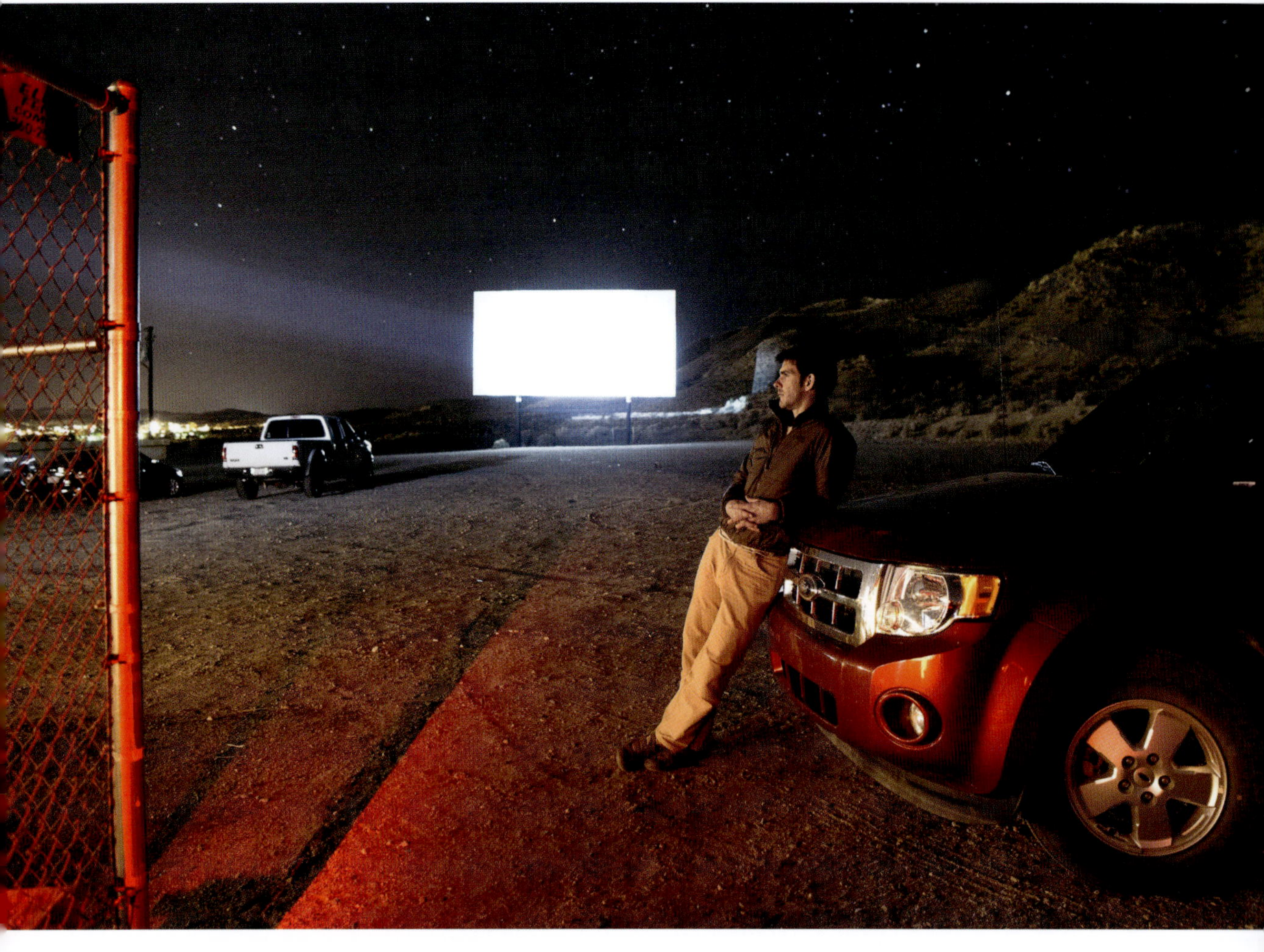

Scott Martin at the Bartsow Drive-in. 4 seconds, f5.6 at ISO 6400. Canon 5D MK II, Rokinon 24 mm, f1.4 lens. We were on a road trip photographing the California desert when Scott noticed the seemingly abandoned drive-in. It turned out that they were just about to open, and we stayed so Scott could do a time lapse during the movie. This portrait was missing something until I hit the fence with a red LED light, adding a splash of color that tied in with the car, and added a diagonal shadow leading back into the image.

that you don't need to light the entire scene from the same position. Just as a commercial photographer would set up multiple lights in different positions, you can achieve a similar effect with a single light by changing locations during the exposure. As long as you wear dark-colored clothing and are careful not to spill the light onto yourself, you needn't worry about walking in front of the camera during the exposure. Of course if the ambient light level is fairly bright, you shouldn't linger in the same place for too long. Eventually, you'll appear as a ghost, especially if you are standing between the camera and object you are lighting.

The reflectivity and color of the object(s) you intend to light also influence how much light will be required. A light-colored or metallic subject needs much less illumination than a dark, non-reflective subject. The difference can be several stops. Trees are notoriously difficult to light, because they absorb most of the light that falls on them. Shiny and wet surfaces are more reflective than dull or dry ones and therefore require less exposure. The night photography pioneers of the 1890s frequently photographed street scenes on rainy nights for this very reason.

The quality of light from a strobe is similar to sunlight. Strobes are a bright, even point source and cast a hard shadow. Flash is best for lighting large, broad areas, like an empty room. The strobe can be fired multiple times from different positions to evenly light a large area. It is difficult to control if you are trying to light a small object in a crowded space. You might want to mask the light with a black card or a snoot—either home-made or a purpose-made product like the Flash Wrap to prevent light spill. A flashlight is softer, more diffuse, and easier to use on a small, localized area. If you want to highlight one object in a busy scene, a well-aimed flashlight (especially if modified with a snoot of some sort) will do the job nicely. Changing the position of the flashlight during use will overlap any shadows, softening or eliminating them altogether. Keeping the flashlight in a fixed position will cast a hard shadow. Shielding your flashlight with a black card, or shade made out of gaffer's or duct tape, can help to prevent the camera from picking up the light source if you're using it inside the frame. The width of the beam of light can also be controlled this way. Cardboard tubes such as a paper towel or gift wrap roll make convenient light modifiers, or you could make a more durable one out of PVC pipe wrapped in gaffer's tape to make it opaque. If you can find a tube that is just slightly larger in diameter than your flashlight, it can be attached to the light so that you can use the light and snoot together with just one hand. A little tape on the end of the light can help to make a snug fit. The longer the tube, the narrower the beam of light coming out the other end.

The positioning of the light plays a significant role in the quality of light. Frontal lighting that is perpendicular to the subject is flat and obscures detail. As mentioned earlier, on-camera flash is an example of this type of lighting, which is why it is best to avoid it. Light directed from oblique angles will emphasize the texture of any surface and bring out detail. This kind of lighting is much more dramatic than frontal lighting and almost always makes for a more successful photograph. While you're light painting, you see the light from the position of the light, not from the camera's perspective, so it is helpful to have someone assist you with the lighting; you will be able to remain at the camera and have a better sense of how it is going to look in the picture. Two photographers working together, taking turns at the lights and camera, can make for a more productive session. Collaborating and exchanging ideas is a great way to learn light painting and can truly enhance the experience.

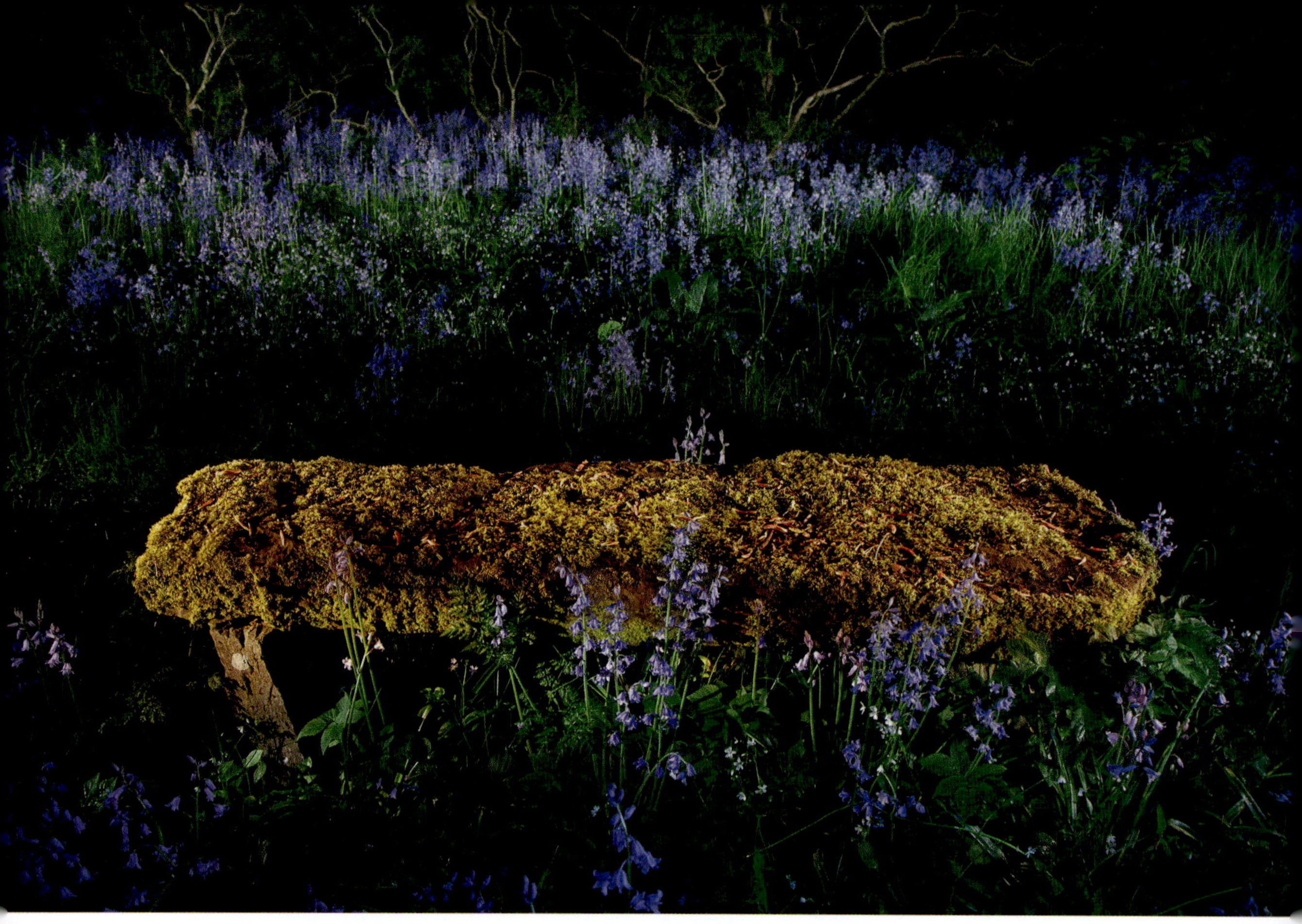

"Moss-covered Bench and Bluebells," Evie, Orkney, Scotland. 5 minutes, f5.6 at ISO 100. Canon 5D MK II, 24 mm f2.8 Canon lens. Side lighting from left and right with warm and cool lights. I first tried this shot with a single light source—an incandescent flashlight—but it was lifeless and monochromatic. Using a cool LED light on the vegetation and a warm incandescent on the mossy bench proved to be just what was needed to make it come to life.

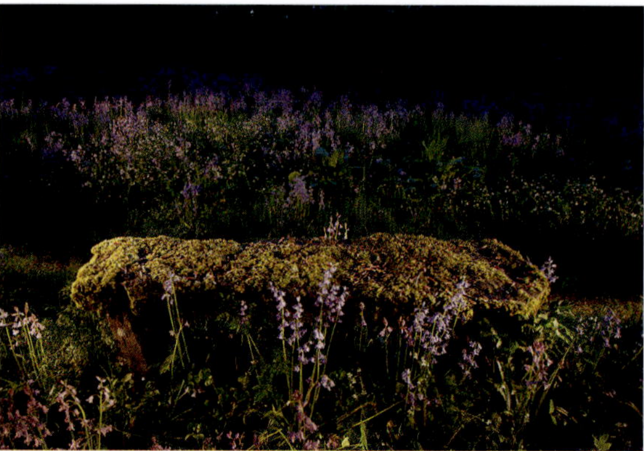

The same image illuminated with only a warm light source.

COLOR

Color can have a strong psychological impact on your photos. Its use can be subtle or dramatic. In particular, complementary or opposite colors in the spectrum can be used to highlight or isolate certain aspects of your image. Different sources of light have different color temperatures, and the selection of a light should not be made randomly. Most incandescent flashlights have a color temperature of about 2800 K, which is close to the 3200 K tungsten white balance. Flash has a color temperature of approximately 5000 K, or daylight white balance. LED lights can range from 2900 to 7000 K, but the majority of LED flashlights are in the 5000–7000 K range. Consider whether you want your added light to blend in or to contrast with the ambient light. In typical urban areas with predominantly warm sodium vapor lighting, cold flash or LED lights will stand out. Although the light added from a tungsten-balanced source will not match exactly, it will be more subtle than the light from a bluer source. Areas lit with metal halide lights will have a similar color balance to LED lights and flash. If you want your lighting to simply fill in a deep shadow, use a light that is similar to the ambient light. If you want to emphasize something, use a different colored source. The color of the object to be illuminated should also be taken into consideration. It seldom makes sense to light a warm-colored object with a cool-colored light, or vice versa. For example, painting a red car with a cool LED light would probably not look very good. The one exception to this rule of thumb is foliage, which can be lit with either warm or cool light as the situation demands.

You can also add color by placing lighting gels in front of your flashlight or strobe. Gels block part of the visible spectrum of light, allowing only light that matches the color of the gels to pass through. Because the gel will block some of the light from your source, you'll need to compensate with either more time with the flashlight, multiple pops of the flash, or increasing the power of the flash. Different colors reduce the light output by varying amounts. For example, yellow and amber gels will let much more light pass through than deep blue, green, or purple gels. Some of the most saturated colors reduce light output by as much as four stops. You can calculate the difference, using the transmission data supplied by the manufacturer, by measuring the light intensity both with and without a handheld light meter, or just by trial and error. Lighting gels come in individual 20 × 24-inch sheets or in the more practical 3 × 5-inch and 1× 3-inch sample packs from Roscolux. The sample packs are ideal because for a minimal investment you'll get over a hundred different colors. The 3 × 5 size is more versatile because it will cover a wider array of lights. The smaller size fits perfectly over most flash heads, but the pieces are too small to use with many flashlights. Before you venture out into the field, disassemble the swatch book and choose five to ten colors to carry with you. You may find it helpful to laminate the smaller pieces, as they are thin and can be awkward to handle, especially in windy conditions. If carried intact, the swatch book becomes cumbersome and frustrating to use. Lumiquest makes a compact gel holder that attaches to your flash head with Velcro, holds the gels in place, and stores the ones you're not using with the flash. Double-stick

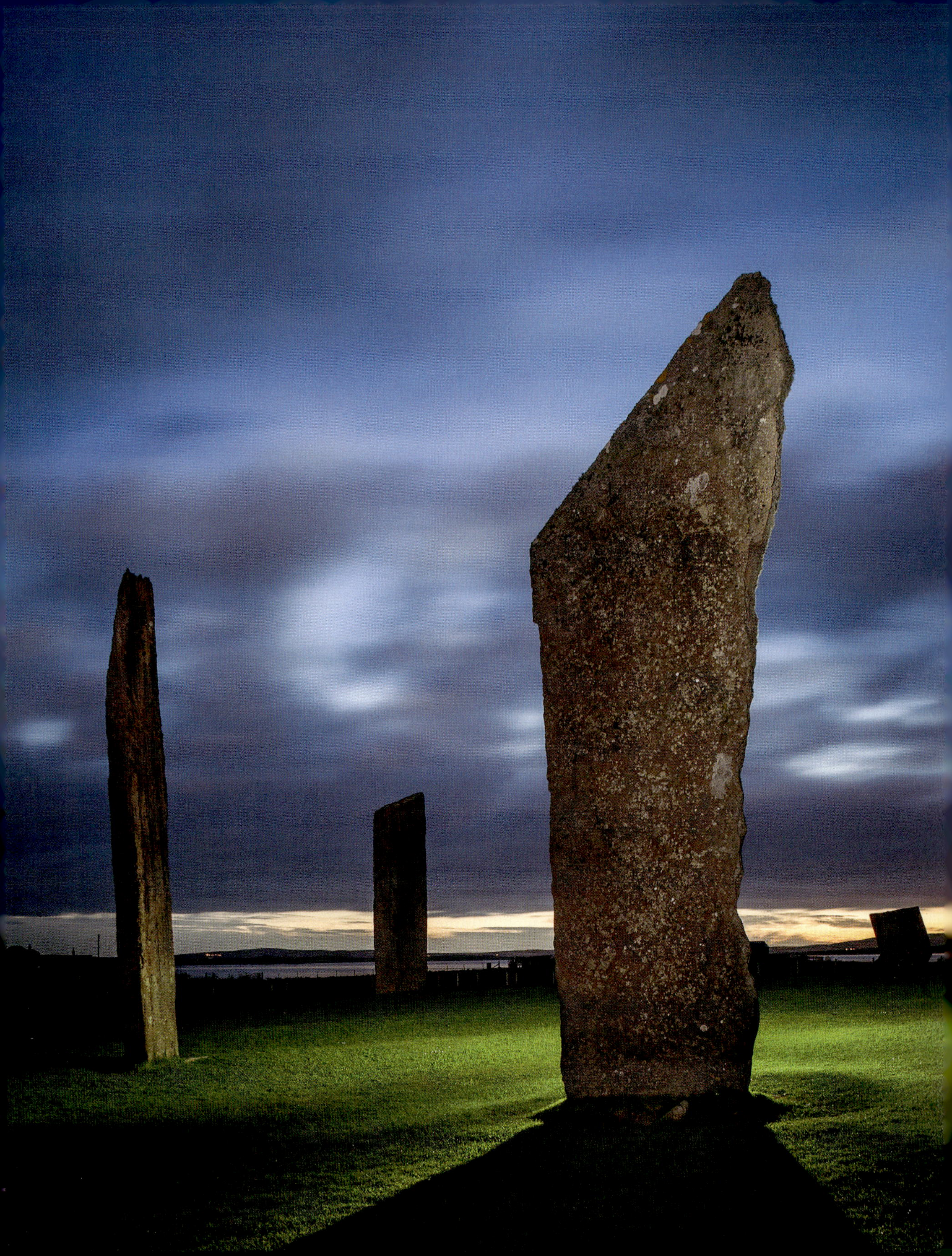

"Stones of Stenness," Orkney, Scotland. 30 seconds, f8 at ISO 800. Canon 5D MK II, 28 mm f3.5 PC Nikkor lens. Shot about 11:30 pm near the Summer Solstice—about an hour after sunset. Light painting with a warm LED flashlight on the stones, and backlighting with the light placed directly behind the tallest one. The 30-second exposure didn't give me much time to light, but I had no choice as my intervalometer had died a few minutes earlier.

tape on your flash head or flashlight bezel will work as well, but will occasionally need to be replaced as the adhesive wears out.

There really is no right or wrong way to approach light painting, but it does take time to learn how to anticipate how a shot will turn out and to develop the confidence to pull it off. You'll want to develop your own ideas and style, but looking at the work of other photographers, and shooting with others, is a great way to learn. Learn to pre-visualize your images as your visual voice matures, but don't become so fixed on an idea that you close yourself to new possibilities when they arise. There is an ever-growing global community of light painters online to explore, learn from, and to share your images with. All of the photo-sharing websites, as well as Facebook and Google+, have multiple groups for light painters. See the resources section for a partial listing. Now it is time to explore the fascinating world of drawing with light. Chapter 9 presents images by several of the leading light painting photographers working today— from Los Angeles to Finland!

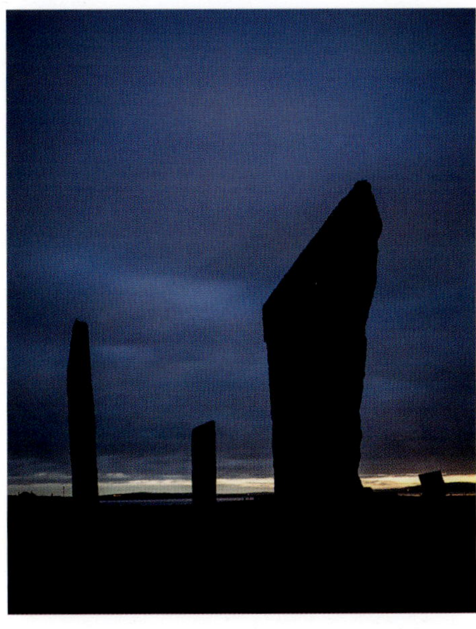

"Stones of Stenness," Orkney, Scotland. 30 seconds, f8 at ISO 800. Canon 5D MK II, 28 mm f3.5 PC Nikkor lens. The same exposure without light painting.

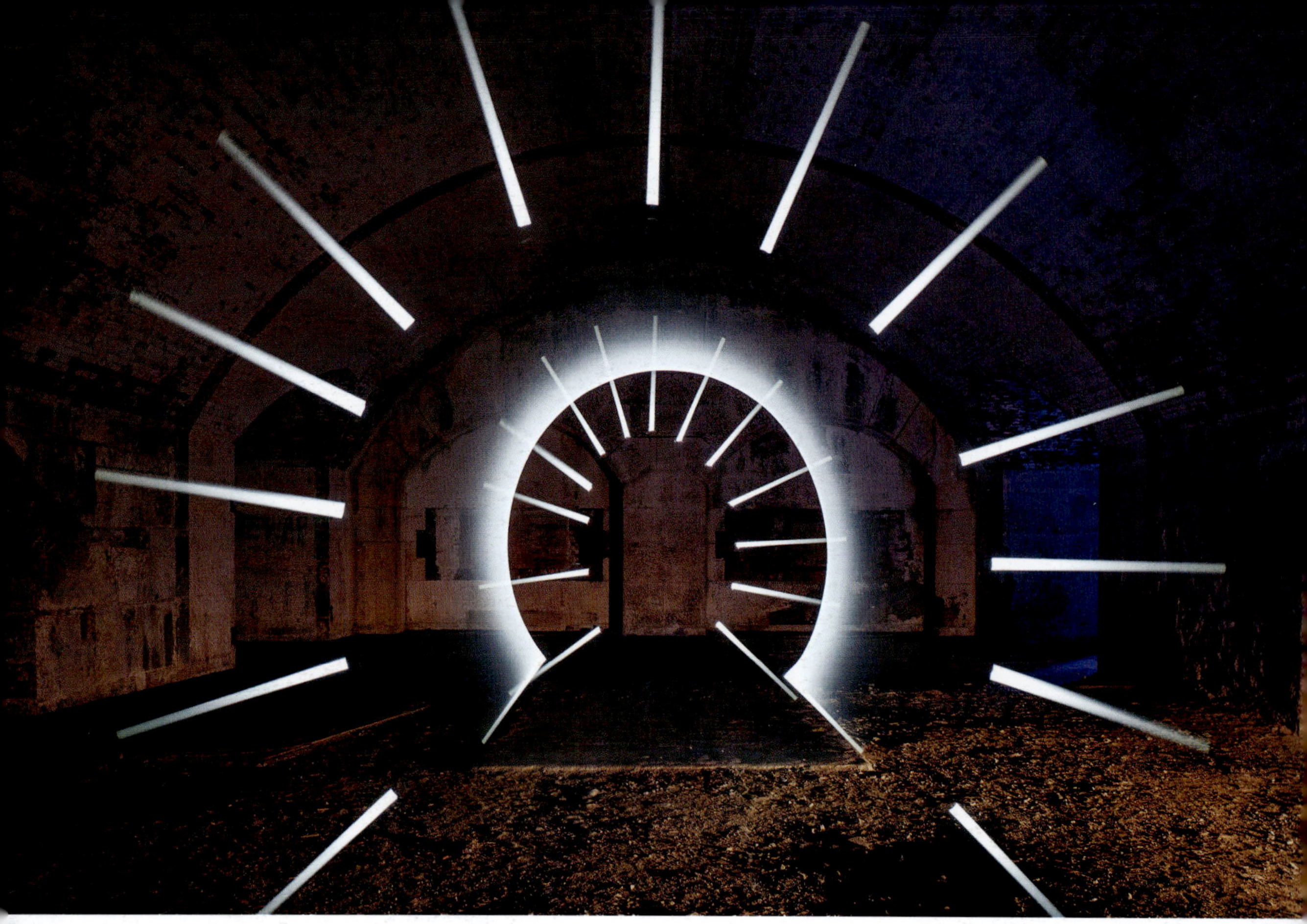

"Stargate," Fort Warren, George's Island, Boston Harbor Islands. 238 seconds, f5.6 at ISO 1600. LED light wand, incandescent flashlight, weak daylight. Inspired by the light drawing artists in the next chapter, I made a light wand out of acrylic tubing, a Roscolux diffusion gel, and an LED flashlight and took it to George's Island when invited by some friends with a boat. Aligning and spacing the various light forms was very challenging, and it took many attempts to achieve this final version.

DRAWING WITH LIGHT—SUBJECT IS LIGHT

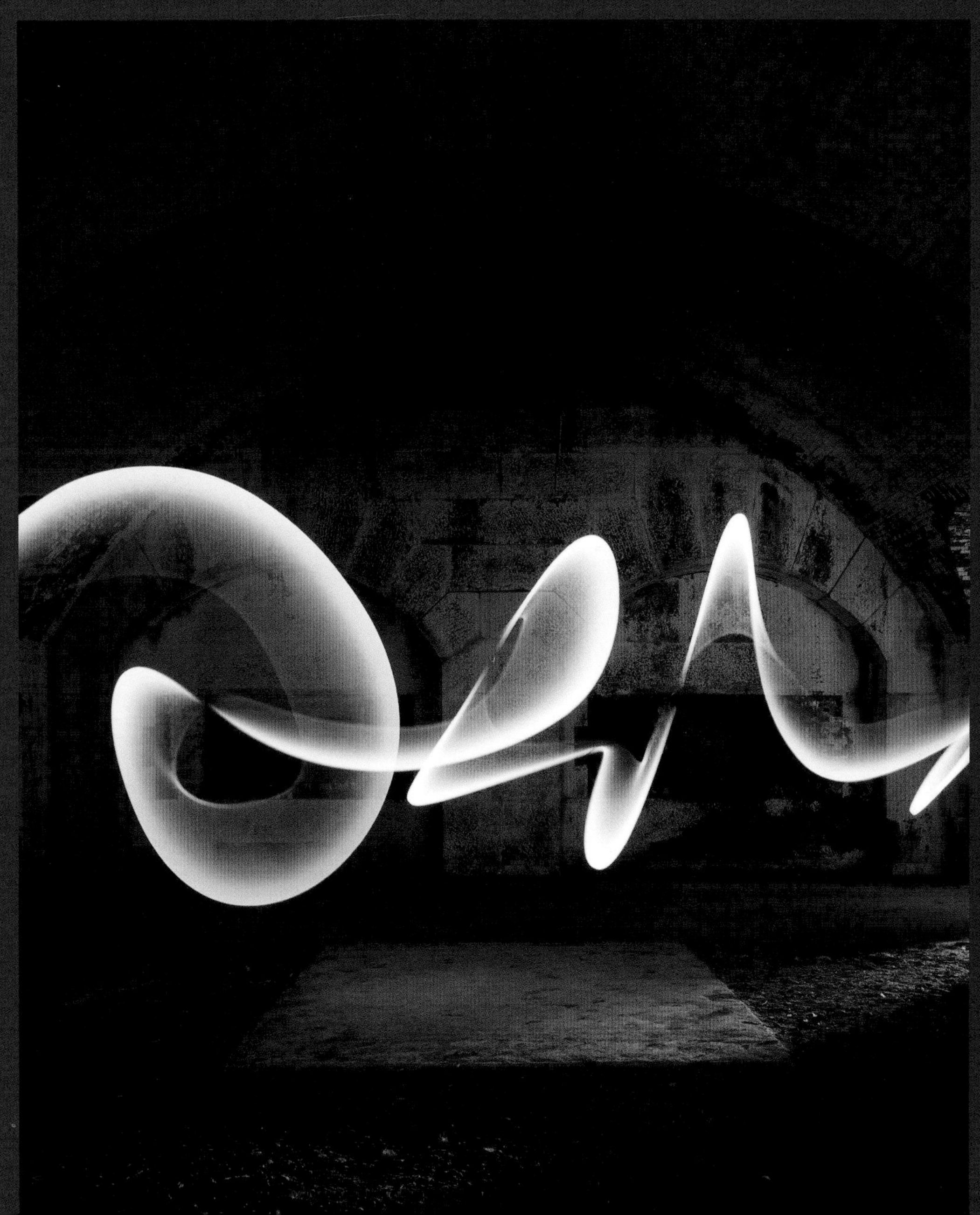

9

Many artists who draw with light use the generic term light painting to describe what they do. This chapter uses the term light painting, which may include both painting with light and drawing with light techniques. It can be confusing, but it doesn't really matter what you call it. This chapter introduces various techniques where a light source is used to create subject matter rather than illuminate a subject.

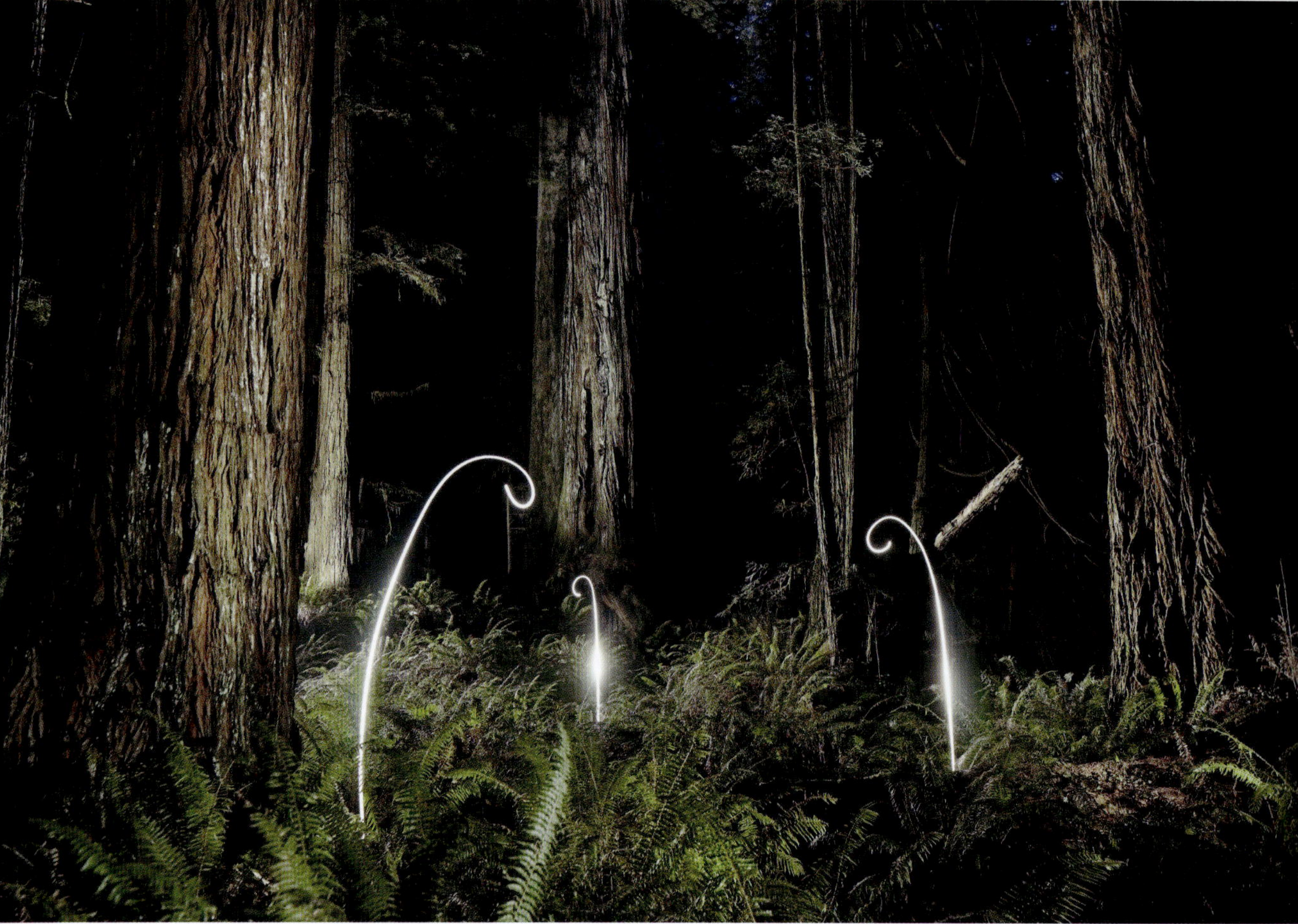

Jens Warnecke and Cenci Goepel, "Lightmark No. 114"

Location: Redwood National Park, Oregon
Settings: f5.6, ISO 50, 342 seconds
Phase One P45, 55 mm lens
2 small incandescent flashlights

Jens and Cenci liked the curly appearance of the young ferns that were covering the ground beneath the huge redwoods, so they decided to plant some more.

Light drawing is a specialized type of light painting where the light source is generally pointed back toward the camera, or at least shown in the image, and used like a pen or pencil to draw lines or forms with light. The range of images that can be created using light drawing techniques is incredibly broad and limited only by the imagination. Drawing with light has become an increasingly popular form of night photography in recent years, and there are numerous light painting and light drawing groups on the various photo-sharing sites for inspiration. See the resources section at the end of this book for a partial listing.

Style is paramount in light painting and light drawing. As you explore the world of light painting and drawing, you'll see that the best artists working in this medium have distinctive styles that are readily recognizable. Often these artists work thematically with a series of images using techniques and concepts that they have developed over time. With time and practice, you too will find your own style. Developing a "look" for your images is not a simple task, and it probably will not happen quickly. At the same time that you are working on your style, you'll probably be finding your visual "voice." What you say is as important as how you say it. Putting style and substance together in a way that the resulting images speak to the viewer is the sign of a mature artist. When you are first starting out, your work is likely to be inconsistent, and this is completely normal. But as your light drawing and painting skills improve, you'll get better at anticipating, or visualizing results, and gain more control over the lighting. Reaching the point when you can both control the image and the lighting—and anticipate the results of your efforts— is a worthy goal, but it is good to remain open to surprises and the unexpected. Sometimes images that come together spontaneously and without a lot of planning can be even more rewarding than those that are planned in advance and carefully choreographed, but with mediums like night photography and light painting, a "decisive moment" is the exception rather than the rule. In the end, it is being true to yourself, and making images that you feel good about that really matters.

If you spend some time looking at light painting on photo-sharing or social media websites you'll see that styles and techniques are frequently assimilated and adapted by others. In interviewing light painters for this chapter, most felt that it was natural to try and figure out how images were made, but that blatant copying of their styles was disrespectful, especially when strikingly similar work is posted without attribution to the original artist. For the most part, light painters are enthusiastic about collaborating and sharing, and have a welcoming and supportive community. We invite you to share your images and become a part of that community.

This chapter showcases the work of some of the best-known light drawing artists working today, with descriptions of their techniques and comments on the evolution of their personal styles. Each of these artists reveals the methods used to create the featured images and the inspiration behind the images. Some artists provide more technical information while others are more inspirational. The purpose of these guest sections is not to teach the reader how to make photographs like these talented artists, but to show how these images and the styles of the artists evolved, and to encourage thoughtful exploration and experimentation of the medium of light painting and drawing. Throughout this book, I have emphasized developing and utilizing the technical skills to become a successful night photographer. Technical proficiency is the foundation of all good photography but it is only a foundation. Without an openness and curiosity to look at the world and inside yourself for inspiration, photographs will most likely appear meaningless or superficial at best. This is not to say that every image has to have some profound spiritual message, but passion, vision, or at least intention and awareness are required for photographs to transcend beyond the ordinary.

Many, if not most, of the readers of this book will have been introduced to photography in the digital age, with little knowledge of film-based photography and the craft of large format, black and white Zone System photography. Ansel Adams and Fred Archer developed the Zone System in 1940 as a way for photographers to systematically express the way they visualized an image in print form. In other words, by using the Zone System, a photographer has complete control over image values, and the ability to render light and dark tones as the photographer imagines them, not necessarily as they actually appear. The Zone System is highly technical, and involves film testing, plotting curves on graphs, sensitometry, and with precise metering of individual parts of a scene to calculate the exposure. Finally, exacting control over the development process theoretically produces a perfect negative. In a way, the Zone System is a film photographer's version of SOOC (Straight Out Of Camera), getting everything right in-camera, with a goal of as little darkroom manipulation as possible to achieve the photographer's vision!

I'm bringing this up because I'm reminded of a certain type of photographer that I used to encounter with some frequency back before digital photography had taken over. They were typically white men in their fifties, sixties, or seventies, who were or had been engineers. They shot 4 × 5 or 8 × 10 black and white film. Many of these photographers embraced the use of Adams' Zone System out of a love of geekery. To them, the science and mathematics of the Zone System was something that their analytical minds could understand, much more so than the creativity required to see a scene before their eyes and visualize a different result. These photographers dedicated tremendous amounts of time to testing film, taking densitometer readings, and plotting curves, but often gave little thought to the images they made. The result of course was technically perfect but the dry, boring photographs were difficult to relate to. The point is that to be a good photographer, day or night, or a light painter or light drawer, a healthy mix of technical competence and creativity is required.

DARREN PEARSON—DARIUSTWIN.COM

Darren Pearson became interested in light painting and light drawing in 2007 after seeing one of Gjon Mili's photographs of Picasso drawing a centaur in midair with a light pen. Like many of the best-known light artists, Pearson, who uses the name Darius Twin online, connected to the light painting community on Flickr, initially drawing inspiration from the images he saw there, but quickly becoming one of the most influential artists working with light painting on the web. He is probably best known for his light drawings of animated skeletons. Pearson's *Light Goes On* animated video of skateboarding skeletons is perhaps the world's most viewed light

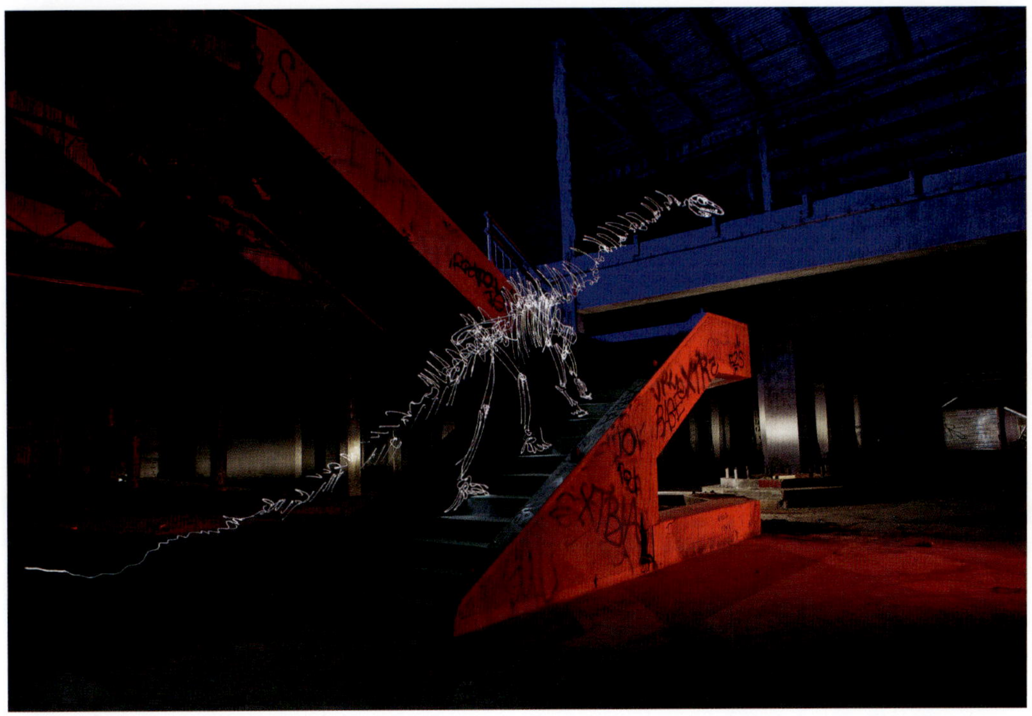

"Amargasaurus"

Location: Hawthorne, CA. 8/4/14
Settings: f5.6, ISO 100, 355 seconds
Canon 6D, and 24-70 mm f2.8L lens
DIY LED pen, LED Lenser P7QC, Dorcy spotlight

Darren says: "I used a small LED pen to illustrate the dinosaur. It is a DIY tool I use often, which is basically a few batteries connected to a push-button and LED light duct taped together and a LED Lenser P7QC on red and blue settings for the coloring along with my assistant Sean who used a high-powered Dorcy Spotlight for the background."

"This place was perhaps the largest area I've ever attempted to photograph at night. Imagine a long abandoned mall where you're the only person there. It was haunting to say the least, and eerie sounds of metal and concrete would groan as we walked into the hollow structure. It became obvious I had to illustrate something large enough to compete with the space!"

drawings. The product of over a year's effort, Light Goes On began as a series of animated gifs and was eventually developed into a crazy 1-minute video that quickly went viral on YouTube, and was reposted on countless other websites. (You can watch the video and several others on Pearson's website, DariusTwin.com.) He had hit on something new, because no one had made such complex light painting animations before. Light Goes On had raised the bar of what light painting could be, a fact that was recognized by a producer commissioned by Honda to produce a commercial for the 2014 Civic, who in turn hired Pearson to do one of his trademark skeletal animations for the commercial.

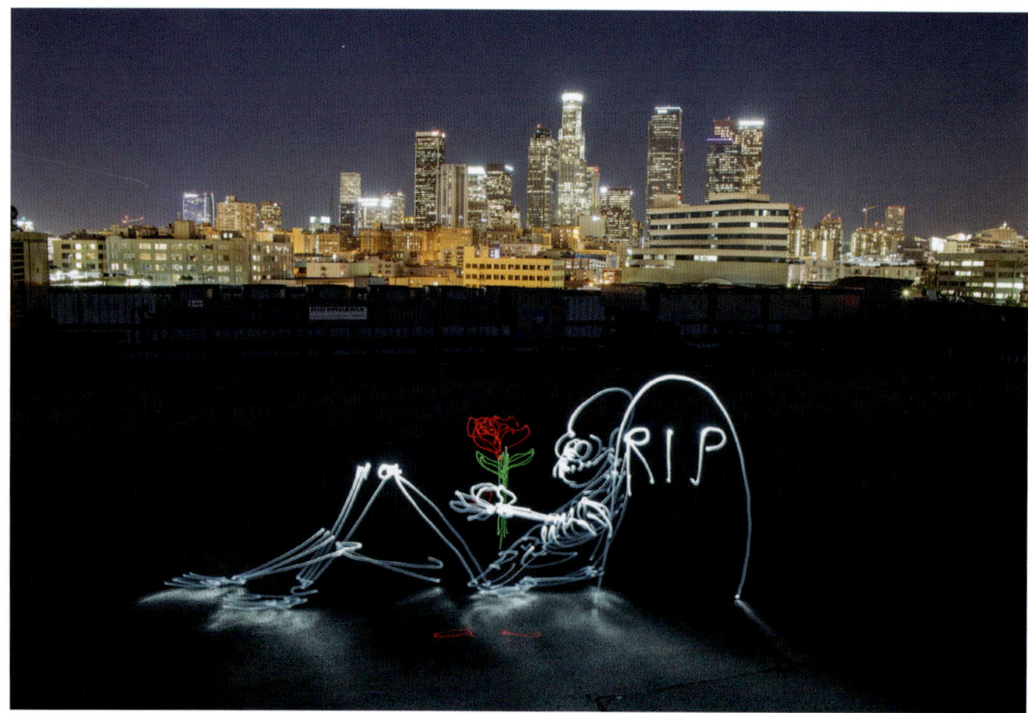

"To Live and Die in LA"

Location: Downtown Los Angeles, CA. 11/15/13
Settings: f13, ISO 100, 164 seconds
Canon 6D, 28 mm Zeiss 2.0 Distagon T
Coleman Max LED, red and green keychain LED lights

Pearson says: "For this shot, I originally decided to pay for parking at the highest garage in Little Tokyo in downtown LA and just shoot it from the top of the building. Once I got to the top there was a guy parked right in the spot I wanted to shoot from smoking a blunt and gazing out at an awesome view of the LA skyline. I set up close by and shot a few less than stellar images. We talked a little about photography and before long I realized that the best view of LA was not from this garage, but on the rooftop next to it. So I bid my new friend farewell and entered the mall across a bridge, climbed to the roof of the next building and shot this image."

Pearson considers himself to be an illustrator, photographer, and a filmmaker, depending on the project he's working on. He tends to work thematically, and many of his figures are animals, skeletons, or dinosaurs, which he aims to bring to life within the frame. His methodology has evolved over a period of years, and he describes working with imaginary spatial templates to orient his figures in space. His first step is to consider the location and the kind of figure that would fit there, and what it would do, and then to find the right placement within the space. He sometimes makes sketches first and starts on location with high-ISO testing. He establishes the exposure and then starts to work on the illustration. It often takes many attempts to get the figure just right—both the way it is drawn and the way that it fits within the frame. His lighting tools are simple; a light pen made by a friend, a couple of LED flashlights, and occasionally some electro luminescent (EL) wire. He takes care to get a good exposure, but is more concerned with creating a striking image than a technically perfect one.

DENNIS CALVERT—DENNISCALVERT.NET

Dennis Calvert discovered night photography and light painting out of plain curiosity. He began experimenting with long exposures as soon as he bought his first camera. A few months later, he came across the work of Trevor Williams and the German light art collaborators known as LAPP Pro, and something clicked. He's been using light painting and drawing ever since. Calvert practices what has become known as SOOC. He does not apply any postprocessing at all to his images as a way of proving that all of the effects were achieved in-camera. Many night photographers and light painters try to minimize postprocessing by spending extra time in the field to make sure that everything is just the way they want it when the image is recorded, but few take it as far as Calvert, who says that SOOC is part of what makes light painting fun for him. Of course if there is no postprocessing, everything has to be perfect in-camera—not just the lighting. Calvert is meticulous; he calls what he does, "well planned and choreographed long exposure photography, with an element of controlled chaos."

Calvert says that light painting is a form of escapism for him, but at the same time he says that it helps him to connect his experiences with the word around him. He occasionally collaborates with other light painters but mostly enlists his wife and a few close friends to be his assistants and models. He states that his working method is simple—dream and then make. He has ideas for the things that he would like to do and then tries to figure out how to make them happen. The burning figure image featured here is a perfect example. Ingenuity, curiosity, and persistence are common qualities of all of the light painters in this book, and most likely among any light painter who has done more than wave a few flashlights around.

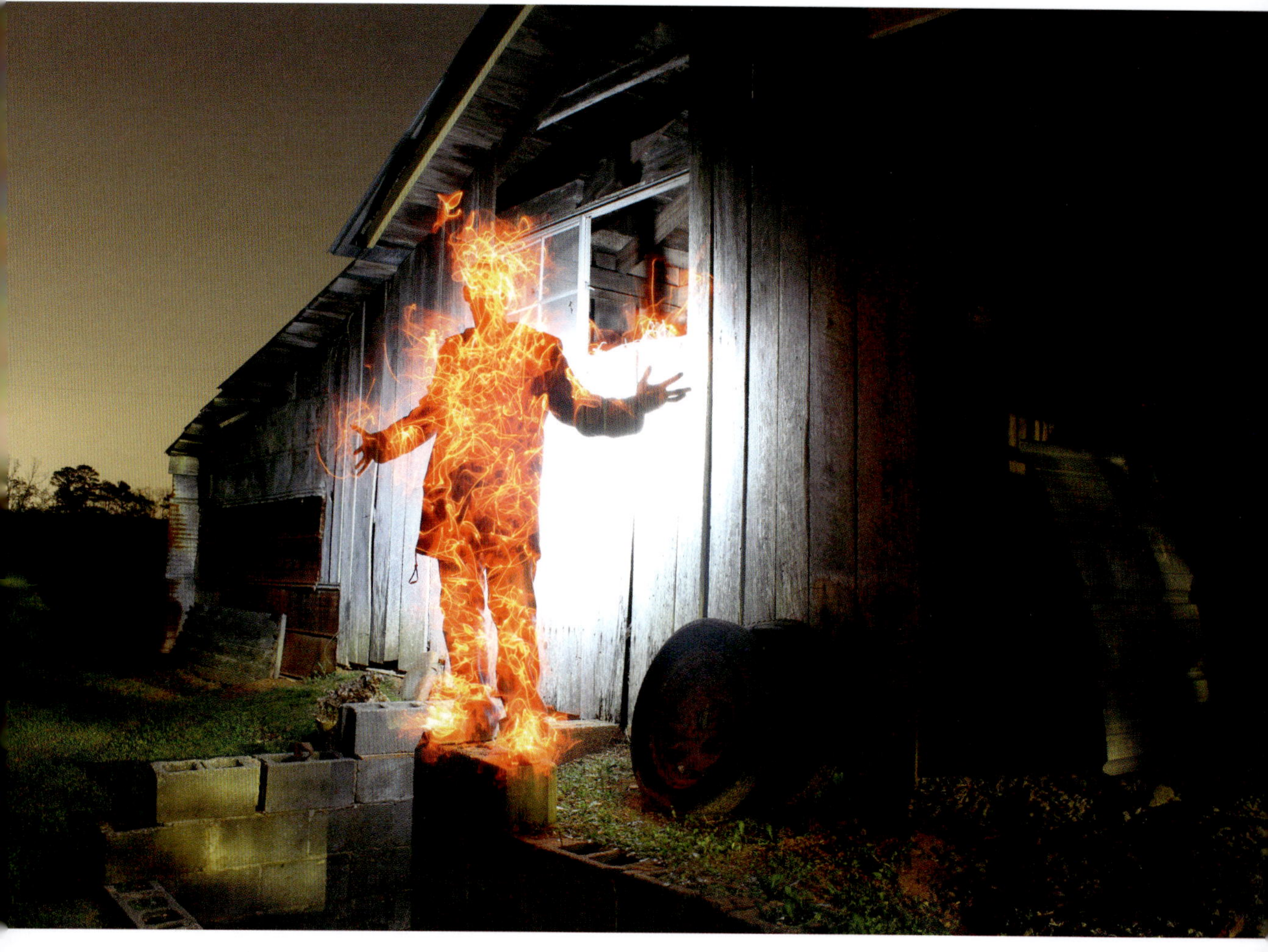

"DC1 Thermodynamic Engineering"

Settings: f6.3, ISO 800, 190 seconds
Canon 7D, and 18-55 mm lens
Remote triggered flash, battery-powered glow stick

Calvert wanted to create the effect of a burning figure without sending anyone to the hospital, and came up with a technique using a battery-powered glow stick. After determining the composition and the ambient exposure, he overexposed the area on the building behind him with a remotely triggered flash that was synced to fire when the shutter opened. The flash was attached to his back and pointed at the wall. This creates the silhouette of the figure. He then took an orange battery-powered glow stick and waved it around in the area where he had been standing when the flash went off. The shadow of his body kept the area where he had stood underexposed so that all you could see was the "fire" in the image. He says that while he tried to be careful with the placement of the fire, coloring outside the lines didn't matter because accidents will not show up in the washed-out area due to the overexposed background. "It's not precision work, but spatial awareness is helpful," he said.

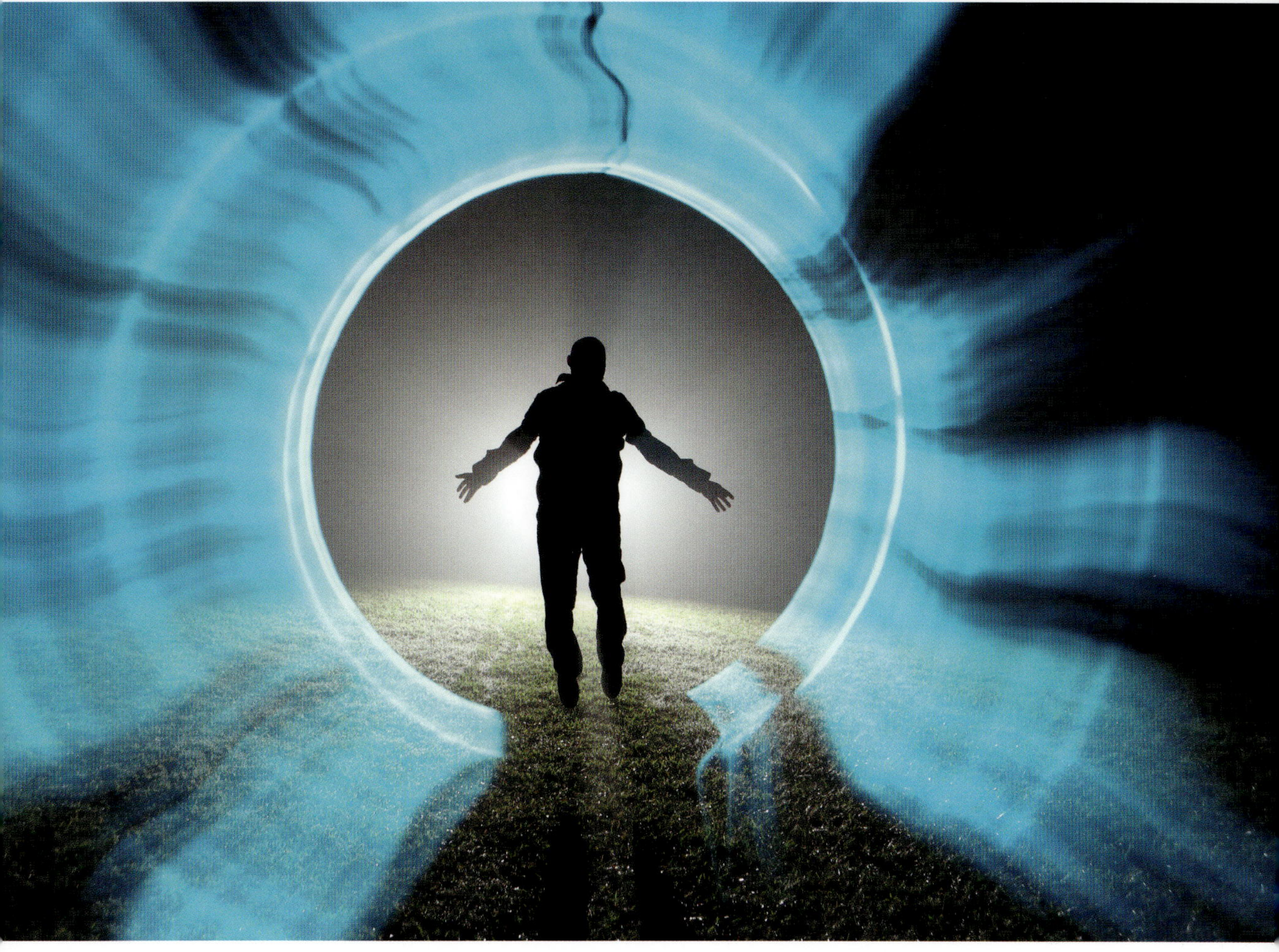

Untitled

Settings:f5, ISO 1250, 14 seconds
Canon 5D MK III, 24-70 f2.8L lens
Canon speedlight, battery-powered glow stick

This image was inspired by fog. As Calvert says: "I really dig fog. A lot. For this one, the idea was simple and the execution was fast. It's only a 14-second exposure. Here's how it went down. First, I set up a speedlite at 1/4 power, with a wireless trigger about 25 feet in front of the camera. I zoomed the flash out to 24 mm to get a nice wide dispersion of light through the fog, and set it to trigger on the first curtain."

"Next, I opened the shutter with an RC-1 remote set for a 2-second delay and timed my jump with the flash. It was really a pretty pathetic jump, but the back lighting threw my shadow out in front of me and made it look like I had really got some air. Finally, I held a hula-hoop with EL wire taped to it in front of the camera and moved it away from the lens 3 or 4 feet. That was it."

Calvert says that his tools and techniques have become simpler and more straightforward the longer he works at light painting. It is a strategy that seems to work for him.

Light Painting Tool

Calvert used this home-made tool to make the blue ring in the previous photo. It consists of EL wire around a hula-hoop, with a paint roller handle for when he wants to spin it. He did not use the roller handle for this image.

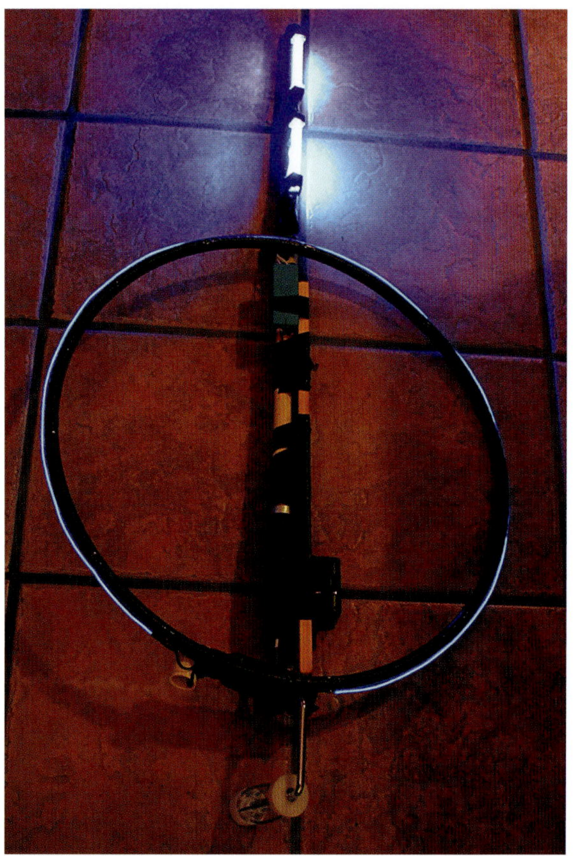

Calvert says that his work has occasionally been copied by others—something that seems inevitable when your work is posted online—but he isn't bothered by it. In fact, he's happy that his work has had enough of an impact that others would want to copy it. He says that art is a form of communication, and being mimicked is simply an answer to his call. He adds that the tools he uses are increasingly simple, and that the concept of an image is far more important than the tools used to make it.

HANNU HUHTAMO—HANNUHUHTAMO.COM

Hannu Huhtamo is a Finnish photographer who is best known for his flower-like light forms that appear in cold, dark places in the Arctic night. He experienced his first brush with light painting in the mid-1990s while taking promo photos for his band by drawing simple lines and figures with a lighter during long exposures. Fast-forward to 2008 when he bought his first DSLR, and then saw his friend Janne Parviainen's light drawings, and ever since then he has been hooked on light painting. Huhtamo says, "It quickly developed into an addiction and I had to do that almost every night. There is something really magical in it." Huhtamo's signature figures are some of the most ethereal and mysterious light paintings ever produced, but his technique is simple. He doesn't hesitate to share his technique with other people despite the number of people who have attempted to copy his work. He's in agreement with most light painters that learning from what others do is a fundamental part of light painting, but that an even more important part of developing a light painting style is to learn from what others have done, and then move on, and make something new.

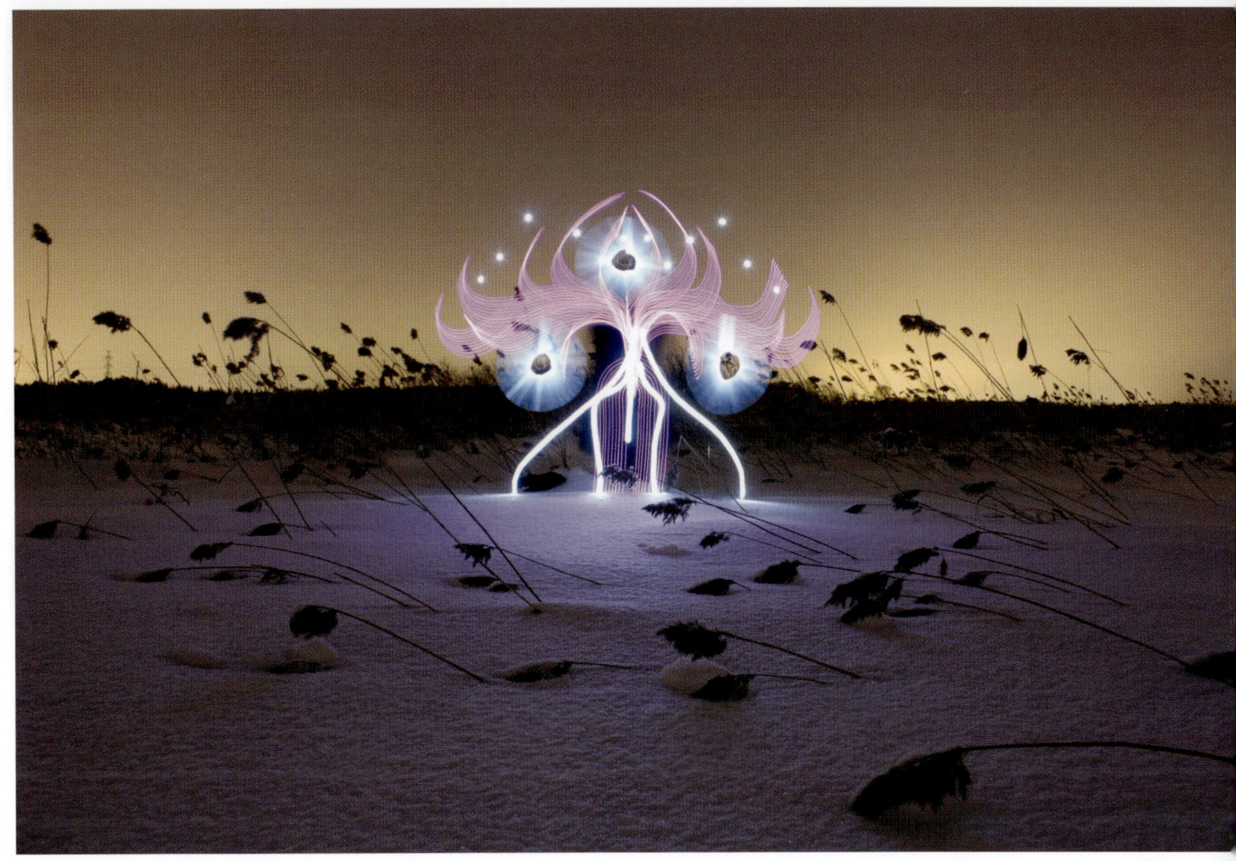

"Stranded"

Settings: f6.3, ISO 100, 92 seconds
Canon 450D, EF-S 18-55 lens
DIY tools and LED penlight

Huhtamo says: "It was –18 C degrees with a bone-chilling wind. All the beaches in Helsinki were covered with thick layers of ice and snow. I really had to scramble along the shoreline to get the shot done. I wanted the foreground to be pristine, without any footprints. After composing, focusing, and checking my camera's settings I asked my friend to open the shutter so I could concentrate on my light work. I used my self-made tool for the stripe shaped trails. It is made out of a paint roller and battery-operated LED strip. It gives that 'wingy' look that I use quite a lot in my work. Next, I created the blue 'irises' with a LED flashlight that has plastic blue cone on the end. Those bright star-shaped spots and lines on the lower part of the figure were made with an inexpensive LED flashlight."

Huhtamo creates light forms that become integrated with the environment where he's photographing—they become part of the landscape. He calls his forms light flowers, or luminous beings. Others have said his light drawings look like aliens or spiritual creatures, but that really isn't his intention. Still, he says that whatever the viewer makes of his work is fine with him and that any reaction is a good one as long as there is a reaction.

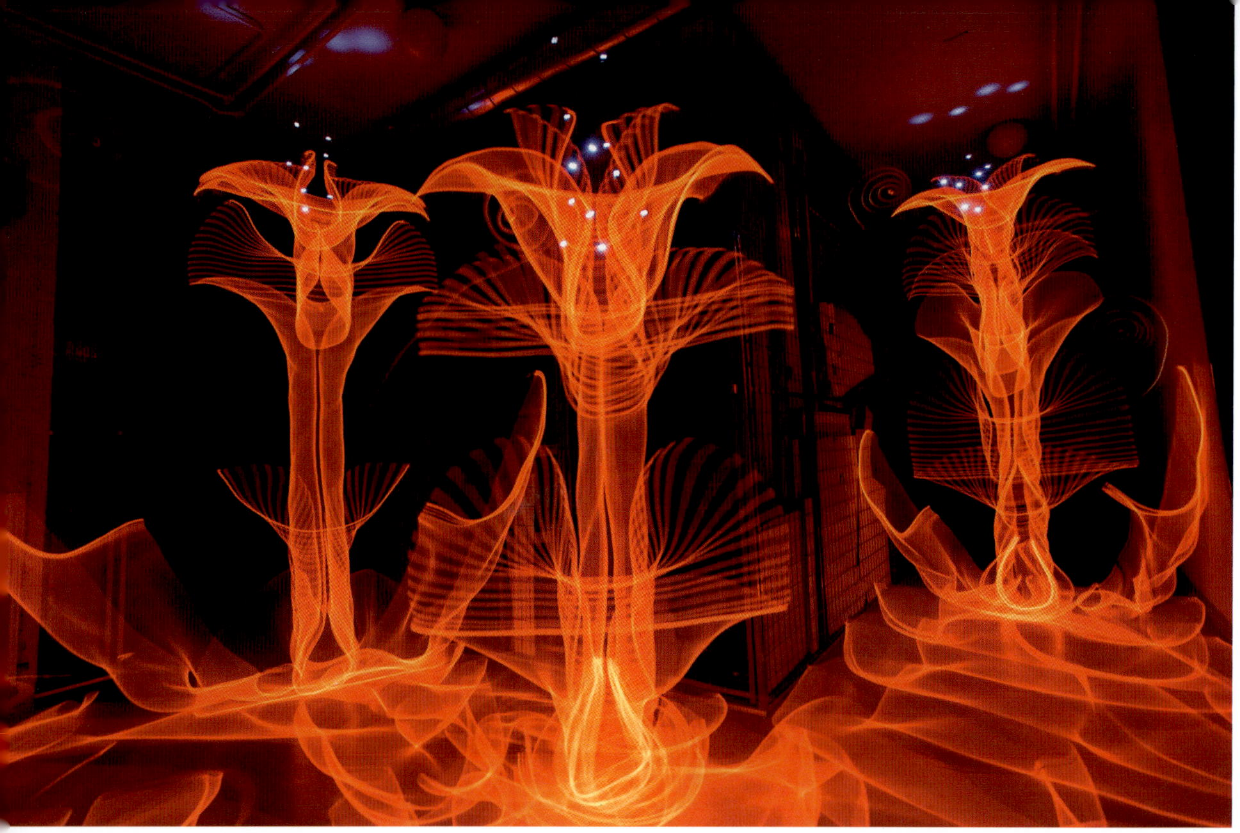

"Releaseduction"

Settings: f6.3, ISO 400, 494 seconds
Canon 5D MK III, EF 17-40 mm f4L lens
DIY tools and LED penlight

Huhtamo says: "The basement of our house offers a peaceful and dark environment to try out new light forms and techniques. First I did some sketches on paper and planned the composition. I wanted to do more than just one light flower, like they were taking over. I used a 1-meter piece of red EL wire and held each end in one hand. A small key chain LED light was used for the starry bursts on the upper parts of the flowers. I start the drawing from the ground and raise the EL wire slowly upwards by bending it to various shapes while I raise it. I control the length by covering the EL wire with my sleeves. The title is a play on words, a variation of 'Released Seduction.'"

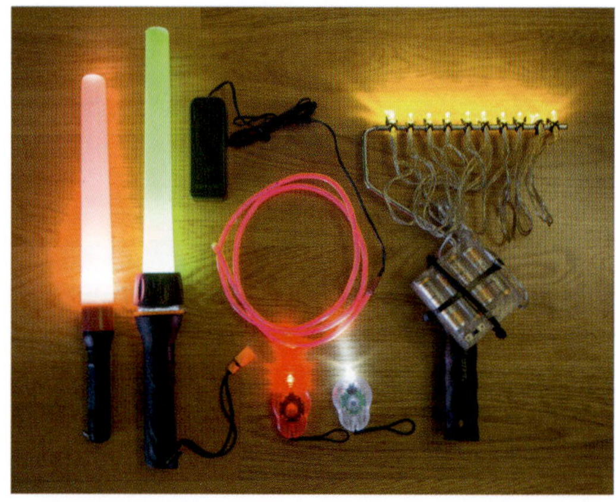

Light Painting Tools

Some of Hannu Huhtamo's light painting tools. From left to right: two flashlights with plastic cones, pink EL wire, two keychain LED lights, and DIY paint roller with battery-powered LED holiday lights.

Huhtamo is inspired by nature and makes many of his images outdoors in the long, cold winters of his native Finland. He also works in urban environments that are often interiors of abandoned buildings. He says that light painting energizes him, and the process puts him into a meditative state as he concentrates to create his balanced, symmetrical forms. Often he starts with sketches, but also improvises during the process as his light forms take shape. He tries to make them as three-dimensional as possible to give them more life. One of the things he likes best about light painting is that it is one of the few mediums where you can draw in three-dimensional space. Huhtamo is not technically a SOOC purist—he does not use Photoshop but does optimize his images for printing. Mostly he works alone but is part of a light painting collective called Valopaja, who do live performances and light painting workshops for children and disabled people.

IAN HOBSON—LIGHTPAINTING.ORG.UK

Ian Hobson is a photographer and light painter from the north east of England who takes inspiration from prehistoric rock carvings found in the British landscape. His diverse interests and talents have led to some truly original work. As you can see from the text that follows, he uses a custom-made Camera Rotation Tool (CRT) and home-made light wands with controllable RGB LED lights to great effect. Hobson's first experience with light painting was in the late 1980s when he was commissioned by a local music venue to create images for projection. He used slide projectors and smoke to create beams of light that he photographed with slide film. Photography and light painting took a backseat to his other interests until 2009 when the main focus of his photography was recording the prehistoric rock carvings of the British Isles. The ancient carvings were eroded and difficult to photograph, so he began searching for effective ways to light them, and stumbled across the blossoming world of light painting online.

Hobson says that:

> The majority of my works are related to my interest in prehistoric "Cup and Ring" carvings, which is in turn informed by my studies in neuroscience. The prevalent motifs in the carvings are dots, concentric circles, spirals, and zig-zags, all of which are fundamental parts of basic human visual cognition. These motifs are sometimes referred to as "entoptic" forms, and are spontaneously generated by the human nervous system. As such they represent to me a continuity of the human experience that transcends time, which I find fascinating. The brains of people thousands of years ago shared elements that we still experience today. Add to this the fact that the carvings are very permanent features, and that light paintings are by their nature extremely transient and ephemeral. I find the combination of the two concepts provides a satisfying and mutually complementary contrast.

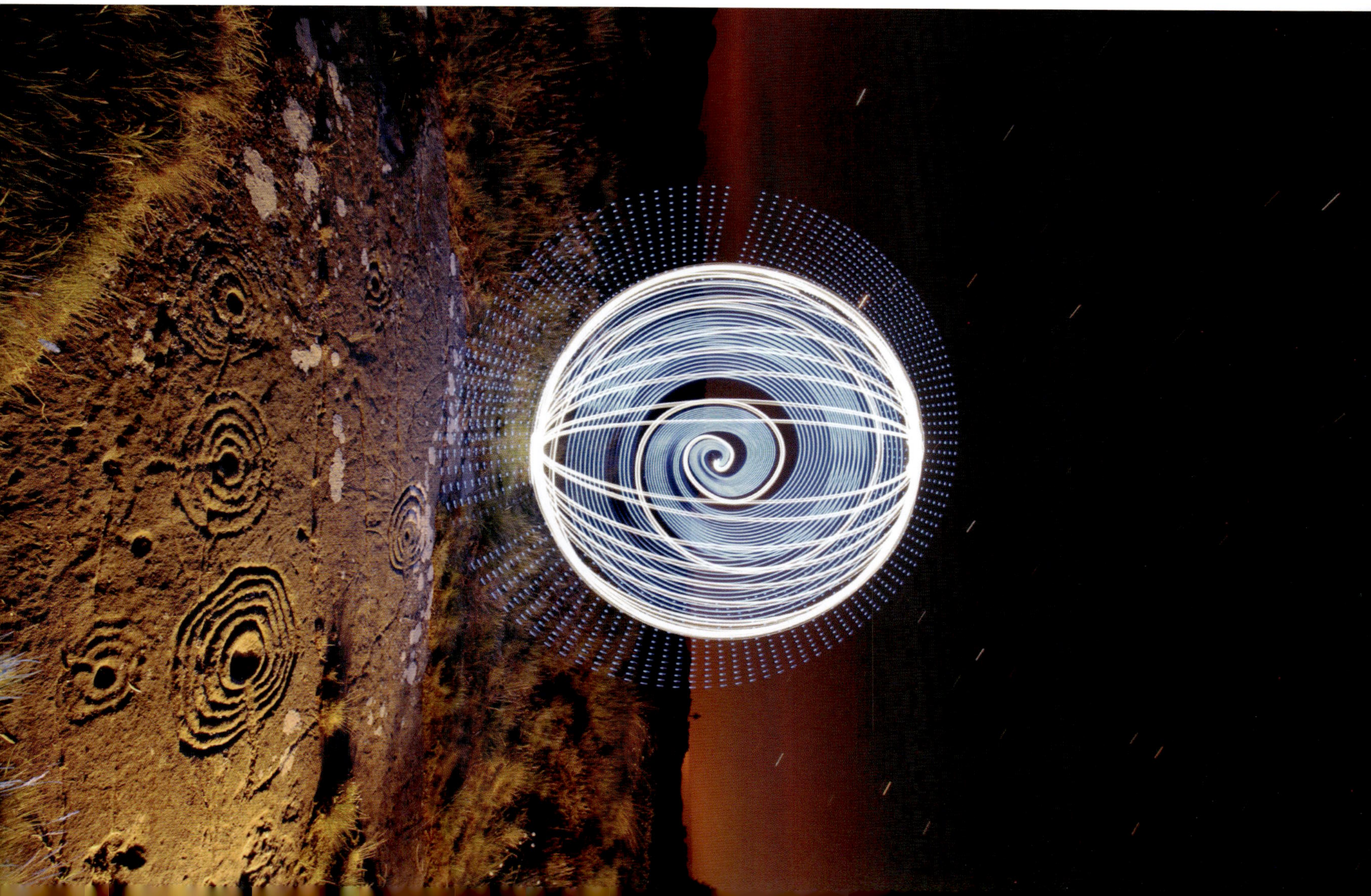

"Weetwood Orb"

Settings: f7.1, ISO 400, 275 seconds
Digital light wand, incandescent flashlight

Hobson says: "Waving lights over the 3500 year old 'Cup and Ring' carvings at Weetwood Moor in Northumberland, UK. In the past, this kind of activity has caused concern among the local farmers, who can see the lights in the distance and get baffled wondering why poachers are signaling to each other in technicolour."

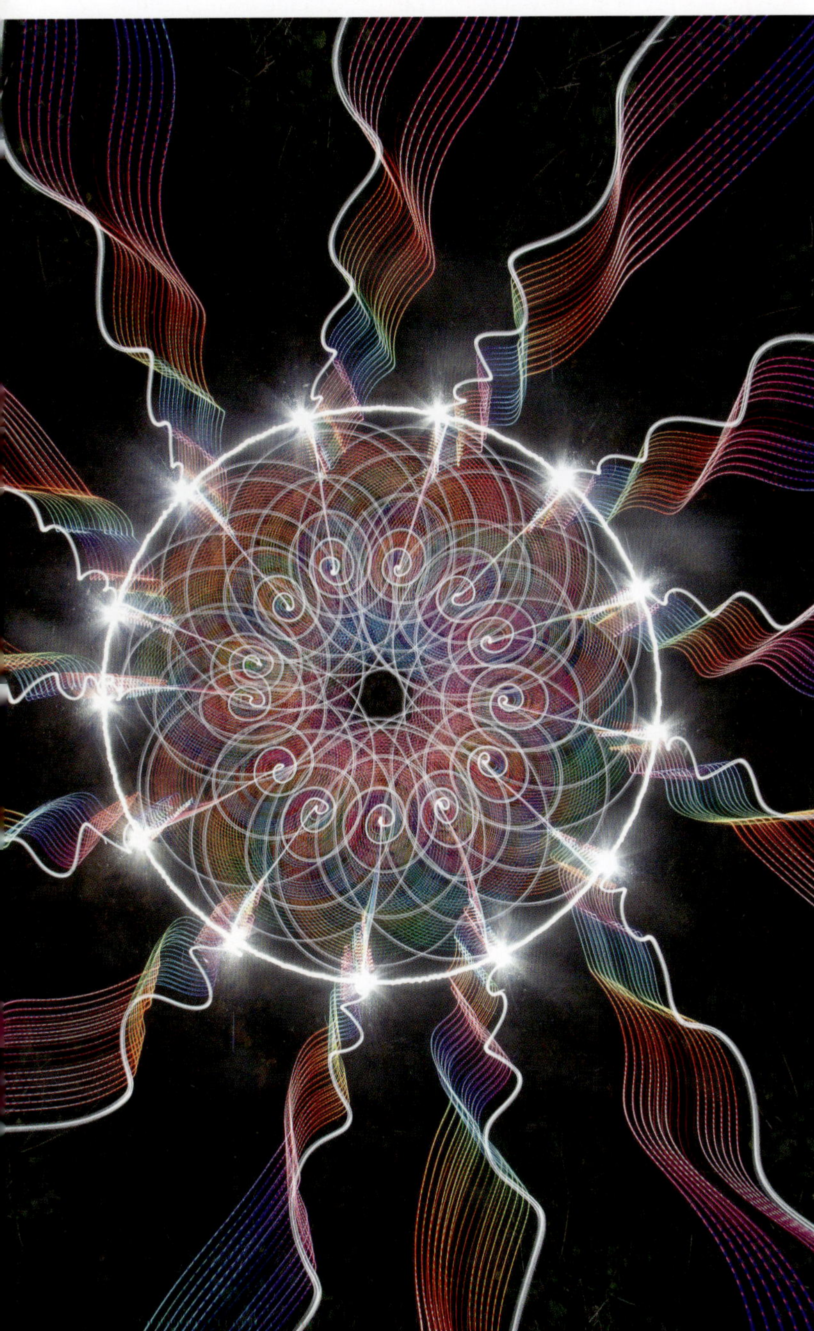

Camera rotation outdoors

Settings: f9, ISO 100, 309 seconds
Digital light wand, CRT

Hobson says: "Waving LEDs at the camera, and rotating it on the CRT, set up on a disused 19th-century waggonway. A marker was placed on the ground, then the LEDs were waved in a spiral, and walked towards the camera. Then the camera was rotated, and the process repeated until the camera had made a full revolution. I'm fairly chuffed with this one; it generated the real dopamine release in my brain when I got to the back of the camera to see what was on the screen. All the more chuffed as it worked first time."

Another aspect of light painting that appeals to me is the fact that it is now possible to create images that look like they are possibly computer generated, but without recourse to a computer. I like this idea as CGI is now so developed that it can convincingly mimic real life. It is fun to turn the concept on its head and make real-life mimic CGI. As a result, I prefer not to do any postprocessing of the images, and I'm even reluctant to print them, as I feel the images lose some of their impact if they have to rely on reflected light (i.e. light bouncing off the paper onto the retina of the viewer) as opposed to the light emitted directly to the eye from a LCD screen. I think this also allows scope to forgive the minor "errors" in light painting images that show them to be products of the real world, and not perfectly symmetrical CGI artifacts.

I am at present having a fine time exploring the possibilities of a custom made "Camera Rotation Tool" that creates some nice smooth concentric circles by allowing the camera to be rotated around the axis of the lens. A repeated sequence of rotating and pausing, combined with some jumping about waving lights during the pauses, helped to produce one of the images shown here."

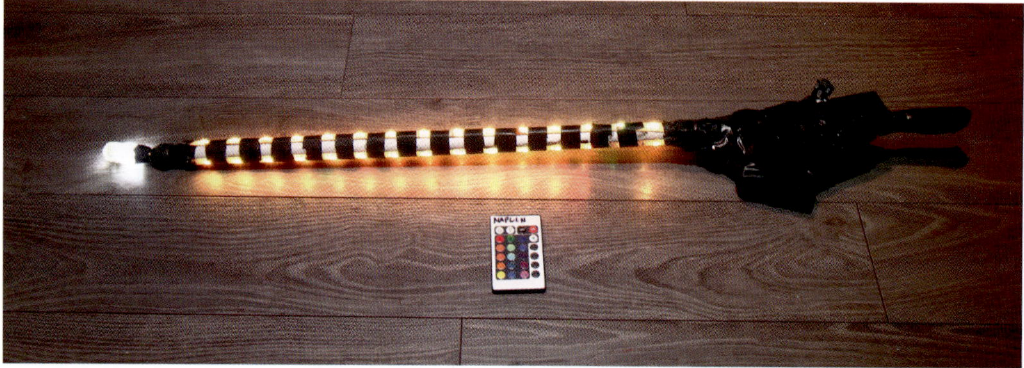

Digital Light Wand

Hobson says: "My 'go-to' light painting tool. It is three strips of RGB LEDs, with a remote control for colour, brightness and a couple of sequenced flashing modes. There's also a 12V car bulb on the end, with its own separate switch. This can be removed and replaced with similar bulbs of different colour. The strips are powered by 2 × AA and 1 × 9V battery, same again for the end bulb. The key element is that it is exactly the right size to allow me to hold it and for it to reach to the ground, and that the switches are in just the right place for ease of access and operation. The downside is it looks like a right old dog's dinner being held together with tape, but I kind of like that aspect of it. It has been tweaked numerous times, and is in a state of constant flux, with bits being added and readjusted to alter the quality of line it produces."

JANNE PARVIAINEN—JANNEPAINT.COM

Parviainen is a Finnish photographer and painter who started light painting by accident when he inadvertently took a continuous series of 8-second photos while walking home one night with his camera. Impressed by the patterns the streetlights had created in the photos, he began experimenting drawing with his camera by pointing it at the Moon or streetlights. Later, he placed his camera on the ground and made light drawings with his phone. That was enough for him to want to explore light painting as an art form. Trained as an oil painter, Parviainen was excited by the possibilities this new medium offered. He enjoys the freedom he has with light painting,

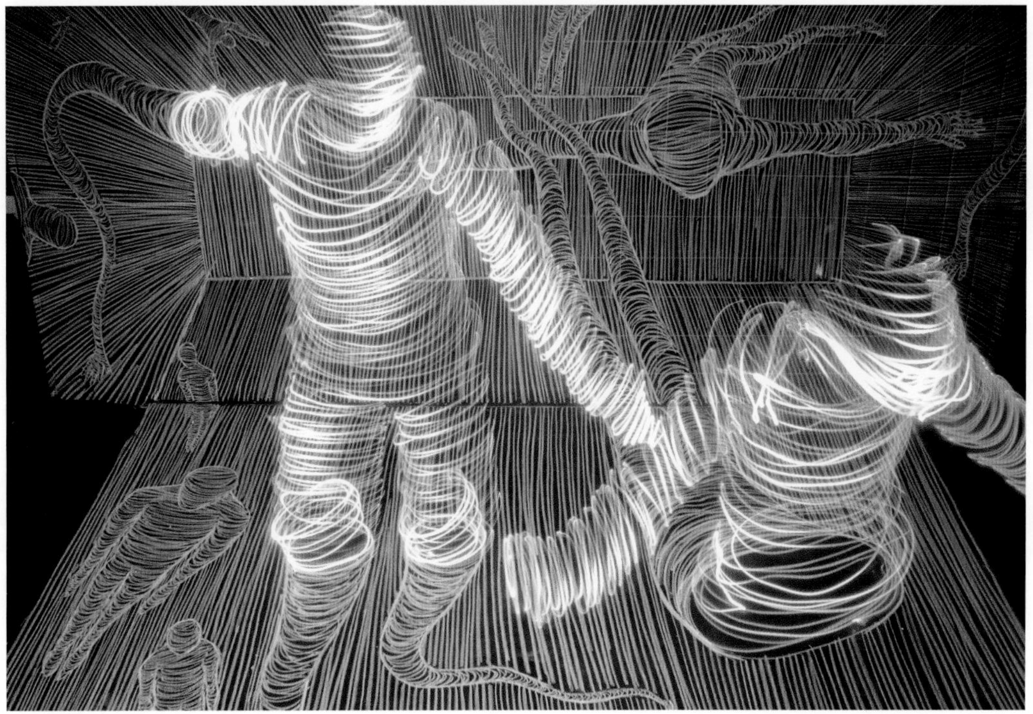

"Voices of the Ether"

Settings: f14, ISO 100, 410 seconds
Sony A850 Camera
LED finger light

Parviainen says: "I made this photo in my studio so I could precisely control the light. I have two large blackboards in my studio which I placed in a corner against the wall. I had made a small sketch of how the characters and the perspective would look as a guide. At first I tried to find the right postures for the figures and the exact spots where the chalk drawing continues from the light drawing. Drawing the basic outlines is always the most time intensive part since the lines should maintain the same perspective despite the 90-degree angle change between the blackboards. Even a small difference in the viewpoint causes the illusion to fail. This photo took almost five hours to execute, around three and a half hours for the drawing and one and a half for the light painting. I decided to go with the black and white effect since it hides some of the tone differences between the charcoal and the light painted parts. I did the light painted figures by tracing my body with a white-colored led light while sitting on the right spot."

especially the ability to paint in three-dimensional space. He also enjoys the adventurous aspect of light painting and night photography—exploring new places, going out at night when everyone else is safely at home, and seeing and experiencing things that no one else does.

Parviainen is both fascinated and repulsed by mass consumption and waste in contemporary societies, and he often photographs things and places that have been left to rot or rust, and turn back to the dust from which they came. Like other night photographers who photograph

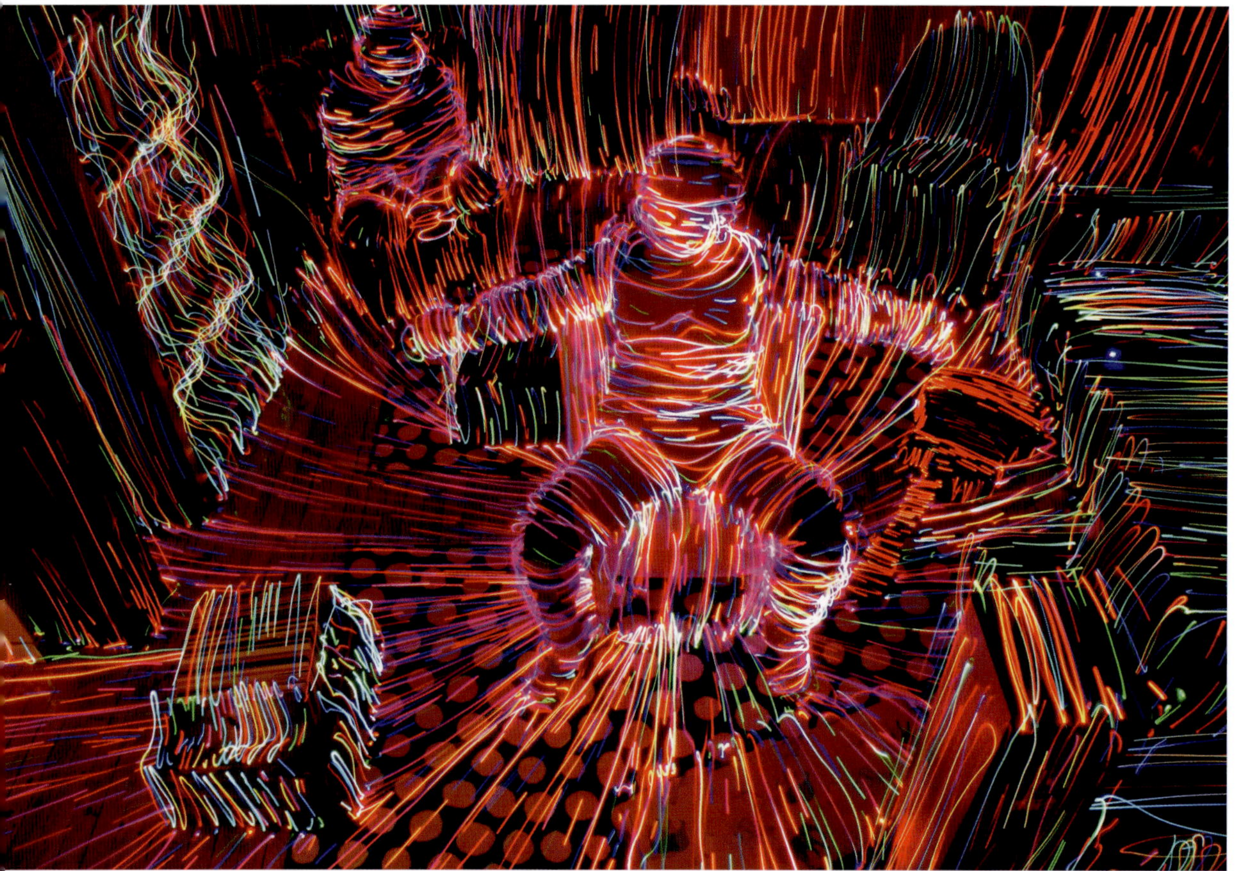

"You Gave Away My Everything"

Settings: f9, ISO 100, 244 seconds
Sony A850 Camera
Color changing LED light

Parviainen says: "This photo was born out of frustration with being homebound with a bad case of the flu. Both my wife and I had been sick for a long time, and felt restless. I set the tripod up on top of the kitchen table to get the bird's eye perspective, and used my wife for the model in both positions, tracing her first in one position and then the other with the color changing light. I then traced the entire room with all of the lines moving towards the figure on the chair in the middle of the room."

abandonments, he finds a strange beauty in what we leave behind, and imagines these places as they once were. Some of his best-known images feature his "light-man" character—an animated human figure drawn with horizontal lines of light that has been frequently spotted in many of the abandoned places he photographs. Another series of images called "Light Topography" involves tracing or outlining the surfaces of an interior space with light. The image, You Gave Away My Everything, is an example. More recently, he has been combining drawings on paper with light painting to create perplexing images that in some ways are reminiscent of M.C. Escher's surrealist drawings. The technique uses spatial illusion to blur the lines of where light ends and chalk lines begin. Creating the drawings is painstakingly tedious and time consuming, because he has to get the alignment and proportions exactly right or the illusion won't work. Voices of the Ether and Lost in Translation are two images from this new series.

JASON PAGE

Jason Page came to light painting in much the same way as Janne Parviainen—by accident. One night in 2004, he bumped the camera during a long exposure of the Moon. When he saw the streak of light on the camera, he had an epiphany that led him to become a light painter. At that time, he thought that he had created something entirely new, and didn't even realize that what he was doing had a name. Several years later, he came across the work of Eric Staller, and then Dean Chamberlain, whose work made a huge impact on him. He was reminded of a dream he had experienced as a child, and Chamberlain's imagery made him realize that through light painting he could get back to the magical place he had found in the dream. The two have become friends and Page describes having a conversation with his mentor as being equivalent to a year of light painting college.

"Light painting is an art form," Page says. "To call light painting a photographic technique would be like calling painting a canvas technique, or drawing a sketch pad technique." He's so passionate about light painting that he has created a website that is a meeting point for the world community of light painters. LightPaintingPhotography.com was born out of years of accumulating research on the subject and its history. It features the work of many of the greatest luminaries in the field, and resources for people interested in the subject. His extensive research on the history of light painting has been referenced in countless articles and on other websites. Page also worked for three years to develop a universal connector to attach light modifiers to just about any flashlight. Because many light painters make or at least modify their own tools, he wanted to come up with a way to make those tools work with almost any flashlight. In true DIY spirit, any home-made brush can be attached with a plastic soda or water bottle-threaded neck. The product was released in October 2014 and is available along with a number of light painting brushes at the product website: lightpaintingbrushes.com.

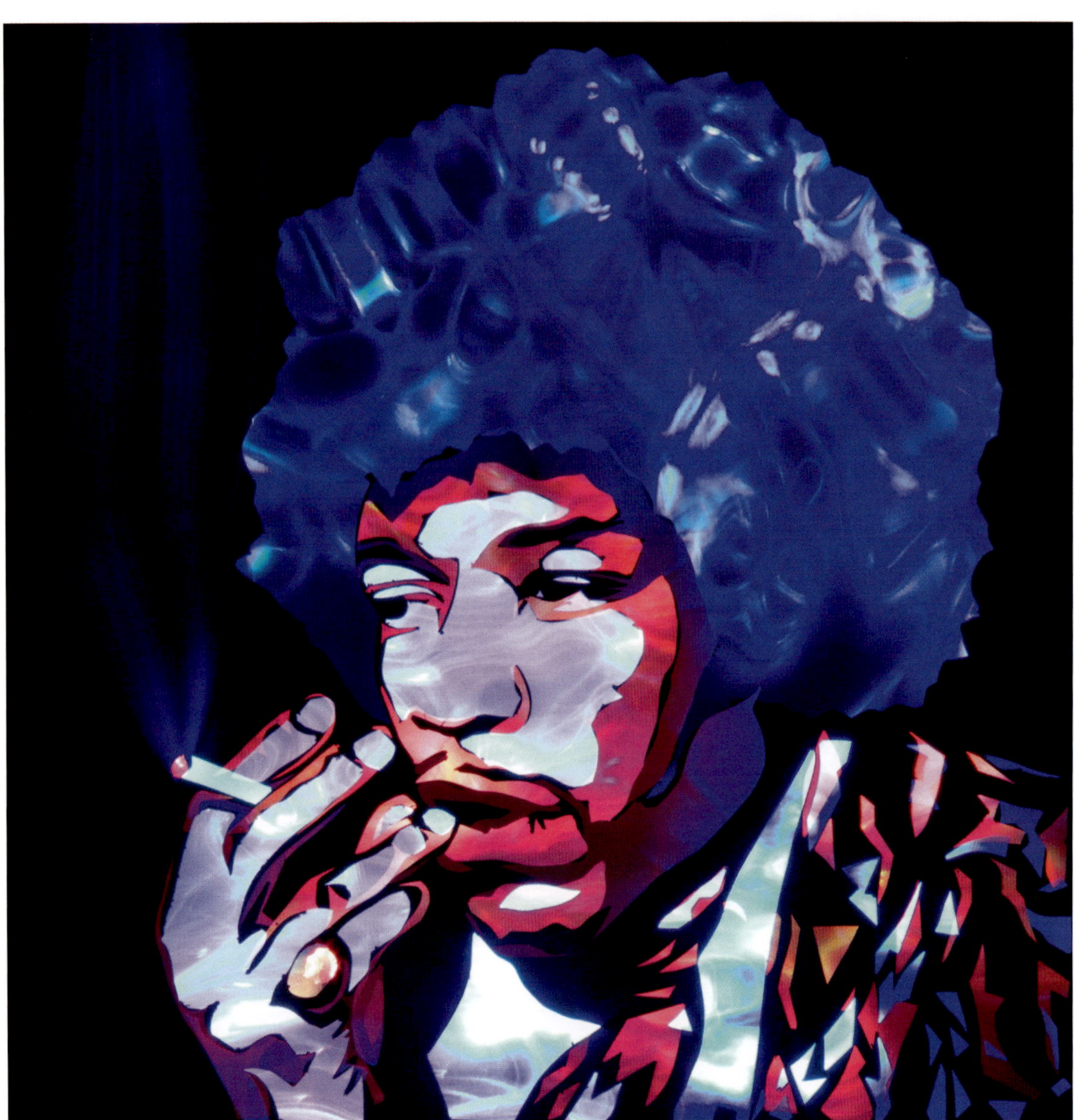

"Jimi Hendrix"

Settings: f25, ISO 100, 220 seconds
Canon 60D Camera
Several Coast LED flashlights, EL wire, light painting brushes, filters

Page says: "This is an image from my Icons series of 'Light Prints.' It was created inside my studio in complete darkness. The process to make this image is similar to screen printing but instead of creating an image with ink I created this with light. I first found a portrait of Jimi Hendrix and deconstructed it into more than 10 individual parts. For each of the parts I then created a glass plate with only select sections of the glass remaining translucent. During a long single exposure I shine lights through the translucent sections of the glass into the camera. I then remove one plate and replace it with another, I repeat this process until all of the sections of the image are recorded by the camera in one single exposure. To create this image I used Coast flashlights of varying lumen outputs, brushes from the Light Painting Brush System and many custom filters to create the different colors and textures in this image. To create the smoke effect from the joint I used a single strand of white EL wire."

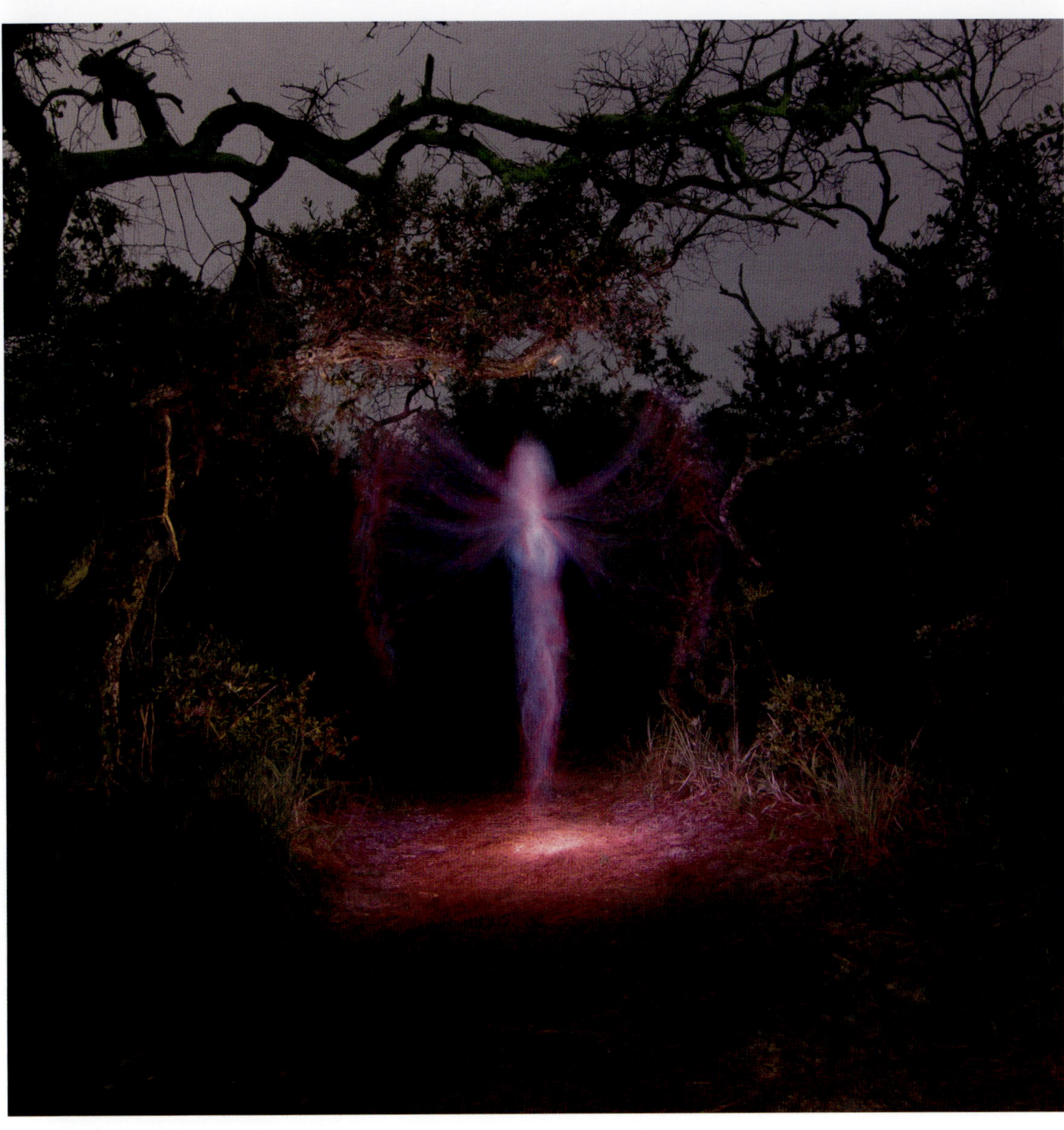

Jonathan Dickinson State Park Apparition

Settings: f5.6, ISO 100, 349 seconds
Canon 60D Camera
Several Coast LED flashlights, EL wire, light painting brushes, filters

Page says: "This image was created on a hot and muggy night with lots of mosquitoes biting me in South Florida. The light painting apparition was created using four strings of EL wire attached to a single battery-operated inverter. The colors that I used were pink, purple, blue, and white. By using a single inverter I was able to easily turn on and off the four different colors of EL wire all at the same time. I opened the shutter of my camera, wearing all black I walked into the scene and first created the apparition by turning on the inverter to illuminate the EL wire, then I waved the strands in a back and forth motion to create a soft light texture for the body. I then turned the EL wire off and repositioned myself to begin to form the wings. Once in position I turned the EL wire back on and held it horizontally. Slowly I changed the elevation from high to low creating the wing shapes. I repeated the same motion for both sides to create the wings."

Page's Icons series uses an ingenious blend of light painting, photography, and printmaking technologies to make what he calls Light Prints. Using either iconic images of pop culture figures or his own images, he deconstructs them into separate parts, very similar to how screen prints are made. The primary difference is that instead of ink, he uses light to make his prints, which are recorded in-camera in a single exposure. Recently, he's been working on a new series of images called Apparitions, which are ghostly figures that appear in the landscape that are created with EL wire. EL wire is a thin copper wire coated in a phosphor that glows when an alternating current is applied to it. There are varying lengths and thicknesses and it is available in many different colors. EL wire is powered by connecting it to a battery-operated inverter. It is inexpensive and available on Amazon and eBay. EL wire is great for creating a fire, fog, or smoke effect, and it can even be shaped and molded to create complex light patterns. Hannu Huhtamo also uses EL wire extensively in his work. It is fairly fragile and the inverters in particular are notorious for breaking. Fortunately, a 6-feet length with an inverter costs less than $10.

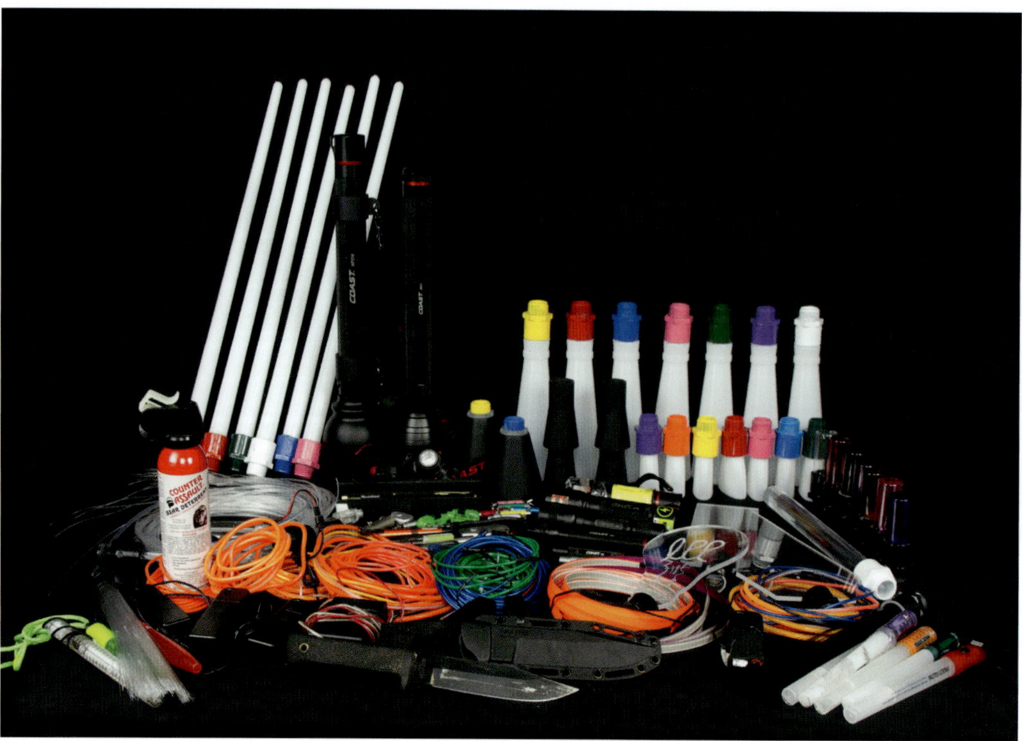

Jason Page has a lot of lights. As the founder of LightPaintingBrushes.com, he has designed and built a variety of light painting tools.

JULIEN BRETON—KAALAM.COM AND DAVID GALLARD—DAVIDGALLARD.COM

Julien Breton is a calligrapher and David Gallard is a photographer who collaborate together where they live in Nantes, France. Breton, who also goes by the pen name of Kaalam, discovered light painting in 2007 in the work of Marko93, a French graffiti artist who also works with light painting. Breton has been a calligrapher working on paper since 2001 and more recently he has been using 3D modeling software. He was interested in combining gesture and movement with calligraphy on a large scale, and light painting was a revelation in that it provided exactly what he was looking for, which enabled him not just to work on a larger scale but also to work in three dimensions. The skills he had developed on paper translated well to light drawing, and combining

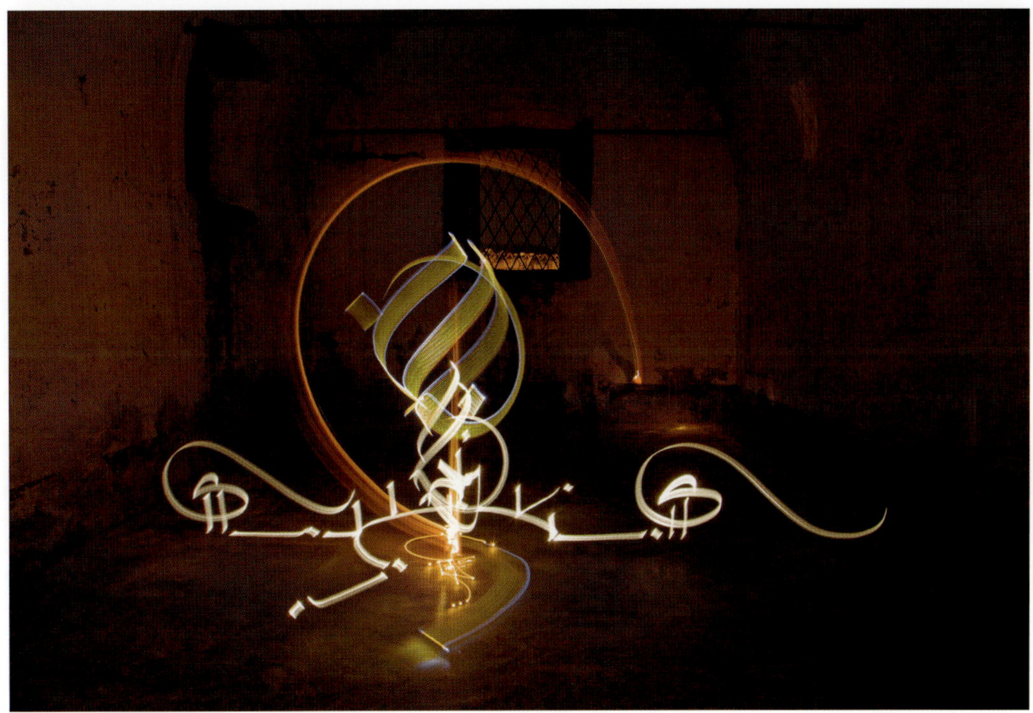

"Faite de chaque tableau une ouverture sur le monde," Franciacorta, Italy, 2011

Calligraphy and photography: Julien Breton aka Kaalam

EXIF not available

Breton says: "I was one of 10 international artists participating in a workshop and exhibition in Franciacorta, Italy. The goal was to produce work that in some way related to the workshop venue. As the place was closed at night—the only time I can work, I had to spend the entire night locked in the building! I took the opportunity to do longer more complex work than usual, and to try to improve my ability to create a three-dimensional perspective. One of the biggest challenges in my work is that without reflections of my lights, it is impossible to know where the calligraphy occurred within the frame. For that reason, I often work close to the ground. The reflections of my lights give a point of reference or context to the calligraphy. I learned to use pieces of tape as markers to help me align the various light elements."

the light calligraphy with Gallard's photography provided a background for his work. The location where a photograph is taken is much more than a background however. The two collaborate closely and the calligraphy is site-specific—designed for the space where the image is created.

Breton describes his light painting as "art of the moment." He says his style of calligraphy is a fusion of Roman and Arabic script, but when he draws with light, he feels like a Chinese calligrapher. The photographs begin when Breton has an idea for a light drawing, which he usually sketches on paper, and then practices with light until he feels that he has got it right. He says that all of the movements need to have the same energy. At that point, the two get

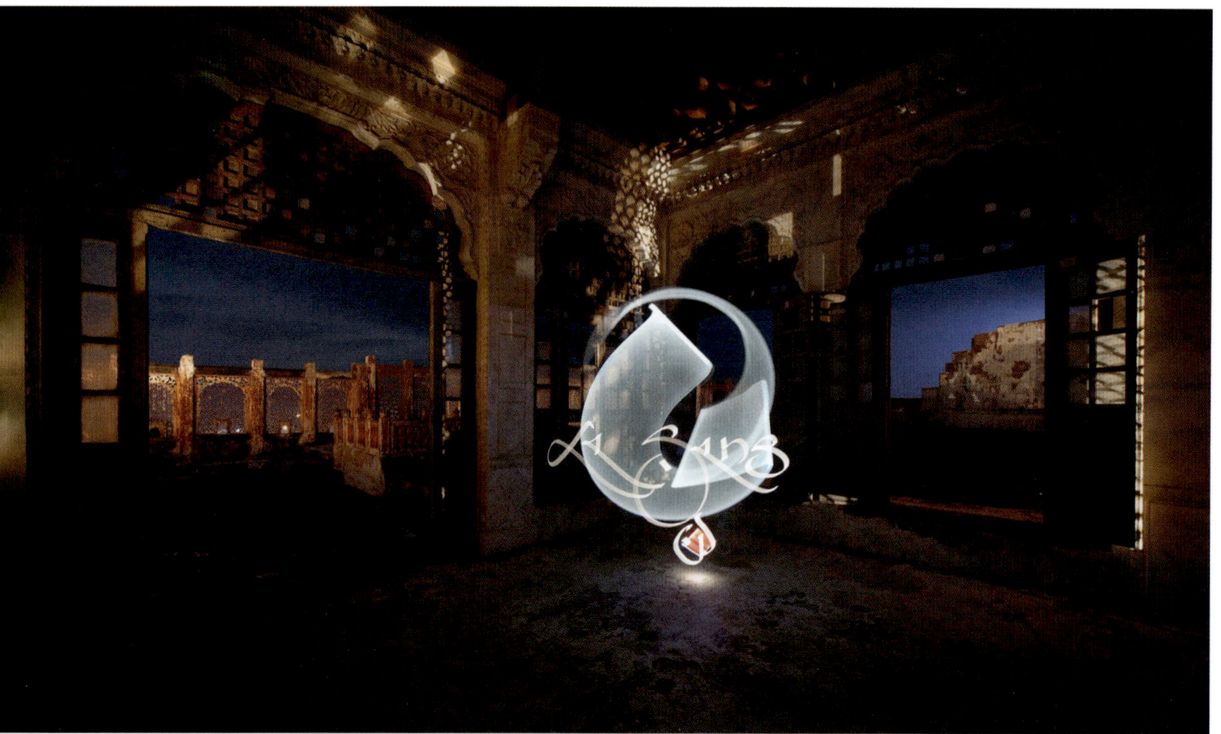

Le Sens, Roman calligraphy, India, 2013
Calligraphy: Julien Breton aka Kaalam
Photography: David Gallard

Settings: f5.6, ISO 100, 138 seconds
Nikon D800, 14 mm lens
LED lights with diffusion wands of differing lengths

Breton says: "Le Sens was made during a trip to India for the International World Sufi festival. We performed our show combining light painting and Indian Kathak Dance. The location is the Merranghar Fort in Jodhpur. We had planned to make the image on the roof, but just as we started it began to rain heavily. We were hoping to have some lightning bolts in the frame, but instead had the lightning illuminate the room and fill it with wonderful shadows."

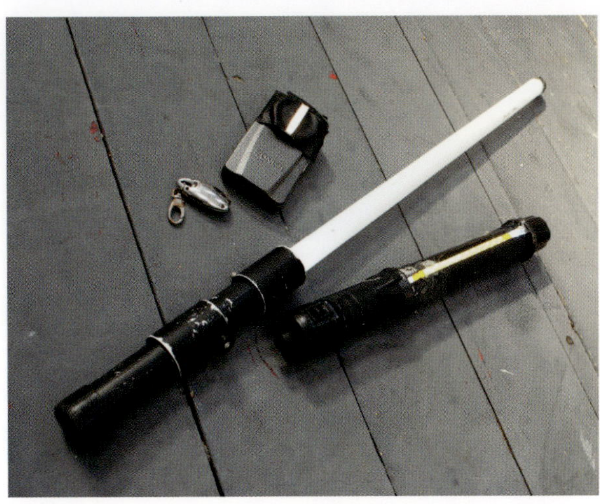

Julien Breton's light painting tools. Breton creates his amazing light paintings with these few simple tools.

together, find a suitable location, and work through the details of orienting the light drawing within the composition, the exposure, and any additional lighting for the background.

Breton also performs in front of a live audience, and the pair started a dance company called Turn Off The Light that combines dance and light calligraphy. They produce a 40-minute show during which time they do 17 different light paintings with dancers, which has been presented in locations ranging from France to India. Through their work, Breton and Gallard hope to help bridge the divide between Arabic and western cultures.

STU JENKS

Stu Jenks is a writer, musician, and photographer who lives in Tucson, AZ and has been photographing at night and drawing with light for nearly 20 years. Jenks marches to the beat of his own drum, working independently, and without much concern for trends or fashion. His work is well known, but he's not really associated with the broader light painting community represented in this book. He stands apart also in that the work presented here was shot on film, although he does shoot digitally as well. His work in different mediums is highly personal, revealing, and part of a lifelong process of personal exploration. The following paragraphs are an excerpt from Stu Jenks' book Flame Spirals—the story of how the image, Owl's Head, Arizona, came to be. The following excerpt is not intended to be instructive as such; it is an insight into the creative process of an artist who uses light drawing in his work.

The Tortillitas are an unassuming mountain range northwest of Tucson. The Torts have neither tourists nor spectacular views, but they do have many statuesque saguaros, a good number of stately ocotillos, and the ubiquitous prickly pear cactus. Add to that a few grazing cows, still fewer tortoises, numberless lizards, a pack or two of roving javelinas and an occasionally

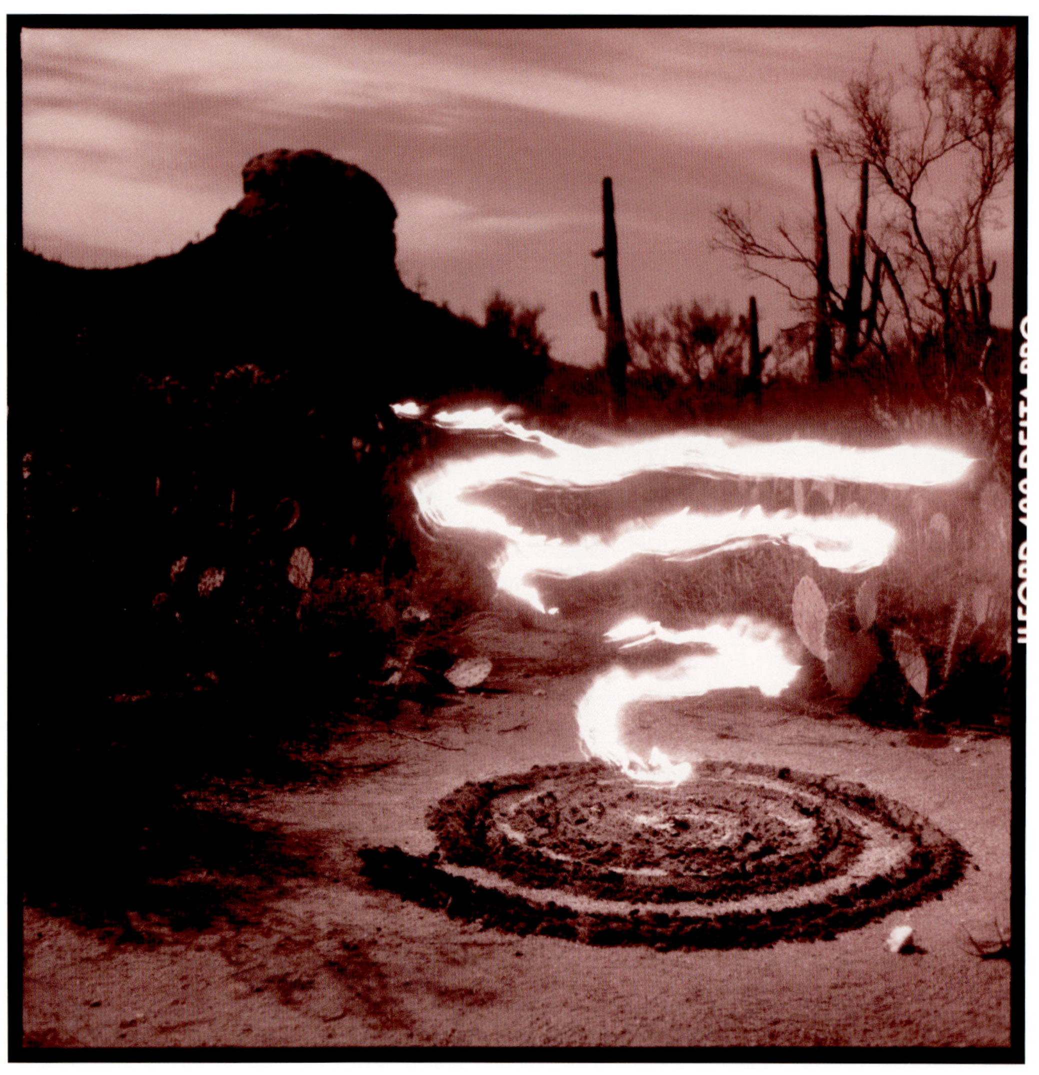

"Owl's Head," Arizona

Settings: f5.6, ASA 400, 15 minutes
1956 Rollei twin lens reflex camera, 80 mm lens
Ilford Delta 400 black and white film
Coleman liquid camp stove fuel, Zippo lighter

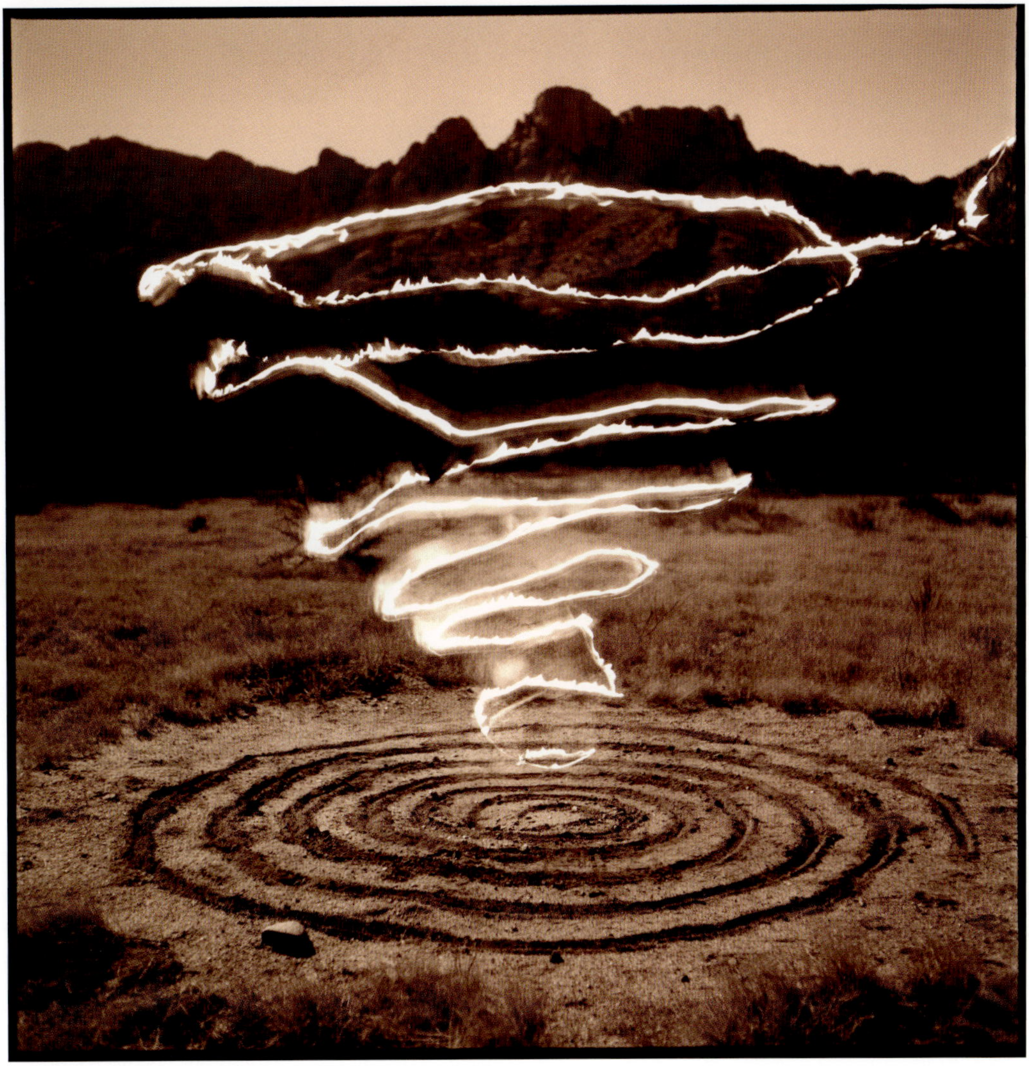

"Catalina State Park," Arizona

Settings: f5.6, ASA 100, 20 minutes
1956 Rollei twin lens reflex camera, 80 mm lens
Ilford Delta 100 black and white film
Zippo lighter

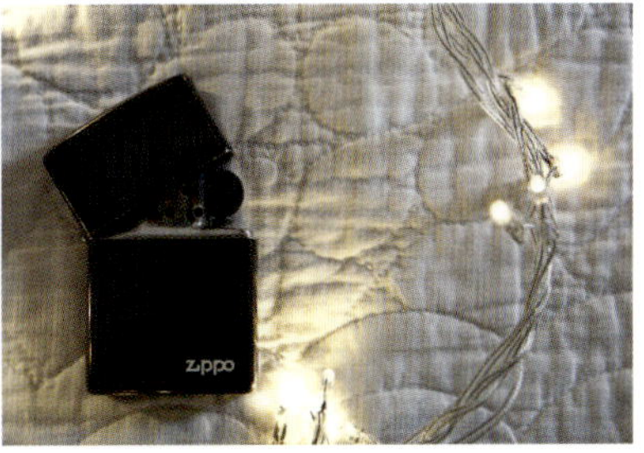

Stu Jenks' lighting kit

Stu uses two primary tools for all of his light painting and drawing—Zippo lighters and a hula hoop wrapped in battery-powered Christmas lights, a tool he made for his "Hoop Dancing" series.

strolling coyote. Overhead, during the day, a disinterested raven may say your name, and a soaring red tail hawk may circle you on her way to finding a slow mouse.

This night I drive out with the waxing Almost-Full-Moon just rising above the Catalina Mountains to the East. The windmill is hard to find, but I eventually see the silhouette of its blades and turn onto the dirt track. I engage the four-wheel drive and motor slowly through the palo verde and mesquite trees. It's summer frog season and toads jump away from my tires and headlights as I cross the washes. Some nights the eyes of javelinas glow in my high beams. Not tonight. Just hopping frogs.

Owl's Head is a prominent rock peak in the Tortillitas. Looking like a thick thumb pushing through the ridge line. Owl's Head has yet to look like an owl's head to me. No matter, it's still a fine peak. I drive up and down the dirt track, in and out of washes, through the trees and cactus that hug the track. Just a bit more driving and I park my truck in a spot where I've often come. It's so quiet I can hear the blood pumping through my veins. Ten miles to the West, a freight train blows its whistle. Two longs, a short and a long. The full moon is higher now, but Owl's Head is still in full shadow. I step near a small fire pit I dug for the cooler winter nights, but I build no campfire tonight. Just a ways from the fire circle, I use a stick to dig a spiral into a flat patch of ground surrounded by prickly pear and mesquite. It doesn't take too long to carve the spiral. I've made a good number of spirals in my day. I set up my Rollei on its tripod and compose a shot. I then pour Coleman white fuel into the trough of the earth spiral. I'm going to try a little experiment, something I've never done before. The idea is to light the fuel, let it burn down a bit and photograph it with the flames gently lapping the ground. I know that white fuel is very volatile, and I have my fire extinguisher close by, just in case, but I'm not that worried. It'll be fine. I strike a wooden match from a safe distance and lazily toss it onto the Coleman-soaked ground spiral.

FAA-TOS-SHEE-YA-YAA! The white gas explodes with a sound that has at least five syllables. Flames rise fast and hard to about seven feet high, and they don't look like they're going to burn down any time soon. Damn! I grab the extinguisher, holding it in my hands at the ready. Oh crap! The Coleman fuel is not burning away. I can see the headlines now. "Local Artist Admits To Causing The Owl's Head Fire." The accompanying article would read something like:"Stu Jenks, local Tucson artist and photographer, turned himself into the Pinal County Sheriff Department yesterday. He admitted he accidentally started The Owl's Head Fire, which has to date consumed 100,000 acres of virgin desert land and is threatening nearby ranches. Many head of cattle are presumed dead. The smoke can be seen as far away as Phoenix."

The flames finally die down to a gentle roar, then begin to flutter out. Thank God. After a few more minutes, I touch the ground. It's still hot. Shoot. I take some water I have in my Pathfinder and splash it softly on the earth spiral to cool it down. As an interesting byproduct, the water softens the spiral very nicely. Hmm. Maybe one of my flame spirals will be good here instead. A hell of a lot safer I can tell you that.

My old Rollei still sits on its tripod, no worse for wear from the hot fire and the dense black smoke. I check the composition again. I like it. I then calculate the exposure time necessary at 15 minutes based on the light from the moon, with an f stop of 5.6, using Ilford Delta 400 black and white film. All set. My Zippo lighter is in my pocket. I open the shutter of my medium format camera. I then walk into the camera's field of view. I light my Zippo near the ground, then draw a spiral upwards in the air with the flaming lighter. At the top I click it shut, step out of the frame, and walk behind my camera. In seconds the flame spiral registers on the silver negative. I'll wait fifteen minutes or so before I close the shutter, allowing time for more light to enter the lens so that the details of the ground spiral and Owl's Head in the distance become visible on the film.

Some nights I dance to ambient music playing from my Pathfinder's CD player. Other times I pray and meditate, or read a book, or simply just sit. This night I go for a bit of a walk down the dirt track, listening to the trains and the sound of my own blood, now pumping a bit louder due to The Coleman Fuel Experiment. I'm thankful I haven't set the desert on fire, and hopeful I have created a bit of a mystery on black and white film.

VINCENT DELESVAUX—WWW.DILIZ-LIGHT.COM

Vincent Delesvaux (aka Diliz) has always drawn and doodled in school when he was bored like so many other kids. He began light painting in 2008 after a trip to Spain where a friend introduced him to the light drawings that Picasso made for Gjon Mili in 1949. For two years he worked alone, refining his skills and experimenting with different techniques without much awareness of what others were doing. Then in 2010 he discovered the world of light painting on Flickr and then Facebook.

A restless spirit, Diliz can't keep still. He light paints and photographs to disperse his energy and to express his thoughts and emotions. Through his images, he explores his own fears, dreams, and joys. The work is personal, but is meant to be shared; it is both fulfilling and a release. Diliz works in series to be able to explore both themes and techniques more fully than single images would permit. Never satisfied, he says that working in series allows him to explore concepts and ideas and to take them all the way to completion. He says that the many different aspects of who he is as a person come through in the different series. The Inside Out series includes multiple images of Delesvaux's hands, and shadows of his hands and arms, which are made using a technique he learned from his friend Quentin Bischoff. The images are dark and mysterious and leave the viewer with lots of questions. Another series, Sixty Seconds To Find An Exit, is made with sparklers and the title refers to completing a light drawing in the time it

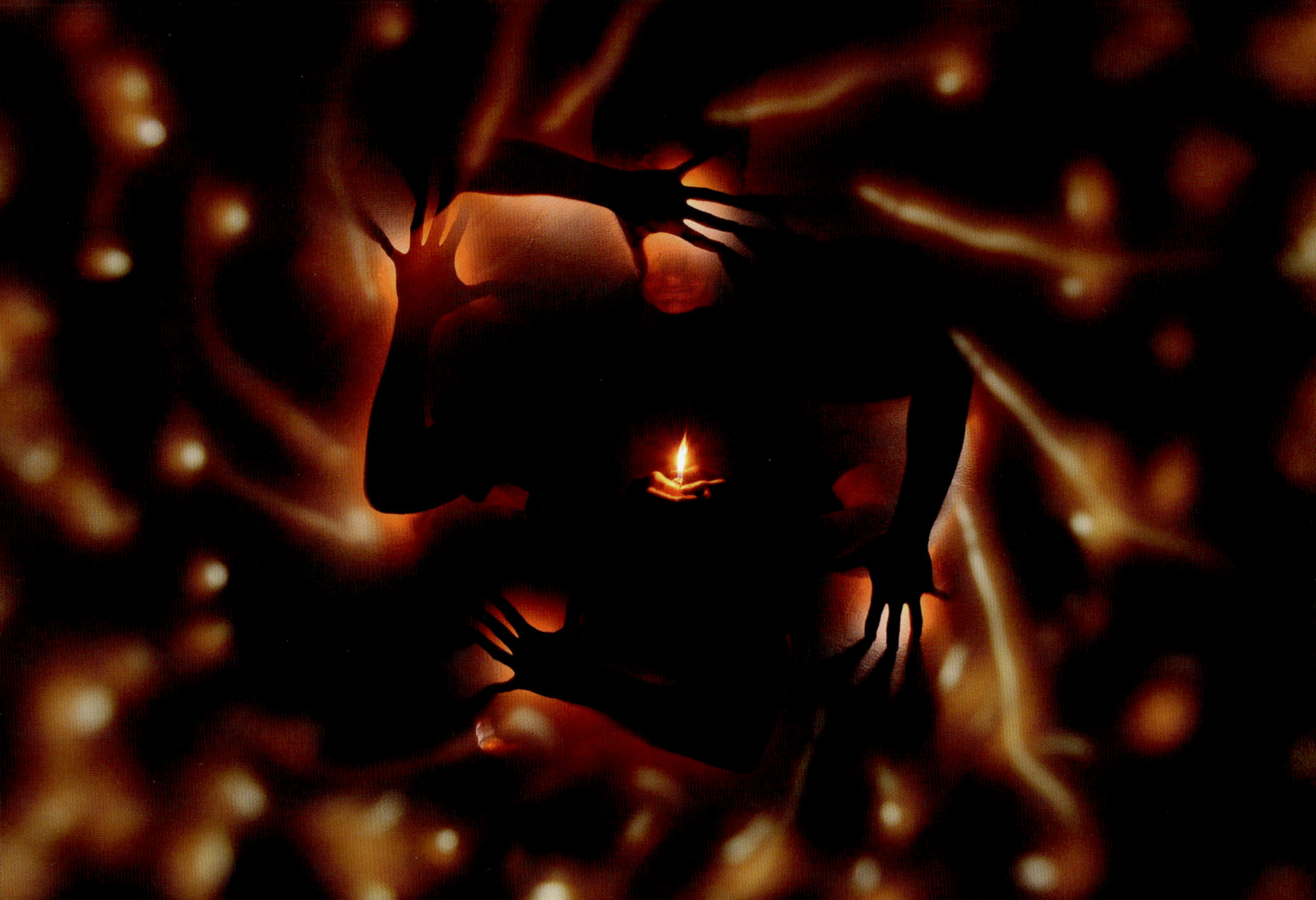

"Fire Play With Me"—Inside Out series

Settings: f11, ISO 250, 86 seconds
Nikon D700
LED flashlight, lighter, LED ring diffused with a T-shirt, gels

Diliz says: "The image began with holding the lighter to illuminate my face, and the flame in the center. Then I put my fingertips on the wall, and moved a small light from underneath my hand down along my arm. I repeated this process three more times, and then used the disc with a circle of flashing LEDs wrapped in a T-shirt for diffusion, moving it around in front of the camera to create the fuzzy dots of light around the outside of the frame."

---

takes for the sparkler to burn out. Each drawing is made with a single line, and after the drawing is completed Diliz has to find an exit for the burning line before the sparkler extinguishes.

All of the images were made strictly in-camera, not replicated in Photoshop. Like most other light painters, Delesvaux prides himself on creating his light painting and drawings in real time rather than in postprocessing, but he does shoot RAW files and develops them to make them look their best. He says that the performance (light painting) is important, but it is transient. The image is what endures and what matters most. He's been influenced by the work of others, but says that as light painting is something done by hand, it is more a product of experience rather

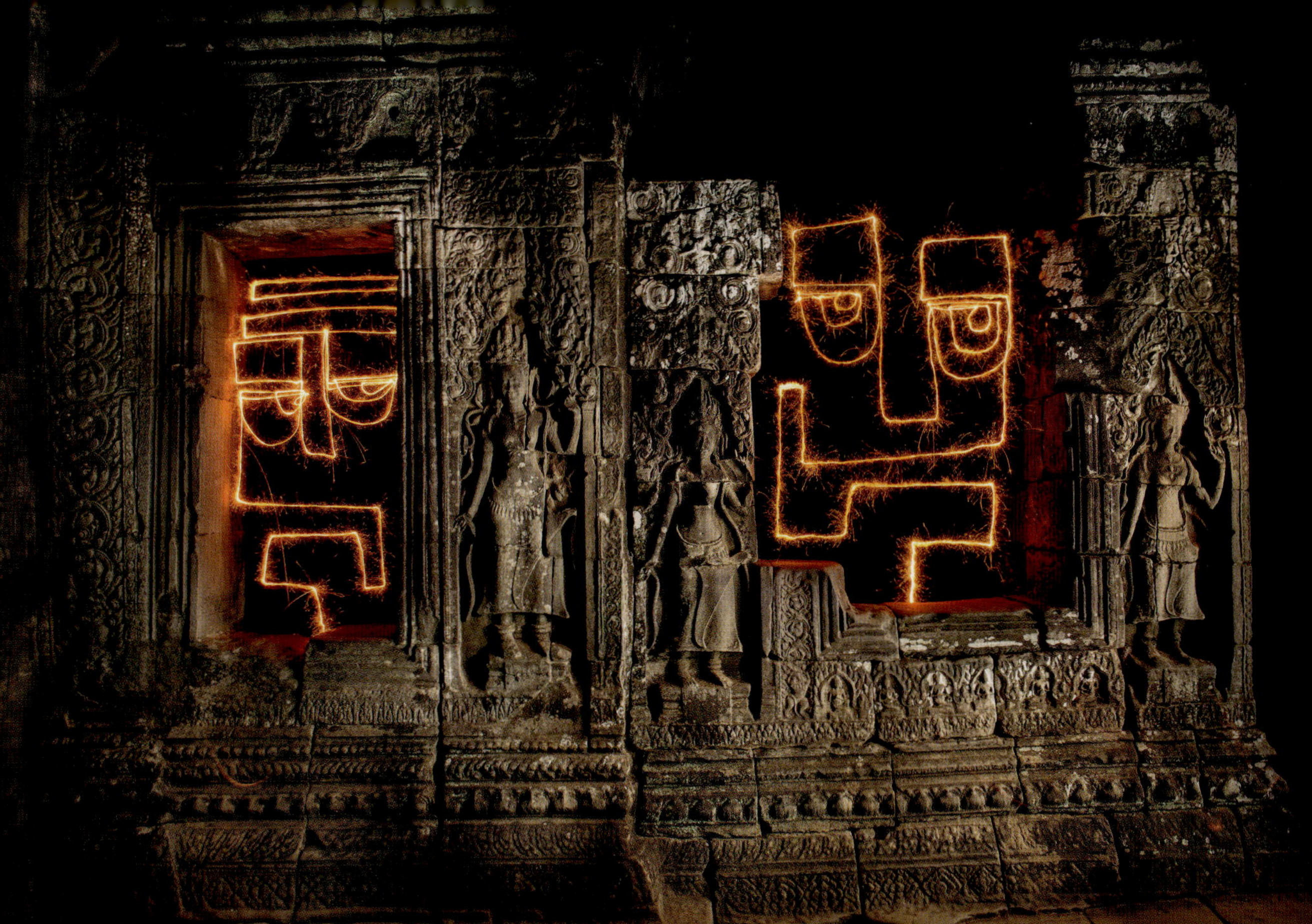

"Jealousy"—Sixty Seconds To Find An Exit series

Settings: f13, ISO 100, 169 seconds
Nikon D800, 24-70 f2.8 lens
LED Lenser M7 flashlight with warming gel, sparklers

Diliz says: "The greatest challenge in making this image was getting to the location: Bayon Temple from Angkor Thom in Cambodia. After a 1-hour bike ride through the jungle, I arrived at the temple to find it locked and guarded. Fortunately, the guards eventually fell asleep, and I was able to sneak in and make some exposures. I don't want to think about what would have happened if I had been caught inside. I first lit the facade of the structure sweeping from left to right with a flashlight, and then went inside and created each of the faces in a single line with one sparkler for each face. The challenge is not only getting the spatial relations right without any frame of reference, but also creating emotion in the faces without seeing what I'm doing."

than of appropriation. He tries to push the limits and boundaries of what he can do and works spontaneously, responding to the space he's photographing with shadow and light.

I hope that you have found this sampling of light drawing and light painting artist's work to be inspiring. There are links to the artist's websites in each of their sections, but I encourage readers to find them on social media and photo-sharing websites too, because that's where you'll find their most recent work, and you'll also be able to connect with the light painting and drawing community at large. Perhaps you have noticed the glaring omission of female

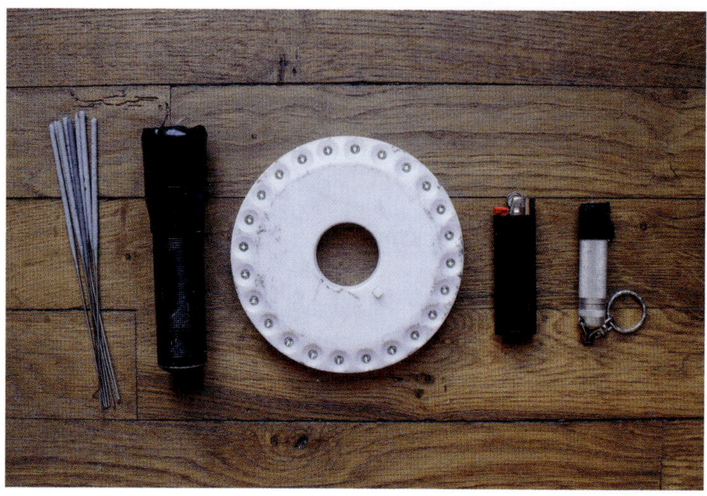

light artists from this chapter. Over the years, I've had close to a 50:50 ratio of men in my night photography classes and workshops, but of the ones who take to light painting, the great majority are men. This seems to be true in the broader light painting world too. With the exception of Vicki DaSilva (featured in the history chapter), Cenci Goepel (who makes up half of the German light painting duo LightMark), and an Australian woman who goes by the name of TigTab (you can find her on Flickr; she wasn't available to participate in this book), there doesn't seem to be many women who have established themselves as light painting artists. The artists included in this chapter reflect the light painting community at large.

By the time you have reached this far in the book, you'll have learned that night photography requires working methodically and deliberately. A productive night means that you come home with 5 or 10 good shots, not gigabytes worth of images. Spontaneity is not usually a part of the process, but careful planning and attention to detail lead to successful images. Persistence and hard work are key to progress, but it is tempting to look for shortcuts along the way. If you are lucky enough to have a talented friend who can help to get you started, then that's a great way to learn. There are many options to take classes and workshops on night photography and light painting. When I studied at the Academy of Art University with Steve Harper in the late 1980s, Steve's was the only night photography class I could find anywhere in the country. In 1998, when Tim Baskerville and I taught our first workshop at Rayko Photo Center in San Francisco, we seemed to be the only ones teaching the subject after Steve retired. Now, there are classes, online courses, and workshops across the United States and in many other countries as well. There are workshops that specialize in astro-landscape photography, full moon night photography, Northern Lights, light drawing, and light painting, and even light painting in automotive junkyards. Night photography and light painting are more accessible than ever, thanks to the technological revolution of the past 15 years. The equipment we use—from cameras and lenses, to flashlights and batteries—has all evolved and matured, putting night photography within the reach of almost anyone, and the unparalleled access to information we enjoy on the internet makes learning and sharing easier than ever before.

Studying the work of others, or what Michael Kenna calls "standing on the shoulders of giants," has long been a tried and tested method to learn new skills and to achieve a new understanding of the world around us. Most of us learn by observation and repetition. This chapter is a testament to that very fact, and is why I've included the work of so many other night photographers in this book. I want to expose my readers to some of the many possibilities that exist within the world of night photography, and show that there is no one way to do it. I've never tried to teach my students how to do what I do, but to give them the techniques and inspiration to express themselves creatively. I hope that this book does that for you. It is tempting to try to replicate images that inspire us, and that in itself is not a bad thing, provided it is only part of a learning process. In the late 1930s, the great English photographer Bill Brandt recreated some of Brassai's famous night photographs of Paris by posing his wife as a prostitute! If that's not a testament to the lengths night photographers will go to for their art, I don't know what is.

Real growth as a photographer or as an artist comes from absorbing what you learn from others, and then taking that knowledge and making it your own. Take it to the next step, go beyond what you have seen others do, and follow your own creative spirit wherever it may lead. There will always be dead ends and paths that lead to frustration, but when you finally nail that shot you've had in mind for so long, or have been working on for hours, you will find true satisfaction and an understanding of why so many people have come to love the art of night photography and light painting. There are no unbreakable rules, and in the immortal words of a little green Jedi master—"Do, or do not, there is no try." Get out there, open your eyes, open the shutter, and dance around waving lights in front of your camera until the wookies come home.

Contributors and Resources

The following photographers have all contributed to this book in one form or another.
I encourage you to visit their websites so that you may further explore the world of night
photography and light painting.

Tim Baskerville	www.thenocturnes.com
Alister Benn	availablelightimages.com
Julien Breton	http://kaalam.fr
Russell Brown	www.russellbrown.com
Dennis Calvert	http://denniscalvert.net
Vicki DaSilva	www.vickidasilva.com
Vincent Delesvaux	www.vincentdelesvaux.com
Michael Frye	www.michaelfrye.com
David Gallard	http://davidgallard.fr
Steve Harper	www.flickr.com/photos/sharper24/
Ian Hobson	www.lightpainting.org.uk
Hannu Huhtamo	www.hannuhuhtamo.com
Stu Jenks	http://stujenks.tumblr.com
Keith Kiska	www.phototrekker.com
David Lebe	www.davidlebe.com
Jürgen Lobert	www.leyetscapes.com
Scott Martin	www.martinphoto.com
Jason Page	www.jasondpage.com
Troy Paiva	www.lostamerica.com
Janne Parviainen	http://jannepaint.wix.com/jannepaint-2
Darren Pearson	www.dariustwin.com
Michael Shainblum	www.shainblumphoto.com
Eric Staller	www.ericstaller.com
J. Michael Sullivan	www.haywood-sullivan.com/photography/
Rick Whitacre	www.whitacrephotography.com
Trevor Williams	http://www.tdubphoto.co

NIGHT PHOTOGRAPHY AND LIGHT PAINTING WORKSHOPS

*Lance Keimig teaches workshops and classes around the United States, and leads photo tours featuring night photography to Scotland, Ireland, Cuba, and Iceland for Northern Lights tours. He also offers one on one and private small group classes to individuals and organizations such as camera clubs. The workshops include full moon, astro-landscape photography, and light painting opportunities: www.thenightskye.com

*Scott Martin co-leads night photography workshops with Lance Keimig: www.martinphoto.com, www.on-sight.com

*Tim Baskerville leads night photography workshops in various US locations, and holds night photography community gatherings in Vallejo, CA: www.thenocturnes.com

*Troy Paiva teaches night photography and light painting workshops in the California desert: www.lostamerica.com

*Gabriel Biderman leads night photography workshops in a variety of US locations, mostly on the East Coast: http://www.ruinism.com

*Noel Kerns teaches light painting and night photography in Texas: http://www.noelkerns.com

*Mario Rubio has been teaching night photography in Spain for years: http://www.fotografonocturno.com

Dave Morrow leads night photography workshops specializing in astro-landscape photography in the Pacific Northwest: http://www.davemorrowphotography.com

Michael Shainblum offers private astro-landscape photography workshops: www.shainblumphoto.com

David Kingham offers astro-landscape photography workshops in the US: www.exploringexposure.com/2015-photography-workshops

Brad Goldpaint offers astro-landscape photography workshops in the US: http://goldpaintphotography.com

Mike Berenson teaches night photography workshops in the American Southwest: www.coloradocaptures.com/night-photography-training

Royce Bair offers workshops emphasizing Milky Way photography in various southwest locations: http://intothenightphoto.blogspot.com

Denis Smith occasionally offers light painting workshops in Australia: http://www.balloflight.com.au

NIGHT PHOTOGRAPHY RESOURCES
Lance Keimig's website has a selection of free PDFs of articles, charts, and checklists that can be printed and carried in your camera bag to be used in the field. These can be found on the Books page of TheNightSkye.com.

Tim Baskerville founded The Nocturnes in 1991, and it's still going strong. A knowledge base, online and real world community of night photographers: thenocturnes.com.

NIGHT PHOTOGRAPHY MEET UP GROUPS ARE SPRINGING UP ALL OVER THE US
Boston: http://www.meetup.com/GBNight/
http://www.meetup.com/NewEnglandNightPhotographers/
New York: http://www.meetup.com/NYNight/
Salt Lake City: http://www.meetup.com/NightScape-Photography/
Virginia: http://www.meetup.com/Night-and-Low-Light-Photography-Group/

LIGHT PAINTING RESOURCES
LightPaintingPhotography.com is a comprehensive resource for information on light painting, created by Jason Page.

The Light Painting World Alliance was founded by Sergey B. Churkin in Moscow in 2011. It is a well-organized member organization that presents light painting conferences and events around the world: www.lpwalliance.com

Jason Page saw a need and developed a system of light painting tools which are available at: lightpaintingbrushes.com

The Protomachine is an incredibly versatile light painting tool for people serious about light painting. Troy Paiva and Tim Baskerville use it extensively in their work: protomachines.com

Pixelstick is a programmable light painting tool that virtually prints images in midair out of lift: thepixelstick.com

A Spain-based light painting tool company: herramientaslightpainting.com

NIGHT PHOTOGRAPHY EBOOKS
Troy Paiva
Light Painted Night Photography

Jim Goldstein
Photographing the 4th Dimension: Time

Mark Bowie
The Light of Midnight

David Kingham
Nightscape

Alister Benn
Seeing the Unseen

NOTE
I can personally vouch for the workshop leaders marked with an *. I'm making a broader listing but have no direct experience with the untagged instructors.

Index